Merry
Christmas 07
Grandpa

Love Stephen
Glenn
Morrgan

D1617212

FULL
CIRCLE

DEATH AND RESURRECTION IN
CANADIAN CONSERVATIVE POLITICS

FULL CIRCLE

DEATH AND RESURRECTION IN
CANADIAN CONSERVATIVE POLITICS

BOB PLAMONDON
FOREWORD BY **LAWRENCE MARTIN**

KEY PORTER BOOKS

Library and Archives Canada Cataloguing in Publication

Plamondon, Robert E.
    Full circle : death and resurrection in Canadian conservative politics / Bob Plamondon.

ISBN 1-55263-855-3

1. Conservatism—Canada. 2. Canada—Politics and government—1984–1993. 3. Canada—Politics and government—1993–2006. I. Title.

JC573.2.C3P53 2006   320.520971   C2006-902906-7

The publisher gratefully acknowledges the support of the Canada Council for the Arts and the Ontario Arts Council for its publishing program. We acknowledge the support of the Government of Ontario through the Ontario Media Development Corporation's Ontario Book Initiative.

We acknowledge the financial support of the Government of Canada through the Book Publishing Industry Development Program (BPIDP) for our publishing activities.

Key Porter Books Limited
Six Adelaide Street East, Tenth Floor
Toronto, Ontario
Canada M5C 1H6

www.keyporter.com

Text design: Martin Gould
Electronic formatting: Jean Lightfoot Peters

Printed and bound in Canada

06 07 08 09 10 5 4 3 2 1

To Marian

I'm sorry this took a little more time than I thought.

CONTENTS

FOREWORD

BY LAWRENCE MARTIN

CANADIAN CONSERVATIVES HAVE had a turbulent, luckless and losing history woven in cycles of despair. When the party occasionally did triumph in elections, the prize was quickly squandered. R.B. Bennett was derailed by the biggest depression the country ever saw. John Diefenbaker's mismanagement of a golden opportunity was catastrophic. Joe Clark, unbelievably, dismantled his minority government in nine months. The party was jinxed. A death wish seemed to hover it. If further proof was needed, it came later in the 1980s. Brian Mulroney had seemingly put an end to the long run of grief. He'd won a record shattering majority in 1984 and seemed well on his way to another robust victory. He had built a coalition of the West and Quebec. Not since John A. Macdonald had the party been so comfortably situated in power.

But as if further proof of an eternal curse was needed, Preston Manning chose this advantageous moment to launch a full-scale revolt in the form of the creation of a new conservative party—one which would splinter the old and send conservatives into nearly a generation of new turmoil, virtually guaranteeing the Liberals a slew of majority victories under Jean Chrétien.

While many could have imagined a protest party being launched when Pierre Trudeau was in power and inflicting the West with assaults like the National Energy Plan, few could have foreseen it happening when the party controlled the power levers and when, as

Brian Mulroney could well argue, many Western grievances were being addressed.

The Mulroney Conservatives not only lost their Western base. The Quebec end of the coalition was shattered as well. Lucien Bouchard bolted the party over a dispute over the Meech Lake Accord and formed his own splinter party, the Bloc Québécois.

The old party was divided in a way it never had been before. More than that, its collapse had left the unity of the country imperilled. There was but one dominant governing party and in Reform and the Bloc, two regionally built formations riding a wave of regional grievances.

The astonishing story of the crash of conservatism and its rebirth is the subject of Bob Plamondon's *Full Circle*. The author comes at it with a unique perspective. Party insiders sometimes do such books. Academics sometimes do them and often it is journalists who take up the challenge. Plamondon provides the advantage of bringing all three perspectives to the table. He has taught at several universities, he was a party insider, having run once for the Tories and worked for the party in elections and leadership conventions. In researching the book, he has done the journalists' labour, interviewing more than thirty key figures in the drama.

His voyage through the last two decades brings new twists and astute analysis to the narrative. Because the post-Mulroney conservative factions could never manage to pose a legitimate threat at winning power, they were hardly the subject of a profusion of books and studies. Plamondon's is the first to chart the fall and rise with such thoroughness.

Having created the Reform Party, Preston Manning was soon to learn that as a right-leaning Alberta-based rump, he could not win on the national level. He was an historian of sorts. History, as Plamondon amply records, demonstrated that the Conservatives only won when they built coalitions to broaden their tent. Manning had narrowed it.

Having divided the right, the Reform leader, with a straight face, now launched a bid to unite it—to fold the party that he had only just broken into two back into one. Canadian politics had seen a lot of chutzpah, but rarely anything to match the gall of this. Manning didn't quite see it this way. He tells Bob Plamondon that his creation of Reform (later turned into the Alliance) may well have saved Canada.

For Canadian conservatives, what he had created had the look of despair. In 2003, as the Liberals were moving to replace Jean Chrétien with Paul Martin, polls told the story. The Liberals were in the 50s, the Progressive Conservatives were at about 15 per cent and the Reform/Alliance was closer to 10.

But the utterly depressing prospects were ironically what saved the right. Neither of the leaders of the two conservative parties had anywhere to go. For the Tories, Peter MacKay was crippled by the backroom dealing he had engaged in to win the leadership. The Orchard affair, for the first time, gets a full hearing in this book. As Plamondon points out, leadership conventions have often been marked by secret plots and secret deals. The pact between MacKay and the left-wing Tory David Orchard took on a more sinister life than the others.

For the future of conservatism, it was good that it did. Without this albatross, MacKay might well have determined he could have led the Tories back to glory.

But now, in what was probably the pivotal decision in the entire piece, MacKay quickly decided he would surrender his leader's status and the entire status of his party for the sake of trying to achieve unity on the right. He did so knowing he would break the pact with Orchard, earning him yet more condemnation on that score. He knew he would alienate party stalwarts like Joe Clark forever. He was closing down a party with a century and a half of history. He was surrendering his leadership status without even being afforded one chance of going to the polls.

For things to come full circle, Stephen Harper had to bow down as well. That would only come about if he too saw scant hope for growth. Fortunately for merger prospects, the party was just as immobile under him as previous leaders. Harper lacked personal appeal, a public personality, but was strategically adept and had a capacity to compromise. Realizing that despite the big edge in seats his party held over the Tories he couldn't make gains without them, he plotted his own party's demise as well, being prepared, in so doing, to be conciliatory on some of the party's right-wing leanings.

Full Circle details the story of how the surprisingly quick merger was conceived and executed. What effective authors of history do is get underneath the running accounts of journalism. to provide new information, insights, and meaningful context.

Plamondon's account reveals how an obscure event, the Perth–Middlesex by-election in May 2003, changed Stephen Harper. It reveals special moments, such as the fateful one when MacKay came across Harper in the Commons corridor and uttered the words, "You and I have to talk:" It shows how Belinda Stronach, credited in the media as a significant player in the merger, was in fact of little significance. How Brian Mulroney was pulling the strings telling everyone how Jean Chrétien had been going to bed every night saying, "*Merci beaucoup*, Preston Manning:" How Harper emissaries shocked the Tories in initial secret merger meetings in a hotel room booked under the name "John Macdonald" by being prepared to give away the store on almost every demand the Tories put forward.

The merger produced little initial excitement—and not much of a jump in the opinion polls for the new Conservative party. But Canadians politics was dramatically altered by this event. The right was unified and it was unified in such a way—with MacKay letting Harper have a free run at the leadership of the new party—that it gave the West the prominence it had long sought. The old Progressive Conservatives had sometimes been almost indistinguishable from the old Liberals. Not the new party.

Difficulties lay ahead after the merger. Harper's leadership was in question after he let a chance to win the 2004 election slip away. But he recovered and the new formation held and it got the big break in the form of a governing party scandal that opposition parties thrive on. In the 2005 election, it took advantage.

In just two years, the conservatives in Canada had moved from their ruinous divided status and some 40 percentage points behind in the polls to unity and to strength. Against all odds—with a leader who so many in the press and the public had written off as a dud—they had moved to governance.

All had changed. From the bottom of the pit they had climbed to the top. They now had hope, legitimate hope, that their history of grief was over. They now had hope, legitimate hope, of a long and wedded future, one which would change the country.

PREFACE

I WANT READERS TO UNDERSTAND my political background and why I decided to write this book.

My first two votes went Liberal. But Pierre Trudeau's mismanagement of the economy, financial irresponsibility, and constitutional recklessness convinced me that I am a conservative.

In 1984, I walked into Dan Chilcott's Ottawa Centre PC campaign office with nothing to offer but enthusiasm. As that campaign progressed, I found my niche in politics formulating policy and writing speeches. Following the 1984 election, I served on my local PC riding executive and later became its president. Professionally, I earned my designation as a chartered accountant and became an assistant professor at the University of Ottawa. There I began to research and write about what I called "Debt, Deficits and Dangerous Complacency." I was the Progressive Conservative candidate for Ottawa Centre in the 1988 election, was not elected, and returned to my passion for public policy. I voted for Kim Campbell as PC party leader, and in the 1993 election I was recruited to work in the Conservative war room, handling economic issues. Undeterred by the decimation of the PC party, I volunteered as an adviser to Jean Charest on tax policy and economic matters.

After the second consecutive Chrétien majority win, and with Joe Clark the leader of the PC party, I was unsure how to best serve the conservative cause. In 2000, it looked like the Canadian Alliance had the upper hand. I recall one particularly uncomfortable scene when my local PC candidate, Beverly Mitchell, knocked on my door and asked to put up a lawn sign. I had been in her shoes less than a decade earlier, but I knew that I would be voting for Stockwell Day, and I declined her request. I was a conservative more than I was a member of any political party and would readily have voted for a merger of the PC and Alliance parties at that time had it been an option. By 2003, the prospect of new leadership within the PC party brought me to the inner circle of Peter MacKay's campaign.

After watching the Liberals win their third consecutive majority government, and with the Paul Martin juggernaut on the horizon, conservatives seized the unexpected opportunity to unite. I didn't expect this new Conservative party to sweep to power, but I was optimistic that conservatives would once again become a relevant political force in Canada. As I raised my hand to indicate my approval of the merger, I thought of the political upheaval Canadians had witnessed over the previous decade. I wanted to understand why the conservative movement fell apart and how it then came back together. I thought that there must be important lessons to be gleaned from this process. With Conservatives in oppostion, I decided to write this book.

My timing was good. For the sake of history, the battle-weary veterans of the PC–Reform–Alliance civil war were ready to tell their stories. Even those deeply engaged in conservative politics will be stunned by what took place "behind the scenes."

I wanted the book to be more than a chronological account of key events and milestones. The death and resurrection of Canadian conservative politics is an emotional story, and I chose to craft it around the failures and triumphs of the three key figures who had the most to do with the division and reunification: Preston Manning, Stephen Harper, and Peter MacKay.

I began my research with print sources on the Canadian conservative political movement over the past twenty years, including a detailed review of books, documents, newspaper accounts, speeches, speaking notes, correspondence, and internal party memoranda. But the substance of this book comes from almost fifty in-depth interviews, conducted in person and via telephone. Most interviews were recorded. Only a few times was I asked to go "off the record." A few people asked that their contributions be used as background information rather than for attribution, and these people are not included in the list of those interviewed. I am grateful to everyone who shared with me their insights and experiences. For the record, and in alphabetical order, those interviewed include: David Angus, Madeleine Ashe, Yaroslav Baran, Roxanna Benoit, Rick Byers, Geoff Chutter, Jeff Clarke, Barry Cline, Stockwell Day, Doug Earle, Graham Fox, Frank Graves, Tom Jarmyn, Denis Jolette, Noël Kinsella, John Laschinger, Marjory LeBreton, Paul Lepsoe, John MacDonnell, Elmer MacKay, Peter MacKay, Preston Manning, Lawrence Martin, Shaun Masterson, Don Mazankowski, Doug McLarty, Lisa Merrithew, Rick Morgan, Geoff Norquay, Terrance Oakey, David Orchard, Bill Pristanski, Duncan Rayner, Marjaleena Repo, Gerry St. Germain, Werner Schmidt, John Weissenberger, Huw Williams, and Jim Williams.

A few technical notes. Footnotes are not used for quotes obtained during these personal interviews; nor for economic and financial data obtained from Finance Canada, nor election data obtained from Elections Canada. All other quotes and information are footnoted, and the footnotes appear at the bottom of each page to make them accessible and useful. There is a Timeline of Key Events at the back of the book. In the word "conservative," a small "c" denotes conservative thought or philosophy and a capital "C" denotes the political party. The term "Tory" is synonymous with the Progressive Conservative party and its antecedents, but the term is also used as a label for the Conservative party that was recognized by Canada's Chief Electoral Officer on December 7, 2003.

ACKNOWLEDGEMENTS

Without the advice and encouragement of Lawrence Martin, this book might never have seen the light of day. He helped me navigate the publishing process, and introduced me to Rick Broadhead, who became my literary agent. He graciously and directly rejected the first fifty or so titles that I proposed, but contributed *Death and Resurrection* to the subtitle. I am deeply indebted to him, not just for writing the foreword, but also for helping to steer this project at every critical juncture.

An historical account of this period would be pretty dull without people who were willing to expose their personal involvement, good or bad. I am grateful to the nearly fifty people who shared their insights and experiences. Some even suggested lines of inquiry, made introductory calls, and set up interviews.

Some of the people I interviewed are epic figures whose service to conservative politics warrant their own books. Senator David Angus is among the most colourful, engaging, and encouraging men I have ever met in the party. The Right Honourable Don Mazankowski, John Diefenbaker's last seatmate, is an icon whose contributions are matched with a wonderful capacity for story-telling. Senator Marjory LeBreton has lived many lives in the party. She has been and is close to several leaders of this country, yet she remains grounded in mainstream Canada. Senator Gerry St. Germain is forthright and insightful. He bears the scars of taking a bold and early stand on the merger of the parties.

I am grateful to several friends and colleagues who read through various random notes and rough drafts and provided comments, especially Graham Fox, Jim Lambe, Bill Pristanski, Paul McAneney, Susan Snider, and Mark Sutcliffe. France Lepin is a meticulous researcher and aspiring writer who painstakingly read every word of the early manuscript. Arguing facts with France is useful only if you enjoy being proven wrong. I am indebted to France for the many hours she contributed to this project.

I am also fortunate to have two nearly lifelong friends whose talents I was able to exploit. John Usborne, who never waters down his opinions, made sure my conclusions were clear, strong, and well supported. He eagerly read everything I sent him. Kurt Rufelds is both my friend and teacher. Whatever I know about writing, and how much work it can be, I learned from Kurt. His contribution to this book was enormous.

When I first spoke with my agent, Rick Broadhead, I told him I had two conditions only. The first was his enthusiasm. The second was getting the book into the marketplace in the fall of 2006. He delivered in spades, and we laughed our way through almost every hurdle.

At Key Porter, Clare McKeon edited the book for publication. I have no doubt that she has, from every author, a 99 per cent acceptance rate on her suggested changes. If my mother reads this book and concludes that my writing has improved, it is because of the nature and extent of Clare's work. She was a joy to work with.

This is my second major book. Both have coincided with my wife's pregnancies and the first three months of our children's lives. I did not plan it that way, and need forgiveness for vanishing on occasion when the crunch was on. I could not have written this book without Marian's love and understanding. I have a wonderful life with Marian, Nathaniel, Charlotte, Megan, and Michael. I hope my children will draw some inspiration from what hard work and dedication can produce, especially when the television is turned off. And, kids, in case I haven't mentioned it lately, say no to drugs, keep your mind and bodies healthy, and your hearts open.

Readers may contact the author at: full_circle@sympatico.ca

CHAPTER 1

POINT OF NO RETURN

I T WAS EARLY IN THE MORNING of a crisp October day. Peter MacKay, member of parliament for Pictou–Antigonish–Guysborough, was alone in his modest New Glasgow constituency office. His staff had yet to arrive for the day's work of helping constituents with the bureaucratic problems they had encountered with their government. This should have been a moment when the thirty-eight-year-old newly elected leader of the Progressive Conservative Party of Canada could put his feet up on the desk, reflect on his success over the past year, and feel satisfied. But in the quiet of this early autumn morning what he felt most was the burden of history.

The years of work that had brought him to the position of party leader could never have prepared him for the decision he was about to make. This decision would determine not only his future, but also the fate of his party and perhaps the country.

Some five months earlier, in May 2003, when Peter MacKay won the leadership of his party, he had imagined going head-to-head in the leaders' debates with Liberal prime minister Paul Martin and Alliance leader Stephen Harper. Confident that the voters would reject a tired and corrupt Liberal government, and hopeful that the regionally based Canadian Alliance party would falter, MacKay wanted to offer voters his vision for Canada.

The dilemma conservative voters had faced over the previous decade and more was that they had two parties from which to choose: the Progressive Conservative party, known from the earliest days of the country as "the Tories," or the Reform–turned–Alliance party. The two were of the same mind on many issues and consequently split the conservative vote. The other federal political parties were of course delighted that conservatives were fighting among themselves. Conservative division allowed the Liberals to win three successive majority governments "without breaking a sweat." Unless and until conservatives put an end to vote splitting, Liberal hegemony could continue indefinitely. For three elections, democracy had not functioned well. Not only did voters not have a meaningful choice in parties, but also the Opposition was weak and ineffective. This was not how Canada's parliamentary system was supposed to work. With another election expected in the next six months, conservatives were dreading yet another futile trip to the voting booth.

Despite the conservative civil war, however, many members in the PC and Alliance caucuses liked one another. They had worked together constructively on various parliamentary committees and they shared many of the same views on public policy. There was some divergence in the area of social policy, but no more than might be expected in a broadly inclusive political party. The tougher obstacle was emotional. Many Tories remained bitter that Preston Manning and the Reform party had split the conservative family in 1993. There was, they felt, a price to be paid for their humiliating defeat in 1993 when the PC party had been reduced to just 2 seats from the 169 it had won in 1988—the worst drubbing for the Tories since Confederation![1]

For a time after the 2000 election, the prospect of a single conservative party seemed possible. While the Alliance party had received a record number of votes and seats in the House of Commons in 2000, a dozen of its most influential and articulate MPs later left to form the Independent Alliance Caucus. Five members

---

[1] Previously the low mark for the Conservative party was 39 seats, which occurred in 1935 when the Reconstruction Party split the conservative vote.

soon returned to the Alliance party, but seven stayed out to form the Democratic Representative Caucus (DRC). The DRC soon joined with the PC caucus to form an entity that the Speaker of the House of Commons officially recognized as the PC-DRC. The Tories were hoping that the Alliance party was about to implode, leaving the PC party, or the PC-DRC, as the only political option for Canadian conservatives. But following the breakdown of merger talks between the PC and Alliance leaderships in 2002, most DRC members left the Tories and returned to the Alliance fold. The battle for supremacy and survival in Canadian conservative politics would wage on.

When the Alliance party was falling apart in 2002, Stephen Harper returned to partisan politics to lead and reinvigorate the party. Harper had begun his political career working for a PC member of parliament in 1985. Initially inspired to help a small-c conservative government implement sweeping economic and political reforms, Harper left Ottawa a year later, frustrated by what he saw as the brokerage politics that dominated decision making in Ottawa. A short time later Harper joined with Preston Manning to become a key figure in the creation of the Reform Party. While Harper was the policy brains behind Reform, and had been elected to Parliament in 1993, he left the world of partisan politics in 1996. The move to a right-wing advocacy group allowed Harper to articulate more freely his conservative vision for Canada. When Harper returned to partisan politics and won the Alliance leadership in 2002, he was intent on immediately seeking a merger with the PC party. However, the only thing PC leader Joe Clark then wanted was for the Alliance party to submit to his leadership.

The polls looked bleak for every party except the Liberals in 2003. Nevertheless, to virtually every political observer a merger between the PC and Alliance parties before the next election was inconceivable, for three key reasons.

First, in the summer of 2003 both the PC and Alliance parties had new leaders who had never been tested in a national campaign. It was natural for MacKay, thirty-eight, and Harper, forty-two, to want at least one opportunity to take their respective parties into a general election. For a merger to happen, one or both would have to surrender leadership, not something most politicians do willingly.

Second, in May 2003 MacKay signed a written agreement with fellow leadership candidate David Orchard. While Orchard came to the leadership convention with the support of only 25 per cent of the delegates, that was enough to determine who would win the contest. Their written agreement precluded the possibility of a merger with the Alliance party. MacKay saw the no-merger provision of the Orchard deal as innocuous, not only because it was party policy at the time, but because it was inconceivable to him that a merger with the Alliance in the near term was even a remote possibility. MacKay thought that each party would try to build national support in the coming election, and then try to starve out the other party until one died on the vine. In his mind, MacKay was in a fight to the death with Alliance. To settle this issue, an election was necessary.

Third, the election was expected in the spring of 2004. In the summer and fall of 2003 it was unimaginable that the emotional, organizational, and policy gulfs that remained between the two parties could be bridged before the next election. While MacKay and Harper knew that a single mainstream national conservative party would emerge from the divided quagmire that had become the conservative movement, nothing hinted that a merger was possible in the foreseeable future. Beyond the intentions and actions of the party leaders, for a merger to happen an agreement would have to be ratified by the membership of both parties. In the case of the PC party, approval was required by two-thirds of the membership. MacKay knew that the 25 per cent of the party members drawn to David Orchard would definitely be opposed, as would many other long-time Tories.

Despite these formidable challenges, however, MacKay and Harper launched a process in the summer of 2003 aimed at exploring methods of co-operation between the parties. Stunningly, what began with modest goals of co-operation and, optimistically, an agreement to find a formula to end vote splitting then eclipsed even the wildest expectation. A full-scale merger was on the table. Most surprising to

MacKay, the proposed agreement included virtually every element that was central to the beliefs and values of a Progressive Conservative. In fact, the aims and principles proposed for the new party were lifted word for word from the PC party constitution. The legacies from the Reform party and Alliance constitutions were virtually unrecognizable in the proposed agreement.

By Thanksgiving weekend, there was only one main area where agreement could not be reached: how to select the party leader. Stephen Harper wanted a simple and democratic one-member one-vote system. MacKay wanted every member to have a vote; but he also wanted each riding to be given the same weight when the votes were tallied. The one-member one-vote system would naturally encourage candidates to spend their time and energy where the party was strong. MacKay feared that very small riding associations, located in regions where it was difficult to sign up party members, would be ignored, thereby hampering the party's ability to build a truly national base of support. However, this was not a purely academic question related to governance. The political imperative was that one method favoured Harper's chances of winning the leadership of the new party, and the other favoured MacKay's.

Harper and MacKay had drawn their lines in the sand on the leadership selection issue. Despite a successful negotiation on every other front, MacKay was not prepared to compromise on this final issue. Walking away from the negotiations on this point of principle would have been easy, if not a relief, for MacKay. But Harper was convinced a merger was the only way the Conservatives could defeat the Liberals. He came to this conclusion in the spring of 2003 when, despite his best efforts, the Tories won a key by-election in a rural Ontario riding. The Alliance came in a very distant and disappointing third. After the by-election defeat, Harper was inclined to agree to almost every condition MacKay imposed, so long as the country ended up with one conservative party and there would be a leadership contest.

Over the Thanksgiving weekend, Harper assessed the risks and then agreed to the equality of riding condition. It was not an easy decision. He was risking his position as leader, and there was also a legacy of democratic populism in the Reform and Alliance parties that was not evident, at least on paper, in the new party. By merging under MacKay's conditions, Harper was also equating his 66 MPs with the twelve-member PC caucus.

MacKay had a far tougher decision to make. His was the party with the legacy from Confederation. His was the party that had roots and appeal in all parts of Canada. His was the party with the deep emotional scars, and for which ratification of a deal was anything but certain. His was the party with momentum, with polls showing 17 per cent for PCs and only 11 per cent for the Alliance. Even though Harper had given in to every one of MacKay's demands, and there was nothing left that MacKay could ask for, it was still a gut-wrenching decision.

During his six years as a federal politician, life and events had seemed to come at MacKay at full speed. There were few moments when the world slowed down long enough to allow focus on a solitary issue. But this quiet October morning in his constituency office was one of those moments.

MacKay felt burdened by the history of his party. Tory contributions had been woven into the fabric of the nation, and MacKay could not be certain that a new conservative party would connect to the legacy with which he had been entrusted. MacKay was worried about whether this new entity would even be called the "Tory" party. Would it be the party of Sir John A. Macdonald, Sir Robert Borden, R.B. Bennett, John Diefenbaker, and Brian Mulroney? Or would it become the party of Preston Manning? Every time MacKay walked past the busts of former PC prime ministers at PC party headquarters he could sense accusatory eyes watching him. MacKay wondered if these men would applaud his moves, or would they be spinning in their graves?

MacKay took comfort in the counsel that was available to him from former prime minister Brian Mulroney. MacKay understood that, as well as advice, Mulroney had enough sway in the party to defeat a proposed merger if such was his will. But Mulroney was supportive of the merger. And then there was MacKay's father. Elmer MacKay was an elder statesman of the party, elected to the House of Commons on seven occasions and serving in the cabinets of two prime ministers. It was Elmer MacKay who resigned his seat in 1983 so that Mulroney could enter the House of Commons through a by-election as the member for Central Nova in Nova Scotia. In retirement, however, Elmer MacKay still felt the scars from the battles with the Reform party in 1993. The elder MacKay initially opposed the merger.

MacKay knew that among the senior people in the party, some would support the merger and some would oppose it. Some of his twelve-member caucus had already spoken out against a merger after news of the negotiations had been leaked to the press. MacKay realized he would never get unanimity on the issue. He was going to be criticized no matter what he decided. This was not a time for consultation and persuasion; this was a time for leadership. But if he signed the agreement, MacKay's leadership would be finished. If party members voted yes, the merger would proceed and he would no longer be leader. If they voted no, his leadership would be in ruins and he would have to resign.

MacKay removed short-term political consequences from his decision criteria. Party financing, the recent polls, and the dynamic of Paul Martin's likely advent as leader of the Liberal party were not on his mind. Even his own leadership and agreement with David Orchard were not factors in this decision. This decision was more important than the career of Peter MacKay.

His mind was drawn to both the history and the future of Canada. What was right for his party? What would Sir John A. Macdonald want him to do? Most important, what was right for Canada?

CHAPTER 2

CONSERVATIVE COALITIONS

A POLITICAL PARTY THAT DOES not understand the reality of competition and strategy in a parliamentary democracy is doomed to failure.

An election is like a hockey game. It's not about who has the fastest skaters, the hardest shot, or even the toughest players. What matters most is which team puts the most pucks in the net. Similarly, it's not the smartest leader, best ideas, or most energetic team of candidates that matters. It's who gets the most votes. Politics is about beating your competition. Politics is about winning.

And here's the score: Liberal party eighty-four, Conservative party fifty-five—that's the number of years since Confederation that each of the parties has held government. Since 1900, the score firms up seventy-five to thirty-one in favour of the Liberals. No wonder the team in the red sweaters is known as Canada's "natural governing party," and arguably the western world's most successful political franchise.

Under Canada's parliamentary system, one rule of the game is that the party with the *confidence* of the House of Commons is asked to govern. This is a rule that Liberals understand very well, certainly far better than do their Conservative competitors. In a country as geographically, linguistically, culturally, ethnically, philosophically, and economically diverse as Canada, Liberals have figured out that they could never win the number of seats required to gain this confidence by speaking to a narrow range of interests, grievances, or communities. To win, a party needs to build a coalition of interests. Some call it a "big tent": a place that can comfortably and peacefully accommodate a large number of voters. This might seem onerous; however, it is anything but a negative. Coalition building helps keep the country united. A system built on the foundations of confidence and consensus also helps isolate extreme positions, making it very difficult for extreme views to find a voice in decision making. At its core, a system that requires consensus for success helps promote harmony, understanding, and tolerance.

The Canadian parliamentary system also places a premium on getting the right number of votes in the right places. For example, in the 1979 election Progressive Conservatives under Joe Clark received 35.9 per cent of the popular vote, while Pierre Trudeau's Liberals earned 40.1 per cent of the vote. Because so much of the Liberal vote was concentrated in the province of Quebec, however, it yielded fewer seats than the Tory vote did. This is a prime example of how pointless it can be to build a political tent with too many of its inhabitants concentrated in one place.

Victory in a local constituency means the winner has one more vote than the second-place finisher. It doesn't matter if a candidate is running against one opponent or twenty; the rule is "second place plus one wins." In a three-way race a candidate might conceivably get elected with slightly more than one-third of the votes cast. Put ten legitimate candidates on the ballot and the winning threshold can be much lower. Winning a seat by ten thousand votes or one hundred produces the same result.

All of this may seem obvious, but some political parties fail to understand the importance of strategy and coalition building, or are simply not prepared to do what is required to win government. Take the federal New Democratic Party, Canada's left-leaning socialist political party. While it takes more than 100 seats to win even a minority government, the NDP has never won more than 43 seats in a general election. Most NDP candidates know they are going to lose even before they register with the Chief Electoral Officer. Losing election after election doesn't seem to bother the NDP. Unlike some of its provincial counterparts, it continues to serve up the same policies and strategies that have produced defeats in every election. The leader may change, but the result stays the same. The party seems more interested in making a point and offering convictions with limited appeal than in electoral success. The NDP is less of a political party than it is a movement. NDP members might get more from government if they became a think-tank rather than a political party. A think-tank could infiltrate the Liberal party and steer it further to the left in the political spectrum. Instead, the NDP hopes for a minority parliament where it might extract a few legislative concessions from the government, in exchange for votes in the House of Commons, which is precisely what happened in the spring budget of 2005. It is an incredible undertaking—putting a political party on the map—to produce such a limited result. Of course, it risks a much more adverse outcome. For example, in the 1988 election, which was a virtual referendum on the Free Trade Agreement (FTA) with the United States, Mulroney was able to retain government and implement the FTA with the support of only 42.9 per cent of the electorate. The combined vote of the Liberals and New Democrats, both of whom strongly opposed the FTA, was 52.3 per cent. Had they fought as one party, free trade may never have come into force.

The fate that befalls the left-leaning NDP one election after another could easily apply to Canada's conservative movement. When conservatives become too narrowly focused, or if they veer far right, or if they fail to appeal to voters in all parts of Canada, they have no chance of winning. Politics 101 states that in a parliamentary democracy, a party with extreme views is sure to fail.

Another way to guarantee defeat would be to divide a coalition of common interests. A single party might win a substantial number of seats with 40 per cent of the vote; but a common voting block that is split into two parties, with each earning 20 per cent of the vote, will win none. When western conservatives established the Reform party, they split the conservative vote with the PCs, ensuring successive Liberal victories. As the Reform and PC parties painfully learned, it is futile to pitch two tents on the same site. The structure of our parliamentary democracy punishes those who divide political coalitions. However, Canadians who consider themselves conservative are far from a homogenous group.

In a classic sense, conservatives tend to support traditional values, established order, and free market approaches to economics. But the variants of conservatism in Canada run wide and deep, offering any number of inherent conflicts, contradictions, and inconsistencies.

There are *conservative nationalists* who oppose foreign direct investment and the liberalization of trading laws. *Fiscal conservatives* generally advocate minimal government intervention in the economy, balanced budgets, and low taxes. *Monarchist conservatives* follow British traditions, pledging loyalty to Queen or King. *Libertarian conservatives* espouse absolute free will, while *social conservatives* believe strongly in pro-family positions, including laws to protect the unborn and the traditional definition of marriage. Canadian conservatives have traditionally been more respectful of the rights and responsibilities of the provinces, as set out in the Constitution, than have the other political parties. Conservatives are also known as *Tories*, a term sometimes prefixed with the colours red and blue. *Red Tories* are thought to be more progressive conservatives who advocate a more activist and compassionate government that will address the social ills of the day. *Blue Tories* follow a stronger free enterprise model of minimal government. Canadians have also been known to follow a form of *populist conservatism*, a belief that places the decisions of government more within the control of citizens and less under the dominance of the political elites. To name but a few more, there are *Burkean conservatives, neo-conservatives, economic conservatives, cultural conservatives, moral conservatives, intellectual conservatives,* and *environmental conservatives.* There are even *liberal conservatives* and *democratic conservatives*, as in the Reagan democrats who crossed party lines in 1980 and 1984 to support the Republican (that is, conservative) American president.

Amidst this multitude of conservative options exists a reality that is ignored at significant peril. Conservative leaders, in Canada or elsewhere, cannot hope to be successful by preferring one element of the conservative brand. The successful leader is judged not by an ability to carry the flag for a particular faction, but by an ability to draw the wide range of conservative factions together with a common cause and vision.

It is inevitable that internal battles will be fought among like-minded people in a broadly based political party. It is natural that any one faction of a party would want to prevail. Blue Tories want to draw a much harder line on reducing the influence of government in the affairs of the nation, while Red Tories believe their willingness to accept more government involvement is a more compassionate and effective approach to government. Since most elections in Canada are decided in the centre, rather than the far right, the Red Tories think their approach offers the best strategy for winning. This may be true, but when they ignore the needs of their Blue Tory friends, they fail to take into account the big picture.

Successful Conservative leaders realize that every dimension of the movement must be represented in a single party. Successful leadership is not about letting one side of the movement dominate, but about fostering unity among a very broad and multi-faceted coalition of conservatives. Collective success comes from accepting and embracing the movement in its widest possible form.

The conservatives who have risen to the rank of prime minister with majority governments can be counted on one hand: Sir John A. Macdonald, Robert Laird Borden, Richard Bennett, John Diefenbaker, and Brian Mulroney. Only two won successive majority governments: Macdonald and Mulroney.[1]

Conservative victories have been achieved only when the party and its leader have built coalitions representing the various factions of conservatives from all parts of the country. Before exploring the political challenges and disunity that beset conservatives over the past two decades, as well as the reformation of the

---

[1] Robert Borden won one majority as a Conservative and another as the leader of a coalition of Conservatives and Liberals in a Union government.

movement in 2003, it is worth reflecting upon Canada's most successful conservative leaders and the coalitions that brought them to power.

SIR JOHN A. MACDONALD

Canada's first prime minister was, arguably, the master of bringing diverse interests and people together. Sir John A. Macdonald built coalitions not just to form a government, but also to establish a nation. Macdonald became a Father of Confederation by bringing together English and French, Reformers and Conservatives, Canadian nationalists, and big business into one political party.

Macdonald's most significant and lasting achievement in nation building was the drawing together of English and French. Macdonald recognized both the diversity and unity of Canada when he said: "Let us be English or let us be French . . . and above all let us be Canadians."

Those who view Macdonald as a great Conservative statesman must understand that he did not win government on the basis of pure ideology or an uncompromising vision. His greatness came from a broad and inclusive vision for Canada and a capacity to cobble together a diverse stream of interests. He was not always noble; his most frequently used currencies to sway public opinion, and the party faithful, were patronage and cash. But for all his well-known faults, he was engaging and charming.

Macdonald was no stranger to compromise as a strategy to build support. As much as he wanted a strong central government, he understood that for Confederation to happen provinces required strong powers. Yet Macdonald could clearly see the destruction from the Civil War to the south, fuelled largely by a dispute over states' rights. Nonetheless, Macdonald and his fellow Fathers of Confederation made the many compromises required to gain the confidence of French Canadians. When Quebec was worried about being outnumbered in a federal parliament that was based on representation by population, it was granted special status assuring the province a minimum of 65 seats in the federal legislature. Quebec would also be given the distinct power to protect the French language and culture. It remains unclear if the

Fathers of Confederation, in making these compromises, were limiting the protection of the French language to Quebec, or if they envisioned a bilingual and bicultural Canada.[2] However, the key here is that what was ultimately offered was enough to bring Quebec into Confederation. Macdonald did not insist on the equality of provinces; he compromised and built a coalition that the people would accept.

We think of Macdonald as the first leader of the Conservative party. While Conservatives lovingly claim Sir John A. Macdonald as exclusively one of their own, however, the party he represented in Parliament was officially called the Liberal-Conservative Party. Today it would seem something of an insult for the word "liberal" to be attached to the legacy of Sir John, let alone having it appear first in the party name. But Macdonald led a party with a liberal prefix because he needed to build a coalition that could lead and win the country. The liberal moniker stayed with the party until the end of the nineteenth century, when the name became the Conservative Party.

The central theme in the various compromises that allowed Macdonald to build a sometimes diverse coalition of disparate interests is that he knew what it took to win. And that's precisely what he did in winning six of the country's first seven elections, all victories with a majority government.

SIR ROBERT BORDEN

Robert Laird Borden came from a family of Nova Scotia farmers, although it was clear from a young age he was more inclined to books than pastures. It was not that he lacked discipline or a strong work ethic; quite the opposite. A successful lawyer, Borden was a reluctant entrant to the world of politics, and an even more reluctant leader. When the call came to lead the party in 1901 he modestly responded that he had neither the experience nor the qualifications, but accepted anyway on the condition that the party simultaneously appoint a committee to search for a permanent replacement.

---

[2] It was not until 1969 that the federal parliament passed the Official Languages Act establishing a new vision for a more bilingual Canada.

Borden would lead the conservatives in opposition for more than a decade and lose two elections before becoming prime minister. During his period in opposition he honed his public speaking and debating skills, although these were both facets of politics he never enjoyed. Caucus unity was an even greater challenge, as the party carried deep divisions concerning religion, language, and policy.

In Borden's first election defeat, the Tories lost 5 seats, including Borden's. A by-election was quickly arranged, which the Liberals did not contest as a matter of courtesy. Borden began to focus on policy and prepared a platform that featured Senate reform, public service reform, tighter restrictions on immigration, ownership or regulation in the communications and transportation sectors, and the unimpaired maintenance of provincial rights. Those of conservative persuasion were not impressed with such an activist platform. Neither were the voters. In his second campaign as Conservative leader, Borden managed to gain 10 seats, which left him 64 seats behind the Liberals.

Soldiering on, Borden faced two key policy questions: the establishment of a Canadian navy and free trade with the United States. Borden wanted a more independent Canadian navy while many caucus colleagues preferred continuing to support the British navy with cash. On the second issue, Prime Minister Wilfrid Laurier had staked out his ground with a free trade proposal, which won him instant support from Canadian farmers, fishermen, and others who were tired of paying high tariffs. Borden, supported by a clutch of conservative premiers, opposed free trade based on fears of a loss of sovereignty and detachment from the British empire. "Canadianism or Continentalism," was Borden's slogan for the 1911 election campaign. Business interests—those protected by the tariffs—were also at the ready. Borden built a coalition of those opposed to free trade, which included anti-reciprocity Liberals. As distasteful as this was to many die-hard conservatives, this would not be the only time Borden would look to Liberals to secure government. On September 21, 1911, the Conservatives won 133 seats to the Liberals' 86.

Borden pursued an activist government that proposed marketing and export assistance for Canadian grains, as well as a national highway system (one of the early uses of federal spending powers in areas of provincial jurisdiction). The Liberal-dominated Senate thwarted many of Borden's measures, as well as a proposal for a more independent Canadian navy. Senate obstruction almost led to a snap election, with an elected Senate as the only issue.

But on August 4, 1914, everything changed. The world was brought to war, and in Canada partisanship gave way to co-operation as Conservatives and Liberals worked together to pass the War Measures Act.

The war lasted much longer than anyone anticipated. Income tax was imposed as a "temporary measure" to fund the war effort, and government intervention in the economy became widespread. Canada matured during the First World War and, through its sacrifice and contribution, asserted its independence under Borden. No longer content to follow the lead of the British, Canada insisted on and obtained a role in military strategy as well as in international affairs.

Borden had made an unbreakable bond with Canadian soldiers fighting in the trenches and vowed to give them the nation's full support. He stood up for Canadian troops and threatened not to send soldiers overseas unless Canada was properly consulted on the deployment of its forces. Supporting Canada's troops also meant conscription. He knew it would be divisive for the country so he invited Liberal leader Wilfrid Laurier to join him in a coalition government. Laurier vacillated, then eventually refused. Borden sought the support of conscriptionist Liberals and eventually formed what he called a "Union" government. On December 17, 1917, the Unionists won 153 seats to the Liberals' 82. Borden's government included 114 Conservative and 39 Liberal members. Twenty Liberal seats came from Quebec. Clearly, Borden faced huge political problems over conscription in Quebec, coupled with the issue of French language schooling outside Quebec. It would be a generation or more before Quebecers would, if only temporarily, embrace Conservatives.

In the 1917 election, Borden's victory was aided by extending the vote to women who were of immediate relation to soldiers. After the election, legislation was passed to extend the vote to all women and to guarantee female workers equal pay for equal work.

Borden also insisted that Canada be represented at the Peace Conference. When offered standing to represent all British colonies, dominions, and the like, Borden refused. He wanted a place for Canada alone, although he secured standing for a number of Britain's allies at plenary meetings.

After the war, the Union government began to disintegrate over budget matters and the Winnipeg General Strike. Borden was tired and disinclined to fight another election and officially retired on July 1, 1920.

Borden was a hard-working, earnest, and decent man who cared passionately about Canada and its independence. But it was not just the strength of his character and convictions that earned him respect and the prime ministership. He understood that for the sake of his country, let alone his party, he needed to reach out to everyone, even Liberals, to provide the unity and leadership the country required.

RICHARD BENNETT

Richard Bennett was fifty-seven years of age when he became leader of the Conservative party on October 20, 1927. At the time the party was both disorganized and in poor financial condition.[3] Bennett invested his own financial resources and built a party organization that was efficient and innovative. An effective opposition leader, Bennett built national support by establishing links with Ontario premier George Howard Ferguson and Quebec Conservative party leader Camillien Houde.

Ultimately, party organization and networking were less impor- tant in Bennett's success in the 1930 election than was the hardship

---

[3] Much of the content that informed this section dealing with R.B. Bennett came from the Dictionary of Canadian Biography Online, hosted by Library and Archives Canada and written by P.B. Waite. Other content is from Michael Bliss, *Right Honourable Men: The Descent of Canadian Politics from Macdonald to Mulroney* (Toronto: HarperCollins, 1994).

facing voters. Canada was suffering from the stock market crash of 1929 and the subsequent collapse in commodity prices. Unemployment was on the rise, and a devastating drought in Western Canada further depressed the national economy and spirit.

Bennett ran on an interventionist platform that promised employment in Canadian industries through tariff protection coupled with a program of public works. What he offered was a shot of hope with a bad economics chaser. Voters chose hope and gave Bennett a mandate on July 28, 1930, with the election of 137 Conservatives, 91 Liberals, and 17 others.

In a move that would make modern-day economists cringe, Bennett implemented heavy tariffs, hoping to create markets for Canadian producers and to keep Canada independent of the United States. The economy failed to improve; in fact, it worsened. Bennett responded with more tariffs, more direct relief for the unemployed, and more public infrastructure programs. Unemployment reached 27 per cent of the workforce. Remedial measures were implemented, including legislation to help farmers avoid foreclosure. Marketing boards were established to help secure better prices for farm products.

Bennett also attacked some of the pillars of capitalism. He established public broadcasting, the Bank of Canada, unemployment insurance, the Canadian Wheat Board, and a national infrastructure program, and he enhanced old age pensions. He believed in labour unions and in improved working conditions.

With his government's popularity at record-low levels and an election looming, he launched a new plan that took dead aim at laissez-faire capitalism. One of his cabinet ministers, Henry Herbert Stevens, was forced to resign over his remarks about the capitalist system. While out of cabinet, a disgruntled Stevens formed a new political entity called the Reconstruction Party.

The election was called, and Bennett went down to defeat. At first glance the results were devastating, with the Liberals rising from 88 seats to 171, and the Tories collapsing from 137 to 39. However, it was not a higher Liberal vote that caused the devastation to the Tories. The problem was the Reconstruction Party, which received 8.7 per cent of the popular vote and cut deeply into conservative support. It was a case of vote splitting, 1930s style.

There is no doubt that R.B. Bennett was an accomplished, intelligent, ambitious, and hard-working man. He invested substantial sums of money in the Conservative party and brought many innovative approaches to the art of politics. He was also very moody, but for this it is hard to blame a prime minister governing during a great depression.[4]

Bennett was not much of a coalition-builder while out of office and a one-man band while prime minister. He was also not much of a conservative. His electoral success was based largely on good timing. He was a single-term prime minister, but the extent of his defeat can be blamed on party disunity and an overcrowded ballot, with the Reconstruction Party dragging the Tories down. Yes, history probably had some important lessons the Tories could have learned, to avoid the debacle of 1993.

PROGRESSIVE PARTY

Before turning to John Diefenbaker, it is worth reviewing the events that led to the change in the party's name, from Conservative to Progressive Conservative. The change occurred after Bennett's tenure and during a twenty-three-year period when Conservatives were out of power. To understand the significance of the name change, we need to look at the history of the Progressive Party.

The Progressive Party was a significant force in federal politics in the early 1920s. At its peak, it was the second largest party in the House of Commons, winning 65 seats in the 1921 general election.[5] Preston Manning credits the Progressive Party with pressuring the government to pass the 1930 constitutional amendment that

---

[4] Bennett was also reported to have a disease called "phimosis," which involved a tight foreskin that could be very painful at erection. Some historians have offered this as an explanation for his dour mood and his status as a life-long bachelor.

[5] This included 21 in Ontario, one in New Brunswick, 5 in British Columbia, and 38 on the Prairies.

transferred the ownership of natural resources from the federal government to the prairie provinces. Many similarities can be found
between the Progressive Party of the 1920s and the Reform party of
the 1990s. Both were western-based and populist. Both believed in
similar approaches to democratic inclusiveness. They shared a distrust
of mainstream political parties and advocated giving more power
directly to voters through initiatives such as referendum, recall, and
more free votes in the House of Commons. Both parties were heavily
influenced by social issues with identifiable spiritual dimensions. The
Progressive Party supported free trade, and was a voice against the
power and interests of big business, particularly in the sectors of transportation and agriculture. The Progressive Party carried a more
agrarian influence than Reform, likely because of the era in which it
existed. On matters of social policy, both Reform and the Progressives
were strongly conservative. Finally, Reform and Progressives built
voter support on what was otherwise the electoral base of the
Conservative party while in government.[6] Unlike Reform, however,
Progressives were able to establish some popularity in Ontario.

Among the more notable Progressive politicians was John
Bracken, who served as the Liberal-Progressive premier of Manitoba
from 1922 to 1942. When Bracken was elected leader of the federal
Conservative party on December 11, 1942 (at a convention in which
John Diefenbaker was a candidate), he insisted that the party be
called the Progressive Conservative Party of Canada.

Many Canadians believed that the term *progressive* was added to
indicate a more compassionate form of conservatism. The history
of the Progressive Party shows that this was not the case. When the
2003 merger of the PCs and the Alliance was analyzed, critics cited
the dropping of the *progressive* moniker as evidence of a hard shift
in policy to the right. The implication was that if the party was no
longer *progressive*, then perhaps it had become *regressive*. The

---

[6] "It was obvious, by early 1920, farmers were turning away from the [conservative]
Borden government. . . . And farmers were starting to back the Progressive Party."
J.L. Granatstein et al., *Nation: Canada Since Confederation.* (Toronto: McGraw-Hill,
1990), 282.

Progressive Party was historically a closer cousin to the Reform party than it was to the so-called Red Tories, who thought of themselves as the progressive wing of the party. When John Bracken changed the party name in 1942, an important historical connector to Progressive—some would say Reform—values was symbolically lost.

Unfortunately for conservatives, the name change was of no clear immediate electoral benefit, as the Progressive Conservative Party did not achieve power for fifteen years, until John Diefenbaker led the charge in the election of 1957.

JOHN DIEFENBAKER

"Dief the Chief," as Diefenbaker was affectionately known, was a different brand of conservative. He was certainly far removed from the central-Canada businessman image of a conservative. A firebrand populist, Diefenbaker was a performer of the highest order.

Using inspiring and visionary language, Diefenbaker put forward a national economic development program that appealed to the regions of Canada. Evoking images of Sir John A. Macdonald's vision of westward expansion, Diefenbaker spoke of a National Vision to provide Canadians with control over their economic and political future. He offered to improve infrastructure and provide financing that would lead to the opening of Canada's northland and the development of its national resources.

Diefenbaker was a spirited and lively sixty-one-year-old campaigner. In 1957 the electorate was fed up and ready to throw the Liberals out of office. In addition to harvesting those that wanted change, Diefenbaker built alliances with Leslie Frost's Ontario Conservatives and Quebec premier Maurice Duplessis and his Union Nationale party machine.[7] Diefenbaker's platform drew in the regions of Canada, and his coalition was attractive enough to business to sustain traditional conservative loyalties.

---

[7] Bliss, *Right Honourable Men*, 193. Duplessis' Union Nationale Party was the entity that emerged from a merger of the Conservative Party and the Action Libérale Nationale in 1935.

The Tories earned a minority government in 1957 under the campaign slogan "It's time for a Diefenbaker government." He beat the Liberals by a mere 7 seats—112 to 105—with other parties holding the balance of power with 44 seats.

While Diefenbaker appeased the business community, he was hardly a free trader. He pursued the foolish policy of diverting 15 per cent of Canada's foreign trade from the United States to the United Kingdom. Diefenbaker was highly interventionist in economic and social policy with a legislative program that included farm price supports, housing loans, aid for development projects, increases in civil service salaries, and a strong dose of regional economic development.

His government lost the confidence of the House less than ten months after his 1957 minority victory, but was awarded a massive majority government on March 31, 1958. In his first campaign as prime minister, Diefenbaker's populist and charismatic message caught the public's mood, and he triumphed, winning 208 of 265 seats, 50 of which were in Quebec. After the victory, Diefenbaker declared, "The Conservative Party has become a truly national party composed of all the people of Canada of all races united in the concept of one Canada."[8]

His success in Quebec was due to the strength of his personality and the help from Premier Duplessis. Support from Quebec was surprising, given Diefenbaker's "One Canada" policy. Diefenbaker believed Canada was a dominion and a confederation of provinces, not that it comprised *deux nations* and that Quebecers were a distinct race. The Quebec coalition would not last long.

Diefenbaker's conservatism is rooted in his monarchist traditions and libertarian beliefs: he believed the power of the state needed to be controlled to protect the rights of the individual. This approach fit well with his egalitarian one-nation belief and his populist appeal. Diefenbaker's beliefs, and his preacher-styled oration provide an interesting comparison to Preston Manning, the first and only leader of the Reform party. While Manning took his views on democratic

---

[8] Library and Archives Canada, Dictionary of Canadian Biography Online: www.biographi.ca (accessed July 10, 2006).

inclusiveness much further than did Diefenbaker, there was a certain similarity between Diefenbaker's populist approach and Manning's "common sense of the common people." The Chief had a common and colourful touch, perhaps most evident when he would don the ceremonial robes and headdress of an honorary native chief.

Diefenbaker broke new ground in a number of areas. As prime minister he gave the vote to status Indians. He appointed the first Indian, James Gladstone, to the Senate; he also appointed the first woman to grace the cabinet table, Ellen Fairclough, as secretary of state. Under his leadership, parliamentary debates were fully accessible in English and French for the first time. His record as prime minister includes the passage of the Bill of Rights (although without a constitutional amendment the Bill did not apply to any of the provinces). Evidence of the symbolic qualities of the Bill was a "notwithstanding clause" that permitted Parliament to override the guarantees contained therein. A "notwithstanding clause" was also incorporated into the Canadian Constitution of 1982.

Ultimately, the Diefenbaker coalition was tenuous and could deliver only one majority government. The coalition, to a large degree, was built on matters that were intrinsically temporary: a desire for a change in government, the powerful and colourful personality of a leader, traditional support from provincial conser-vatives, and finally the help from a soon-to-be-deposed government in Quebec.

Diefenbaker's powerful personality was a double-edged sword. Like one of his Liberal predecessors, Mackenzie King, Diefenbaker frequently had his sanity questioned. As historian Michael Bliss reports in his review of Canadian prime ministers: "Everyone said the unstable old man [Diefenbaker] was paranoiac, and many felt righteous and sane enough to cast the stones that drove him from office. 'Sometimes I really do believe he's crazy,' Leslie Frost, the Premier of Ontario, said to Eddie Goodman, a leading party organ-izer in 1961. 'Why only sometimes?' Goodman responded."[9]

---

[9] Bliss, *Right Honourable Men*, 186.

His efforts to draw people to his cause and build consensus were hampered because of his basic distrust of others—including experts such as the governor of the Bank of Canada. He abhorred ambition within his party and demanded nothing less than complete loyalty.[10] His skills were better suited to the podium and the campaign trail than to the management of people and government.

Diefenbaker's massive majority was reduced to a minority government in the June 1962 election, in which the popular vote with the Liberal party was tied at 37 per cent. His minority government lasted less than a year when, on April 8, 1963, Lester Pearson's Liberals assumed government in another minority parliament.

Diefenbaker remained leader of the party until September 9, 1967, when he was replaced by a former premier of Nova Scotia, Robert Stanfield. The Chief remained in Parliament, however, last winning office in the 1979 election that brought Joe Clark to the office of prime minister. Diefenbaker encouraged, inspired, and cajoled parliamentarians of all stripes during his days on the backbenches. Don Mazankowski, deputy prime minister in Brian Mulroney's government, was Diefenbaker's last seat mate in the House of Commons. It was an appropriate pairing because Diefenbaker was Mazankowski's idol and had inspired him to enter politics: "I am a Conservative because of John Diefenbaker. He gave the West its place in Confederation and he did things for western Canada that made me feel a part of this country. He also opened the party to guys with names like Mazankowski, Epp, and Schmidt." Mazankowski also remembered Diefenbaker as a man of humour and humility. After Mazankowski nervously delivered what he thought was a horrible maiden speech in Parliament, Diefenbaker quipped: "Young man. That was a great speech and you are doing just fine." Seeing that Mazankowski still wondered whether he belonged in Parliament, Diefenbaker continued. "Don't worry. For the first six

---

[10] In his autobiography, Diefenbaker included an appendix listing all MPs who signed a declaration of loyalty to him as leader, as well as those who did not. John G. Diefenbaker, *One Canada: The Tumultuous Years*, 1962–1967 (Toronto: Macmillan, 1977), 301–302.

months you will be wondering if you really belong here, but after that you will question how the rest of us got here."

Historians like to blame craziness for Diefenbaker's defeat, and few bother to lay the blame for his demise on the rise of the conservative-minded Social Credit Party. When Diefenbaker swept the nation in 1958, Social Credit won only 2.6 per cent of the national vote and no seats. In 1962, Social Credit surged in Quebec, received 11.7 per cent of the vote, and won 30 seats. Had these votes gone Conservative, Diefenbaker would have won a comfortable majority. Even in 1962, the combined PC and Social Credit vote eclipsed that of the Liberal party by 3.1 percentage points. According to Mazankowski, Ernest Manning was a key figure in the fall of Diefenbaker's minority government in 1963: "When the chips were down in the Diefenbaker years it was Social Credit that brought the downfall. It was Ernest Manning who persuaded Socred leader Robert Thompson to 'pull the pin' on the Diefenbaker government."[11]

As the coalition that brought Diefenbaker to power fell apart, Conservative vote splitting between the PC and Social Credit parties helped elect a Liberal government under Lester B. Pearson. Conservatives would face a similar problem when the next generation of Conservatives came to power.

BRIAN MULRONEY

After Sir John A. Macdonald, the next greatest conservative coalition builder is Brian Mulroney.

The son of Ben Mulroney, the chief electrician for Baie Comeau, Quebec, Martin Brian Mulroney was born on March 20, 1939, the third of six children. Brian shone brightly from an early age and was a natural leader and public speaker. He became active in politics at St. Francis Xavier University, taking the role of Conservative prime minister in its model parliament. While studying law at Laval, he was elected vice-president of the Conservative Students' Federation.

---

[11] Robert Thompson was a five-term MP: the first three with Social Credit and the final two as a Progressive Conservative.

Mulroney caught the attention of Diefenbaker and took on the unprecedented role of student adviser to the prime minister. David Angus, whom Mulroney appointed to the Senate in 1993, was a Young Progressive Conservative (YPC) colleague of Mulroney: "I met Mulroney at a PC convention when Diefenbaker was in power. Before I met him, Diefenbaker had talked to me about him. Imagine a sitting Prime Minister recognizing a student in that way. Brian was a magnet."

Mulroney faithfully supported the party's efforts throughout the 1960s and early 1970s. While he had a national presence, his passion was Quebec, where electoral prospects for the Tories were weak to non-existent. By the time Robert Stanfield stepped down as leader in 1976, many in the party had identified Mulroney as a potential leader.

FROM HIS DAYS IN THE YPC, Mulroney had an incredible network right across the country. However, his only link to the PC caucus was Patrick Knowlan, the MP from Annapolis Valley, Nova Scotia. The 1976 convention did not go well: some refer to the movement to defeat the two business-oriented Quebecers, Claude Wagner and Brian Mulroney, the first- and second-place candidates on the first ballot, as the "great gang bang." Mulroney was devastated. It was seven years before the position of leader came open again. During this period, Mulroney spent time licking his wounds, establishing a high profile and lucrative business career, and raising a family. He maintained his political contacts, including people such as Peter White, Frank Moores, and Sam Wakim—men who were anxious to oust Joe Clark as party leader.

What made Mulroney most distinctive to the party was that he was a Quebecer. Only once in its history had the Conservative party ever tried a Quebecer as party leader, and that was for only eighteen months at the end of the previous century.

Mulroney delivered what was, to that point in his life, his most important political speech on June 10, 1983, the day before party delegates would choose their next leader. The speech dealt not with policy and vision; rather, it was about the grand coalition that would bring Conservatives at long last out of the wilderness and into power:[12] "Our major purpose . . . in being here is to drive the Liberals from office and bring about a majority Progressive Conservative government." Mulroney called party unity a pre-condition to victory, and pledged to follow an eleventh commandment: "Thou Shall Never Speak Ill of Another Conservative." Recognizing the breadth of conservatives represented in the party, Mulroney said, "There shall be no incivility because of divergent views . . . there shall be no ideological tests of purity, absolutely none."

Mulroney boldly challenged convention delegates to face up to a historical reality: "Why is it that when we put on our hats as federal Conservatives . . . everyone says we are a bunch of losers? . . . [O]ur area of weakness in French Canada, time after time, decade after decade, election after election, has staggered this Party and debilitated the nation." Invoking the memory of Sir John A. Macdonald and his coalition of west and east, English and French, Mulroney said, "Let us accept [Macdonald's] invitation and let us recreate that grand alliance, and in the process, together we shall build a new Conservative Party and we shall build a brand new Canada."

What Mulroney was really saying was, "elect me as leader and I will deliver seats from Quebec." Given Liberal hegemony in Quebec, few believed this was possible. But Mulroney's credentials were impressive and his confidence was brimming. His appeal to soft Quebec nationalists was unspoken, but very real and legitimate. The party could also verify Mulroney's Quebec bona fides by the large number of Quebec delegates he brought with him to the 1983 leadership convention.

To win the leadership Mulroney built a cross-country network of support, but it was far from complete. He won the convention, but it took four ballots to do so, beating Joe Clark 54 per cent to 46 per cent. It was hardly a commanding win. Mulroney reached out immediately to the other seven leadership contestants, all of whom represented different conservative constituencies. In his convention

---

[12] It is noteworthy that the only policy plank in Mulroney's speech with a specific objective was to eliminate the deficit by 1990.

acceptance speech, he publicly indicated his desire to work with friend and foe alike. Erik Nielsen, the party's interim leader, was at the podium after Mulroney had been declared victorious. Nielsen reminded the delegates that Mulroney had not been *his* first choice. Without missing a beat, Mulroney announced that Nielsen was *his* first choice as deputy leader. In that instant, Mulroney showed the discipline, wisdom, and grace that would inspire loyalty and draw the Conservative family together.

As a master coalition builder, Mulroney understood he could begin to unite his party by reinvigorating the failed leadership candidates. David Angus recalled that the day after the convention, Brian had lost his voice. "He called me into his suite at the Château Laurier and whispered, 'I understand the party is in terrible shape. I want you to do an audit. We have to clean up the place.' More important, the first thing he did, as party leader, was to make sure none of the candidates had a debt. There were some huge amounts owing, by Crosbie, Clark, Wilson, and others. We scheduled ten dinners across the country and we cleaned everything up. We built up a tremendous amount of goodwill among the candidates and in the party."

Mulroney then turned his attention to party finances. "He didn't want to go to the people of Canada to elect his party and him as prime minister if we didn't have our own books balanced and if we didn't have a frugal mindset," said Angus. "We had to be able to present a responsible financial position, which we did." It is ironic that, having placed such a premium on getting his party's financial house in order, Mulroney would be so heavily criticized when it came to dealing with the government deficit.

Mulroney recognized that his coalition had four distinct blocks. While he would deliver the Quebec contingent, he would rely upon deep conservative Atlantic roots, the free enterprise crowd from the West, and the "big blue machine" from Ontario. He counted on the provincial party machines to deliver the conservative vote in the regions of the country in which he was least familiar. "There were a lot of Tory Premiers to work with," said Angus. "Premier Lougheed (from Alberta) was always supportive behind the scenes. But Quebec was the key to this thing. The Créditistes were no longer active, and Brian had a tremendous network in Quebec with an organization on the ground. We had organizers from the Quebec Liberal Party and the Parti Québécois. Brian seemed to know everybody."

But Mulroney had a trump card that appealed nationwide: Canada was ready for a change.

Mulroney understood that for a party in opposition, coalition building could be a far-reaching and quiet exercise. In 1984, for example, it is unlikely that long-suffering Tory voters from the West would have thought of themselves as joining forces with soft Quebec nationalists. Conservatives in Quebec were too rare and unknown to be fully appreciated. This might help explain the surprise and disappointment of western conservatives when the Conservative government they had waited more than thirty years to elect stood for recognizing Quebec as a distinct society in the constitution.

While the Liberal party was choosing its new leader in the spring of 1984, Brian Mulroney and his wife, Mila, embarked on an extensive cross-country tour with little or no publicity in the national press. Mulroney dubbed this his "small town strategy." It was unusual for party members to have a leader in their hometown except during an election. "I am leaving a series of pearls in all these communities across Canada. The moment that the new PM calls an election, the pearls will be strung together. Then just watch us!" This was Mulroney in action: reaching out to bring in new people. He made the newcomers feel they were part of a grand and noble coalition that would lead Canada to a brighter future.

Conservative provincial premiers were integral to the Mulroney coalition and to his 1984 summer tour. In the excitement of the tour, New Brunswick premier Richard Hatfield told Mulroney he was worried because up to six of his senior cabinet ministers confided they wanted to resign to run federally. Mulroney promised that he would only take two.

Mulroney inspired his coalition with his leadership style and engaging personal qualities: a legendary Irish charm, a wonderful capacity for storytelling, and an endearing if not unhealthy dose of

loyalty. He was also a great campaigner, seizing a tremendous opportunity to deliver a knockout punch during the national leaders'
debates with Prime Minister John Turner on the issue of patronage.

To ensure a massive victory in Quebec, Mulroney delivered the
now famous "Sept-Isles speech" that laid the groundwork for the
Meech Lake Accord. Mulroney drew support from every quarter of
Quebec. In some regions, he tapped into the Parti Québécois network for help; in other areas, provincial Liberals took the lead. It was
a remarkable and unstoppable coalition that came to be known as
Mulroney's "Blue Thunder."

Results from the 1984 election were better than even the most
optimistic conservatives could have imagined. Mulroney earned a
popular vote of just more than 50 per cent, the first time a true
majority in popular vote had been recorded in a Canadian election
since the Diefenbaker sweep of 1958. By comparison, Trudeaumania
in 1968 had produced a popular vote of 45.5 per cent, which was
Trudeau's best result as Liberal leader. Under Mulroney,
Progressive Conservatives won 58 of 75 seats from Quebec. In the
previous twenty years, Conservatives had never won more than 8
Quebec seats.

It was anyone's guess how long the Mulroney coalition would
last. In 1984, one leading columnist boldly predicted that
Mulroney's Conservatives had a lock on power until at least the turn
of the century. However, building a coalition from the opposition
benches was one thing. Keeping it together while in government was
quite another.

CHAPTER 3

LIFE BEFORE NATIONAL POLITICS

AMONG A CAST OF THOUSANDS, three leading characters come to the fore as having the greatest influence on the division and reunification of the conservative movement over the past two decades. They came to politics through different paths, although there are some similarities worth noting. Exploring their personal motivations for entering politics and looking at their early influences will provide some interesting insights into the visions and choices that mark their political careers.

So, who are Preston Manning, Stephen Harper, and Peter MacKay? And what did they bring with them to national political life?

PRESTON MANNING

Preston Manning came to national politics with all the credibility and sophistication that we would expect of the son of one of Canada's right-wing political icons. Ernest Manning not only directed *Canada's National Back to the Bible Hour*, a radio broadcast syndicated to more than ninety outlets, but was also, for twenty-five years, the Social Credit premier of Alberta.

Born June 10, 1942, Preston was raised in the evangelical Christian tradition. His faith is deep, profound, and the foundation of his life. From a very young age, Preston lived with a strong sense of civic duty. This is not something he picked up casually over time at the dinner table. He had a small side office in the Alberta

Legislature beside his father's. While other kids played in the streets after school, Preston did his homework in the office next to the premier. As a child, Preston was immersed in more than the family farm; he was entrenched in the family business of politics and religion. He read the Alberta statutes as a way to understand what his father did for a living. The accomplishments of the senior Manning helped instill in Preston a strong sense of destiny, a high dose of ego, and a legacy on which to build.

Preston's older brother, Keith, was the victim of oxygen deprivation at birth. Keith was unable to attend school and suffered from seizures and arrested mental development. He died in 1986 at the age of forty-six. Manning describes the suffering of his brother as his family's "greatest sorrow." Sometimes a struggle of this magnitude draws a family together, but Preston confided that his was not a particularly close or emotionally supportive family. In his second autobiography, Preston laments the difficulty he had expressing his emotions and passions about Canada, and this difficulty appears to have limited his ability to connect with Canadians about his most deeply held convictions. In this regard, his childhood appears to have left its mark.

Parents of five children, Preston Manning and his wife, Sandra, have struggled with how best to integrate their faith with a life in politics. In his first autobiography, Preston devoted an entire chapter, called "The Spiritual Dimension," to the subject of faith. One approach Manning has followed is to "work Christianity with the urgent or existing public agenda...trying to influence it from within the application of one's most deeply held values."[1] Manning wrote words to this effect in the constitution of the Reform Party of Canada, under section 11, which stated: "We believe in freedom of conscience and religion, and the right of Canadians to advocate, without fear of intimidation or suppression, public policies which reflect their most deeply held values."[2] However, on matters of

[1] Preston Manning, *The New Canada* (Toronto: Macmillan, 1992), 104.
[2] Reform Party of Canada: Statement of Principles, section 11.

morality and conscience, Manning is a fervent democrat and believes that citizens, not politicians, should determine public policy on matters such as abortion. Even though his faith and conscience would consider the procedure abhorrent, he would vote for legislation that would enable the procedure if that were the clear will of his constituents.

Manning was raised to be suspicious of the intentions and deeds of the mainstream political parties and was deeply rooted in the populist political traditions of Western Canada. The Social Credit movement, where his father left his mark, heavily influenced Manning. In addition, Manning cites the Progressive Party and the Canadian Commonwealth Federation (CCF, which later became the left-wing federal New Democratic Party) as sources of inspiration. Although there is nothing in the Social Credit name that implies conservatism, most historians would agree that it was a conservative party through and through; it just had a different name.

Manning's appreciation for the power that can be unleashed by a populist movement is not academic or theoretical. He grew up with it. His father, at the age of twenty-six, was one of fifty-six Socred candidates who were thrust into power in the provincial election of August 22, 1935, a scant five months after the party was founded. When Preston Manning talks of a spark that can ignite a prairie firestorm, he only has to think of the rapid and overwhelming ascent of Social Credit in Alberta in 1935. If it could happen once, thought Preston, it could happen again.

Manning also carried with him a sense of destiny, a belief that he would one day form and lead a populist western-based political party. This would be his vehicle to transform the alignment of traditional political parties and ultimately reshape the country. From this perspective, the formation of the Reform Party of Canada was not a question of if or why, but a question of when. Manning waited for the right conditions to launch the new party for nearly two decades before Mulroney's 1984 election victory.

Manning might well have been permanently turned off by mainstream political parties when he saw his father's cherished and aging

Social Credit Party replaced in Alberta by the vibrant and youthful Progressive Conservative party under the leadership of Peter Lougheed. Preston thought enough of Lougheed during the Socred twilight to advocate a merger or coalition between Social Credit and the provincial PCs. And thus, in the mid-1960s, Preston Manning led a process similar to the one that would ultimately bring the Canadian Alliance and Progressive Conservative parties together in 2003. Small groups of emissaries from both the Socreds—represented by Preston Manning and Erick Schmidt—and the PCs—represented by Joe Clark and Merv Leitch—led these strictly confidential negotiations. The meetings went so far as to suggest a new name (Social Conservative), produce a statement of principles, and choose party colours. In the end, however, the leadership of each party concluded it did not need the other party to win government. Lougheed won the next election, and the PCs were proven right.

Preston Manning was stung by how the traditional parties treated his father's predecessor, William Aberhart. As the retired Social Credit premier, Aberhart was nominated for an honorary doctorate from the University of Alberta. The partisan Liberal members of the university senate refused to ratify the nomination. According to Preston, "Liberal members of the Senate, still smarting from their electoral defeats at Aberhart's hands, could not bring themselves to be magnanimous towards their old foe."[3] This incident might well have been on Preston's mind in the late 1990s when he was seeking co-operation from the federal Tories his Reform party had decimated in the 1993 general election.

The Liberal party was kinder to Preston's father than to Aberhart. Ernest Manning resigned as premier of Alberta, then was appointed in 1970 to the Senate of Canada by Pierre Trudeau, where he served for thirteen years until his retirement on September 20, 1983.

Although a conservative by nature, Preston Manning was never an advocate or supporter of the Progressive Conservatives. Like his

---

[3] Manning, *The New Canada*, 10.

father, he was ensconced in the Social Credit Party. He ran for federal Parliament as a Socred in 1962 at the age of twenty, when Diefenbaker went from a record-breaking majority to a thin minority government. The Socreds received a substantial portion of the conservative vote, rocketing from zero seats in 1957 to thirty seats in 1962. Manning lost to Progressive Conservative candidate William Skoreyko, who had more than twice as many votes as Manning.

With his father out of office, Preston decided to lay low. Rather than join the only conservative option available in Alberta, he bided his time. He believed that every generation or so, an opportunity would arise that would invite fundamental reform of political parties and institutions. This sense of destiny was imparted to Preston by his father and was articulated in Ernest Manning's book on political realignment, which they researched and wrote together in 1967.[4]

A central thesis of the book was that meaningful political choice did not exist in Canada because the federal Progressive Conservative Party and the federal Liberal Party were ideologically indistinguishable. What was needed, argued the elder Manning, was a social conservative movement, which he said would bring "the humanitarian concerns of those with awakened social consciences to the economic persuasions of those with a firm conviction in the value of freedom of economic activity and enlightened private enterprise."[5] The belief that the Liberals and Conservatives are indistinguishable was alive and well in Preston Manning twenty years after it was posited in his father's book.

While a small-c conservative by nature, Manning never attempted to influence or ingratiate himself within the Progressive Conservative party. He resisted efforts by Joe Clark and others in 1972 who wanted him to run as a PC candidate in Pembina, Alberta. Manning thought very little of the PC party and wondered "whether

---

[4] Ernest C. Manning, *Political Realignment: A Challenge to Thoughtful Canadians* (Toronto: McClelland & Stewart, 1967). Although the listed author of the book was Ernest Manning, in his biography Preston Manning takes credit for the research and initial writing of the book.

[5] Ibid., 63.

the Conservatives had been born under an unlucky star, with a con-
genital inability to govern themselves, let alone the country."[6]
Manning had a different approach. "Rather than participate politically... through either of the traditional parties, I would wait,
complete my political and economic education in the real world, and
become politically active again if and when the winds of the Western
reform tradition once more began to blow."[7] While surely a conservative, Manning was more influenced by populism than by the
world's great conservative leaders of the era, such as Ronald Reagan
in the United States and Margaret Thatcher in Great Britain. His
heroes were more likely to be Canadians who countered established
norms and order, for example, Louis Riel, Joseph Howe of Nova
Scotia,[8] and the visionaries and builders of Quebec's Quiet
Revolution. Preston Manning, remember, was a reformer.

Manning could not implement his plan while the Liberals were in
power because most western Canadians had pinned their hopes for
reforming their national government on the Progressive Conservative
party. In the five elections before 1984, Progressive Conservatives had
won 95 seats in Alberta, to the Liberals' 4. Even the Trudeaumania
sweep of 1968 did little to threaten the Tory dominance of Alberta politics. When Joe Clark's short-lived conservative government went
down to defeat in 1980, the Liberals elected only two MPs in Western
Canada. Westerners must surely have been wondering if they would
ever have influence in Ottawa. It was this perceived repudiation that
gave rise to the phrase often quipped by Preston Manning and Reform
party supporters: "The West Wants In."

Some might be surprised that the West wanted in after Pierre
Trudeau introduced the destructive National Energy Program (NEP)

---

[6] Manning, *The New Canada*, 91.

[7] Preston Manning, *Think Big: My Adventures in Life and Democracy* (Toronto: McClelland
& Stewart, 2002), 24.

[8] Joseph Howe was a journalist and politician. He played a major role in winning
responsible government for Nova Scotia in 1848. A reformer and anti-Confederate,
he ultimately accepted office in Sir John A. Macdonald's cabinet on offer of "better
terms" in 1869.

on October 28, 1980. The NEP increased Canadian control and ownership of the energy industry while shielding the country, and the
East in particular, from rising oil prices. The NEP imposed price controls and federal taxes on oil and gas production, which most
Albertans and many Canadians thought was an intrusion into provincial jurisdiction. Companies operating in the oil patch responded by
leaving the province, increasing unemployment in Alberta. "The NEP
wiped the Liberals out of the West for a generation," said Preston
Manning. In the early 1980s, the NEP was a rallying cry for the loud
and growing voices of western discontent, most of which found a
home in the Progressive Conservative party.

When Brian Mulroney was elected to office in 1984, Preston
Manning was forty-two years old. We can conclude from Manning's
writing that he never wanted Brian Mulroney's PC government to
succeed. For the twenty years before Mulroney was sworn in,
Manning had been advocating a new western-based, conservative-
minded, populist movement. The national political spotlight would
soon be shining upon him.

STEPHEN HARPER

Not much is known about the childhood of Stephen Harper. That in
itself says something about Harper's approach to public life. Harper
declines to be interviewed on such matters, and he has yet to write
an autobiography. Most of what is known publicly is gleaned from
interviews with family members, boyhood friends, and political
associates in whom Harper has confided. The most penetrating
examinations of Harper's youth are found in the biographies by
William Johnson and Lloyd Mackey.

Most people think Harper grew up in a dynamic and prosper-
ous Alberta. Yet Alberta is one of the few places in Canada where
you don't have to be born and raised there to be *from* there. You're
not an islander if you were not born and raised in P.E.I., but
Alberta is different. No one would doubt that Stephen Harper is an
Albertan through and through. But that's not where he was born
and raised.

Born April 20, 1959, Stephen Joseph Harper is the son of Joseph and Margaret Harper. He has two younger brothers, Grant and Robert. His mother and father met at their local church. His father was a chartered accountant who worked most of his life for Imperial Oil. Stephen grew up in the Toronto area, in Leaside and Etobicoke, within a loving, supportive, and happy family. He has family roots in Atlantic Canada, where he spent many of his childhood summers with his grandparents in New Brunswick. He was a quiet and thoughtful child, and it would have been unimaginable for him to come home from school with anything but an A+ in his report card. Nevertheless, one of his teachers noted that he was a difficult student to teach and perhaps hard to be led. Given his academic success, we can imagine that Harper's intelligence and impatience posed a challenge to his teachers.

Failure is an outcome Stephen does not accept easily. Combine his top grades, strong work ethic, diligence, discipline, love of cats over dogs, and interest in politics, and you have the makings of a classic nerd. It is unlikely that many of Stephen's classmates are surprised he has risen to the highest office in the land.

Stephen won the gold medal for top high school marks when he graduated from Richview Collegiate Institute. While excelling at academics, he suffered from asthma, which limited his ability to compete in certain sports. Nonetheless, Stephen was active and a member of his school's cross-country running team. Like most high school students in Canada at the time, he was not a political activist, although he did join the Liberal party at the urging of his friend Paul Watson. This was more a matter of convenience than conviction. The local Liberal youth club Watson led needed at least twenty members to attract the local MP and Liberal cabinet minister Alastair Gillespie to attend a meeting. "Stephen Harper was a friend at the time, but definitely not a Liberal. I roped him in because I needed the numbers."[9] According to Watson, Harper was anything but intimidated when he met the Liberal heavyweight in

---

[9] Andrew Duffy, "Stephen Harper: A political life in three movements," *Ottawa Citizen*, January 28, 2006, B3.

person: "I can't remember what Stephen asked, but I do recall how much he seemed to enjoy sparring with a Rhodes scholar and cabinet minister. And as usual, Stephen was probably the smartest person in the room." Although he thought and talked like a conservative, Harper had a certain intellectual admiration for Trudeau, Watson claims. Stephen's first political campaign as an activist came under the Liberal banner: he supported Alastair Gillespie's re-election campaign. But Harper's flirtation with the Liberal party would not last.

Spiritually, Stephen Harper appears to be the product of his own thinking and experience, rather than something rooted in childhood. In 1995 Harper remarked, "I'm not the person who was born with a particular set of values and has held them my whole life. I like to think that the values I hold today are in the process of a life of education."[10] Reflecting on his teenage years, Harper noted, "I would have been an agnostic, central Canadian liberal. And my life experiences have led me to come to other conclusions about both life and political values . . . both intellectually and spiritually."[11]

With high expectations, Harper enrolled at the University of Toronto to study business. Shocking many, including his family, he dropped out of university after only two months. Claiming he didn't know what he wanted to do, Harper ended up in Edmonton, Alberta, in 1978, where he landed an administrative job at Imperial Oil, the company for which his father had worked. After a few years in the workforce, he returned to university, pursuing a bachelor's degree in economics at the University of Calgary. In speeches, Harper has said, "I didn't have the personality to become an accountant, so I became an economist." Not a comment on his father's chosen occupation, it's a rare display of humour from a very serious and determined man.

His degree was in economics, but his passion was politics. Academically he was aligned with conservative leaders of the present and conservative intellectuals of the past. But it took Pierre Trudeau

---

[10] Lloyd Mackey, *The Pilgrimage of Stephen Harper* (Toronto: ECW Press, 1995), 47.
[11] Ibid.

and the National Energy Program to convert Stephen Harper from academic conservative to partisan activist. The NEP's intrusion into areas of provincial jurisdiction also inspired him to study the constitution and the separation of powers between the federal and provincial governments. You could say he was an economist who often thought like a lawyer.

With limited experience but great fervour, Harper and his girl-friend at the time, Cynthia Williams, signed up as volunteers in the 1984 campaign of Calgary West Progressive Conservative candidate Jim Hawkes. Not that the incumbent MP needed the help: he had won each of the two previous elections by more than 17,000 votes and would win in 1984 by 31,816 votes, with more than six times the number registered by his second-place Liberal opponent. However, even in a sea of volunteers and an atmosphere of over-whelming confidence, Harper stood out. So much so that, when Harper graduated from university the following year, Hawkes brought him to Ottawa to work as his legislative assistant. Recalling his early encounters with Harper, Hawkes remarked, "He demonstrated interest and competence. He had good skills and a good mind. When I had a vacancy, he was the first person I thought of."[12] Harper would be returning east, but he hardly felt as if he were going home. Although raised in Ontario, he had evolved into a western Canadian, a transformation that was made complete by the NEP. Harper went to Ottawa, not with cowboy boots and a ten-gallon hat, but with an intellect with a can-do western attitude. He was ready to take a hard look at the current political realities and exercise all the discipline required to bring fundamental change to national government.

PETER MACKAY

First elected to office at the tender age of thirty-two in 1997, Peter Gordon MacKay belongs to a new generation of technologically savvy politicians. But this fresh-faced and dynamic parliamentarian

---

[12] Duffy, "Stephen Harper."

received his primary education in a one-room schoolhouse with no running water, a wood stove, and a two-seat outhouse.

"I caught the tail end of the one-room schoolhouse," boasts MacKay of his good fortune. It was an antiquated beginning, but MacKay describes it as idyllic: "It was like being on the set of an old-time movie. It was perfect." MacKay thinks many of his generation in rural Canada grew up this way, but in 2006 it's not a story many forty-year-old Canadians can tell.

Peter remembers the ruggedness and simplicity of the schoolhouse. His hats and mitts were littered with scorch marks from the school's wood stove. All he had to do to be first in his class was beat Beverly York, the only other student in his grade. To this day, Peter can recall the names of every student in the school, and tell you how their lives have evolved.

For the record, Peter MacKay, born on September 27, 1965, on Temperance Street in New Glasgow, Nova Scotia, was the second of four children of Elmer and Macha MacKay. Reflecting on his youth, Peter points out that he was lucky enough to have two additional sets of parents. Indeed, MacKay is as likely to tell stories about his grandparents as he is about his mom and dad.

His maternal grandfather, Bradin Delap, was born and raised in Rye, Ireland. He was a distinguished and decorated man who served in two world wars and retired from the navy as a commander. He then went to work for Western Union and led the team that laid the first transatlantic cable. The first picture transmitted across that cable was of Peter's grandmother holding his mother. Ultimately, world travels gave way to a more peaceful setting and life as a blueberry farmer in the Annapolis Valley of Nova Scotia. Braden was a loving, affectionate, and playful man. Whenever the MacKay children would pinch some blueberries from the bushes, Bradin could be heard loudly complaining about "those damn mice," just so he could enjoy the giggles from the MacKay kids lurking nearby.

Peter's paternal grandfather, Gordon MacKay, was a machine of a man who often performed legendary feats of toughness and

strength. During the depression, when work was scarce and complaints were few, Gordon would impress the locals with his
endurance. One memorable day he hauled some heavy equipment
between neighbouring farms on his already callused back, the work
you would expect of a heavy horse. When he reached the laneway
leading to the barn, a crew of three came to take his burden. "Don't
touch it," Gordon warned. "I'm taking it all the way." In many ways,
he was a twentieth-century version of mythical lumberjack Paul
Bunyan. He was a playful man who loved his grandchildren, but he
could also be tough. He had a task-oriented and business-minded
approach to getting things done, and done right. But he also would
help those who were down on their luck. If someone in the community was facing hard times, particularly if they were a visible
minority, he would go to the town office and pay their taxes. He
owned the local lumber mill and would often send construction
materials to hard-working farmers who couldn't make ends meet.
He hired dozens of new immigrants to Canada, mostly Estonians, to
work in the woods, paying them in advance. When he was practicing
law, Peter would emulate his grandfather by doing pro bono work.
On one occasion an elderly black man whom Peter had helped with
a charge for petty theft thanked him by saying, "I know who you are.
You are the grandson of Gordon MacKay."

A daily presence in Peter's life from the start, Gordon MacKay
taught Peter how to fish, ride a bike, and change a flat tire. Gordon
was also his taskmaster. "He was affectionate and fun; but he was
also all about hard work." If Peter got the sense that life was no
dress rehearsal, it was from the lessons imparted by his grandfather. What seems surprising is that through his youth, the
often-impatient grandson never once tasted the consequences of
letting his parents or grandparents down. "The one thing I would
never want to hear from my dad or grandfather was that they were
disappointed. To this day, that would be the most cutting thing they
could say."

As a young man, Peter had the presence of mind to tape-record
his grandfather, to recall the many amusing and heroic stories and to

preserve and revere his voice and persona. The mementoes on display in Peter's office connect him with his grandparents.

Macha Delap, Peter's mother, met Elmer MacKay at Acadia University. They were married in 1961 and took up residence first in New Glasgow, where Peter was born. They ultimately settled in the old MacKay homestead in Lorne, in Pictou County, Nova Scotia. For the early years of his life, Peter lived in a world contained within a one-mile radius bounded by his grandfather's lumber mill, the gristmill, the outbuildings and barns, the one-room schoolhouse, the apple orchard across the street, and, of course, the fishing stream. Elmer MacKay describes his young son as the quintessential Canadian lad. "He was kind, hard-working, conscientious, and never complained. He always wanted to do what was right." Elmer recalls a telling incident: "When Peter was about twelve years of age his grandfather let him drive his truck in the back woods. Peter was backing up with the door open and caused some damage. Peter felt bad and gave his grandfather the twenty dollars he had and told him he would get more. Peter's conscience will always guide him to the right thing." Although his family had means, Peter was not spoiled either with material goods or praise.

Life took a different turn when Peter was six. His dad, a popular and respected community lawyer, was recruited to be the Progressive Conservative candidate in a federal by-election in Central Nova on May 31, 1971. This was a seat the Liberals were supposed to win. They had finagled the by-election by offering the sitting PC member, Russell MacEwan, a judgeship if he would resign. The Liberals recruited a high-profile broadcaster named Clarrie Mackinnon to carry their banner. It was a tough campaign in a place where everyone knew about hardball politics, the sort of place where the Liberal from the adjacent riding had earned the nickname "godfather." That's what they called Liberal heavyweight Allen J. MacEachen, the man who desperately wanted the Liberals to take Central Nova from the Tories. The benefits of having the godfather on your side were noticeable: "You knew right away from the quality of the pavement which riding you were in and who was in government," said Peter MacKay. But the residents of Central Nova proudly shunned the Liberal government's goodies and sent Elmer MacKay to Ottawa with a healthy surplus of votes.

The life of a parliamentarian was different in the 1970s: MPS would stay in Ottawa for months at a time, returning home only when the House was not sitting. Elmer's absences were hard on Peter, and hard on the MacKay marriage; under the stress of politics, it didn't last two more years.

Macha MacKay took Peter and his siblings to the Delap homestead in Wolfville. It was only about 250 kilometres from Lorne, but to Peter it felt like the other end of the earth. Being closer to his maternal grandparents was the only thing that redeemed the move. He particularly looked forward to the summers when he would return to Lorne to be with his other grandparents and his father. Lorne was a place to make hay, plant vegetables, fish, and play sports. Peter's father was one to make sure that play followed work. "He would give me a list of things to do and there would be an accountability session later to see what had been accomplished," MacKay said. He maintained regular contact with his dad after his parents' divorce; his grandfather Gordon often drove to Wolfville to pick up the MacKay children for the regular trek to Lorne. Peter's heart remained in Lorne. It still does.

Peter's mother was a left-leaning social activist. She rebuilt her post-marriage life by earning a master's degree in psychology and pursued her passion for international justice and issues of women's health. With the help of her parents, who often stepped in to care for the four MacKay children, Macha was able to travel and then share her experiences from the Third World with her children. She would often bring home visiting University of Acadia students for supper; the students came from countries of which most people had never heard. The education Peter received by being exposed to his mother's world was every bit as valuable to his outlook on life as were his more formal studies. As a woman of social conscience, Macha was not blind to the harm done by well-intentioned governments that claimed to be helping the less fortunate. Peter had a sense she was more comfortable with non-governmental organizations than she would have been working for a government agency.

Macha never remarried. Elmer MacKay, on the other hand, married twice more and had another daughter, Rebecca, whom Peter considers as full a sibling as Cethlyn, Mary, and Andrew.

Peter was always involved in sports, with a passion for hockey, football, baseball, and rugby. Not known for raw talent and finesse, he was skillful as a mucker and grinder, someone who would tough it out in the corners, fighting for an edge against any opponent who came his way. Peter's rough-and-tough sportsman side is offset by a not-so-well-known aptitude for art and drawing, a passion he studied at university and something to which he might well return if the day ever comes when he doesn't feel the need to be so engrossed in politics.

Despite a father in cabinet and a community-minded activist mother, Peter was adamant in his youth that he was not going to be a politician. He knew from experience that achieving the life–work–family balance could be next to impossible. Even today, it seems this struggle persists. "I really don't want to miss having a family. It weighs heavily on my mind," said MacKay. The divorce and the love from his grandparents explain why MP Peter MacKay introduced Private Member's Bill C-309 to amend the Divorce Act. Had it not died on the order table, the bill would have given interested grandparents automatic legal standing in divorce cases, entrenching an undeniable interest.[13]

Peter was a steady student who accomplished the trilogy of a strong B average, an active social life, and a daily dose of sports. His passion for competitive team sports eclipsed any interest in politics that one might expect in the kid of a politician. Beyond talking politics around the dinner table or on the long drives between his parents' homes, Peter showed little interest in partisan activity. He shunned any form of student politics. His first meaningful exposure

---

[13] Thirty-eighth Parliament, first session, edited Hansard, n. 038, Friday, December 3, 2004.

came when he was seventeen, in the 1983 by-election in Central Nova. Peter's father, Elmer, resigned the seat so Brian Mulroney, newly elected leader of the PC party, could enter the House of Commons. Peter worked as driver for Mila Mulroney and her assistant, Bonnie Brownlee. He enjoyed the glamour of driving powerful and beautiful people past the local ball fields where his friends were playing, but what he remembers most about the by-election was when hockey legend Bobby Orr came to the riding to help Mulroney. Such was Peter's early superficial involvement in politics.

Peter went to Carleton University for his first year of undergraduate studies and to play varsity football. He thought moving to Ottawa would allow him to spend more time with his father. (Elmer had resigned his seat in 1983 in favour of Brian Mulroney, but he ran successfully for the same seat in 1984, when Mulroney ran in Quebec.) But it didn't turn out that way. Football was also a problem, as he was red-shirted and didn't play.[14]

After spending a second summer working in the High Arctic on supply boats, Peter returned for second-year studies at Carleton and another round of football tryouts. Within a few weeks, Peter was told that his grandfather MacKay was dying. A gnawing feeling that he was not where he was supposed to be overcame him, so he packed his bags and returned to Wolfville. Returning home to Nova Scotia in a time of personal crisis and stress would become a pattern repeated many times in Peter's life. Peter finished his undergraduate degree at Acadia and graduated in 1987 with a bachelor of arts, majoring in history and politics.

"I always wanted to be a trial lawyer," MacKay had declared in his high school yearbook. It was a good choice for a competitive rugby player. However, he thought he would always be a defender, not a prosecutor: "That was probably my mother's altruistic influence; that it was a noble thing to do." He studied law at Dalhousie University and was called to the bar in 1991. It was not long, however, before

---

[14] The phrase "red-shirted" describes a student athlete who does not participate in any competition during the academic year.

MacKay fell into his father's footsteps and set up a private practice in New Glasgow. His law office was above the local pizzeria, not more than a few blocks from where his father had set up his practice. "I had some clients who were the sons of the people my father defended: for him it was bootlegging, in my generation it was drugs." He gained some international experience early in his legal career on a six-month contract in Kassel, Germany, where he gave legal and strategic advice to Thyssen Henschel, a large defence contractor.

Returning to Canada, MacKay took per diem legal work for the Crown prosecutor's office. The office was short-staffed because of an inquiry into the Westray coal mine disaster, and within months Peter was brought on full time. "It seems throughout my entire life, I don't wade into things. For some reason or another, I always get thrown into the deep end. But it can be a great way to learn," MacKay said.

Working as a Crown prosecutor exposed Peter to a host of public and community interests. He worked with the police, victim advocacy groups, government agencies, and with people in deep crisis and conflict. "It showed me a much bigger world than I had worked in before." He learned to be discreet and to use careful judgment. The failings of the criminal justice system confirmed MacKay's politics. His mother's commitment to social and environmental justice had left its mark on his thinking, but MacKay came to the conclusion in his mid-twenties that his overall thinking was fundamentally conservative. MacKay believes in being tough on crime, and in particular on young offenders. He is tight-fisted, or as his friends say, "He has nickels in his pockets as heavy as manhole covers." His frugality applies to taxpayers' money as well as to his own, which is just the way his constituents want him to be. He also carries the work ethic, community mindedness, and entrepreneurial interests of his grandfather. Put it all together and you have what MacKay calls a "practical conservative." His mother is a frequent and meaningful sounding board for him, although she might disagree with her son's vocation.

As a Crown prosecutor, MacKay handled everything from shoplifting to first-degree murder cases. Although it may not have been apparent at the time, being in court and making arguments daily turned out to be good training for the House of Commons. He even made it to the Supreme Court of Canada, arguing a precedent-setting case concerning the police seizure of video gambling equipment where no warrant had been obtained. As he is inclined to do, MacKay describes the setting with a metaphor to sports: "If I had been a ball player, it would be like playing in Yankee Stadium."

Peter felt he had found his niche. He loved the job and the people he worked with. But he was summarily fired as a Crown prosecutor on March 4, 1997, because of a perceived conflict between being a non-political public servant and being a candidate for political office.

THEY ARE ALL CONSERVATIVE POLITICIANS, but they are substantially different men. MacKay is the most sensitive, Harper the more temperamental, and Manning the most detached. When it comes to religion, Manning is in a league of his own. In their spare time MacKay talks sports, Harper conservative economic theory, and Manning Canadian history. If you were out for an enjoyable and fun dinner with the three of them, you would want MacKay to do most of the talking.

Manning and Harper would be more likely to sign up for a debate, especially if the subject is dry and requires a painstaking amount of research. MacKay is the Boy Scout of the three, a dutiful soul who never wants to disappoint. If they were not in politics, Manning would lead a think-tank, Harper would be a tenured and well-published university professor, and MacKay would be commissioner of the National Hockey League.

In the mid-1980s, the paths of Manning, Harper, and MacKay had yet to converge. Brian Mulroney was about to make his mark on the nation.

CHAPTER 4

MULRONEY LEADS CANADA, MANNING LEADS WESTERN DISCONTENT

J OE CLARK'S NINE-MONTH TENURE as prime minister aside, in 1984 the federal Progressive Conservatives had not formed a government for a generation. Not since John Diefenbaker was prime minister in 1963, twenty-one years earlier, had the Tories tasted real and lasting power. Brian Mulroney changed all that.

In the September 4, 1984 federal election, Progressive Conservatives took 211 out of 284 seats. It was a stunning and over-whelming victory that few predicted.

With such a huge majority, Mulroney was expected to transform government and the nation. The government moved quickly on a number of fronts to secure some easy wins to demonstrate that the direction of government had changed. It eradicated the much-hated National Energy Program (NEP) and repealed the Petroleum Gas Revenue Tax, issues of greatest concern to westerners.[1] It replaced the restrictive Foreign Investment Review Agency (FIRA) with Investment Canada, which had a mandate to promote, rather than repel, foreign direct investment. It took steps to reduce government subsidies, and it identified Crown corporations for privatization. It steadily improved relations with Canada's allies, particularly the

---

[1] Not every element of the NEP was immediately cancelled. For example, it was not until 1990 that the government began to sell its equity stake in Petro Canada. In 1985, Petro Canada acquired Gulf Canada's refining and marketing operations in Ontario and the West.

United States. And it established a renewed spirit of co-operation with provinces that would ultimately lead to a unanimous agreement to amend the Canadian constitution. There was a litany of accomplishments that Mulroney could parade in front of conservatives and Canadians to demonstrate that his government was making a constructive difference.

Turning the nation's finances around was another matter. To western Canadians in particular, dealing with the deficit was as much a sacred trust as protecting old-age pensions was to seniors. "The fiscal conservatives particularly in Alberta expected the Conservatives to balance the budget, reduce the taxes, and reduce the debt," said Preston Manning. "When everything went in the opposite direction [Mulroney] just lost that whole constituency right there."

But what was Mulroney's record on the deficit? Did the Reform party happily exploit a myth, or did the PCs deserve rebuke for failing to balance the budget?

ON ENTERING OFFICE THE MULRONEY government faced a projected $42 billion deficit and a burgeoning level of public debt. While there is little doubt that finance minister Michael Wilson ushered in a new era of responsible financial management, progress on deficit reduction was slow, if not invisible.

Before Mulroney came to power, Liberal finance minister Marc Lalonde had seemed more concerned with putting the federal deficit into perspective than actually dealing with it. In April 2003, Lalonde wrote, "High interest rates and the recession have raised the federal deficit substantially. With the recovery expected to be moderate and gradual and with the international oil market outlook as weak as it is now, large decreases in magnitude of the deficit will not be easily achieved.... I do not hold the view that the deficit must be brought down immediately.... There has been ample room for the federal government to finance the deficit without causing an increase in interest rates.... The deficit must be brought down to lower levels as appropriate for the economy."[2] In other words, Lalonde was telling the country that dealing with the deficit was for some other finance minister at some other time.

Contrast the words of Marc Lalonde with those of Michael Wilson. In a document tabled in the House of Commons on November 8, 1984, barely one month after the change in government, Wilson reported, "For too long, the government has ignored the causes of the problems and has dealt only with the symptoms. For too long it has allowed the fiscal situation to deteriorate and the debt to increase . . . we must put our fiscal house in order so that we can limit, and ultimately reverse, the massive build-up in public debt and the damaging impact this has on confidence and growth."[3]

The Liberal government saw debt as a tool to manage the economy. Wilson said that the deficit and the debt were the problem. When Wilson made this statement, government projections were calling for deficits over the ensuing four years to be in the range of $34 to $36 billion. In a November 2004 statement, measures were announced that would reduce government spending by about $4 billion in the short term.

Wilson's first full budget came in May 1985. Actions were specified to reduce the deficit, including the de-indexation of various tax items and social payments. Under Wilson's budget proposals, only increases in inflation beyond three percentage points would be automatically reflected in key elements of the tax and social security system. At the same time, to spur investment and job creation, the government announced a $500,000 lifetime capital gains exemption. The change in direction and policy from the previous administration was stark and clear.

Tough measures to control spending were coupled with an increase in tax revenue. (De-indexation was a method of increasing personal income taxes.). But the deficit was still projected to be in

[2] *The Federal Deficit in Perspective* (Ottawa: Finance Canada, April 1993). Extracts are from Finance Minister Marc Lalonde's preface.

[3] Michael H. Wilson, *A New Direction for Canada: An Agenda for Economic Renewal* (Ottawa: Finance Canada, November 8, 1984), 1–2.

the range of $32 to $35 billion over the next few years. The actions might have seemed bold, but the results were modest.

Those who thought some quick-fix belt-tightening and a change from the big-spending Liberal ways would solve the problem were severely disappointed. Even with Conservatives in power there was no plan or reasonable expectation that the deficit would be eliminated in the foreseeable future.

Finance Minister Wilson wanted to lead on the deficit problem, but a number of people in the Mulroney government were not convinced Canadians were up for a stiff round of belt-tightening. Geoff Norquay, a PC party scribe and policy guru since 1981, was one of many who were frustrated by the government's inability to persuade Canadians of the severity of the deficit problem in Mulroney's first term as prime minister.

Norquay had been a leading backroom figure in the party for more than thirty years. His career in the policy field began with stints in the Ontario and Alberta governments. Before signing on with the PC party, he was director of research for the Canadian Council on Social Development.[4] When he was hired as research director for the PC party, he was interviewed by MPs who both supported and criticized party leader Joe Clark. (Such was Clark's command of the caucus in 1981, after the electoral defeat of February 18, 1980.) After the 1984 election, Norquay took on various responsibilities in the office of the prime minister, including speech writing and policy development. He "held the pen" for Jean Charest and the party during rebuilding efforts after the 1993 campaign and became a frequent commentator and panelist for the party in the national media. He served as communications director for Belinda Stronach in her run for Conservative party leader and for Stephen Harper when he was leader of Her Majesty's Official Opposition.

---

[4] The Canadian Council on Social Development (CCSD) is a non-governmental, not-for-profit organization founded in 1920. Its mission is to develop and promote progressive social policies inspired by social justice, equality, and the empowerment of individuals and communities.

Norquay contends that the government was way ahead of the public in its desire to tame the deficit. "People forget how just about every element of Canadian society vehemently and vigorously opposed doing anything about the deficit. The first response [to cutbacks] of the CBC was to publicly announce that the first thing they would do was to close the television station in Baie Comeau [Mulroney's hometown]. There was controversy in the press that went on for months about killing a study on seagull eggs as part of cutting back. Just about every institution in Canadian society opposed what we were trying to do, including corporations. The Catholic church was at war with the government of Canada over social and economic policy. No one wanted to deal with this."

As it was, the government did not hold firm on its plan to de-index old-age pensions. The change in position can be traced to a pledge made by Mulroney during the 1984 election, to treat government social programs as a "sacred trust." The pledge was made in an attempt to quell fears that a Conservative government had a hidden agenda and would "slash and burn" government spending on the altar of the deficit. Mulroney comforted voters before the election by assuring them that savings would be found elsewhere in the system. Even hard-line western conservative John Weissenberger, a key figure in the creation of the Reform party who considered deficit reduction a priority, questioned the decision to target seniors' programs. One event galvanized public opinion against Mulroney on the pension issue: an unplanned confrontation with a sixty-three-year-old Solange Denis, who was protesting outside Mulroney's Langevin block offices. The prime minister was caught off guard when Denis said, "You made promises that you wouldn't touch anything . . . you lied to us. I was made to vote for you and then it's goodbye Charlie Brown."[5]

"We cut tail and ran," said Norquay.

---

[5] Human Resources Development Canada, "The History of Canada's Public Pensions," http://www.civilization.ca/hist/pensions/cpp-a68-ip_e.html (accessed July 18, 2006).

Despite the lack of visible progress on the deficit, by almost every objective measure Mulroney and Wilson had changed the course of government finances for the better. The problem for Conservatives was that it took expertise on government finances to understand what they had accomplished.

Governments are like oil tankers: very hard to turn. In fact, most government spending is subject to long-term commitments that make it difficult to institute any sort of quick fix. In 1984–85, 23 per cent of all spending was on interest. The government could hardly reduce spending by repudiating its debt. About 22 per cent of all spending was payments to individual Canadians for universal social programs: Old Age Security, Unemployment Insurance, and Family Allowance. The "sacred trust" promise made it difficult to reduce these costs. Besides, Canadians would only be prepared to cut payments to individuals once they were satisfied that government waste and inefficiency had been addressed. Transfers to provincial government for health care, education, social assistance, and equalization amounted to about 17 per cent of all spending. (The Mulroney government had no mandate to cut in this area.) Other transfers amounted to 13 per cent of spending. National defence accounted for 7 per cent and Crown corporations almost 6 per cent of all government spending. That left about $12 billion for all other government departments and agencies, about 11 per cent of the total. The pool of $12 billion is what Canadians thought could be trimmed to resolve a $40-billion deficit. Those who thought that cutting out the waste and inefficiency in government operations would eliminate the deficit had limited insight into the nature of government spending.

The Conservative plan to reduce the deficit had three elements. First, a growing economy would produce higher revenues. Second, program spending would be limited to increases at or below the rate of inflation. Third, selected spending cuts would be made in low-priority areas. Taken together, these three elements would slowly strengthen government finances without causing any great shock to the economy. The plan was incremental, and not exciting.

Holding spending increases to the rate of inflation might not seem particularly ambitious, but it would be a Herculean achievement given what had transpired in the previous two decades. From 1968 to 1984—the Trudeau years—the average increase in program spending was 13.1 per cent per year. In the early and mid-1970s, the average increase was more than 17 per cent per year. The record year was 1974–75. Trudeau's minority Liberal government was being propped up by the NDP, and program spending increased by a whopping 27.9 per cent. Out-of-control spending and persistent deficits took their toll on government finances. During the Trudeau era, Canada's national debt increased tenfold, from $19.2 to $194.4 billion.

During Wilson's first year as finance minister, program spending *decreased* by $800 million, or 1 full percentage point. The reduction was modest but nonetheless earth-shattering: the brakes on spending had clearly been applied. In the first four years of Conservative administration, program spending increased on average 3.8 per cent, one-third the level of the increases of the previous administration. Relative to the size of the economy, program spending in Mulroney's first term declined from 18.5 per cent of GDP (gross domestic product) to 15.7 per cent. Had government spending maintained the same share of the economy during Mulroney's first term, the size of the deficit would have been at least $17 billion higher than was ultimately recorded.

Spending control is only one side of the deficit equation, although this was clearly the side that most Canadians wanted the government to pursue. Nonethless, government revenues increased during Mulroney's first term by some $33 billion, rising from 15.7 per cent to 16.9 per cent of GDP. Economic growth was the primary reason for higher revenues, although the government also imposed "temporary" surtaxes and the de-indexation of various tax elements to help bring the deficit down.

All this left Canadians confused. Revenues were rising, the government talked about being tough on spending, but the country was still plagued with huge deficits. The problem, which most Canadians did not understand, was the debt.

To help understand the burden of debt, it is worth looking at what happened to government operations from the 1960s to the 1990s, excluding interest on the accumulated debt. For most of the 1960s, the government had healthy operating surpluses, with revenues exceeding program spending by more than $5 billion. In the 1970s, the federal government spent $16.3 billion more on programs than it recieved in revenues. This meant that for an entire decade there was no residual revenue to pay the interest on the debt. In other words, Canada borrowed every cent needed to pay the interest on the debt. In the early 1980s, before Mulroney came to power, operating deficits totalled $36.9 billion. In 1984–85, the operating deficit was $12.2 billion. By the end of Mulroney's first term, that operating deficit had been converted to an annual surplus of $7.6 billion, a turnaround of $19.8 billion.

Despite remarkable improvements in the operating position, the deficit by the end of Mulroney's first term remained stubbornly high, at $27.9 billion. The big financial problem was the debt. The government tried to claim some success, citing that relative to the size of the economy, the deficit had shrunk almost in half, from 8.3 per cent to 4.6 per cent of GDP.[6] Yet it was easy for opponents of the government to ridicule any boast of progress, as the overall debt load during this period had risen from $194 billion to $314 billion, an increase of 62 per cent. Relative to the size of the economy, the debt rose in each year of Mulroney's first term, from 43.2 per cent of GDP in 1984–85 to 51.3 per cent in 1998–89.

Relatively high interest rates, designed to combat inflation, exacerbated the problem of the debt. The average interest rate on Canada's outstanding debt during Mulroney's first term was 11.6 per cent. Compare that with the rate for 2004–05, which was 6.8 per cent, a difference of almost 5 per cent. Such a difference on a $314-billion debt in 1988–89 would have produced a dramatically

---

[6] By international standards, Canada had made significant improvements in the financial balances (the deficit or surplus). While these figures necessarily include the results of provincial governments, for 1984 Canada was 3.4 percentage points higher than the G7 average (7.8 per cent to 4.4). By 1988, the differential had been reduced to 1.4 percentage points.

different bottom line. But the government and the people wanted a balanced budget, and not even the most optimistic forecaster could predict a balanced budget over the short or medium term.

The Mulroney government deserves substantial credit for making significant progress in turning the finances of the nation around. It took control of government spending, limiting increases to below the rate of growth of the economy. It brought in more money from a growing economy and from selected tax measures. It turned a $12.2-billion operating deficit into a $7.6-billion operating surplus. Had the Mulroney government, throughout its first term in office, maintained the previous Liberal government's relative level of spending and taxation, the deficit would have been more than $60 billion. Because of the debts in place when Mulroney took office, the best it could accomplish at the end of its first term was to reduce the deficit to $29 billion. Canadians, and western Canadians in particular, were not impressed. It was hard for Mulroney to explain to even the most sophisticated observers that such a deficit was an accomplishment.

CERTAINLY PRESTON MANNING WAS SOPHISTICATED, and he understood government finances. But Mulroney's accomplishments were of little consequence to Manning. Future deputy prime minister Don Mazankowski could see that: "Manning was always organizing something." From his writings and activities, one could conclude that Manning was inclined to be unimpressed with Mulroney even before he was sworn in as prime minister. Some might go so far as to say Manning wanted Mulroney to fail. If Mulroney and his massive majority could not deliver the sort of government demanded by western Canadians, suggested Manning, then maybe the country needed an alternative. His alternative.

Most westerners could readily list their disappointments with the Mulroney government's first term: patronage abuses, political scandal, perceived slowness in responding to western grievances about the National Energy Program, and even the government's general sensitivities towards Quebec. The much-hated deficit was enough to make western blood boil. But even these issues, taken together, were not enough for westerners to turn on the new Conservative government so early in its mandate. There was not yet enough of the groundswell Manning was looking for to launch a new political movement. But that did not mean Manning was not trying.

At a meeting on October 17, 1986, Manning made the case to some senior oil industry executives "for a new federal political movement dedicated to reforms that would make the West an equal partner in Confederation."[7] It was a speech Manning had been delivering in his mind and in public for the past twenty years. Manning expressed his view that the West would produce something new provided it had the leadership and funds to do the job. Not everyone was convinced. Manning remembers, "One of the people in there was a pollster, David Elton, who at that time was head of the Canada West Foundation. I used him as a pollster in some of my consulting work, and he was intimately familiar with polling data, particularly in Western Canada. David was sympathetic to what I was saying but said, 'Look, my heart is with you but my head will tell you that there is absolutely no proof in the polling data that there is a market for a new political party of any kind in Western Canada.'" While there was agreement at the meeting that a gathering of like-minded westerners would be a good start for a new political movement, they realized they still needed a spark to fan the flames of discontent. That spark came not more than two weeks later, ironically on Halloween.

On October 31, 1986, the Mulroney government announced that a maintenance contract for Canada's CF-18 fighter jets was being awarded to Canadair of Montreal, Quebec. This award overruled the recommendation made by a panel assembled to evaluate competitive bids. The panel had determined that Bristol Aerospace Ltd. of Manitoba had submitted the superior technical and financial bid.

The decision by the Mulroney government was not just about economic development for Quebec; it was hardball politics. Politicians from Quebec had lobbied Mulroney, who wanted Quebec

---

[7] Manning, *Think Big*, 27.

to be happy. In the five elections before 1984, Conservatives had won only 12 out of 372 seats contested in Quebec. Mulroney wanted to show that electing 58 Tories from Quebec in the 1984 election had made a difference. With no political roots in Quebec, the Tories were anxious to build something that would last into the next election and beyond. Shaun Masterson worked in the Prime Minister's Office at the time. "It was clear from the discussions that this would be controversial. But our coalition in Quebec had no roots, and we were trying to build something that would be sustainable."

Mulroney knew a "Quebec Round" of constitutional talks lay ahead. One of his key election planks was to have Quebec sign the Canadian constitution with honour and dignity. If he was sensitive to Quebec's need for economic development, the constitutional talks might go that much easier.

Mulroney was mindful of the large number of companies that had fled Quebec in 1976 when the sovereignist Parti Québécois was elected. He wanted to reverse that trend and be able to point to some success stories that would spark the attachment of Quebecers to Canada. He argued that his decision to award the contract to Canadair was in the national interest because the technology embedded in the CF-18 contract would be used by Canadair to create manufacturing jobs in Canada. According to Don Mazankowski, "The guys in Winnipeg had no use for that technology. The issue that the government had to wrestle with was what became of the technology; who could make best use of the technology. Most public servants in the Defence department said it was the right decision in terms of insuring that the technology could be utilized in the most effective way."

Mulroney concedes his government suffered from the CF-18 decision because of a tremendous failure to communicate effectively the reasons for the decision. As a consequence, the feelings of western resentment towards Quebec, which had until then been kept just below the surface of public discourse, were legitimized. Preston Manning could capture and exploit the anger over the CF-18 decision to build the movement he had been hoping to lead.

Communication specialists in the Prime Minister's Office knew the decision was trouble. "I was very much in the minority in warning anybody who would listen about the hugely damaging consequences of the CF-18 decision," said Geoff Norquay.

The process by which the government made its decision was never explained, but it would be logical to conclude that Mulroney made the call on his own. Norquay recalls, "I went to the Priorities and Planning Committee and to full cabinet for four years and I don't recall any discussions about the CF-18 issue."

When one region of the country feels it has been harmed by a government decision, the government often tries to help in other ways. "Little is known about the CF-5 contract that went to Winnipeg that same year. It was a bigger dollar figure than the CF-18 contract," said Mazankowski.[8]

But Mazankowski was also realistic about what the CF-18 decision meant. "I knew it would be trouble. I knew it would be a difficult sell." Speaking of its impact on Preston Manning's ability to build and mass forces with the Reform party, Mazankowski said, "The CF-18 decision didn't help. That was an issue that gave Manning's movement momentum."

So Quebec might have been happy, but the West was outraged. Some groups, such as the Western Canada Concept, talked openly of separation. "That is just one of many insults to the West which cannot be effectively answered by the present federal political parties which are directed from Central Canada. The Canadair contract was a billion-dollar bribe to the voters of Quebec and demonstrated once again that Western separatism is justified."[9]

The CF-18 decision reaffirmed what many Canadians thought about federal politicians: they favoured Quebec over other parts of

---

[8] This was not the first time the Mulroney government would placate a region that had suffered economically as a result of a larger government decision. For example, when the military base in Summerside, P.E.I., was closed, it was not long before the government announced that a new tax-processing centre would be located in that region.

[9] "Western separatist party to make federal bid," *Globe and Mail*, November 3, 1986, A5.

Canada. In a late 1986 poll by Environics Research, 67 per cent of those surveyed expressed the view that the federal government favoured one region and did not treat all regions fairly. In the West, 83 per cent held this view, and Quebec was identified as the number-one beneficiary.[10] The poll also revealed a serious decline in Tory support in Western Canada. The poll pegged Conservative support at 35 per cent, well below the 69 per cent the Tories had received two years earlier from Albertans in the general election. Westerners were saying that not much seemed to have changed between Liberal governments of the past and the Conservative administration of the present.

Manning knew that the CF-18 decision was a gift:

> It was a significant contract in its own right, but it was the symbolism of it all. The West felt the Liberals always bent over backwards to accommodate Quebec and didn't even hear what the West was saying. Here were the new guys, the different guys, the different guys who were going to do it different, doing exactly the same thing. They made a big thing about having western guys in the cabinet, but then they send [Manitoba MP and minister of national health and welfare] Jake Epp back to Winnipeg to try to convince Winnipeg that this somehow was in the national interest. This just added insult to injury. I think there were enough other ingredients [to launch Reform]. The CF-18 thing had its biggest impact in Manitoba, although it was seen as a symbol across the West. I think the biggest driver was still the fiscal thing. But the CF-18 was icing on the cake.

David Angus thought the reaction of Manning and others in the West to the CF-18 was excessive:

---

[10] Michael Adams and Donna Dasko, "Tories Favour Central Canada, Majority of Canadians believe," *Globe and Mail*, December 31, 1986, A1. The survey was conducted by Environics Research Group Ltd. between December 8 and 23 with a sample of 1,938. The national result is considered accurate to within 2 percentage points 19 times out of 20.

Mulroney was focused on separatism in Quebec and he told the western group to run the country. Mazankowski was the chair of the cabinet operations committee, which was a new thing that Mulroney had invented. No matter what Mulroney did to help the West, all they would remember was the CF-18 decision. We were getting out of that business. Canadair had been disadvantaged because they had to swallow de Havilland. They were the beginning of Bombardier Aerospace. But it was a symbolic thing. We gave Manitoba way more compensation for not getting the contract. Why was it that the CF-18 decision became the only thing? They said we were anti-west and that was just plain wrong.

While few can recall how the CF-18 decision was made, or discussing it beforehand, the announcement certainly caused a commotion in the Tory caucus. Gerry St. Germain was PC caucus chair at the time: "I don't recall much discussion about CF-18 before the decision was made, but it definitely caused an uproar in caucus. It was the symbolism of the thing, another sop to Quebec at the expense of western Canada. It was the only time I ever agreed with Norman Atkins.[11] We both told the prime minister at the time that it was the wrong decision." St. Germain believes the CF-18 decision was historic. "I knew most of the founders of the Reform Party, many of them former RCMP. I asked them, 'What was the one factor that caused you to join Reform?' CF-18 comes up ten times out of ten."

THERE HAD BEEN TALK OF SEPARATION in western Canada before. Various attempts had been made in the 1970s and early 1980s to launch western-based protest parties; most of the attempts used Pierre Trudeau as their punching bag. Many promptly flamed out, usually because of their extreme positions or because of the suspicious characters involved in their formation.

---

[11] Norman Atkins, who was summoned to the Senate on July 2, 1986, was Mulroney's campaign chair in 1984.

Manning would have nothing to do with these protest movements. He sought a far-reaching and overwhelming populist wave of
discontent. Also, significantly, he did not argue for separation: he
wanted a "New Canada."[12] Why did Manning, a man of clear conservative persuasion, not seek to enlighten Mulroney and his western
cabinet ministers of the error of their ways? Why, with Mulroney in
office for only a few short years, did Manning not seek to reshape the
Progressive Conservative party? Because this approach ran counter
to his political strategy. Manning wanted to work from the outside.
He was more comfortable protesting and agitating than governing.
He wanted to lead a grassroots mainstream protest party that would
shake up the political elite. Timing was critical to the launch of his
new venture, and it took patience: ". . . rather than getting on the tail
end of the populist movements produced on the Canadian prairies
during the depression, I would wait for the next one. By 1986, there
were signs that another populist movement was in the making in
western Canada."[13]

It is ironic that Manning, a conservative, had to wait until the
Progressive Conservatives were in power for his protest party to take
hold. Trevor Harrison, a professor of political science at the
University of Alberta, observed the incongruity of the rise of right-
wing populism and the Reform Party of Canada coinciding with the
election of a Conservative government: "Within a short time, the
Tories dismantled state-nationalist economic policies, decentralized
political authority and control, and generally followed a pro-business
agenda. What was the effect of this political change upon the western
region . . . ironically right-wing populism gained in momentum!"[14]

Manning believes that Liberals have generally been better than
Conservatives at responding to western grievances. "Whether
Mulroney had behaved differently, or if Trudeau had behaved differ-
ently, maybe Reform wouldn't have happened, or more likely it

---

[12] *The New Canada* is the title of Manning's 1992 book.

[13] Manning, *The New Canada*, 7.

[14] Trevor Harrison, *Of Passionate Intensity: Right-Wing Populism and the Reform Party of Canada* (Toronto: University of Toronto Press, 1995), 4.

would have happened fifteen years later. The traditional parties are just slow-moving anyway. The success of the traditional parties, to a large degree, depends on their ability to recognize these movements and accommodate them—or fails to recognize them and accommodate them. In the twentieth century, the Liberals have been more the ones who have picked up these movements and tried to accommodate them. The Conservatives have been slower at it." Nowhere in this statement does Manning talk about governing. Shaking things up seems to be his goal.

Manning knew that the CF-18 decision engendered mistrust and disappointment that cut a wide swath across the western electorate. Resentment of the Progressive Conservative government in western Canada was at an apex. Mainstream westerners could no longer simply blame the Liberals. Manning knew that westerners were hungry for a legitimate and credible voice that could articulate western resentment. He remarked, "The hotheads talked about separation; cooler heads sought better alternatives, but the conditions for a full-blown prairie fire were present. The time for 'waiting for something to happen' was over. Something was happening. It was time to act."[15]

The Reform party was not the brainchild of disgruntled Progressive Conservatives. The origins of Reform can clearly be traced to the latent forces of the Social Credit movement. Like Reform, the Social Credit party had clear western roots. It was formed in the early part of the twentieth century in western Canada to combat the more powerful industrial class of the East. In Alberta, Social Credit governed from 1935 to 1971, principally under the leadership of premiers William Aberhart and Ernest Manning. Beginning in 1952, Socreds governed British Columbia for thirty-six of thirty-nine years.

Federally, the Social Credit party has existed since 1935. In the early 1960s it held as many as 30 seats in the federal Parliament, consistently ranking ahead of the New Democrats. The last time Social Credit or Créditistes had members in the House of Commons was

---

[15] Manning, *Think Big*, 27.

during the short-lived thirty-first Parliament led by Joe Clark. The 1979 election left Clark only 6 seats short of a majority government, precisely the number of seats held by Social Credit under the leadership of Fabien Roy. On the fateful night of December 13, 1979, a vote of confidence was held on the Clark government, and Social Credit members either abstained or failed to show up for the vote. It would have taken very little effort on Clark's part to gain the support of the small Social Credit caucus, but he had decided to run his government as if he had a majority, and he ignored the otherwise "conservative" Social Credit MPs. In effect, Social Credit defeated the government. As Elmer MacKay recalls, Clark was not concerned about bringing the Socreds on side. "We could have won them over by giving them a few perks in office and by increasing their profile. And as a guy who likes to win, I told Clark we should make common cause with Socreds. They were not difficult people to deal with. But Clark thought it would be like Diefenbaker in 1958; going from a minority to a huge majority." History shows that Socred members would regret their decision to defeat the Clark government, as they have not held a seat in Parliament since. Many people remember the legacy and the glory days of Social Credit; no one more so than Preston Manning.

Manning and many of his followers were influenced by the writings of Peter Brimelow, especially his 1986 book *The Patriot Game*. The essence of the "patriot game" is to use the fear of Quebec's separation as an excuse to control the national political agenda, largely to the benefit of a class of mostly Liberal political elites. Brimelow predicted in the book that new splinter parties would emerge, that the fate of Confederation was anything but certain, and that elections would take the form of Russian roulette.

It was somewhat unexpected for a populist free-enterprise prairie politician to lead on issues related to Quebec. But Manning was a dedicated historian with a passion for the country's constitution and the rule of law. He was also brave and not worried that he might be criticized for speaking out. While most observers would say that Reform was able to flourish because of Mulroney's perceived

inadequacies, Manning gives the initial credit for the Reform revolution to another Quebec politician. "Trudeau laid the seeds for
separatism . . . by insisting that the federal government, and not the
Quebec government, be the guardian of the French language and
culture. He was on a collision course with Quebec nationalists [for
that], plus from the way he repatriated the constitution."

Manning signalled that the day of the realignment of the conservative political movement was pending. In the book he and his father
researched and wrote, ominous counsel was offered to conservatives
under the heading "Consideration of One Remaining Alternative":

> Anyone who speaks or writes about the subject of political
> realignment is open to the common misinterpretation that he
> is advocating the formation of another political party alto-
> gether apart from those presently in existence. I wish to make
> it very clear that this is not what I am advocating in this thesis.
> I do not believe that the formation of an entirely new political
> party is the best way to meet the serious national political
> needs of the present hour. Nevertheless, having regard to the
> prevailing political mood of the Canadian people, present
> national party leaders and federal politicians, especially those
> affiliated with the Progressive Conservative Party of Canada,
> should take cognizance of the following fact: if the Canadian
> political situation continues to degenerate, and if the cause of
> conservatism continues to suffer and decline, not for lack
> of merit or a willingness on the part of the Canadian people to
> support modern conservative principles or policies, but rather
> because of unnecessary dissention among politicians and par-
> ties, the idea of establishing a wholly new political party
> committed to the social conservative positions will find an ever
> increasing number of advocates and supporters among a con-
> cerned and aroused Canadian public. [16]

---

[16] Manning, *Political Realignment*, 86.

The establishment of Reform was the fulfillment of that prognostication. The brand of conservatism Mulroney offered failed to meet Manning's conditions for not organizing a new political party. To Preston Manning, the Mulroney government had fallen into Brimelow's Patriot Game and was ignoring western concerns: "The Mulroney Conservatives tried to accommodate the Quebec bloc by making his [Mulroney's] own deal with the nationalists. He hoped that things like Meech Lake would accommodate them. But I don't think Mulroney ever understood the western movement. There wasn't much of an attempt to accommodate it."

PRESTON MANNING AND STEPHEN HARPER shared a distrust of and disappointment in the Mulroney administration, but they came to this common conclusion from different perspectives. Manning expected Mulroney to fail, perhaps even hoped he would fail, while Harper was filled with enthusiasm after helping Tory MP Jim Hawkes get elected in 1984. Manning scrutinized Mulroney's actions, looking for a political opening for himself and a western-based populist movement; Harper travelled to Ottawa to work as Hawkes's legislative assistant. Then Manning's and Harper's views began to converge.

Ottawa did not impress the young Stephen Harper. It was relatively early days in the Mulroney administration, and Harper began his year-long sojourn with high hopes for a fundamental conservative transformation of the workings of government. He hoped to find Parliament a place of ideas, debate, intellectual stimulation, integrity, and respect for the taxpayer. Instead he discovered a phony environment filled with trivial and meaningless chatter and policies designed not to offend the masses. Harper had no interest in playing the Ottawa game of glad-handing and networking. While others went to restaurants and bars, he went to the parliamentary library. The keen young conservative had set his sights on reforms to the unemployment insurance program.

Like almost every intern who works as a parliamentary assistant, Harper told his boss that he had no interest whatsoever in seeking elected office. But many interns who make such a statement are hiding personal ambition, and if they get the chance to seek elected office they will take it. Harper is a case in point.

Harper saw Conservative leadership that meekly compromised in the name of a broader coalition as a failure. Fed up and lonely, he returned to the University of Calgary to pursue post-graduate studies. He was not entrepreneurial or particularly motivated by money; he was a man of ideas, an intellectual who could easily have pursued a comfortable life as a university professor. As Jim Hawkes said: "Everyone thought his future lay in proceeding to a doctorate in economics and to a career in university, something that would also give him the opportunity to advance policy ideas."[17]

But Harper was still very much a partisan and wondered how he could help persuade Mulroney and the PC party to shift to the right and follow a purer form of conservatism, like that being pursued by Ronald Reagan and Margaret Thatcher. Harper felt there was not much cause for optimism in this mission; in his view, the Red Tories, those in the middle and perhaps the left of the political spectrum, were in charge of the PC party. In his view, the leadership of the party lacked political will. Nonetheless, his first instinct was to work within the PC party to try to move it to the right of centre by building a "Blue Tory" network.

"The Blue Tory network was basically two guys: Stephen and me," recalled John Weissenberger, a colleague of Harper's at the University of Calgary and the man considered to be Harper's best friend.[18] Like Harper, Weissenberger was an easterner who went west in the early 1980s to pursue studies and a career. Harper and Weissenberger met while they were volunteers for the Calgary West PC Association in 1988.

"The idea behind the Blue Tory network," said Weissenberger, "was to find a home for philosophical conservatives, who did not exist at the time within the PC party. There was not, to our minds, a

---

[17] Duffy, "Stephen Harper."

[18] The night Harper became prime minister in 2006, Weissenberger and his wife were among a handful of people who watched the returns unfold in the home of Stephen and Laureen Harper.

strong philosophical base to the party, especially compared with what was happening to conservative parties around the world. The PC party, in our estimation, was a very broad brokerage party that was trying to copy the Liberal party in terms of its positioning within the political spectrum."

Weissenberger and Harper developed terms of reference for their Blue Tory network and identified caucus members they thought might support it. "These were the caucus members that to average PC members would have been referred to as the dinosaurs," said Weissenberger. "But what we really wanted to attract was younger people to the cause." In the 1980s, there was no Internet or blogging; communication and outreach were more painstaking.

The dinosaurs had another name for themselves: the 1922 Club. According to Gerry St. Germain, the club was patterned after a rump of the Tory caucus, formed in 1922 in Great Britain out of a huge majority government, not unlike the one Mulroney had earned in 1984. The Canadian version of the 1922 Club consisted mostly of western members with strong right-wing social conservative views on issues like capital punishment. Mulroney acknowledges that he had "Reformers" in his caucus. However, once inside caucus exposure to the legitimate interests and concerns of members from other parts of the country persuaded most of them to accept a more moderate and inclusive national vision.

It is clear that Harper and Weissenberger wanted to remain politically active, and their first choice was to work within the structure of the existing system, that is, the PC Party of Canada. It is equally clear that Harper did not underestimate the challenge of remaking the PC party from within. Within the party, he and Wiessenberger would have been but a couple of faint voices. While they may have been accused of being dogmatic and youthfully uncompromising, they understood they were in a "big tent" political party that was supposed to represent a broad spectrum of political views. The problem, as they saw it, was that small-c conservatives were essentially ignored or, worse, derisively labelled as right-wing Neanderthals. "There is a difference between being a conservative and making honourable compromises, and being a centrist," said Weissenberger. "A lack of conservative philosophical grounding caused the PC party to be not much different from the old Liberal party."

Weissenberger added, "But the whole Blue Tory network thing got short circuited." That's because Robert Mansell, head of the economics department at the University of Calgary, introduced Stephen Harper and John Weissenberger to Preston Manning. This was no chance introduction: Manning had asked Mansell for his best and brightest student, and Mansell thought of Harper. He was, recalled Mansell, "A reluctant politician—an ideal politician in my sense."[19]

To both Harper and Weissenberger, Manning sounded like a principled conservative; he had credibility in the West, was articulate, and was prepared to give two young and inexperienced conservative idealists a chance to spread their wings. Manning could provide an easier route for the University of Calgary students to hatch their network. "Had we carried on with the Blue Tory network [within the PC party], we would have been going against the party establishment. We would have been going against the flow. We were willing to work inside the party to try and change things, but it seemed to us the path of least resistance was to leave and try and effect change from the outside," said Weissenberger.

Harper and Manning both felt that something was wrong in Ottawa. Harper was intrigued with Manning and travelled to Vancouver to attend an assembly Manning helped organize. Prime Minister Mulroney had directed the PC party to avoid the assembly. But Harper and Weissenberger felt no disloyalty in attending and contributing. "I get annoyed when . . . Stephen and I are called turncoats and traitors for leaving the PCs," said Weissenberger. "We did not leave for any personal advantage and had no expectations of personal gain. We went into the wilderness and filled a void. We just thought it was the right thing to do and we did it." The meeting would lead to the creation of a new political party that would change the course of Canadian history.

---

[19] Mackey, *The Pilgrimage of Stephen Harper*, 20.

The Western Assembly on Canada's Economic and Political Future was held in Vancouver May 29–31, 1987. Under the banner "The West Wants In," about three hundred delegates and observers discussed issues such as regional fairness, balanced budgets, Senate reform, and free trade. Progressive Conservatives thought the West was already "in." After decades of underrepresentation during the Trudeau years, western conservatives filled the government benches and cabinet seats like never before. Yet it was not western people Manning wanted in, it was popular western ideas. The assembly was no meeting of flaming radicals. The creation of the Reform party was careful, deliberate, thoughtful, and professional.

To establish an organized response to western alienation, four options were debated: (i) work with a traditional party; (ii) create a focused pressure group; (iii) create a new federal political party; and (iv) the non-offensive category "other."[20] While there were four options on the table, however, the outcome was never in doubt. "Preston had the objective right away of forming a political party that he would lead," said Weissenberger. "It is a fair comment to say that this was his objective back in 1967."

Preston Manning and others tried to argue that the new political party would be different and would not be ideologically focused. Trevor Harrison, in his book on the rise of the Reform party, paints a different picture. "Despite Manning's call for balance, the ideological mix of the new party had already begun to congeal around certain right-wing principles."[21] Harrison cited comments from delegates and reporters to support his conclusion that assembly participants "were almost uniformly social and economic conservatives" who were "dominated by old-time Socreds dying for another kick at the political cat."

The young Stephen Harper went to the assembly with a manifesto called "A Taxpayers Reform Agenda," which he concocted with Weissenberger. Their agenda included eleven one-sentence propos-

---

[20] The category "other" was considered less inflammatory and extreme than presenting delegates with the stark alternative of the breakup of Canada.

[21] Harrison, *Of Passionate Intensity*, 111.

als that were true to conservative principles. But Harper's right-wing perspective was at odds with the message Manning delivered to the assembly. Manning advocated a populist movement that would, in theory, appeal to the left, middle, and right of the political spectrum. He may have sounded like a conservative when he complained about the Mulroney government being out of touch with western Canada, but he was not trying to form a party of the right. Manning, an evangelical Christian, also spoke of social conservative issues, which were nowhere to be found in Harper's manifesto.

Despite Manning's populist urgings, Harper felt he was among true conservatives, and he was comfortable enough to abandon his Blue Tory project to explore what could be done within this new western-based political movement.

The convention that established the Reform Party of Canada took place in Winnipeg from October 30 to November 1, 1987. The 306 delegates were largely from Alberta.[22]

Manning thought Stephen Harper's speech, titled "Achieving Economic Justice in Confederation," was the best of the convention. He credited Harper with ". . . shatter[ing] all the stereotypes (reactionary, backward looking, narrow, simplistic, extreme) that are often applied to a new political party struggling for legitimacy from a western base."[23] Harper demonstrated the extent to which the West gave far more than it received within Confederation. Whether it was transfer payments, regional economic development, unemployment insurance, government employment, or tariff protection, the West was consistently on the short end of the stick. Power, Harper suggested, was concentrated in the hands of eastern elites who sought to perpetuate the welfare state and seek appeasement from Quebec. Those agitated because the CF-18 maintenance contract was given to Quebec-based Canadair, whose bid was higher and whose technology was inferior, instead of to western Canada's Bristol Aerospace, had a cogent and articulate framework in which

---

[22] Ibid., 114. There were 140 delegates from Alberta, 91 from British Columbia, 65 from Manitoba and only 10 from Saskatchewan.

[23] Manning, *The New Canada*, 150.

to situate their angst. No longer, Harper argued, should the country "...be built on the economic exploitation and political disenfranchisement of western Canada."[24]

With the theme "The West Wants In," Manning believed he was laying the groundwork for a national political party. He recalled, "When Reform started, one of the first discussions we had at the founding convention in Winnipeg was, are we creating a regional party or creating a national party? I argued we were creating a national party. We might have to start in one region because that's where we had our roots and our energy, and we had only very limited resources."

The party was founded on principles of openness and inclusiveness, but the process to elect a leader was anything but. Manning faced Stan Roberts, the former president of the Canada West Foundation and Canadian Chamber of Commerce, for the leadership. Delegates were to be registered by Saturday, but the registration was closed early. Trevor Harrison, in *Passionate Intensity*, described the scene:

> As the crucial vote neared, tensions between the two camps increased. Fearing that the Roberts camp was about to bus in a number of "instant delegates," Manning supporters closed delegate registration on the Friday evening. [Frances] Winspear, who was supporting Roberts, stood up before the delegates and denounced the decision to suspend registration. This incident was followed by further accusations from Roberts that association moneys were unaccounted for ... Roberts made a brief emotional statement to the delegates, announcing that he was withdrawing from the race. "It is with deep regret," he said, "that I have taken this step.... This party was founded on the principles of honesty and integrity—those principles appear to have been compromised during this convention." Declaring Manning's supporters

---

[24] William Johnson, *Stephen Harper and the Future of Canada* (Toronto: McClelland & Stewart, 2005), 85.

"fanatical Albertans" and "small-minded evangelical cranks,"
Roberts then stormed out of the convention.[25]

Of the fracas that ensued, Manning remarked, "[The] delegates
seemed pleased with the results. That was all that really mattered."[26]
This statement seems inconsistent with Manning's approach to other
issues. When asked to explain his objection to the Meech Lake
Accord, Manning pointed to the objectionable process under which
the agreement had been reached.

University of Calgary professor Tom Flanagan was an adviser to
Manning and has described Manning's inner thoughts and strategies.
In his book *Waiting for the Wave: The Reform Party and Preston Manning*,
Flanagan provides a somewhat surprising assessment of Manning's
controlling leadership style. He argues that Manning led the nomination process for the party's executive, dealt with staff "one-on-one"
to diminish their ability to override the leader by sheer numbers, and
controlled the formulation of policy.[27] It was an anomaly that a populist party, designed first and foremost to represent its members, was
tightly controlled by one individual. Said Flanagan, "To a remarkable
degree, the Reform Party is the personal project of Preston
Manning."[28]

PRESTON MANNING BELIEVED that the Reform party crossed all
political lines and appealed to masses of Canadians who were disil-
lusioned with the traditional political parties. Manning's Reform
party would, in theory, draw support from the mainstream parties
in roughly the same proportions as these individuals would otherwise have voted. But was Reform a populist party, as Manning
claimed, or was it intrinsically conservative and in direct competition with the Progressive Conservative party?

[25] Harrison, *Of Passionate Intensity*, 118.
[26] Manning, *The New Canada*, 153.
[27] Tom Flanagan, *Waiting for the Wave: The Reform Party and Preston Manning* (Toronto:
Stoddart, 1995), 36.
[28] Ibid., 5.

Manning did not want to accept that Reform was really another Conservative party, because he did not want to debate an inherent and obvious strategic flaw: that the Reform party was splitting votes with the Tories and thereby electing Liberals and NDP members of parliament. Manning also did not want to be accused of cannibalizing the vote on the right. Manning may have hoped the votes had not been split, but the results are indisputable. Stated differently, how could a populist political party rooted in Alberta be anything but conservative?

But what is populism really? Trevor Harrison answers the question in his book on right-wing populism and the Reform party: "In short, populism constitutes an attempt to create a mass political movement, mobilized around symbols and traditions congruent with the popular culture, which expresses a group's sense of threat, arising from presumably powerful 'outside' elements and directed at its perceived 'peoplehood.' . . . Populist unrest results from the delegitimization crises and the resultant de-composition of previous political alliances. The type of populism that emerges (right- or left-wing) is a product of social, political, and ideological elements set adrift by this process and the consequent reconfiguration of alliances designed to resolve the crisis."[29]

The crisis that gave rise to Reform began with a long string of western Canadian grievances, which were inflamed when the supposed savior, the Progressive Conservative party, failed to meet hopes and expectations.

Leading Reform strategist Tom Flanagan, who knows Manning well, agrees that Manning was first and foremost a populist agent of reconciliation and change. "At the deepest level his political career is motivated by a unique personal sense of mission: not, as is often thought, to impose a right-wing fundamentalist agenda on Canadian politics, but to act as a mediator, to bring together the warring factions into which Canadian society has become divided."[30] Flanagan describes Manning as a "human barometer of political dissatisfaction lying beneath the surface."[31]

---

[29] Harrison, *Of Passionate Intensity*, 5, 11.

[30] Flanagan, *Waiting for the Wave*, 2.

[31] Ibid., 3.

Flanagan's impression of Manning is consistent with Manning's view of himself. "I came to the conclusion that if I was ever to be personally involved in politics, I wanted to be involved in a genuine populist movement rather than a traditional political party.[32]

Manning wrote that populism is the "common sense of the common people [that would] allow the public to have more say in the devolvement of public policy through direct consultation, constitutional conventions, constituent assemblies, national referenda and citizens' initiatives."[33]

Yet he acknowledged to Flanagan that both populism and conservatism were intrinsic to Reform. He also recognized that populism is inherently short-lived. Flanagan remarked: "Manning has always emphasized that his populist project, by its very nature, must be accomplished quickly . . . the populist impulse will disintegrate and the party will be left with the conservatism of its members."[34]

The stark reality is that populist movements are inherently transient. The Reform party's original constitution includes this remarkably bold and unprecedented clause: "This constitution shall become null and void, and the Party shall cease to exist, on November 1st, 2000 AD, unless this Constitution is re-enacted in its present or amended form by a two-thirds majority of delegates to a Party assembly held before that date."[35] The Reform party was populist in the way Social Credit was populist when Manning's father was premier. "Manning thinks in terms of a new party sweeping to power on a tidal wave of popular discontent, as Social Credit did in 1935 in the depths of the Depression."[36]

There are two popular conceptions about Manning's political views: that his political philosophy is grounded in his Christian beliefs, and that he is an extreme right-wing conservative. Flanagan counters both. Manning does have deeply held religious beliefs, but

[32] Manning, *The New Canada*, 7.

[33] Ibid., 26.

[34] Flanagan, *Waiting for the Wave*, 4

[35] Reform Party constitution, October 30, 1987, section. 11c.

[36] Flanagan, *Waiting for the Wave*, 36.

he believes that important moral issues should be decided by referendum and not be based on the moral conscience of a political party, its leader, or an individual member. This suggests that Preston Manning would support initiatives to increase access to abortion, obviously anathema to his Christian beliefs, should it be the majority position of his electors.

There is clear contradiction between being populist and showing attachment to any particular political philosophy. Presumably, those who identified themselves as left or socialist would find comfort with the NDP, while those on the conservative right would align with the Progressive Conservatives. Those living in Quebec who believed in separation and a Quebec nation would align with the Bloc Québécois. In its pure form, populism is more a methodology than a consistent stance on a series of issues. For a populist party to survive and succeed there must be a broad consensus that none of the current political philosophies respond to voter concerns. Some suggest the Bloc Québécois is populist because it was born out of political uprising. It is anything but, because it has a well-defined agenda with coherent and consistent policies designed to deliver the destiny it sees for Quebec.

For Reform to work as a populist party it could not be a purely conservative or right-wing party. Manning knew this, which is why he never wanted the right-wing label. He knew that unless he could attract voters away from mainstream political parties right across the country in somewhat equal proportions, his project would fail.

So, was Preston Manning as conservative as his Reform party members? Flanagan doubts this, for a number of reasons. He saw that Manning was fundamentally opposed to deficits and the burden of debt, but that view could easily be held from the left; witness Tommy Douglas, the former socialist NDP premier of Saskatchewan. Manning did not support an end to interventionist supply-management marketing boards and would also continue farm income subsidies. He supported social programs and opposed privatization of pension plans. Manning, said Flanagan, "is eclectic in his thinking, and has a tendency to embrace contradictory positions in a belief that they will be reconciled in some future synthesis. He is certainly not a socialist or even a liberal, but in ideological terms he could lead a centrist party with a favourable orientation to business.... He envisions a dynamic process in which he will recruit centrist or even leftist members, whose presence will change the party's ideological center of gravity, which in turn will make it more hospitable for centrist, leftists and so on. Eventually, he wants Reform to embrace the whole ideological spectrum, just as he wants to become a demographic microcosm of the whole Canadian society."[37]

To some in Canada, populism has a negative connotation. It is seen as a place where disaffected and angry misfits attempt to congregate legitimately because they cannot find a home in any of the mainstream parties. Manning tried his best to avoid this stigma, although he did acknowledge the inherent risk of his undertaking. "There is some academic literature where populism is a perversion of democracy where some demagogue bamboozles the public into support. I acknowledge there is a dark side to that. But that was never what we were talking about. It is a phenomenon that has its dark side but it is a very admirable phenomenon when it works properly." It doesn't always work properly. Brian Mulroney is reported to have warned Manning about the dangers of cobbling together a coalition of the disaffected: "You can build an army of opportunists, but you can never make them march."[38]

Manning was uncomfortable calling himself a populist or a conservative. "I stopped using populism because of the perceived negatives and just kept using democracy, democratic grass roots, bottom up, those types of words." This labelling confusion irritated Manning. "The people that argue that Reform was populist, and to them populism is a derogatory word, they are often people who don't really like democracy but don't have the guts to say it, so they call it populism in protest."

For Manning, Reform fit into a broad historical and sociological context. "There are two parts of the country that innovate politically

---

[37] Ibid., 15, 17.

[38] This quote was attributed to Brian Mulroney in an interview with Peter MacKay.

in the sense of supporting new movements outside the traditional ones ... there are two parts of the country that are systemic changers. One is Quebec with that long list of third parties: Bloc Populaire; Union Nationale; Ralliament des Créditistes; BQ; ADQ. The other of course is the West with its stream: Riel, the independence movement, the Progressives; the depression parties, CCF, Social Credit, and then Reform." Manning believed the urge to be different is somehow innate. "I argue there is something in the juices of these two regions that produce these movements, and will produce these movements sooner or later no matter what." (Brian Mulroney responded to the notion of western juices by saying one could hardly expect western-ers to remain calm when a political leader is telling them on a daily basis that they are being abused and exploited. It was one thing, argued Mulroney, to foment discord. It was quite another to govern the country where a national and inclusive perspective is required.)

The Reform Party of Canada was not established with a neutral ideological bent. The populist methodology was encumbered in the first instance by a number of predetermined views enshrined in its Statement of Principles.[39] These included: a Triple-E Senate (elected, effective, and equal); conserving the physical environment; protecting the family unit; a free-enterprise economy; collective responsibility for the care of basic human needs; balanced budgets; and positive relations with the United States. These were the princi-ples Manning hastily wrote on a sheet of paper that became the Reform party constitution. A truly populist party would not have policy markers in its constitution; rather, it would have various mech-anisms and procedures to prioritize the will of electors and citizens.

Tom Flanagan questioned the legitimacy of populism in the Reform party: "The populist dream of consensus about policy matters is both empirically impossible and logically incoherent ... as a political leader Manning operates with an intuitive grasp of the importance of agenda control, and within the Reform Party he tries to reserve that control for himself."[40]

---

[39] Reform Party of Canada Principles and Policies 1991, 1–4.

[40] Flanagan, *Waiting for the Wave*, 27.

Manning's commitment to democracy also appears to have its limitations. Even within the party's hierarcy, Tom Flanagan reported that Manning exercised de facto control over the nomination of the chairman and officers of the party's executive council and the chairmen and members of all committees "... to ensure that all key positions are filled by reliable loyalists and to isolate mavericks on the council."[41] And when Reform party policy was adopted at general assemblies and conventions, Manning frequently ignored those aspects with which he was not completely comfortable. "The relative lack of concerns with assembly proceedings and decisions stems from Manning's feelings that he is not bound by them."[42]

Ted Byfield, a Reform party founder[43] and creator of the *Alberta Report*,[44] did not believe Manning was a populist and suggested he was more interested in control and power: "It always seems to me that [Manning] is always advocating something [populism] that is incompatible with his own instincts.... And I think that will likely get him into trouble before he's finished, too, because it isn't his [first] instinct. [Preston] is the authoritarian of the first order, [just] as his father was..."[45]

THE ARGUMENTS THAT ULTIMATELY led to the merger between the Progressive Conservative and the Reform-Alliance parties were as valid throughout the 1990s as they were in 2003 when the merger was consummated. The parties were eating each other's lunch.

Preston Manning was never comfortable with Reform being placed on the right wing, as in pro–free enterprise and minimal gov-

---

[41] Ibid., 28.

[42] Ibid., 30.

[43] Harrison, *Of Passionate Intensity*, 82. Harrison credits Ted Byfield, Preston Manning, Stan Roberts, and Francis Winspear as the group that "took the first step in creating an alternative right-wing party."

[44] Ibid., 51. Harrison describes the *Alberta Report* as "Western Canada's most prominent and consistent organ for the dissemination of conservative values."

[45] Ibid., 217.

ernment, or the left wing, as in redistribution of wealth and state-run social programs. He thought that Conservatives on the right had "hard heads and hard hearts," while the New Democrats on the left had "soft heads and soft hearts." His political goal was to be "hard headed and soft hearted." Yet in his autobiographies, Manning provided no evidence that Conservatives were hard-hearted. Instead, he pointed out that 60 per cent of government spending while Mulroney was in office was on social programs, hardly the measure of a hard-hearted politician. In elections to come, Reform party platforms would cut heavily in these areas.

Manning was alone in arguing that Reform was not on the right of the political spectrum. Trevor Harrison said: "The data support the widespread contention that Reformers are, in general, disgruntled Tories or previous supporters of other right-wing parties. The party's 1989 delegate survey found that 78 per cent of the delegates identified themselves as previous Tories, 5 per cent Socreds, 5 per cent Liberals, and just over 1 per cent Confederation of Regions members. Similarly, the 1992 delegate survey found that over 79 per cent had voted Tory in 1984, while 46 per cent did so again in 1988, compared with 36 per cent who shifted to Reform."[46]

Reform members were far to the right of the Progressive Conservative party. Yet Manning didn't even want to say he was a conservative. "Stephen Harper and I were conservative and could see the obvious contradiction," said John Weissenberger. So could the media. They viewed Reform as ultraconservative. Denying reality made Canadians suspicious of Reform. "The critics would say you are not calling yourself conservative, but you have nothing but conservative policies," said Weissenberger. "It seemed to Stephen and myself that this was an untenable position. That left us open to the accusation that we had a hidden agenda."

It is hard to imagine a more ideologically driven party or leader than Preston Manning and Reform. The party's 1989 convention

---

[46] Ibid., 201. Harrison points out that Reform's figures do not add up to 100 per cent.

survey found that on a 7-point scale defining left–right ideology (left=1, right=7), Reformers placed themselves at 5.08; the Canadian electorate at 3.74; the federal Conservatives at 3.5, the Liberals at 2.63, and the NDP at 1.85.[47]

While Reform party members viewed themselves far to the right of the PC party, most western conservatives saw Reform as more innovative than extreme. John Weissenberger thought an average member of the PC party was not much different from an average member of the Reform party. What was different was the apparatus and the leadership. Reform party members could see their conservatism represented in the Reform party. What they saw in the PC party was decision making and leadership dominated by centrist Red Tories. Reform party members by and large represented a view of Canada that was strongly anti-government, anti–social welfare, and anti-Quebec (as in opposed to official bilingualism in the federal government, distinct society status, or vetoes for Quebec in the constitution).[48]

Manning did not agree with Harper, Flanagan, Weissenberger, and others who said his populism lacked a philosophical ideology to sustain his political beliefs. In 2006, he looked back at the Reform movement:

> I always felt there was an ideological commitment [to Reform]...[beginning with] a principled commitment to small-c conservative economics. We had people who were social conservatives, in the current meaning of that phrase, who had principled commitment to those positions. We had Reform-oriented federalists who had a principled conception of federalism and were trying to implement it federally. We had all of those elements that were principled and value-driven. We had an equally strong commitment, at least I did, to democracy. I think of democracy itself as an ideology and so we had a commitment to that.

---

[47] Ibid., 205.
[48] Ibid.

It was astonishing to hear Manning say in 2006 that small-c conservative economics were fundamental to Reform, because almost everything he said before 1997 suggested his was not a party of conservative persuasion.

In 2006, Manning also defended his populist notions, suggesting they were integral to democracy:

> I used to argue we were a coalition and the way you make coalitions work is you have to reconcile these other principled positions if they are reconcilable, which I argued they were. And the way you reconcile them is using democratic processes. You get everybody in a room; you have a representative assembly; you let everybody have their say, nobody gets shouted down and told you can't talk about that here. But at the end of the day we have a vote and that's the position we have until it's changed. My commitment to democracy was ideological, partly, but also a process commitment as the way you reconcile these other views, which are not incompatible, but still need some reconciling.

Manning felt he was leading a party where democratic mechanisms were used to establish policy within a philosophical orientation towards conservative economic and social issues, such as family values. Also intrinsic to his views was a position of federalism that was fundamentally egalitarian.

Other senior Reform activists for example, Harper and Flanagan, were uncomfortable that party members could choose policies and positions that were inconsistent with conservative philosophy. Manning, however, was entirely comfortable with that outcome. "I think the people who objected to populism, and would have described themselves as ideological, were mainly hard-line fiscal conservatives. That was the kind of party they wanted to create. I agued there was certainly a place for that and we were committed to that. We were the guys who crusaded on budget balancing when the pollsters said you couldn't get votes that way. But there were other dimensions to our ideology: the social ones, the constitutional ones, and democracy itself."

GENERALLY, REFORM AND MANNING would have anything but a warm welcome from federalists in Quebec. Manning rejected the notion that Canada is a product of two founding peoples—English and French—arguing instead for a single nation of equal provinces. He offered Quebec equal status with other provinces. In Manning's words, "Reformers believe that going down the special status road [for Quebec] has led to the creation of two full-blown separatist movements in Quebec... and this road leads to an unbalanced federation of racial and ethnic groups distinguished by constitutional wrangling and deadlock, regional imbalance, and a fixation with unworkable linguistic and cultural policies, to the neglect of weightier matters such as the environment, economy, and international competitiveness."[49]

On a practical level, Manning's view gave little regard to how Quebec might embrace Canada. As far as Manning was concerned, if Quebec was not prepared to accept equality with other provinces, then another arrangement should be negotiated:

> Either all Canadians, including the people of Quebec, make a clear commitment to Canada as one nation, or Quebec and the rest of Canada should explore whether there exists a better and more separate relationship between the two.... If, however, we continue to make unacceptable constitutional, economic and linguistic concessions to Quebec at the expense of the rest of Canada, it is those concessions themselves which will tear the country apart and poison French–English relations beyond remedy. If the house cannot be reunited [on the basis of equality] then Quebec and the rest of Canada should openly examine the feasibility of establishing a better but more separate relationship between them, on equitable and mutually acceptable terms.[50]

---

[49] Manning, *The New Canada*, 305.
[50] Ibid., 224.

One could easily imagine a very short and largely agreeable debate in which Manning would be pitted against former separatist leader Lucien Bouchard or Jacques Parizeau. Based on questions asked and answered, all parties might come to one conclusion: Quebec must leave Canada. At least Manning was prepared to call their bluff, if bluff it was.

Preston Manning opposed the 1987 Meech Lake Constitutional Accord for a number of reasons, the most important of which was the difficulty it would pose for the establishment of a Triple-E Senate. Manning thought it unlikely that Quebec would agree to accept a formula that gave equality to every province in a new legitimate Senate, and that gave Quebec only 10 per cent of the representatives. Manning was unimpressed that the Meech Lake Accord required the prime minister and provincial premiers to place Senate reform on the agenda of upcoming conferences.[51]

The statism inherent in allowing Quebec to promote and defend itself as a distinct society with special powers was also of concern to Reform.[52] Manning made no specific argument about the difference acknowledging Quebec as a distinct society would make to the daily lives of western Canadians. What did Albertans care if the courts of the land interpreted the constitution to recognize the inherent obligation of the Quebec government to protect its language and culture? Even without the distinct society clause, Quebec, and other provinces, could impose whatever language laws they wanted under Trudeau's constitution by simply invoking the notwithstanding clause. Ultimately, Manning and the Reform movement grew tired of having progress on important national issues thwarted because central Canadian elites needed to deal with the Quebec question.

---

[51] The Meech Lake Accord mandated a review of "the role and functions of the Senate, its powers, the method of selecting Senators and representation in the Senate."

[52] The Meech Lake Accord responded to five demands made by Quebec as conditions for signing the constitution. These were: veto on constitutional amendments; limits on federal spending power; greater role in immigration policy; role in the appointment of Supreme Court justices; recognition of Quebec as a distinct society.

For decades, federal Liberal governments had been intruding into areas of provincial jurisdiction by using federal spending powers. This was a huge frustration to many provinces, including Quebec. Manning wanted to scuttle the federal intrusions and return the responsibility and taxation room to the provinces.[53] It is unfortunate that Manning was never able to articulate his views in French. If Manning had a legitimate ally on respecting the Canadian constitution and the allocation of powers between the federal and provincial governments, it should have been Quebec nationalists such as Lucien Bouchard. Manning recalled: "We always felt that if we could ever have communicated that in Quebec, or found an ally who could have communicated it, there was a very interesting commonality between western Canada and Quebec on that issue. Of course I was crippled there by not being bilingual."

Manning and Harper were prepared to take their vision of Canada into Quebec. "We called our view a new federalism: not the status-quo federalism of Chrétien and the Liberals; not the kick at the pieces approach of the Bloc; but a reformed federalism. We talked about rebalancing the powers where you respected the provincial governments in their area of jurisdiction. You got the federal government out of these areas, you vacated the tax room that they occupied and gave it to the provinces," Manning explained. But it was hard for Reform to be heard in Quebec. Reform was seen as the party that led the fight against Meech Lake, the party that would not allow Quebec to be recognized as a distinct society.

To be clear, the Meech Lake Accord was not an influence in the initial meetings that led to the founding of the Reform party. The Meech Lake Accord was signed on June 3, 1987, just after the Vancouver Assembly that led to the launch of the Reform party.

---

[53] The federal and provincial goverments tax many of the same sources, such as personal income and sales. In rebalancing the finances of the federal and provincial governments, one approach has been for the federal government to reduce its tax rates while provincial governments raise their rates on the same source. The overall tax paid is the same, but tax is being shifted from one government to another. In other words, the federal government "makes room" for the provinces to increase taxes.

THE FIRST ELECTORAL TEST FOR REFORM came in 1988, when Brian Mulroney's government faced the electorate for the first time. Speaking in 2003, Mulroney recalled his puzzlement at the prospect of facing Preston Manning and the Reform party on the ballot, given his government's record at responding to western grievances:

> We had not run a perfect government. We had made mistakes. But, as I arrived in Alberta to begin the campaign I felt reasonably confident, however, of taking on this coalition of Free Trade opponents: unemployment was down; growth was strong; the NEP was abolished; FIRA was eliminated; the wave of privatization had begun; we had negotiated the Canada–U.S. FTA, an initiative ardently sought by Western Canada for generations; we had three Albertans in Cabinet in positions of great influence: Messrs. Mazankowski, Deputy Prime Minister; Clark, Foreign Affairs; Andre, Government Leader. I was running the most conservative government since Prime Minister St. Laurent and our government had responded more fully to western Canadian aspirations than any other in modern history. Imagine my surprise, therefore, to find that, running against us and cutting into our vote at the centre and centre-right, was Preston Manning and the old Social Credit Party, then dressed up under a new name, the Reform party. This was the beginning of the division of conservative forces in Canada. At the very moment the centre-right was gaining effectiveness in Canada, Mr. Manning chose to launch a new party, split the vote and give rise to the political fragmentation we know today.[54]

The election was dominated by debate over the Free Trade Agreement with the United States. Liberal leader John Turner said opposition to the FTA was the "cause of his life." In the free trade

---

[54] Notes for an address by the Right Honourable Brian Mulroney, Progressive Conservative Leadership Convention, the Crowne Plaza Hotel, Toronto, Ontario, May 30, 2003.

debate, Reform was on the same side as the Tories. Conservative-minded voters feared that placing a protest vote with Reform might defeat the PCs and thwart the trade deal. Those who might otherwise have voted Reform instinctively knew the consequences of splitting the conservative vote. Mulroney would later remark, "Had Westerners truly split the conservative vote in 1988, Canada would never have had free trade, something the West had wanted for the past 125 years. As it was, a number of NDP were elected in 1988 because of vote splitting."

Don Mazankowski recalled that Reform certainly made its presence felt in 1988, but that the election battle lines were drawn around free trade. "I ran in seven election campaigns. That one was the most satisfying because it was clearly an issue-oriented campaign. One side was going to win and one side was going to lose and Canada was going to take a different track. That is the real genius of the Mulroney government." If western alienation was real, this was not the election where it was safe to give it expression.

The major issue that Reform brought to the electorate in 1988 was financial mismanagement, specifically the inability of Mulroney's government to balance the books.

Much of the Reform effort was focused on the riding of Yellowhead, Alberta, where Preston Manning took on Joe Clark, then minister for external affairs and a former Tory leader. It was clever and politically savvy for Manning to pick such a high-profile opponent. No one expected Manning to win, but the contest gave Manning the opportunity to debate and ridicule a former Conservative prime minister in local debates and on local media. Such encounters would be played across the country, giving both Manning and Reform some much-sought-after publicity.

Author Graham Fraser describes a campaign event where Preston Manning squared off against Joe Clark:

> Manning . . . was cheered when he told the audience to send the old parties a message, and that his election would be a warning to MPs across Canada. "If you [Clark] will not faithfully repre-

sent those who elect you, you will be replaced by someone who will." This was the issue people questioned Clark most closely about. They opposed bilingualism and favoured capital punishment: he [Clark] had supported bilingualism and voted against capital punishment. "How can we vote for you if you don't vote for us?" one member of the audience asked.[55]

Manning tapped into the anger and feelings of alienation that existed in western Canada. Voters in the West remembered well the decision by Mulroney, with his western cabinet ministers by his side, to award the CF-18 maintenance contract not to a Manitoba company, but to a Quebec firm. Reformers campaigning in Manitoba distributed pamphlets telling voters, "Don't Get Mad, Get Even."

For a first attempt in a strategically difficult election, Reform performed remarkably well. It received slightly more than 2 per cent of votes cast nationally and 8.5 per cent of votes cast in the 72 ridings in which it fielded a candidate. The Tories won 25 of 26 Alberta ridings, but Reform captured 15.3 per cent of the vote, with support from both urban and rural ridings. Preston Manning placed second in Yellowhead, reducing Joe Clark's popular vote from 74 per cent in 1984 to 45 per cent in 1988. Manning lost by a margin of only 6,640 votes.

While the Free Trade Agreement was secure, Alberta had still managed to cast a meaningful protest vote, a warning Progressive Conservatives should have heeded. Reform had shown that it was not a fringe party.

One of Reform's most successful candidates was Stephen Harper. There was some awkwardness to this campaign because Harper was on the same ballot as Jim Hawkes, his former boss and one of his political mentors. Hawkes had recognized Harper's potential four years earlier in the 1984 campaign, when Stephen led the youth volunteers in Calgary West. Hawkes had brought Harper to Ottawa to work as his legislative assistant, and they had spent many hours

---

[55] Graham Fraser, *Playing for Keeps: The Making of the Prime Minister* (Toronto: McClelland & Stewart, 1989), 410.

together discussing the nation, policy, and political strategy. Harper felt sufficiently uncomfortable facing his former boss that he called Hawkes before the election to ask if his candidacy would bother him. Hawkes acquiesced to Harper's candidacy. (It is difficult to know what would have happened had Hawkes objected.) Harper had already formed the local Reform constituency association and had been acclaimed as its candidate. Most likely the call to Hawkes was simply an indication of respect. Harper was in the 1988 campaign for better or worse.

As the party's first chief policy officer, Harper had been instrumental in crafting Reform's 1988 election platform. Drawing inspiration from the manifesto of British prime minister Margaret Thatcher, the Reform platform was clearly more conservative than populist, although elements of both streams of thinking were clearly in evidence in the thirty-six-page document. (It is noteworthy that a populist party would have a chief policy officer; you would expect its platforms would be assembled from the grassroots and not entrusted to a single person.)

Harper and Hawkes could hardly disagree on the principal election issue, free trade. The Liberals did Stephen Harper no favours when they turned the campaign into a virtual referendum on the FTA. Yet Harper finished a respectable second in the election, with 16.6 per cent of the vote, compared with Hawkes's 58.5. It was an easy win for Hawkes, but his popular support was 16.2 percentage points lower than it had been in 1984, about the same level given to Harper. This suggests the conservative vote held together between 1984 and 1988, although vote splitting had no consequence on the outcome.

For many reasons, the 1988 results should have made the Tories nervous, but instead they were joyous. They had focused entirely on John Turner and the Liberal party. "After the [leaders'] debate I figured we had lost it," said Mazankowski. "It looked at times like the Liberals might win. But that's when Mulroney turned on the afterburners and he went to work. Then there was no looking back." Mulroney secured another majority government, winning 169 of 295 seats.

The Tories felt they could ignore Manning and Reform without consequence. After all, they won 7 of 14 seats in Manitoba, the province that was supposed to punish them for the CF-18 decision. The Tories felt they had an unshakeable grip the West. "They loved us out west," said David Angus. "The oil barons of Calgary, they loved Mulroney. We got rid of the NEP. They gave us lots of money. They got everything in spades."

While the Tories may have kept the oil patch, however, the battle for the hearts and minds of mainstream westerners was another matter. So although Reform had no seats, everyone seemed happy. For the moment, that is.

CHAPTER 5

PC DEMISE, REFORM RISE

THERE WAS NOT MUCH suspense on election night 1988 in the riding of Beaver River, Alberta. This was a new riding, the result of electoral boundary adjustments. The PCs knew they could chalk up a win without so much as knocking on one door or putting up one lawn sign. Like other rural Alberta ridings, Beaver River was a seat the Tories could not lose even if they tried. PC candidate John Dahmer, who had unexpectedly spent most of the campaign in hospital, won decisively, with 13,768 votes. Reform party candidate Deborah Grey, a political novice trying to make a point, finished in fourth place with 4,158 votes.

Sadly, five days after the election, the bone cancer that had sidelined Dahmer from the campaign took his life.

Less than four months later, on March 13, 1989, the voters who turned out for the by-election to fill the vacant seat sent a decidedly different message to Ottawa. Deborah Grey, who had been a campaign afterthought less than four months earlier, swept the riding and outpolled her PC rival, Dave Broda, by a margin of almost two to one. Grey received nearly as many votes as her PC, Liberal, and NDP opponents combined. This was a watershed day for Preston Manning and the Reform Party of Canada.

By-elections are rarely kind to a governing party. Even so, the extent of this turnaround in Beaver River demanded in-depth analysis. Some thought the reason for the poor PC showing could be voter resentment over the failure to disclose John Dahmer's illness during the campaign. "There was a certain amount of anger that we didn't level with the electorate. But the seriousness of his illness only became known during the campaign," said Deputy Prime Minister Mazankowski. Having just won a second majority government Mulroney was nonplussed by the loss. And his western cabinet ministers were more likely to produce a long list of measures they had implemented to address western grievances than to try and understand the rising sentiment of alienation that Reform was exploiting. The Mulroney government ignored the warning signs evident from the Beaver River by-election.

On by-election night, Grey was blunt. "We have the chance now not to be totally ignored by Ottawa and Quebec."[1] Manning explained that the Reform win was due, in part, to voter frustration with official bilingualism. While the Reform win raised a few Tory eyebrows, Manning predicted the Tories would not do much soul-searching about their loss of popularity in the West. He was right: the Tories lamely excused the loss in Beaver River as a by-election anomaly, and said the Reform party was the lucky beneficiary of an isolated and predictable protest vote.

Deborah Grey was a schoolteacher. Although her great-grandfather had been a Liberal MP and her great-uncle had been Liberal premier of British Columbia, Grey had no practical experience in politics. She acknowledged that she was a Tory and had voted Tory all her life. But in 1988, she thought there was "something in it that just didn't ring true."[2]

Before her first trip to Ottawa, Grey admitted she was unprepared for the scrutiny of the media and the functioning of Parliament. "Every night when I go to bed I think, 'Holy man. Am I able to do all this?'"[3] Fearing that a serious mistake by Grey could be fatal to the party, Preston Manning implored Stephen Harper to go to Ottawa as

[1] Peter Bakogeorge, "Reform Party supporters in this federal riding," Southam News, March 14, 1989.

[2] Peter Bakogeorge, "When Parliament resumes Monday, the newest MP," Southam News, April 1, 1989.

[3] Ibid.

her parliamentary assistant. Harper was in the middle of graduate studies at the University of Calgary and was disinclined to return to Ottawa, a place he found meaningless and trivial. However, Manning was persistent, and Harper was ultimately persuaded.

He helped Grey navigate through her new life as an MP and continued to advise Manning on policy development and the Reform platform for the next election. He also completed his master's degree in economics, with a thesis on the political and economic cycles of federal budgeting.

Grey described Harper as "bright as a whip . . . a good strategic thinker. But intense."[4] In her autobiography, *Never Retreat, Never Explain, Never Apologize: My Life, My Politics*, she offered limited praise and criticism of Harper. Perhaps the street-smart Grey resented the unelected graduate student telling her what to read, what to do, and what to say. Harper was not one to be shy about offering his opinion and direction.

Grey's confidence was buttressed by the quality of the material Harper prepared and the speeches he wrote for her. Harper was the party's chief policy officer, and he had the ear of Preston Manning. For all Grey's incredible strengths and her ability to connect with voters on a personal level, she needed Harper's guidance to prepare for parliamentary debates.

Even with a Reform MP sitting in the House of Commons, Brian Mulroney had no clear idea what Reform represented. Mulroney confided to Peter C. Newman, "The Reform Party is anti-everything. There is a really deep-seated racism there. I still don't know what to make of Reform. I know that for the moment it's growing. But these are one-trick ponies. They are not standing on a whole lot of sound ground. It's all negative."[5]

The comment about racism was not entirely partisan bluster. Racism was certainly an issue with Manning. In 1991, he wrote: "If a new political movement can prevent extremism of any kind, partic-

[4] Johnson, *Stephen Harper*, 132.
[5] Peter C. Newman, *The Secret Mulroney Tapes: Unguarded Confessions of a Prime Minister* (Toronto: Random House, 2005), 245.

ularly racism, from taking root in the first place, it will save itself and its members of minority communities an infinite amount of trouble later on."[6] Manning described a host of measures to deal with some of the extreme elements that had been surfacing in Reform, such as candidate questionnaires specifically designed to resist the infiltration of racist forces. Unfortunately for Reform, these measures were not universally successful.[7]

In the late 1980s, senior Tory strategists were dismissive of Reform. But other voices in the Tory party warned of the peril that lay ahead. PC party president Gerry St. Germain recalled heated discussions at meetings of the PC Canada Fund (the fundraising arm of the PC party) in 1989:

> Guys like Jake Epp and myself, we told them what was happening. We had an aggressive debate. We told them to concentrate some of their resources to try and determine how this Reform party was emerging. But they just dismissed Reform as a bunch of wackos from the West. From what was said, they wanted to castigate them as extremists. They said Reform would never be accepted by Canadians. They thought they could just ignore them and they would go away like a bad cold—but they didn't. Some of us from the West, that knew and understood the West, we were aware what was going on and how deep-rooted this

---

[6] Manning, *The New Canada*, 24.

[7] "In the early 1990s, the party was controversially endorsed by extremist groups such as the Heritage Front and the Alliance for the Preservation of English in Canada (APEC). This was a significant blow to the party's image in many regions of Canada, and one from which they struggled to recover for many years. While the Reform Party had similar views to APEC's on official bilingualism and the role of Quebec in the confederation, the reasons for the racist Heritage Front's endorsement were less direct. In fact, the Heritage Front simply viewed Reform as a vehicle they could infiltrate in order to steer it toward their views, a phenomenon to which many new political parties are somewhat vulnerable. A few individual party candidates did come under fire for having made racist statements; however, the Reform Party itself never proposed or endorsed a racist platform." Source: en.wikipedia.org (Reform party of Canada, "Controversial Links").

movement was taking hold. The status quo figured these guys would go away and die. Even Mulroney wasn't prepared to give an inch.

Mazankowski's strategy for dealing with Reform was innovative. "I said let's not fight them; let's hug them to death to try to bring them back into the fold." But Reform wasn't interested in Tory affection: it had an agenda quite apart from anything the PC government was trying to accomplish. Even had the PC government done everything Manning wanted, Manning was not going to join its ranks. As far as Manning was concerned, the more his ideas were ignored by the Tory government, the better. What Manning wanted most was to make his mark on the national stage and test the political-realignment theory that had been in his head for much of the previous twenty years.

THE NEXT REFORM PARTY ELECTORAL breakthrough occurred on October 16, 1989, when Stan Waters won an Alberta-wide election to determine the province's nominee for the Senate of Canada. This was an unusual and unprecedented election with an unpredictable outcome. Since Senate appointments are the prerogative of the prime minister, a provincial election to determine a prospective nominee had no constitutional standing. However, Alberta's premier, Don Getty, used the Senate election to distance himself from Mulroney, who was unpopular, and to give voice to western calls for a Triple-E Senate.[8] Mulroney initially resisted the pressure to appoint the election winner. Getty threatened Alberta's withdrawal from the Meech Lake Accord, and Waters was summoned to the Senate on June 11, 1990.

With two election victories under its belt, the Reform party was building momentum for a general election. Reform had two articulate and forceful members, who provided an aura of credibility and respect. However, the significance of Grey's election was not clear to Mulroney's government. It had not even begun to ask whether her

[8] Triple-E refers to elected, equal provincial representation, and effective in safeguarding regional interests.

win was risk-free mid-term posturing by the Alberta electorate or a more fundamental realignment of western Canadian politics.

APART FROM THE SUCCESSFUL IMPLEMENTATION of the Free Trade Agreement, Mulroney's second term was anything but joyful.

Despite sustained efforts, the deficit rose for most of Mulroney's second term, ending up at $38.5 billion for the fiscal year end March 31, 2003. The final two years of the Mulroney administration produced the two highest nominal deficits in the country's history. The operating surplus had shrunk from a peak of $12.1 billion, in 1988–89, to $1.5 billion in 1993–94. No longer could the financial mess be blamed on the Liberal government. It was Mulroney's to own.

Annual public debt charges, which were $24.9 billion when Mulroney came to power, were more than $40 billion at the end of his second term as prime minister. Relative to the size of the economy, federal debt stood at 67 per cent of GDP, compared to 43.2 per cent when Mulroney came to power and 51.3 per cent at the end of his first term in office. On a National Accounts basis, which combines federal and provincial finances to permit international comparisons, Canada's debt was 64.4 per cent of GDP, almost 50 per cent higher than the G7 average. The only clearly positive statistic was that the deficit as a per cent of GDP was lower in 1993 (5.3 per cent) than it had been in 1984 (8.3 per cent).

Mulroney was beginning to hear rumblings of discontent from within his party about government finances. Kim Campbell, a rookie MP from British Columbia, was frustrated by her government's unwillingness or inability to tackle the deficit problem. "Much was expected of the first budget of a new mandate [after the 1988 election]. The response from many conservatives was disappointment. When the B.C. Ministers held a conference call to discuss the budget with members of the party executive in the province, we heard almost uniform criticism that it didn't go far enough to restrain expenditures."[9]

[9] Kim Campbell, *Time and Chance: The Political Memoirs of Canada's First Woman Prime Minister* (Toronto: Doubleday, 1996), 116.

In Mulroney's first term, the debt grew, and so did the economy. But in the second term, all key economic indicators turned south. Government revenues, which had grown by an average of 10.1 per cent per year during Mulroney's first term, grew an anemic 2.4 per cent per year in his second term. Revenues decreased by an average of 2.8 per cent for the last two years of Conservative administration. It was of no comfort to Mulroney and Canadians that the recession was worldwide. (Voters rarely take this into account when assessing blame.) Interest rates remained high, which hurt both government finances and consumer confidence. The recession, with its consequential rise in unemployment, triggered automatic increases in public spending on Employment Insurance and other social programs, placing greater strain on the nation's finances.

Undeterred by a weak economy, the Mulroney government bravely tackled the hidden yet profoundly destructive Federal Sales Tax (FST), which was charged at the rate of 13.5 per cent on manufactured goods. The FST was structured in a way that harmed Canadian industry by making exports more expensive, while making imports more attractive than domestic products. It was an archaic system that every government for the previous thirty years had studied and been challenged to replace. Only Mulroney had the courage to reform the system. While there were hints of sales tax reform in the Tories' 1988 election platform, it was not until early into his second mandate that the government proposed replacing the FST with a value-added tax called the Goods and Services Tax (GST).

The GST was a public relations nightmare. It confused and outraged consumers, and imposed a huge compliance burden on the business community. Under the FST, some thirty thousand manufacturers charged and remitted tax. Under the GST, more than a million businesses and not-for-profit organizations were required to register then collect and remit the tax revenues. Most of the businesses drawn into the new system were small and ill equipped to handle the administration of a value-added tax. Mulroney knew he would consume a considerable amount of his political capital by proceeding with sales tax reform. This was something his finance minister had asked for, and anyone who had studied the damaging effects of the FST knew it was the right thing to do. Mulroney had already backed off on a budget measure that would have de-indexed old age pensions. He displayed fortitude in supporting Wilson on the implementation of the GST.

It would have made sense to combine the GST with existing provincial sales tax systems, but only Quebec was prepared to co-operate in this. The GST was profoundly different from the single-stage provincial retail sales tax systems that were already in place. And there were inefficiencies in the provincial systems. But provincial politicians knew they would face trouble if they went along with the federal GST.

Kim Campbell thought that introducing the GST, even if it was the right thing to do, seemed almost suicidal: "In 1990, the Alberta Tory MPs were taking an enormous beating on the subject of the GST, a problem made worse by the PM's appointment of eight additional senators when the Liberal majority in the Senate threatened to defeat the GST legislation. Our Alberta colleagues' solidarity was sorely tested as they watched the Reform Party eat away at Conservative support."[10] Foreign Affairs Minister Joe Clark, who had been targeted by Preston Manning and Reform in the 1988 election, speculated in 1990 that he would not be re-elected in his own riding. Had he not retired in 1993, his prediction would likely have come true.

Abuse of patronage was another problem that continued to plague the Mulroney government. Kim Campbell highlighted one incident in particular that raised voter anger. "The issue that seemed to evoke the most anger was the PM's appointment of John Buchanan to the Senate, which was seen as a last straw by beleaguered MPs. At that time, the former Nova Scotia premier was under attack for alleged improprieties when he was in office."[11]

The nation's unity, a clear win for Mulroney in his first term, was starting to unravel. The Meech Lake Accord had passed the federal Parliament; now it required ratification by all provincial legislatures

---

[10] Ibid., 147.

[11] Ibid., 151.

within the prescribed three-year time frame. Every provincial premier had signed the original accord in 1987, but ensuing provincial elections had brought a different slate of premiers to the table. Premier Frank McKenna of New Brunswick had objections, although these were subsequently, if not painfully, addressed, Manitoba and Newfoundland were more troublesome. The two main provincial opponents were premiers Clyde Wells of Newfoundland and Sharon Carstairs of Manitoba, both staunch supporters of former prime minister Pierre Trudeau and well connected to Liberal leader Jean Chrétien.

Preston Manning had a key role to play in the eventual collapse of Meech Lake. His opposition to the accord placed him in unlikely company: he was on the same side as Pierre Trudeau and Jean Chrétien. Without Trudeau's opposition to Meech Lake, Manning's opposition might have been perceived as anti-French, but with Trudeau and Chrétien on his side, he was safe from that accusation. The death of Meech Lake was not supposed to be on Mulroney's agenda in the second term. Paul Lepsoe, Mulroney's legislative assistant, observed that Mulroney was often criticized for having a certain constitutional obsession. "But Meech wasn't even an issue in the 1988 election. Not to diminish its importance, it was thought to be done in 1987. He didn't intend for Meech to become a huge focus of the government and the nation with all attendant consequences, including the growth of Reform."

When Meech Lake died, Mulroney initiated a second round of constitutional talks that led to a national referendum and a disaster of a different sort. Joe Clark was the lead negotiator for the Charlottetown accord, dubbed the "son of Meech." The effort was a tribute to process but a failure in content, a mishmash of provisions that included responses to many of Manning's long-standing concerns, particularly a Triple-E Senate. Federalist politicians from all parties supported the accord, but Canadians were confused and fatigued by it.

Preston Manning used old-time hardball politics to oppose the accord, an approach that seemed inconsistent with the populist brand of politics he preached. He underminded the accord by calling it the "Mulroney deal." Kim Campbell found this particularly ironic "given the PM's minimal involvement in the development of the agreement, but it played to the widespread public mistrust of Mulroney."[12]

When the accord passed in the House of Commons by a vote of 233 to 12, Deborah Grey cast the sole Reform vote to oppose it. Her vote placed Manning and Reform on the same side as most Canadians, who defeated the Charlottetown accord in a national referendum on October 26, 1992, by a margin of almost 10 percentage points.

Mulroney's approval ratings were at 60 per cent or higher during the 1984 and 1988 elections.[13] By 1992, the Mulroney charm had lost some of its lustre, and his personality had begun to grate on many Canadians. His approval ratings during his second term set record lows.

After the failure of the Charlottetown accord came the introduction of the GST, high interest rates to battle inflation, and the recession. By then, 85 per cent of Canadians disapproved of the job Mulroney was doing. The best election strategy for the PCs was beginning to look like new leadership. Mulroney took his low ratings in stride and quipped, "Every time you make tough decisions you lose friends." He had been making many tough decisions.

In the period leading up to his replacement as party leader, the government was largely immobilized and ineffectual. The spring 1993 budget, delivered by Finance Minister Don Mazankowski, did the party more harm than good. Mazankowski, who was well liked and respected within the Conservative party, was the first westerner to hold the finance portfolio in more than sixty years. If Mazankowski's final budget was an attempt to put a western stamp on the nation's finances and squelch the rising tide of the Reform party, he had clearly failed. David McLaughlin wrote the only book about what might well have been the last election for the Progressive Conservative party. He had this to say:

---

[12] Ibid., 222.

[13] Peter G. White and Adam Daifallah, *Gridlock: Are the Liberals in Forever?* (Toronto: Essence Publishing, 2001), 179.

Finance Minister Don Mazankowski's final budget in April,
1993 simply confirmed the worst. Designed to not offend anyone in the midst of a leadership campaign, its spending cuts,
hotly arrived at within Cabinet, were immediately derided as
insufficient. It was simply a "stand-pat" budget, serving simultaneously to undermine the Party's own base with the business
community and Reform-leaning conservatives by not doing
enough on the deficit, while demonstrating the bareness of the
government's own policy cupboard. It simply confirmed the
deficit as an election issue, to the Party's detriment.[14]

About the budget, McLaughlin wrote:

> The budget had clearly been mishandled and was fundamen-
> tally a mistake. They would have been better off without one,
> allowing the soon to be elected Prime Minister to put his or
> her stamp on the future direction of the nation's finances.
> Leadership contender Jim Edwards went so far as to declare
> the budget a "disgrace."[15]

Only a small circle of advisers knew that the spring 2003 budget
was intentionally half-baked to allow Kim Campbell an opportunity to
put a stamp of freshness on her new government. Mazankowski recalls
that a dramatically new budget was precisely what got Ralph Klein
elected as Alberta premier in June 2003, after his party had been lan-
guishing behind the Liberals in the polls for a considerable period:

> Of course my half budget didn't go far enough because we left
> room for her [Kim Campbell] to do that. We set it all up for
> her. I took a rap for it because I was overruled by the strate-
> gists. That was primarily to allow her to come in and say "now
> here is the tough budget" because that's what people were look-

---

[14] David McLaughlin, *Poisoned Chalice: The Last Campaign of the Progressive Conservative
Party?* (Toronto: Dundern Press, 1994), 4.
[15] Ibid., 87.

ing for. [That was the advice from] the strategists around her, the PMO and the PCO. I had brought in an economic statement at the beginning of the year that should have carried us through, but there were some who believed that we should have a budget. I was in favour of it at the time because I thought it was going to be quite an aggressive budget. But with her about to assume the leadership it was the wisdom of the experts that we leave sufficient latitude for her to demonstrate a new vision and vigorous approach.

There were increasingly evident signs, even from within, that the Progressive Conservative brand was in deep trouble. A survey of 2,200 party members in August 1992 revealed that more than 50 per cent of respondents rated their own government as doing a "poor" job on controlling spending, while 43 per cent offered a "poor" rating for managing the deficit. When asked to rate priorities for the government, fiscal and monetary policy received five times as many first-place votes as employment.[16] The government was failing to meet expectations even among its partisans. These numbers were available to Mulroney and his cabinet ministers and clearly showed the government's vulnerability to defection from within, most likely to Reform. It didn't take much of a strategist to determine where the government would be attacked in the 1993 campaign.

Mazankowski defends his government's economic and fiscal record. Mazankowski attributes the rise in the deficit during the government's second term to declining revenues from a worldwide recession and to the government's battle with inflation. "Canadians didn't think we were cutting the deficit fast enough, but we were fighting inflation. Inflation was the fundamental issue we had to deal with because that is what drove up interest rates, which drove up the carrying cost of debt." The mechanics of inflation and the remedy of higher interest rates were hard to explain and difficult to comprehend. The Conservative spin doctors couldn't persuade Canadians

---

[16] Ibid., 125–126.

that higher interest rates, more expensive home mortgages, and higher lease rates for new cars were in their best long-term interests.

Mazankowski is correct when he says, "We didn't add one red cent to the deficit. Except for the first two years when we turned around the $12-billion operating deficit we inherited from the Liberals, we carried an operational surplus in every year. The debt accumulated because of the debt servicing cost on the debt left to us by the Liberals." Figures from Finance Canada show that the Conservative government of Brian Mulroney recorded almost $50 billion in operational surpluses while it was in power. Mazankowski correctly points out that as a per cent of GDP, program spending was 15 per cent lower in 1993–94 than it was when the Mulroney government came to power.

The measures being taken by Mazankowski and his predecessors to improve government finances and to strengthen the economy were not quick fixes and would take several years to produce results. The weak economy of the early nineties meant that the Conservative government began to miss its financial targets. But, as Mazankowski said, it wasn't long before the difficult structural reforms Mulroney implemented began to pay off:

> The impact of the GST started to pay off. The impact of free trade started paying off. The impact of low interest rates and low inflation started to pay off. The economy started percolating and government revenues increased. That program was laid out for Mr. Martin. As Mulroney has said on many occasions, Mazankowski and Wilson planted the garden and Martin plucked the flowers.

Indeed, the economic record of Mulroney, Wilson, and Mazankowski would stand the test of time. In a 1993 study, two McGill University professors, economist Tom Velk and historian A.R. Riggs, concluded that since the end of the Second World War the best economic record of any prime minister belonged to Brian Mulroney. They updated their study seven years later to include the record of Prime Minister Chrétien, and the conclusion did not change: Mulroney was still "the man to beat."[17] They used eighteen objective and measurable variables, including inflation, unemployment, interest and exchange rates, taxes, deficits, income distribution, growth and productivity. Velk and Riggs examined whether "a leader improves the situation he inherited from the previous government, and outperforms contemporaries in other nations." Of Chrétien, they said, "He inherited an economy whose fundamentals were sound—low inflation, low interest rates, a shrinking government share of the overall economy, a relatively strong dollar and expanding trade."

Could it be that going into the 1993 campaign the Tories had a record that was worth defending? There were strong political and economic reasons for Kim Campbell to articulate a new vision, yet her unwillingness to remind Canadians of the accomplishments of the Mulroney administration tarnished the Tory brand.

The Tories also went into the 1993 campaign without an understanding of what Reform meant by "The West Wants In." Tories responded incredulously to such a claim, citing the unprecedented number of westerners in senior cabinet positions, including such luminaries as Mazankowski, Clark, Tom Siddon, and Bill McKnight. Not since Diefenbaker had there been so many westerners in cabinet. The Tories failed to appreciate that it was not western people Reform wanted; it was western ideas, or more specifically Manning's ideas. Preston Manning frequently argued that while Joe Clark might be a good minister for external affairs, he did not do a good job representing his Yellowhead constituency.

People in western Canada were starting to agree with Preston Manning and the Reform view of Canada. From a base level of 2 per cent support in the 1988 election to the by-election and Senate wins, Reform support was on the rise. In the early 1990s, Reform crested in the polls at nearly 16 per cent. At its peak, Reform could claim a

---

[17] "Mulroney's numbers best in a half century in updated study by McGill professors," McGill University Press Release, June 2, 2000, www.mcgill.ca/files/economics/Press_Release.pdf (accessed July 10, 2006).

higher standing in the polls than the governing PC party, in areas outside Quebec. However, by the time the general election was called
in 1993, Reform support was closer to 10 per cent nationally—still
significant, but lacking momentum. It was also concentrated in areas
where the PC party was naturally strong. Reform was not strong
enough to threaten the insurmountable lead the PCs had enjoyed in
the West for a generation or more.

Mulroney thought his efforts to respect the western faction went
unappreciated:

> I went out there quite often and I sat down to talk to Albertans
> and they were very clear. They wanted more influence in the
> federal cabinet; in the decision making process. And so today
> you have Don Mazankowski in finance, Joe Clark in constitu-
> tional affairs and Harvey Andre as government leader. They said
> they wanted the National Energy Program scrapped; we did
> that. They said they wanted the Foreign Investment Review
> Agency scrapped; we did that. They said they wanted deregula-
> tion of the industry and transportation system; we did that. They
> said they wanted free trade with the United States; we did that.
> We have done it all. I know that no Canadian government can
> or ever will do as much for Western Canada as my government
> did. That I know. Not even Diefenbaker, oh by a long shot. We
> increased grants to western agriculture by 650 per cent in six
> years. We moved the head office of the National Energy Board
> to Calgary. We moved the Western Diversification Office to
> Edmonton. No government in history has ever, ever given west-
> ern Canada this kind of attention and this kind of results. One
> of the reasons why I am quite calm about it all is that I know that
> it's just a matter of time before they'd be saying, boy we were
> better off with Mulroney. But now people propose to vote
> Reform. All they are going to do is elect the NDP. A vote for
> Reform is a vote for the extreme left wing.[18]

---

[18] Newman, *The Secret Mulroney Tapes*, 244–245.

In fact, it was the Liberals who ended up as the prime benefici-aries of Reform votes.

Mulroney said he only ever intended to serve two terms. At the statutory end of his second term as prime minister, on February 24, 1993, Brian Mulroney resigned from office. In response to questions about his record-breaking low approval ratings, Mulroney said, "Obviously, I didn't always succeed but I always tried to do what I thought would be right for Canada in the long term, not what could be politically popular in the short term."[19] Decisive leadership and profound structural change were often unpopular, Mulroney claimed, but they were the responsibility of a prime minister. "Whether one agrees with our solutions or not, none will accuse us, I think, of having chosen to evade our responsibilities by side step-ping the most controversial questions of our time. From free trade, NAFTA, tax reform, the GST, privatizations, deficit reduction, fighting inflation, and lowering interest rates, we have made the decisions that are now strengthening Canada's competitive position."[20]

Mulroney was judged unpopular in public opinion polls. But as time passed, his overall record as prime minister stood up well when he was objectively compared with his peers. For example, in a com-prehensive study of prime ministers in the past fifty years, sponsored by the Institute for Research on Public Policy (IRPP), Mulroney was ranked second, behind Pearson, but ahead of Trudeau, St. Laurent, Chrétien, and Diefenbaker, in that order.[21] A panel of twenty-eight leading historians, economists, journalists, political scientists, and former mandarins determined the ranking. They considered four areas of interest: Canadian unity and management of the federation; economy and the fiscal framework; Canada's role in the world; and social policy. Dale Orr of Global Insight, an economic forecasting think-tank represented in 170 countries, credited Mulroney's policy

---

[19] Remarks by Prime Minister Mulroney, on the occasion of his announcement to resign as prime minister, February 24, 1993.

[20] Ibid.

[21] L. Ian MacDonald, "The best prime minister of the last 50 years," *Policy Options*, June–July 2003.

choices for the rise in Canadian living standards during the Chrétien administration.[22] And in 2006, a panel of leading environmentalists determined that Mulroney was Canada's greenest prime minister.[23]

Mulroney was not expecting much recognition after announcing his retirement, and tributes were in short supply. Nonetheless, he was optimistic about the prospects for a third majority PC government. Without mentioning the Reform party or the Bloc Québécois by name, Mulroney predicted the main combatants for the coming election: "As the economy continues its recovery, and as the regional parties continue their decline, it is very clear that the next election will be fought between the Liberals and ourselves." He also added, "I look forward to the enthusiasm and renewal that only new leadership brings."

KIM CAMPBELL WAS NEW. She was different. She was intelligent, articulate, and persuasive. Even though she only came to the Mulroney administration for its second term, she was given a cabinet post and was branded a potential leader as soon as she arrived in Ottawa. It was a strong beginning. She was also an able minister of justice.

A westerner and the first woman prime minister of Canada, she was so different from what they were used to that many Conservatives didn't know what to make of her. As one anonymous Nova Scotia delegate said at the leadership convention that brought Campbell to power: "I knew we were in trouble when I got to the Tory convention and saw the men wearing pink and drinking bottled water."[24]

It soon became clear that Campbell was incapable of winning a national election. By her own admission, she was overpowered by her election team and unable to assert herself sufficiently to follow the path she thought was right for the country, her party, and herself. In

[22] "Living standards rose under Chrétien: Liberals successes based on good luck, Mulroney policies, economist says." *Ottawa Citizen*, November 25, 2003, D5.
[23] The panel was assembled by the publishers of the magazine *Corporate Knights*.
[24] McLaughlin, *Poisoned Chalice,* 65.

short, she was no leader. Aside from her claim that she "wanted to do politics differently," Campbell was bereft of a vision or a set of clear policies to take to the electorate. Consequently, and despite her obvious strengths, Campbell's one and only election campaign as PC party leader and prime minister of Canada will go down on record as the worst Canadian political performance of all time.

Campbell's inexperience and lack of leadership skills and vision were evident throughout her run for leadership, but the Tories were so anxious for change they failed to heed the warning signs.[25] From the outset of the leadership race Campbell had a seemingly insurmountable lead in public, political, and financial support. Yet Jean Charest, her only serious opponent, still managed to come within 187 votes of Campbell on the second and final ballot.[26] Party members should have noticed the support Charest was receiving from Campbell's home province of British Columbia. "We knew Campbell on the West Coast," recalls then PC party president and B.C. resident Gerry St. Germain. "She was late for everything. It was as if she expected the world to wait for her." When she started to worry about the momentum Jean Charest was building, she told Ross Reid, her campaign manager: "Jean Charest has a strategy, and I want a strategy."[27]

As minister of national defence, Campbell took on the responsibility of replacing the aging Sea King search-and-rescue helicopters with a fleet of modern aircraft. She was, at first, a formidable advocate for the purchase of a new fleet of EH101 helicopters. It was clear to Campbell that her record as defence minister would be defined by this purchase. Yet when her national campaign team advised her to relent and scale back on the unpopular purchase, she was powerless to resist. Campbell later admitted that it had been a mistake to retreat when faced with opposition and that she should have shown the

---

[25] The author was a delegate at the 1993 leadership campaign and voted for Kim Campbell.

[26] The vote was held on June 13, 1993; Kim Campbell won on a second ballot, defeating Jean Charest. The vote was 1,817 to 1,630.

[27] Campbell, *Time and Chance*, 275.

strength of her convictions. Instead, she delivered a speech to party faithful in the summer of 2003 that left most people in the audience scratching their heads. She began with a strong case for favouring the helicopter purchase and hinted that "the lady is not for turning," a phrase forever attached to British prime minister Margaret Thatcher. Campbell then unexpectedly backed down. "Everyone insisted that the helicopters were a terrible political liability. There was no time to argue the issue; the speech was set. Against my better judgment, I put the best face on it I could. It was a disaster. . . . From that point on I was just another politician doing politically expedient things."[28]

Despite weak leadership and various stumbles, however, once she was in office Campbell's personality and new approach to policy won her remarkable support. She attracted some of the highest approval ratings of any prime minister since the early 1960s.[29]

Kim Campbell thought she could win, and so did many other Canadians. "Although our party support had lagged behind the Liberals' for most of the summer," she later wrote, "our own polls now showed us 6 percentage points ahead among decided voters—35 per cent to 29 per cent—and in other public polls we were neck and neck."[30] Few people would say that Mulroney bequeathed a winning hand to his successor, but nor did he bequeath a sure loss. By Labour Day, the election was hers to win or lose.

David McLaughlin wrote: "To her credit, Kim Campbell succeeded in convincing Canadians to give her and her party a second look. Yet, the favourable numbers masked the fundamental lack of vision, strategic thinking, and focus needed to win an election campaign."[31]

GOING INTO THE 1993 ELECTION, Preston Manning was encouraged by the attention his new party was receiving. It had two members in Ottawa, and Manning had led the western charge that helped defeat the Charlottetown accord. Reform hoped to win between 30 and

[28] Ibid., 349.
[29] Ibid., 345.
[30] Ibid., 352.
[31] McLaughlin, *Poisoned Chalice*, 4.

50 seats. Pundits however dismissed this hope as pre-election braggadocio.

For the first time, Reform would run candidates across the country. At a Saskatoon convention in April 1991, later confirmed by a mail-in ballot, Reform party members voted in overwhelming numbers to "go national."[32] To field candidates across the country was clearly what Preston Manning wanted. Also firmly behind the decision to go national was Stephen Harper, who seconded the motion at the Saskatoon convention. Going national was stage one of a plan that would see Reform in a position to win government in 1997. "The thinking was that the wave would keep moving across the country; or it wouldn't," said John Weissenberger.

The decision to go national—an interesting phrase considering the exclusion of Quebec—was of monumental importance. In the early 1990s, it seemed Reform could elect members from the West, but few commentators gave the party even a remote chance of translating western resentment and alienation into a platform it could take across the country. The party's leadership, its principles, and most issues it advanced were all based on "The West Wants In." Conservatives from the Atlantic provinces and Ontario generally did not support the socially conservative agenda advanced by Reform; nor did they follow the hard-line economic message that was fundamental to Reform party policy. The notion of the pure equality of all provinces and the lack of recognition of Quebec's distinctiveness made Reform a non-starter in Quebec.

Had Reform run candidates only in western Canada, where it had a reasonable chance of winning seats, it might have been able to advance its cause and keep the Liberals out of power during the 1990s—if the Tories continued to win seats in eastern Canada, where they had the most support. There might even have been a chance of forming a coalition government between Reform and the Tories. Former PC party president Gerry St. Germain contended:

---

[32] Manning, *Think Big*, 42. Only 42 per cent of Reform party members bothered to vote in this critical decision that would determine the fate of the party and the national political landscape.

"Had Manning just stayed in the West he would have built a tremendous power base." The decision to run nationally virtually guaranteed the election of majority Liberal governments, hardly the intended result.

The decision to exclude Quebec from its plan for a national party seemed to indicate that Reform had already given up on Quebec, or at least didn't want to take the flak for views that were resonating elsewhere in the country. When the decision was made to expand eastward, Manning observed that it was his intention to organize and run candidates in Quebec "just as soon as we were convinced of the interest and intentions of the Quebec people on participation in a new Confederation."[33] It is curious that a serious democrat—not to mention populist—like Manning, a man who wanted to be prime minister of all of Canada, would not feel an obligation to appeal directly to the voters of Quebec with his message of a new Canada. But as John Weissenberger recalls, "There was just no wiggle room for us to get into Quebec."

Nevertheless, Manning thought of himself as a saviour for Canada:

> When the West started to do something different in the 80s, when the winds started to blow, the big danger to those of us here that could see this stuff, and that Mulroney didn't see at all, was one that the West was one charismatic leader away from a full-blown separatist movement here. One of the reasons for creating Reform was to take that energy away from that option. We identified with all the concerns and grievances and alienation and all that. Let's use our energy to try and make federalism work better so that these problems don't exist rather than kick it apart. We had to be very strong on that— let's reform the federation.

Manning took these ideas to the next level, the level of being a true saviour of Canada. He felt he had to be the leader of a national

[33] Manning, *The New Canada*, 294.

party that could win government: "If you stopped half way and only ran candidates in the West, and were not even going to think about trying to get a majority in the House of Commons, you would have blunted that argument [about being able to take energy away from western separatism]."

There was another reason Reform wanted to go national: concern over the influence certain Quebecers held in the PC party. "A lot of the guys in Mulroney's Quebec caucus were hard-line separatists. The Trudeau Liberals had locked up the federalist vote in Quebec, so Mulroney looked for whomever he could get, many of whom had strong separatist leanings. That was something that was a huge concern to Stephen [Harper] and myself in the 1980s," said Weissenberger. He added, "No one in the Reform Party was ever advocating separatism." By going national, Reform leaders thought they would become the sole federalist conservative voice.

Although Manning was a student of history, he seems to have ignored his knowledge of popular protest movements when he assessed the likelihood of building a truly national party. Could Reform win seats in Ontario and Atlantic Canada? Manning answered:

> You could argue that in pre-Confederation period Atlantic Canada, Quebec and Ontario had their Reform parties that were system changers. They were committed to responsible government, but that was another era. Since Confederation, Ontario and Atlantic Canada have gone back and forth [between Liberal and Conservative] and it's Quebec and the West that have experimented. Quebec and the West, from time to time, say, that's not working very well so let's create these system-changing parties.

Manning acknowledged that Ontario and Atlantic Canada would be tough going for Reform.

However, Manning felt growing sense of confidence, not just in Reform, but also in what he thought of as the prevailing sentiment of western Canada:

There was also considerable evidence to us at the grassroots level in the West that westerners themselves wanted us to be a national party. This was part of the new West. The new West is not just interested in solving its own grievances. It's getting to the place where it could take care of itself quite well thank you. We felt we had solutions to the bigger national problems. In solving them we would solve some of our own too. We should aspire to get 155 seats in the House of Commons.

The referendum on the Charlottetown accord was an important dress rehearsal for a national election campaign. During the referendum, Reform established a ground game and began to build an election war chest.

The final plank in Reform's 1993 election strategy was the development of a credible platform to exploit the areas where Progressive Conservatives were most vulnerable. That was perhaps the easiest task of all. Federal finances were in a mess, and the entire country blamed the Mulroney Conservatives for mismanagement. All Reform needed was a credible plan to tame the deficit.

Manning wanted to ensure that Canadians understood him before the 1993 general election. Like many politicians who want to be taken seriously, he presented his thoughts, his vision, and some personal information in a book. Written in 1991 and published in 1992, *The New Canada* had three parts. The first traced the influences that helped to shape Manning's life and approach to politics. The second documented the birth, construction, and intent of the Reform party. In the third, Manning offered his vision for a new Canada. In his preface, he appealed to Canadians who were dissatisfied with the status quo: "Whether 'left out,' 'driven out,' or 'wanting out,' Canadians are alienated from the life, politics, economy, and decision making of their own country, and Reformers began to see this as the one common characteristic shared by their compatriots from sea to sea."[34] Pretty appealing stuff.

---

[34] Ibid., vi.

"The leaders of Canada's traditional federal parties continue to think of the country as 'an equal partnership between two founding races, the English and the French'...their approach to national unity is to grant special status to those Canadians [read, "Quebec"] who feel constitutionally or otherwise disadvantaged. This is Old Canada—and it has become 'a house divided against itself.'"[35]

People who felt that the current political dynamic wasn't working could attach themselves to Reform. It seemed to be a credible vehicle for their hopes. But Reform was appealing to a baser emotion: anger. An appeal to anger might attract every extremist unable to find a home in the traditional parties and looking for refuge in a movement that defined itself as untraditional. Manning was up front about his views towards Quebec, which ensured him a loyal following from a substantial band of western Canadians. Unfortunately for Manning and Reform, the band included some people who were racist and bigoted.

Manning had to fight the accusation that he was providing a home for the intolerant, and this was disheartening for a man of deep faith and introspection who was fundamentally a true democrat. He was anything but racist and held no ill will to any Canadian. He was simply articulating a different vision for Canada, a vision based on an interpretation of Canadian history and a constitution that were out of synch with most Canadian elites.

Reform had the good fortune to be wildly underestimated by the Progressive Conservatives both before and during the 1993 campaign. David Angus, at the time leader of the PC Canada Fund, recalls his first meeting with Preston Manning in 1988:

> We brought Manning down to speak at the Mount Royal Club. Harper was there as well. I had heard that Manning was a yahoo, but I was impressed. I could relate to a lot of the issues he was talking about. It was all very cordial. He is smart and certainly not scary. But I didn't fully realize what was

---

[35] Ibid., viii.

going on with the Reform party. Just before the 1993 election, my fellow board members on the PC Canada Fund from the West were warning me that these guys from Reform were going to sweep the West. I had no idea the impact they were going to have.

Kim Campbell visited the Governor General on September 8 and asked him to dissolve Parliament so that a general election could be held on October 25, 1993. Stumbling out of the gate, Campbell told reporters waiting outside Rideau Hall, the home of the Governor General, that Canadians might have to wait until the turn of the century before meaningful and sustained progress would be made on unemployment. Politicians—especially when stumping— are supposed to inspire hope, not deliver grim doses of reality. Even though her statement would turn out to be historically accurate, the media jumped all over her supposed gaffe, an early indication that they were intent on giving the prime minister a rough ride during the campaign.

It was clear from the outset that the PC strategy was to ignore Reform. On day nine of the writ period, Campbell toured Alberta and did not even mention Preston Manning. "Reform were not yet deemed a significant threat. To this point, at least, no comprehensive strategy to deal with the Reform threat had even been pulled together by the campaign," Campbell wrote.[36] National support for the Reform party stood at around 10 per cent for much of 1993, then slowly began to rise after the election was called. This should have caught the attention of the Tory strategists, but it didn't. They continued to underestimate Preston Manning until it was too late to make a difference.

With polling numbers starting to sag, the Tory brain trust thought exposing Reform to the public would be good for PC political fortunes. They "acutely wanted him to participate fully in both English and French debates on the assumption that it would

---

[36] McLaughlin, *Poisoned Chalice*, 197.

illustrate his unfitness as a national political leader."[37] But the nerdish-looking Manning was more of a politician than they thought, and very capable of a clever turn of phrase. (He was not unlike Ross Perot, who ran for president of the United States first in 1992 and then in 1996 under a Reform party banner. Perot largely denied George Bush senior a second term as president.) Criticizing the expensive and transitional 1993 Liberal infrastructure program, Manning said, "It's like trying to start a 747 with a flashlight battery." He commented on the mounting federal debt: "If you want to get out of a hole, the first thing to do is stop digging." These statements cleverly connected Reform with mainstream voters.

Reform started to receive more exposure, but the exposure Reform got was not quite what the Tories had in mind. Earlier in the year the Reform party had published its platform, which included a "zero-in-three" plan to eliminate the deficit. On September 23, 1993, the *Globe and Mail* editorial scrutinized the Reform plan under the headline "The only deficit plan we've seen." The plan clearly stood up to the scrutiny of the *Globe*'s editorial board. All of a sudden, Reform could no longer be castigated as extreme and scary. The party had been given instant credibility courtesy of one of Canada's most prominent national newspapers. The editorial also helped underscore the public's widespread view that the Tories had a dismal record on financial management and no plan to fix the problem. Tory assumptions that public exposure would reveal Reform as "lunatic fringe" were deeply shaken.

The *Globe* editorial shook Tory campaign headquarters badly.

> It's early days yet, but in our view the campaign offering the best value for money so far is Preston Manning's.... Quite simply, Reform is the only party that has yet shown a credible commitment to getting control of the national debt: a commitment made credible by its detailed "zero-in-three" plan to halt the growth of public debt. Ms. Campbell is at pains to display

---

[37] Ibid., 226.

how emotionally committed she is to the task, but can't tell us
how she would go about it.... Ever since Mr. Manning first
unveiled the Reform plan last spring, it has set the standard by
which other parties must be compared. It cuts deeply, but judi-
ciously. It would entail no genuine hardship to anyone, nor
would it harm essential services. Yet it would succeed in
pruning $19 billion—16 per cent—from current program
spending over three years.... Whatever its other failings,
Reform is the only party to have taken the measure of the debt
problem, and has come the furthest way to grasping its solution.... As important, Reform is the one party to date to trust
Canadians with the truth. Indeed if there is one party who is
truly offering "hope," that much-advertised elixir, it is Mr.
Manning's: hope that the economy might one day break out of
the death spiral of high debt and higher taxes, as much as the
hope that Canadian politics might climb out of the slough of
cynicism and deception in which we have been wallowing for
so long. The other parties might do well, as Mr. Manning
advises, to "take notes."[38]

The Reform plan would cut $5 billion (net) from the
Unemployment Insurance system, $3 billion from Old Age Security,
$1.5 billion in transfers to provinces, $4 billion in subsidies to business and special interest groups, and $5 billion in general from
government departments and Crown corporations. Reform contended that these cuts, combined with projections for revenue
increases from a growing economy of $16 billion, would balance the
budget in three years. The plan was easy to criticize, but at least
Reform had a plan, when the Tories were offering nothing.
    William Johnson, in his biography of Stephen Harper, revealed
that officials at the department of finance secretly helped Reform
concoct its deficit-elimination plan. Presumably finance officials
were as impatient with the lack of progress on the deficit as were

---

[38] Editorial, *Globe and Mail*, September 23, 2003.

most Canadians.[39] However, this may not be as nefarious as it sounds, because government departments often help MPs from all parties conduct research on public policy.

The 2003 PC election team had put all its eggs into one basket. The basket was not the Conservative record over the past nine years, not a plan for the future, and not a comparative analysis of the weakness of the opposition. The basket was Kim Campbell. And the team was selling her style, her gender, and her new, more consultative way of doing politics.

Campbell's performance on the campaign trail was nothing short of abysmal. She did not speak to the hopes and dreams of Canadians when she said unemployment and the debt would remain high for the balance of the decade. In a statement at the launch of the election, Campbell said, "But there is more to economic success than bringing the deficit down."[40] This was music to Preston Manning's strategic ears. Even if the prime minister had a point, she gave her opponents and the media any number of opportunities to bring her down.

Despite the gaffes, in the first few weeks of the campaign Tories were still running neck and neck with the Liberals, and Reform was registering only modest support out West. Polls were telling PC strategists that unemployment was the most important issue, more important than the deficit by a factor of five to one.

On September 23, the same day the *Globe and Mail* ran its editorial praising Preston Manning's zero-in-three deficit plan, Campbell was pressed by reporters about a so-called hidden agenda on social programs. The prime minister said, "The first budget of the new government would be in February of '94, and Parliament will come back this fall. I think there is ample opportunity to engage Canadians in a serious dialogue and to work with provinces to find the best way to deliver those services."[41] This response struck reporters as odd. Did she not think that the best time for dialogue with Canadians on these issues was during an election? Campbell replied:

---

[39] Johnson, *Stephen Harper*, 191.

[40] Campbell, *Time and Chance*, 354.

[41] Ibid., 367.

I think that's the worst possible time to have that kind of dialogue . . . because I think it takes longer than forty-seven days to
tackle an issue that's that serious. It's a very important policy
issue. Now I've stated very clearly that I'm fundamentally committed to preserving quality social programs in this country, to
preserving our health care system. But the issues are much too
complex to try and generate some kind of a blueprint in the
forty-seven days that's available in an election campaign . . . .
This is not the time, I don't think, to get involved in a debate
on very, very serious issues.[42]

Thud. Full stop. Game over. The egg in the basket had cracked!
The Tories were left with nothing with which to fight. There was no
platform and no vision to fall back on, and now, there was no credible candidate.

Campbell knew that there would be few opportunities during
the campaign to repair the damage: "Our campaign should have presented our policy in a way that would have dispelled any fear of a
hidden agenda. For that, we needed a fuller discussion of policy over
the summer. Although we tried to diffuse the issue."[43]

A mid-campaign poll by Ekos Research Associates portrayed the
Tories as the party that pointed to problems it was unable to solve:

The Tories have been successful at convincing the public of the
severity of the debt problem to the politically alienated.
Unfortunately for the Tories, they are not poised to benefit
from this acknowledgement of the centrality of the debt issue
since they are seen by many Canadians as either the authors or
else the one group who could have stemmed the problem.
Hence, they are seen as ill-equipped to solve it in the future.[44]

---

[42] Ibid., 368.

[43] Ibid., 373.

[44] Ekos Research Associates Inc., "A Mid-Campaign Report: The State of the Nation
before the Debate," October, 1993.

The Ekos poll explored the concept of "political alienation," a phenomenon both the Reform party and the Bloc Québécois were starting to exploit. The data showed that Reform voters had a high level of fatigue with the Tory party and were unlikely to switch back.

The PCS became desperate when their poll numbers began to plummet and Reform numbers began to rise. Campaign manager John Tory was worried about the impact of the September 23 *Globe and Mail* editorial and wanted Campbell to meet the *Globe*'s editorial board. Tory wanted to demonstrate that a Campbell government would be serious about the deficit and had a plan to balance the budget. A sound strategy; the problem was, the Campbell government had no such plan. Campbell fumbled the meeting, leaving the *Globe* to conclude that only Preston Manning had command of the issue.

With only twenty days left in the election campaign, the *Globe and Mail* reported that a poll showed Reform ahead of the Tories (20 per cent to 19 per cent), with the Liberals comfortably ahead at 40 per cent. The poll results were one of two front-page stories that day that carried the word "Reform" in banner headlines. The poll predicted that, if the numbers held, on election day the Tories would be reduced to only 35 seats. A stunning result that would be!

Desperation showed its face in a Tory ad that began to air on national television near the end of the campaign. Campbell had been briefed about the ad but had not seen it. The entire nation thought the ad was an attempt to ridicule Liberal leader Jean Chrétien's facial disability. It was a cold and heartless attempt to make Chrétien seem something less than prime ministerial. Predictably, it backfired. But it also provided an opportunity for Chrétien to utter a line he may well have been waiting his whole life to deliver. Speaking in Lunenberg, Nova Scotia, Chrétien said: "It's true that I have a physical defect. God gave it to me. When I was a kid people were laughing at me. But I accepted that God gave me other qualities and I'm grateful."[45] The game was truly over. The Tories went from being badly defeated to annihilated.

---

[45] Susan Delacourt, "Campaign takes the low road," *Globe and Mail*, October 16, 1993, A1.

When Kim Campbell had been sworn in as prime minister, the party was, according to PC Canada Fund chairman David Angus, "flush." Angus noted, "We had money in the bank and a line of credit for a total of $15 million. By the time that election was over, a $15 million plus had become a $10 million minus."

Reform had run a brilliant campaign, scoring high on issues that mattered most to western Canadians. By focusing on its platform and its deficit-elimination plan, Manning sidestepped the many accusations of racism, bigotry, and intolerance. Reform exceeded its pre-writ predictions and won 52 seats in the House of Commons, only two fewer than the Bloc Québécois, who became Her Majesty's Loyal Opposition. The Tories shrunk to a rump caucus of two members, Jean Charest in Quebec and Elsie Wayne in New Brunswick. The two seats were won only because of the popularity of the candidates in their home constituencies.

Reform beat the PCs in popular vote by a small margin, 18.7 per cent to 16 per cent. However, because so much of its vote was concentrated in western Canada, it won 25 times the number of seats won by the PCs.

The Tory demise was so dramatic that the Reform party managed to come in second in 56 Ontario ridings, where it won 20.1 per cent of the popular vote. Reform didn't perform nearly as well in Atlantic Canada, however; it received 13.3 per cent of the vote in Nova Scotia, 8.5 per cent in New Brunswick, and 1.0 per cent in each of Newfoundland and Prince Edward Island.

The early polls gave little indication that the Reform party would do so well. Manning commented on the polls:

> There wasn't a single national pollster even as close as eight months before the 1993 election who predicted that cataclysmic collapse of the Conservatives or the strength of either of the regional parties in the West or Quebec. For some reason there must have been things in people's minds that were predisposing them to those options, but they were not saying it to the pollsters, or the pollsters maybe weren't quite fishing

for it in the right way. When you get those pollsters together, at least the national ones, give them a little to drink, they still shake their heads. Why didn't that show up much more solidly both in Quebec and the West until just almost weeks before the actual election?

The pollsters had no way of predicting what an abysmal failure Kim Campbell would be in a national campaign. Indeed, there is every reason to believe that the Reform party was successful in 1993 because Campbell failed during the campaign. Had Mulroney stayed on as prime minister, holding together the weakened strands of his coalition, or had Jean Charest won the leadership, Manning and his team might well have been held to a handful of seats.

One study of voting defection in the western provinces between the 1988 and 1993 campaigns isolated the source of Reform's support. Relative to the 1988 campaign, the PC party lost 55 per cent of its vote to Reform, double the rate of Liberal defections to Reform, and six times the rate of loss from the NDP.[46] In other words, Kim Campbell's loss was Preston Manning's gain.

David McLaughlin suggested that Jean Chrétien's Liberals won the election by default, then summed up the Tory loss and the Liberal win this way: Tories "refused to put ideas on the table for Canadians to consider because they either had none or did not want to tell what they actually intended to do.... The overriding lesson from the election is simple: ideas do count. Standing for something does matter."[47] Party veteran Don Mazankowski placed much of the blame for the party's demise on the performance of Kim Campbell. "We felt it was time to turn the page and present a new image. Had we known what was going to happen many of us would have stuck around to fight the good fight. We may not have won the election but we sure would have come back with more than two seats."

---

[46] Flanagan, *Waiting for the Wave*, 162.

[47] McLaughlin, *Poisoned Chalice*, 304.

It would not have surprised Canadians had the Tories succumbed to the humiliation and folded the party's tent. They had a mountain of debt and no official recognition in the House of Commons as a political party. Perhaps it would have been better for the nation had they closed shop and let Reform have a clear run at government. But Tory party roots run deep. Also, little was known about Reform and its leader, Preston Manning, and old Tories were wary enough to keep fighting. Yet it was a legitimate question to ask: could and should the Progressive Conservative Party of Canada be given up for dead?

The man who couldn't stop smiling was Jean Chrétien. He had had an awkward run as Opposition Leader and came into the campaign as a clear underdog. Few expected a majority Liberal government and few expected that Chrétien, often dubbed "yesterday's man," would out-campaign Kim Campbell. His party held 177 seats in a 295-seat legislature.

AMONG THE MORE ARTICULATE and forceful of the 52 Reform MPs elected in 1993 was Stephen Harper. In a rematch of the 1988 campaign against his former boss, Harper won in a landslide, earning 52.1 per cent of the vote. Hawkes recieved only 15.3 per cent support, down from the 75 per cent of the vote he received in 1984 when the Reform party was not on the ballot.

Hawkes might well have been bitter that the former apprentice had bested his political mentor. Many Tories were angry and bitter that the conservative family had been divided, leaving faithful Tories out in the cold. Yet Hawkes had a lingering warmth and admiration for Harper's abilities and ambition. Harper had shown respect towards Hawkes: first, he sought Hawkes's permission to run against him. Then, when Hawkes was in the hospital suffering from a serious illness before the 1993 election, Harper visited almost daily.

In 1993, Harper married graphic artist Laureen Teskey. There was a political dimension to the marriage: Laureen first spotted Stephen at a Reform party convention when he delivered one of his many keynote addresses. Laureen had been married before. She was introduced to Stephen by one of his former girlfriends, Cynthia Williams. After their marriage, two children followed: Ben and Rachel. Harper's motivations, which before marriage and family were almost exclusively intellectual, would be grounded and softened with a wife and children. Parents often think their job is to teach their children, without recognizing what they themselves are learning. And Harper was learning something quite valuable: patience.

CHAPTER 6

THE THIRTY-FIFTH PARLIAMENT

ANADA'S THIRTY-FIFTH PARLIAMENT was like no other in terms of the unknowns it held for Canadians. Jean Chrétien, although a fixture in the House of Commons since 1963, was starting his first term as prime minister, prompting the usual questions about where a new prime minister would lead the country. For the first time in history, the Leader of the Official Opposition was a Quebec separatist. Lucien Bouchard's views may have been well known in Quebec and elsewhere, but there were questions about how Parliament, the government, and even the country would work. And finally, Canadians knew virtually nothing about the untested band of new Reform party members and their leader, Preston Manning.

Before the writ was dropped, Preston Manning had been an afterthought in media stories that set the scene for the 1993 campaign.[1] He was a regional figure, known mostly as the rabble-rousing son of a former Alberta premier. But as the campaign unfolded, and with the unprecedented Tory collapse, the nation began to wonder what Manning and his team of western Reformers might be able to do for Canada. Canada's thirty-fifth Parliament would let everyone find out.

Outside Reform party circles and the constituency of Calgary West, few people in Canada had heard of Stephen Harper. He was

---

[1] The "dropping of the writ" refers to the technical opening of an election campaign.

146

still in his early thirties and had just earned a master's degree from the University of Calgary. He had dabbled in the creation of the Reform party and achieved some academic success, but otherwise Stephen Harper's resumé hardly made him a national figure. When he entered the House of Commons as a member in 1993, he had invested more in the study of Canadian history, politics, and economic issues than almost any of the other 294 MPs. He came to Ottawa ready for debate.

Harper was the antithesis of a spin doctor and would never be satisfied preparing a few talking points for Preston Manning on a particular issue. Harper's curiosity demanded a thorough review of the often complex source documents. He knew about the Meech Lake Constitutional Accord because he studied the agreement and all supporting documents. Before he reached an opinion, he reviewed the history of an issue, applied rigorous analysis, and sought validation from conservative principles. He was an intellectual with a mind of his own. He researched issues not just so he could help the Reform party and Preston Manning, but so he could understand the issues. He worked within the structure of the party but formed his own opinions on what was right for Canada. It helped that he was a talented writer with the skill to express his thoughts on complex issues clearly and cleverly, in a manner that was informative, persuasive, and easily understood.

It was evident early on that Preston Manning and Stephen Harper did not agree on some fundamental questions of political philosophy and political strategy. Harper was a conservative, Manning a populist. Harper saw issues from a political spectrum of right and left; Manning saw life from East and West. Harper wanted to build a principled conservative party; Manning wanted to appeal to disaffected Canadians across all political spectrums. Harper could identify with the libertarians; Manning was most comfortable with Christian values. Harper was inclined to leadership and serious debate; Manning was more comfortable consulting and seeking consensus. Harper was thoughtful and analytical, Manning more intuitive and political. Harper was distrustful of political elites;

Manning was prepared to bring professional political strategists into the party. The differences between the party leader and the chief policy officer were daunting.

Harper had always been worried about the influence of social conservatism and evangelical Christians within the party. He believed that the Reform party should not have a position on issues of conscience. He also believed that the party should support free votes in the House of Commons, or find some other democratic form of resolution. Manning held similar views, except he was more comfortable with a Christian perspective, which provided his core beliefs and was the prism through which he viewed all issues.

Harper was out of step with many rank and file Reformers on a number of controversial issues. He supported bilingualism in key national institutions, although he opposed Trudeau's vision of a bilingual Canada in favour of the reality: a predominantly unilingual French Quebec with English dominating in the rest of Canada. Harper thought that provinces should have primary, if not exclusive, authority over matters of language and culture. He opposed controls on immigration based on country of origin, arguing that economic interest should be the sole criterion for admittance.[2] And while he was opposed to both government intervention in economic matters and a welfare state, he was not a zealot for the emasculation of government. Harper's ultimate political strategy was to supplant the PCs with a more principled *conservative* Reform party. Manning was more inclined to seek appeal across all political spectrums.

However, Harper and Manning agreed on one thing: both viewed the Tory party as a visionless creature born of central Canadian elites. Neither trusted the political elites, especially elites who sought special status for Quebec as a strategy to win electoral support. Manning's thinking may have evolved since he first entered the House, but in the thirty-fifth Parliament this was his clear position.

Manning's inherent conservatism allowed him to speak the same language as Harper, and there was an obvious mutual respect

---

[2] Johnson, *Stephen Harper*, 122.

between the two, who seemed to play off each other's strengths: Harper had the keen intellect, and Manning provided the legitimacy and leadership that delivered 52 Reform members to the House of Commons.

In the House, Reform could attack the government of Jean Chrétien for its failures on domestic policy. The deficit was still a problem, taxes were a constant frustration, and the ethical lapses of certain ministers required attention. Yet Reform distinguished itself most on the question of national unity.

Manning and his Reform members made some noble efforts to make friends in Quebec, and Manning at least made an attempt to be understood by Bloc Québécois MPs whose attachment to Canada was officially negative. Sensing that Reform and the Bloc Québécois had some common views about the functioning of the federation, Manning reached out to BQ leader Lucien Bouchard. He recalled the first time he met Bouchard:

> I suggested we have a breakfast. I said we have all these new members who know nothing about your gang. You have all these people that know nothing about us. Let's get them together. You bring the maple syrup and we'll bring the pancakes. It was a cultural event.

> I got up and said to these Quebec Bloc guys: we are a bunch of discontented westerners that don't think the federation is working very well and we can give you a thousand reasons and illustrations of why we think so. And, we are here to change that so it will work better for everybody. Bouchard got up and said: we are a bunch of people from Quebec who don't think the federation is working very well either. But we don't think it can be fixed and we want out.

To his lasting frustration, Manning could not communicate or connect with Quebecers. He felt a kindred spirit with them but could not find the words or language to express that spirit persuasively.

Perhaps it was just bad timing. To this day, Manning can only think, "What if?"

> If these two regions that innovate politically ever got on the same agenda at the same time they could transform the country. And Ontario and Atlantic Canada would probably respect it because some constitutional or federalism changes that made those two parts of the country less discontent would be in everyone's interest. But we have never been on the same wave length at the same time.

Manning saw himself as a modern-day Father of Confederation. He often talked about the great pre-Confederation reformer Robert Baldwin, who in 1848 with Louis Lafontaine led the Great Ministry that established responsible government in Canada. "When I went to Quebec, I only had one speech. It was called 'Où est Lafontaine?' I know there are system changers in English Canada but where are our counterparts in Quebec?" said Manning. It was clear he had donned the cloak of a modern-day Baldwin. Manning said that the most frequent answer he got to his question was, "Bouchard is your Lafontaine." But Manning had already tried Bouchard and been turned down flat. One clever Quebecer told Manning: "We can't pick your Baldwin and you can't pick our Lafontaine." Manning knew he was right. It is an interesting historical footnote, however, to observe that in 1854, Baldwin gave his approval to the merger of the Conservatives and the "Baldwin Liberals." The new party was called the Liberal Conservative Party, and it was the party of Sir John A. Macdonald. Manning saw himself as Baldwin. Was he signalling his "end game": to take over or merge with the Tories?

MOST FEDERALISTS, INCLUDING Jean Chrétien, were committed only to a Plan A with regards to Quebec, meaning that all efforts were focused on persuading Quebecers to affirm their attachment to Canada by rejecting the emotional appeal of sovereignty. When he said there was no Plan B, Chrétien was telling Quebecers his commitment to Quebec was so strong, and his confidence so high, he was not prepared to contemplate the possible consequences of separation. Compare this to a marriage, where talk of separation might make it difficult to rekindle love and fidelity.

Manning was succinct about what he was offering Quebec: "Our position was a two-pronged approach—offer Quebec and other Canadians a better federalism, and we will define what we mean by that, but also make it crystal clear to Quebecers what the consequences of secession will be."

William Johnson, in his biography of Stephen Harper, suggests that it was Harper who pushed Reform into chastising the government for failing to develop a Plan B or take a hard stance with Quebec. Both Harper and Manning countered the view that Quebec had a unilateral right to self-determination. They argued that the rule of law should supercede any romantic notion of a province becoming a nation. The Canadian constitution did not contemplate the dismemberment of the country or any part thereof, and thus does not authorize the federal government to negotiate any other arrangement with Quebec. Consequently, argued Reform, the government of Canada had no authority on the matter, and separation was illegal. According to Manning and Harper, the argument that Quebec never signed the 1981 constitution was specious and had no bearing on the need to apply the rule of law. A province could leave Confederation only if there were an amendment to the constitution specifying how such an outcome would be achieved. This constitutional amendment would require the approval of the federal and all provincial governments, and would likely include specific terms and conditions that some provinces might not like. Accepting a Plan B approach was a hard sell to those who were more comfortable speaking eloquently and emotionally about Canada as a sovereign nation. What Reform was pitching was stone-cold reality.

In 1995, during the Quebec referendum, Prime Minister Chrétien did not find Manning's interventions on national unity helpful or instructive. Chrétien was brimming with confidence that Quebec would vote no to a change in the province's relationship with the country, and saw no need to talk tough with Quebecers. His view had always been, "When the question is clear, Quebec will always vote with Canada." His unwillingness to offer Quebecers special status or distinct society or even a diminished role for the federal government in areas of provincial jurisdiction had won Chrétien the admiration of Pierre Trudeau.[3] Why worry about Preston Manning when Pierre Trudeau thinks you are doing a good job?

As the referendum campaign drew to a close and the polls indicated that those in favour of a new arrangement with Canada were going to win, Chrétien was overcome with fear. So much so, that he became an overnight supporter of distinct society status for Quebec. But he was caught in a dilemma. To scare Quebecers into voting no, he told them the referendum was really about separation (even though that is not what the referendum question asked). With a yes vote, Jacques Parizeau could use the prime minister's statement about separation to say he had the moral authority to take Quebec out of Canada. Until very late in the game, Chrétien never made the ambiguous nature of the referendum question an issue, nor did he suggest he had no authority to negotiate the sovereignty of Quebec.

The need for the federal government to insist on a clear question was precisely what Stephen Harper had been arguing in the House of Commons for the two years before the Quebec referendum. He introduced a private member's bill to that effect in 1993.[4] Like most private member's bills, Harper's went nowhere. However, his judgment on the need for such legislation was vindicated five years after

---

[3] Prime Minister Chrétien, in conversation with the author in the fall of 1995, remarked how proud he was and said, "Even Trudeau thinks I am doing a good job." This comment was made in the middle of the Quebec referendum campaign.

[4] Bill C-141: An Act to establish the terms and conditions that must apply to a referendum relating to the separation of Quebec from Canada before it may be recognized as a proper expression of the will of the people of Quebec.

the referendum, when the Chrétien government used much the same thinking in crafting the Clarity Act.[5]

ALTHOUGH THEY SOMETIMES disagreed on policy and strategy, Manning appointed Harper the Reform critic on the country's most important issues: finance and national unity. While Manning was the lead spokesperson for Reform, Stephen Harper was never far away, lending support and respectability. He was young and articulate, the antithesis of the Reform's public image as a collection of old, cranky, and reactionary white men. Harper was also bilingual.

Still, Manning's autobiography makes frequent references to disagreements and frustrations with Stephen Harper, who "had serious reservations about Reform's . . . belief in the value of grassroots consultation and participation in key decisions."[6] Manning also complained about Harper's ego: he "had difficulty accepting that there might be a few other people (not many, perhaps, but a few) who were as smart as he was with respect to policy and strategy. And Stephen . . . was not prepared to be a team player and team builder."[7] Manning did concede, however, that Harper was the party's best mind regarding policy and strategy.[8]

Their relationship may have been respectful, but it was not warm. Manning understandably resented Harper's public criticism—perhaps even disclosure—of a $31,000 annual clothing allowance, which

---

[5] The Clarity Bill (C-20) was passed by the House of Commons on March 15, 2000 and by the Senate on June 29, 2000. The bill began with a preamble that stated, in part, "WHEREAS the Supreme Court of Canada has confirmed that there is no right, under international law or under the Constitution of Canada, for the National Assembly, legislature or government of Quebec to effect the secession of Quebec from Canada unilaterally; WHEREAS the Supreme Court of Canada has determined that the result of a referendum on the secession of a province from Canada must be free of ambiguity both in terms of the question asked and in terms of the support it achieves if that result is to be taken as an expression of the democratic will that would give rise to an obligation to enter into negotiations that might lead to secession . . . ."

[6] Manning, *Think Big*, 49.

[7] Ibid., 74.

[8] Ibid., 126.

Manning received as Reform party leader. "Stephen Harper and several other caucus members went public with their criticism . . . to the media . . . not to the caucus officers of the Management and Planning Committee or the party's executive council, all of whom were justifiably furious."[9] Party members took a different view. How could Manning be critical of anyone arguing for transparency? The clothing allowance came out of money donated by party members. In addition, the taxpayers of Canada encourage party donations with generous tax credits. The disclosure created problems, which Manning blamed not on himself, but on Harper's "machinations." He acknowledged that part of the problem was his poor relations with caucus.[10] (The incident so bothered Sandra Manning that she withdrew completely from political work and became a real estate agent in Calgary.) The clothing allowance caper was cited as the reason for a drop in donations to party coffers.[11]

When Manning came to Ottawa he gloated about how Reformers were not like other politicians; one of his first gestures on Parliament Hill was refusing a taxpayer-supported driver and limousine. In a well-orchestrated photo-op and with great fanfare, Manning handed the limousine keys to a government employee. The clothing allowance seemed to fly in the face of Manning's anti-politician persona and set a precedent that many Reform members would follow when they opted into the generous MP pension plan—after they had repudiated the perk as excessive.

Manning was distressed by Harper's criticisms and concluded that his chief policy officer was not a team player. Manning thought Harper could be petty, with a tendency to withdraw when he didn't get his way; he remembered that Harper abandoned Reform's Charlottetown accord campaign after Harper was excluded from Reform's steering committee. Manning upset Harper when he brought in Rick Anderson as Reform's new chief strategist.

[9] Ibid., 261–262.

[10] Ibid., 262.

[11] Canadian Press, "Donations to Reform dwindling," *Globe and Mail*, June 10, 1994, A3.

Anderson, an experienced operative from the Liberal party and an easterner, was not the sort of political operative Harper found attractive. Manning wanted Anderson's national campaign experience on the Reform team, even if that meant shunting Harper aside. As a consequence, Harper returned to Calgary in 1993, to work on his personal election campaign and did not support the party in its broader regional campaign.

On January 14, 1997, at the age of thirty-seven, before his first term as an MP was over, Harper stunned the Reform party and the national press gallery when he resigned his seat to become vice-president of the National Citizens Coalition (NCC), a right-wing lobby group. (He eventually became president.) According to Manning, Harper left Parliament and "...gloomily concluded that [Reform] was going nowhere and would likely lose badly in the next election."[12]

Most elected officials who leave office prematurely announce that they are doing it to spend more time with their family. Many of them return to elected politics a few years later, usually after whatever dust was bothering them has settled. But Harper was forthright; he told reporters he did not want to be bound by party discipline and wanted to be free to speak his mind. Harper resigned, and was free to say and do as he chose, while Manning was left to build the party as he saw fit.

During the thirty-fifth Parliament, Manning and Harper failed to address their relationship with the Tories. Manning in particular was preparing for the 1997 election, seemingly oblivious to the surging Tories and the inevitable vote splitting that would crush their electoral prospects in the coming election.

One senior Tory said that when he chose to ride a wave of indignation against the Mulroney government, Manning sealed his fate. "How was it that Manning with so many members could not finish the job? Why did he not seek reconciliation with the remnants of the PC party? Where were his vision and nation-building skills? The answers are that his vindictiveness, lack of vision, and malice prevented any

---

[12] Manning, *Think Big*, 146.

hope of reconciliation. There was no conceivable situation where we would associate with him. By abusing the PC party, its members, and our record, he signed his own political death warrant."

JEAN CHAREST ASSUMED THE LEADERSHIP of the Tories shortly after the election debacle in 1993 and promptly went to work rebuilding the party with his other MP, New Brunswick's Elsie Wayne. "Charest was the franchise. Even in the aftermath of the defeat, he was still viewed by Canadians as the next generation of leader," recalls Tory stalwart Geoff Norquay.

The reality Charest faced in Parliament could not have been more stark. His party had lost the levers of government, and for the first time since Confederation it was not recognized in the House of Commons as an official party.[13] He would have few opportunities to ask questions in the House, and he had virtually no parliamentary budget. The party was $10 million in debt, so there was no money available to hire staff or conduct a leader's tour. Senator David Angus recalls some anxious moments: "We were like a little rump manning the barricades. Sometimes, I even had to go down to party headquarters on a Friday afternoon to help them meet payroll."

However, thanks to nine years of Tory rule, Charest did have a majority in the Senate, and he persuaded the senators to pool their budgets with the leader's in a single fund that he controlled.

Rebuilding the party was a daunting task, and no one would have blamed Charest had he taken a pass. In the past year, he had lost the leadership race to Kim Campbell, and the future existence of the party was anything but certain. However, it wasn't long before Charest confirmed he would take on the challenge, which he did with vigour and determination.

The Tories held their first convention about eighteen months after the 1993 election, in April 1995. Optimistically called "Jumpstart 95," the gathering exceeded all expectations by attracting

---

[13] The minimum number of seats required to be recognized as an official party in the House of Commons is 12.

1,500 delegates from across the country. "It took a full restructuring process to rekindle interest and life in the party," said Norquay. Charest understated the challenges when he told delegates, "Restructuring a political party is very much like the overhaul of a car; to succeed we'll need to do some work on this car again."[14] Most Canadians thought the Tory car had been nearly totalled and might easily have been written off for good had Charest not been willing to serve as the master mechanic.

The 1995 convention was the first stage in the party's Three-R master plan: restructure, rebuild, and finally return (to power, that is). The mandate in the 1995 convention was for the party to restructure itself so it could connect more meaningfully with its grassroots supporters. The delegates debated and adopted a report prepared by the National Restructuring Committee, chaired by Roxanna Benoit and Pierre Fortier. The report was prepared following a series of cross-country meetings involving about four thousand party members. If restructing of this magnitude can occur in a political party only after a massive defeat, then this should have ben the "mother" of all reformations. "We didn't bother to amend the old constitution," said Benoit. "We threw out the old constitution and adopted something completely new."

The reforms gave more influence to rank-and-file members, largely by placing a national council between the members and the executive. The national council would comprise one representative from each of the 295 federal ridings. It may have sounded good on paper, but co-chair Benoit recalls, "There was a 'leap of faith' in what we did. Charest was absolutely worried about the new organizational structure. How could we ever get agreement from 295 riding presidents on anything?"

Other initiatives included a national membership program, greater influence through a bottom-up policy review process and increased transparency and accountability on party finances.

---

[14] Terrance Wills, "Tory convention is first since '93 election disaster; PCs have only two seats, but Charest trying to rebuild with young members," *Montreal Gazette*, April 25, 1995, A1.

During the convention, a few delegates begin to muse about a possible merger with Reform, although most people suggested the wounds from the 1993 campaign defeat were too fresh for any serious discussions to commence. "I'm not saying it's not going to happen," said outgoing party president Gerry St. Germain "but on our side, at this point in time, it's not an issue. I don't expect it to be, either." St. Germain later recalled, "Reality had not yet set in for most of the Tories. But even back then, I had met on occasion with the president of the Reform party, usually on the golf course. I always kept an open dialogue." Leadership contender and defeated MP Jim Edwards chipped in his views to convention delegates: "Both sides are bearing too many scars for talk of a regrouping to be serious at this point."

Stage two of the master plan, rebuilding, was discussed at a major policy convention in Winnipeg in August 1996. About 1,500 delegates debated a comprehensive 114-page report from the policy advisory committee. There was a clear and obvious schism at the convention: many delegates, mostly the youth, sought to push the party further to the right than Charest was comfortable with. The leader summarized his strategy and hope for the convention by asking delegates to produce resolutions that showed "conservatism with a human face." Those seeking a shift to the right wanted to win back hard-line western conservatives who had defected to the Reform party. They also wanted to emulate the success of the Conservatives in Ontario, led by Mike Harris. Ultimately, a number of right-wing measures narrowly passed at the convention, including cutting 10 to 20 per cent in personal income taxes, privatizing CBC television programming, abolishing the firearms registry, and lowering the minimum age for the Young Offenders Act.

Some controversial measures were rejected, including proposals to repeal the recognition of Quebec as a distinct society, allow partial privatization of medicare, do away with employment equity, and adopt union-busting right-to-work policies. The policy split within the party caused conservative commentator David Frum to remark, "The federal PCs are now two parties. The first block is the Harris

Tories, who are some of the most conservative people in Canada. And then there is the Charest party, which is, with the possible exception of the NDP, the least conservative party in Canada. And there's a big gap between them."[15]

Charest was gung-ho for stage one: structural changes that led to a more democratic and accountable party. But he was not so keen on the results from stage two: the policy program had taken the party much further to the right than he was comfortable with. While his discomfort was understandable, he should not have been surprised at the result of letting rank-and-file members decide on policy. People who join political parties in Canada are activists with strong opinions. They are not representative of the Canadian public, or even of those who might identify themselves as supporting a political philosophy. This is particularly true in the Conservative party and the NDP, where activist party members would inevitably steer their parties further left or right than would the population as a whole. If party members want power to implement change, they would be better off picking the right leader, offering that leader the benefit of their views, and letting the leader develop the strategic and tactical plan to win. That's how most successful organizations operate. You cannot effectively run a corporation or a political party by committee.

There was an attempt to finesse the seemingly prescriptive policies being adopted by the party, to gain the flexibility the leader needed to win an election. Roxanna Benoit described it this way: "There is a difference between platform and policy. Policy is ongoing and evolving, while platform is point in time that applies to a particular election." So much for letting the grassroots have their way.

ABOUT SEVENTY RIGHT-LEANING THINKERS, activists, and academics convened in Calgary in May 1996 to try to find a way to unite conservative political forces before the next election. Organized by conservative writers/activists David Frum and Ezra Levant, the

---

[15] "Still the same old Tories: Charest embraces the centre, snubs his youth wing and cedes the political right to Reform," *Western Report* II:33, September 9, 1996, 6.

closed-door meeting, labelled "Winds of Change," was designed to directly connect the divided yet like-minded forces in the Canadian conservative movement.

Practically, conference organizers had set their sights on something less than a full-scale merger. While merger may have been their ultimate goal, the proposition presented at the conference was for electoral co-operation between Reform and the PCs as the best strategy for ending Liberal hegemony. Some referred to this co-operation as "sisterhood."

The specific plan was for local Tory and Reform riding associations across the country to hold joint nomination meetings to determine which one candidate, and which one party, would best represent the conservative cause in the general election. The result should be more Tories and Reformers in the House of Commons who would ultimately come together in a coalition to end Liberal rule. The local southern Ontario Tory riding association of Brant was amenable to the one-candidate approach. Conference organizer David Frum proclaimed, "It's hoped the idea will spread and help bridge the split that has allowed the Liberal party to rule. We have come up with a model of how the unification of the right can proceed. It's an experiment that will open the door to other ridings, especially in Ontario, to adopting similar kinds of techniques."[16]

Party leaders and strategists almost immediately dismissed the idea. Reform's Tom Flanagan said, "The two parties will still end up running separately in the next election, and the Canadian people will decide which one goes forward from there."[17] PC leader Jean Charest said, "I find the whole thing to be not very serious at all. I have no idea how it would work."[18] Even the Reform constituency association in Brant nixed the idea of working co-operatively with its Tory counterpart. Conference participant and Reform MP Ray Speaker said, "Once

[16] "Conference cooks up experiment in uniting the right (Winds of Change)," Canadian Press, May 26, 1996.
[17] Ibid.
[18] "Reform-Tory riding alliance dead, one day after birth (at Winds of Change conference)," Canadian Press, May 27,1996.

the local Reform organization in Brant said no to these matters, then it's dead. That's it." Most partisans involved rejected the notion of surrendering a riding, any riding, to another party; as well, other issues revealed the awkwardness of the proposal. These included which party leader would sign the nomination papers and which platform and policies would ultimately prevail if government was won.

It seemed illogical to Stephen Harper for the PC and Reform parties to be battling over second place. "I can't understand the [PC] political strategy," said Harper. "To the extent they have one, it seems to be everybody's second choice, and in this political system, that's absolutely suicidal."[19]

Although conference attendees discussed various options that would allow each party to build on its respective regional strengths, the conference revealed the deep chasm that existed between the parties on a wide range of issues. The resentment towards Reform for dividing the conservative family was still widespread. In other words, Tories were angry at Reform, a party they felt was motivated by anger.

AS THE 1997 ELECTION APPROACHED, it was clear that both the Reform and PC parties were set for a rematch. This time, the Tories would be better prepared for Reform. Whatever strategy Reform had to wipe the Tories off the political map was unclear. In their divided states, both parties would be gunning for the same conservative vote. As a consequence, the outcome of the election was never in doubt: Jean Chrétien would be re-elected as prime minister. The only question the election might settle was which of the two conservative parties would survive.

---

[19] Wills, "Tory Convention is first."

CHAPTER 7

CHRÉTIEN IN A
NO-CONTEST

O N PAPER, THE REFORM PARTY could claim a substantial victory in the June 2, 1997 federal election. The party went from 52 to 60 seats, an increase of 15 per cent from 1993. More important, Reform rose from the third party in the House of Commons to the official opposition, replacing the Bloc Québécois. The symbolism of removing a separatist party from the official opposition and assuming the government-in-waiting tag of the Opposition was powerful. However, the election result was a disappointment for Reform.

It is hard to imagine how a political party that started from scratch with five people in a Calgary boardroom in 1986 and rose to the status of Her Majesty's Loyal Opposition in a little more than a decade could be considered a failure. But before the 1993 campaign, Reform strategists had set the objective to form government after two elections. At a campaign strategy meeting in July 1993, Manning laid out his grand scheme, which Tom Flanagan summarized:

> The key premise was that this [1993] election was the first stage in a two-election strategy. That is, in this election, the Reform Party would break into the system, and in the next it would win enough seats to form government. Manning explicitly said that he wasn't interested in getting a toehold and then working for forty years to enlarge the caucus. Even more dramatically, Cliff

Fryers said he doubted that the party could fight three or more elections. To an outsider, these seemed like rhetorical flourishes calculated to excite the troops to greater efforts; but in fact they faithfully represented Manning's conception of a populist party that comes to power catching a wave.[1]

The two-election strategy called for Reform to burst onto the national stage, which they had done in the 1993 election. The 1997 election was stage two. This was the election Reform was supposed to win.

Based on the polls in early 1997, it would have been hard to find anyone who would bet that Reform had even a remote chance of forming a government. Since the 1993 election, the Liberal party had been hovering comfortably between 40 and 50 per cent support in the polls. Even though the Reform party had twenty-five times more seats in the House of Commons than the Tories, the polls gave both parties about 10 per cent support in the three years before the 1997 election. Even combined, the Tory and Reform vote was way behind the Liberals. There were as many undecided voters as there were Tory and Reform voters. These were not good times for conservatives of any stripe.

Before the writ was dropped for the 1997 election, however, the Tories had more to cheer about than did Reform. First, they were slightly ahead of Reform. Second, an April 1997 Ekos Research Associates poll showed that the Tories were the most popular second choice for both Liberal and Reform supporters by a significant margin.[2] In fact, Liberal party supporters were three times more likely to switch to the Tories than to Reform. Third, Jean Charest rated much higher than Preston Manning on the issue of trust (27 per cent to 21 per cent), which meant that the Tories had more potential to increase their level of support than did Reform.

Criticized for not having any ideas in the 1993 campaign, the Tories may well have gone overboard in 1997 with a hard-hitting right-wing

---

[1] Flanagan, *Waiting for the Wave*, 136.

[2] Ekos Research Associates Inc., April 20, 1997. The survey was conducted between March 18 and April 9, 1997, with a sample size of 1,535 households.

manifesto called "Let the Future Begin: Jean Charest's Plan for Canada's Next Century." The original draft was crafted by Alistair Campbell and Leslie Noble, two of the whiz kids who had helped orchestrate the Mike Harris Common Sense Revolution in Ontario. But, according to Geoff Norquay, Charest thought the re-baked Harris plan was "extreme and woefully inadequate." He had it rewritten.

Even toned down, the platform still packed a punch, calling for a 10 per cent reduction in personal income taxes and a one-third cut in small business taxes. The Harris strategists wanted the platform to stay away from federal–provincial issues; Charest disagreed. He designed a key platform plank that gave provinces more flexibility in setting tax rates and that transferred "tax points" to provinces. This was one of the first political efforts to fix what is now known as the "fiscal imbalance."[3] While most Canadians paid little attention to Charest's 1997 campaign, it included many policies that governments have subsequently implemented. For example, his pledge to implement a Canadian Covenant in his platform was eventually reflected in the Council of the Federation.

The campaign theme for Reform was "Fresh Start." Wanting to look more like a winning politician, Manning took great pains to make himself look "fresh" by undergoing a personal makeover. He had laser surgery on his eyes and shed his nerdish glasses. His teeth were capped, and his hair was coiffed. He had a colour chart done, his wardrobe was updated, and a voice coach was added to the Reform team. Reporters and political opponents ridiculed this makeover, remarking that while Manning came to Ottawa to change government, it looked like Manning was the one undergoing the change. Manning was clearly pulling out all the stops for this campaign. He was always strong on content, and now he had a new look. The one thing missing was passion, which is not something he could manufacture or fake. In the

---

[3] As the platform document explained, transferring tax points means that the federal government gives to the provinces a portion of federal taxes it collects. In other words, federal tax rates go down and provincial tax rates go up and the total amount of taxes paid by Canadians doesn't change. The difference is that provinces and territories, rather than the federal government, collect the money.

leaders' debates, Manning, with his lack of passion, was in stark contrast to the more youthful, energetic, and emotional Jean Charest. After the debates, Manning acknowledged to his team that Charest had overwhelmed him and that he had let his troops down.

Midway through the campaign, the polls showed that the Tories had rebounded and were expected to replace Reform as the official opposition. The Liberals were still comfortably ahead in a *Globe and Mail*/Environics poll, at 40 per cent. The Tories, at 25 per cent, were substantially ahead of Reform with 18 per cent. The *Globe and Mail* endorsed the Tories as the preferred choice for the nation's official opposition, a dramatic contrast to the 1993 campaign when the *Globe and Mail* legitimized Reform with its endorsement of its "zero-in-three" deficit elimination plan.

In a desperate move to torque up Reform's campaign, the party began to tap into the base anger and resentment many western Canadians felt about the special treatment they believed had been reserved for the province of Quebec. A highly controversial Reform election ad suggested Canada had had enough of national leaders from Quebec. The ad featured Quebec politicians, including Chrétien and Charest, with a red circle and bar over their faces. The symbol was similar to warning labels or highway traffic signs alerting drivers to impending danger. The ad gave Chrétien and Charest an opening to undermine Manning on the national stage. Manning was described as a divisive and bigoted leader attempting to appeal to extreme and destructive forces in certain parts of Canada. But the hard-hitting Reform ad seemed to work; polls showed Tory numbers starting to fall and Reform numbers starting to climb. But in vote-rich Ontario, Reform support was well below the level needed to win seats. That did not seem to matter to Manning. Reform was in a fight for status as the official opposition. Rather than reaching out to the Tories to help defeat the Liberals, Manning had his sights on holding his base in western Canada. It didn't seem to bother members of the Reform party that they were being vilified for running a nasty and racist campaign, although the party did pull the objectionable ad after it had run its course.

Geoff Norquay believes the ad might have helped Reform win some battles, but it ended its chance of ever winning the war: "If you want to chart the beginning of the end of the Reform party, it was the running of those ads. As soon as those ads ran, the vast majority of people east of the Manitoba border said, 'Forget those guys.'" In military terms, Reform bombed the bridges to protect its home turf and solidify its base.

Post-campaign, Brian Mulroney commented on the controversial Reform party ad, reminding Canadians that a leader is someone who builds unity, not division, in the country. He also warned about the intolerance of Reform:

> In the Canadian experience there was John Diefenbaker from the west and myself from the east who sought to expand the conservative base, not by driving people out but by welcoming people in. Neither of us was perfect, God knows, but we built coalitions of like-minded Canadians who believed in the values of conservative governments. And neither of us would ever have countenanced an advertisement which drew big slashes of disapproval through the faces of leaders who happened to be French Canadians from Quebec. The message could not have been clearer or more odious. And Mr. Manning can campaign without success until the streams run dry because every minority in Canada will now be wondering when they will see their pictures on TV screens, simply because they have become the latest symbols of anger and resentment for the Reform Party and its leadership.[4]

Mulroney would later remark, "While it was a natural extension of what he was saying, the guy who authorized those ads in 1997 was no nation builder. He could never be Prime Minister. Never. Nor was he ever going to get his hands on the Conservative franchise and its 135 years of history."

---

[4] Taken from "Notes for an address by the Right Honourable Brian Mulroney; The 2000 GTA Golf Classic," a speech delivered at the Angus Glen Golf Club, Markham, Ontario, June 9, 2000.

Manning confirmed he had no interest in coalition building when he mused about minority government near the end of the 1997 campaign. "In the West, a minority government was not seen as a problem to be concerned about but a result to be welcomed . . . And if a Conservative rump, mainly Red Tories, joined the Liberals to prop them up, so much the better. That's where Red Tories belonged anyway."[5] Leaders like Sir John A. Macdonald and Robert Borden would have reached out to build a national-unity government; Manning was prepared to lose centrist conservatives to the Liberals because of his stubborn discomfort with their stance. By 1997, Manning abandoned his populist dream and accepted the reality that the Reform party was simply a party of conservatives of a different name and colour.

Just days before the election, an Ekos Research poll showed the Liberals with a commanding lead. Those polled predicted that the Tories would form the official opposition. On voting intentions, the gap between the Tories and Reform had narrowed significantly, with Tories at 21.2 per cent and Reform at 17.7 per cent.

By its own design, 1997 was to be Reform's shining moment. Short of winning government, Reform's next most significant objective was to gain a meaningful breakthough east of the Manitoba border and thereby drive a solid nail into the Tory coffin. Before Reform could form a government, the PCs had to be eliminated. The polling results showed this was not going to happen.

The poll was more than a wake-up call for Manning. The wave he was trying to ride to power had dissipated at the Manitoba border. Reform had crashed. "In aggregate numbers, we got a large number of votes in Ontario, more in Ontario than we got in the prairies. The difficulty there was vote splitting," said Manning. After the election Manning started to do the math, imagining what-if scenarios, for example, what if the Tories and Reform were one party and could combine their votes. "It's the same old story of 1993," wrote

---

[5] Manning, *Think Big*, 181.

Manning. "Thirty-eight second-place finishes, and 28 seats where the combined Reform/Conservative vote is more than the Liberals', but no seats. For the Ontario candidates who came in a close second, the results are deeply disappointing."[6]

In 2006, Manning said he had counselled voters in 1997 to avoid the vote splitting that gave the Liberals easy wins. "In the West you could get people to either choose us or choose those guys, but choose one or the other. I used to say that all the time, and people would do that. And they chose us [in the West]. But in Ontario, vote splitting is what prevented us from getting seats." This was an astonishing admission for the leader of a national party. In one breath he claimed to be running a national campaign, fielding candidates across the land; in the next, he said he only wanted votes in ridings that could be won. Why would Manning bother putting candidates on the ballot in unwinnable ridings? There is reason to question Manning's claim that he discouraged vote splitting during the 1997 campaign. There is nothing in the public record or in Manning's autobiography to substantiate the claim. Perhaps he was using the strategic-voting defence to respond to critics who argued that the existence of two right-of-centre parties accomplished nothing more than to hand easy majority wins to the Liberals.

The Liberals had another majority government, even though they secured only 38.5 per cent of the popular vote. With a strong showing from the NDP and Conservatives, as well as the modest pick-up by Reform, Chrétien's majority was reduced to 155 seats in a 301-seat legislature. But Chrétien was still the prime minister, although he had no members from Nova Scotia, 1 member only from Saskatchewan, 2 from Alberta, and 6 from British Columbia. That's 9 out of a possible 71 seats. The saviour for the Liberals was Ontario, where they won a stunning 102 of 103 seats.

Manning secured the role of Official Opposition Leader with 60 seats, but that was small comfort when the plan had been to ride a populist wave right into 24 Sussex Drive.

---

[6] Ibid., 184.

Despite an increase in seats, the popular vote for Reform, at 19.4 per cent, was an increase of less than one percentage point over 1993. Of the 56 men and 4 women elected as Reform MPs, none came from east of Manitoba. Reform lost the lone seat it had held in Ontario.

Worse for Reform was the showing of the Tories. Under Jean Charest's leadership, the Tory vote increased significantly over 1993. At 18.8 per cent, their vote was only six-tenths of one percentage point behind Reform. The Tory seat total rose from 2 to 20, with a particularly strong showing in Atlantic Canada and Quebec.

Charest had performed a minor miracle and resuscitated his party from intensive care, if not the last rites. The Tories may not have been able to compete with Reform for seats in the West, but they managed to poll close to 15 per cent of the vote in Alberta. The fatal flaw for Reform, and the saving grace for Charest, was that Preston Manning made no real effort to appeal to voters east of Ontario. Reform pretended to be a national party, but it had no roots in Atlantic Canada and did not have a message or platform that could generate much support outside its western base. As a result, the Tories outpolled Reform by a factor of 14.7 to 1 in Newfoundland, 25.3 to 1 in Prince Edward Island, 3.2 to 1 in Nova Scotia, 2.7 to 1 in New Brunswick, and 74 to 1 in Quebec.[7]

Charest quickly discovered during the campaign that his most likely wins were to come from Quebec and Atlantic Canada. Adapting to his new audience, Charest opportunistically began to attack the Liberals for their cutbacks to Employment Insurance and regional development programs so he could demonstrate empathy to his newfound eastern friends. It worked. With the ongoing existence of the Progressive Conservative Party of Canada very much on his shoulders, Jean Charest was able to tap into the Tory party legacy, particularly in Atlantic Canada, where conservative support is passed from one generation to the next.

One of those multigenerational Tories on Charest's team was Peter MacKay, who handily won his father's old Nova Scotia

---

[7] In Quebec, Reform ran candidates in only 11 of Quebec's 75 constituencies.

riding.[8] MacKay was a member of the "thin blue line" of support for the Tory party, a force that was hard for Reform to kill, even when it was clear that the pcs were far removed from government.

Despite the life Charest had breathed into the party, there was a tinge of disappointment on election night in Sherbrooke, Quebec, because an early momentum had stalled in the final weeks of the campaign, especially in Quebec. During the campaign there was something peculiar going on in Quebec that would not make sense to Tories until the Quebec sponsorship scandal erupted in 2003. Tory strategist Roxanna Benoit believes the Liberals used the sponsorship program to ensure that they became the only federalist option in Quebec. To assert themselves as supreme, they had to kill Jean Charest and the pc party. "With the sponsorship program, money was flowing into Quebec in 1997 that took away our organizers. They ended up with all the political machinery."

Despite the setback in Quebec, however, there was more joy than sorrow for the pcs on election night. The party had taken its first serious step in the rebuilding process. "We retained one critical aspect in 1997. We remained a national political party," said Geoff Norquay. "We secured votes in all parts of Canada. Because we were a mile wide and an inch deep, we didn't win many seats, but it was a foundation on which we could build."

---

[8] Elmer MacKay won seven consecutive elections in the riding of Central Nova and retired from federal politics before the 1993 election. In 1997, his son, Peter MacKay, won the seat of Pictou–Antigonish–Guysborough, which comprised major elements of his father's riding after boundary redistribution.

CHAPTER 8

MACKAY IN OTTAWA, HARPER AT THE NCC

EVEN BEFORE PETER MACKAY threw his hat into the ring, there were three experienced political combatants vying for the PC nomination in the Nova Scotia riding of Pictou–Antigonish–Guysborough in 1997. The nomination meeting was a raucous affair.

MacKay had not thought of running for politics until the fall of 1996. That was when he first met PC leader Jean Charest. Charest asked MacKay about running as a candidate at a time when MacKay's frustration with the criminal justice system was at its peak. He had prosecuted numerous gruesome cases for murder and sexual assault and had seen the system fail its victims. MacKay was ready to shift his focus towards what he thought was a more direct tool to change the system—politics.

MacKay could rely on his father's good name and political network, but neither could guarantee him a nomination. The riding boundaries had changed substantially since his father had been a member, and Elmer MacKay's old riding now included the county of Antigonish. As much as he wanted to help his son, Elmer understood that it would diminish Peter if he was seen standing in his father's shadow. As far as Elmer MacKay was concerned, his son didn't need much help. "He was a good candidate. Peter had done good things in his community and had no skeletons. He worked hard and was not flamboyant." This seemed to be the right combination for the rural Nova Scotia riding.

More than five thousand residents had bought party membership: an incredible number for a party that had been left for dead four years earlier and reduced to only two seats in the House of Commons. But the eight hundred or so party members MacKay's team signed up were new to the political process, mostly people MacKay had worked with in the criminal justice system. So the nomination meeting, held in a noisy hockey arena, took a full day and the maximum three ballots to settle the contest.

Controversy found MacKay as soon as he won the nomination. On March 4, 1997, he was fired as Crown prosecutor by the Nova Scotia government because the government cited a perceived conflict between being a non-political public servant and being a candidate for political office. MacKay reacted angrily to the firing, suggesting that Director of Public Prosecutions Jerry Pitzul was politically motivated and on a power trip. The publicity surrounding the firing would later prove beneficial in the election, when MacKay could use the incident to position himself as an underdog. MacKay, who offered to take an unpaid leave of absence for the campaign and promised to resign if elected, sued the province for wrongful dismissal. It took four years and a trip to the courthouse steps before the province finally apologized to MacKay. The province also paid a portion of his legal fess and committed to change the legislation to allow doctors, dentists, and lawyers who worked for the province to run for public office.

Beyond his hard work, personal network, and solid reputation as a Crown prosecutor, there were three main reasons MacKay won the 1997 election: Jean Charest, Jean Chrétien, and the "thin blue line."

MacKay defines the "thin blue line" this way: "There were people in Atlantic Canada who simply would not let the PC party die. They were there to hold the fort while the party was under siege. Call it a 'goal line stand' or the 'last sentinels,' but they were committed to the history and traditions of the PC party. There was also no way they would let Reform take hold in Nova Scotia."

Charest was personally attractive to Nova Scotia voters. He was young, articulate, and forward-looking. Jean Chrétien was another matter. He and Paul Martin had dispensed some tough financial medicine to the country. This included measures that were particularly unpopular in Nova Scotia: cutting transfer payments to the provinces and making reforms to the Employment Insurance system. Chrétien had won all 11 seats in Nova Scotia in 1993, and he lost every one of them in 1997. MacKay's voters cared little that the Tory platform in 1997 offered an even stronger dose of right-wing economics. They wanted to punish the Liberals for what they had done.

So MacKay won handily in Pictou–Antigonish–Guysborough with almost 50 per cent of the vote. The Liberal candidate, Francis Leblanc, came in a distant second with only 35 per cent.

"COMING TO OTTAWA WAS A SHOCK TO THE SYSTEM," MacKay said. He had lived in Ottawa briefly while studying at Carleton University, and had even kicked around Parliament Hill while his father was in Mulroney's cabinet. But he had little idea what he was in for when his plane landed in Ottawa in June 1997.

One of the first calls he made was to Madeleine Ashe. MacKay and Ashe had worked together at the Crown attorney's office in Nova Scotia before a family transfer brought her to Ottawa. She had no experience working on Parliament Hill, but MacKay wanted someone he could trust to run his office. There are many around MacKay who admiringly refer to Ashe as "the vault," in recognition of her absolute discretion and because of her steely resolve to protect her boss and his time.[1]

During the orientation session for new MPs on the floor of the House of Commons, MacKay was summoned to a meeting with his leader. Not feeling he quite yet belonged on Parliament Hill, MacKay thought he must have done something wrong, and this was the equivalent of being called into the principal's office. Without

---

[1] Madeleine Ashe has worked continuously with MacKay since his first day as an MP and now serves him in his capacity as Minister of Foreign Affairs as his personal assistant.

much preamble, Charest offered MacKay the job as House leader. As a team player, MacKay readily accepted, even though he knew little of what the job entailed.

Being House leader was a terrific assignment for MacKay—a rookie MP—because it forced him to become an expert on rules and procedures. He was guided in this process by a careful reading of Beauchesne's *Rules and Forms of the House of Commons of Canada* and Erskine May's *Parliamentary Procedure*. MacKay was also educated on parliamentary procedure by John Holtby, a former clerk of the Ontario legislature. On entering MacKay's office for one of their many orientation sessions, the very formal Holtby dismissively remarked, "I have never seen a bookcase in the office of a House leader look so sparse." MacKay took the message to heart.

In the summer of 1997, before the thirty-sixth parliamentary session began, MacKay enrolled in the French language training program offered to MPs and attended an immersion program at the military base in Saint-Jean-sur-Richelieu. Also in attendance was young and forward-looking Reform MP Monte Solberg, first elected in 1993. Solberg helped MacKay prepare for his first days as a member of parliament and helped MacKay understand the concerns of western Canadians and why so many of them had voted for the Reform party. It was useful for MacKay to learn about Reform from an articulate and insightful member who, unlike many other Reform MPs, carried no particular animosity towards the PC party. Solberg and MacKay would occasionally go to the gym together and share a few beers at the end of the day. They were more than colleagues; they were friends. Solberg was the first of a number of important and influential connections MacKay made in the Reform party.

When Parliament convened, the most difficult adjustment for MacKay was the unrelenting and overpowering presence of the media. As a Crown prosecutor, MacKay was trained to say little to the media, from fear of jeopardizing the outcome of a case. But after each question period, he was expected to face a throng of reporters intent on tripping up the rookie PC House leader with rapid-fire questioning.

The functioning of the House of Commons was easier for MacKay to handle. His experience as a prosecutor was put to good use, particularly when Charest asked MacKay and fellow MP André Bachand to take the lead in a case of tollgating by a Liberal fundraiser. Their investigative work, combined with the receipt of a few brown envelopes, revealed that Liberal fundraiser Pierre Corbeil had promised speedy and favourable treatment to government grant applications in exchange for a donation to the Liberal party. Documents were seized from the regional office of cabinet minister Marcel Masse, and Corbeil was convicted of influence peddling. Later, MacKay took a key role when the Opposition was building a case against Prime Minister Chrétien because of the link between his private holding in a golf course in Shawinigan, Quebec, and his involvement in government loans and grants that affected the value of that property.

MacKay's performance in the House of Commons won him instant praise in the media. In his very early days as a parliamentarian, he was given star treatment by the press and was touted as a potential leader. But not all the attention was welcome. Being voted sexiest MP by Parliament Hill staff—a distinction ultimately given for eight consecutive years—embarrassed him. He said he did not appreciate being "trivialized in such a way." Many bachelor MPs might have found the award amusing, but MacKay shunned the notoriety and did not crack even the slightest grin of satisfaction when he was questioned about it.

For MacKay, Charest was a national icon. "There was Charest in caucus, and then there was everybody else." Charest signalled his confidence in MacKay first by making him House leader, then by making MacKay his seatmate in the House. From this perfect vantage point, MacKay studied Charest's combative approach to question period. It was a style MacKay would emulate for its drama and effectiveness.

When Charest resigned as federal PC leader in 1998 to respond to the national call to lead the federalist forces in Quebec, there were some who urged MacKay to go after the top job. Without hesitation MacKay declared himself "wet behind the ears." The candidates vying to replace Charest would spend a lot of time and energy seeking MacKay's support. "I didn't know Joe Clark very well. And I felt we needed a new face to expand the base of the party. I am a competitor and I wanted someone who I thought could win the country," MacKay said. Having met the two main contenders, MacKay chose to support Hugh Segal.

When Clark won, MacKay continued as House leader, although he had supported another candidate. MacKay returned Clark's confidence with steadfast loyalty. "I have an abiding respect for Joe Clark," said MacKay. "He has an incredible work ethic and was always well prepared for whatever task he set his mind to." MacKay's appointment may have rankled other caucus members, some of whom might have been candidates for the prestigious and influential post, for example, Nova Scotian Scott Brison, who had been an early supporter of Clark in the leadership race.

When Clark canvassed his caucus to determine who would be willing to resign so he could enter the House of Commons in a by-election, MacKay readily offered his seat. "Politics is a team sport. Sometimes you have to do things that are not in your personal interest."

As the 2000 election neared, MacKay had a solid reputation as an effective parliamentarian after just three years on the job. He quickly and effectively made the transition from son of a politician, Crown prosecutor, and rookie MP to a political force in his own right. MacKay was a man with a political future.

WHILE MACKAY HAD SERVED his apprenticeship well, Stephen Harper was beginning to look like someone who wanted never again to be a politician.

Freed from the constraints of electoral politics and party discipline, Harper began a new career in 1993 in an environment much closer to the academic life he intended to pursue when he left Ottawa in 1987. Some in the national press gallery were taken aback when Harper gave up the prestige of the House of Commons to work for a lowly right-wing advocacy group, but that's not how the thirty-seven-year-old Harper perceived it. At the National

Citizens Coalition (NCC) he would be free, yea encouraged, to pursue and expound upon the conservative thinking in which he believed so deeply.

The NCC was strongly ideological and philosophically coherent. It described itself as "Canada's largest non-partisan organization for the defence and promotion of free enterprise, free speech and government that is accountable to its taxpayers."[2] Its motto was, "More freedom through better government."

As NCC president, Harper was able to contribute thoughtful analysis and commentary on a range of political issues, most frequently through op-ed pieces in Canada's daily newspapers. He commented often about the state of disunity in the Canadian conservative political movement. He was sympathetic to the need for one principled conservative political party, though biographer William Johnson observed that Harper was not necessarily on the unite-the-right bandwagon. Johnson read a 1996 article by Stephen Harper and Tom Flanagan titled "Our Benign Dictatorship," then noted, "Harper, the contrarian, had argued that this [a merger between the PC and Reform parties] was impossible, and not necessarily even desirable, because of the three quite different political cultures, which, historically, had come together on a few occasions in the Conservative Party since 1896 to enable the party to take power. Harper warned that this conjunction of the three cultures had happened only rarely, when the electors were angry at the Liberals, and had always proven unstable."[3] The three cultures were the soft Quebec nationalists, the conservative-minded populists of western Canada, and the traditional Tories from Ontario and Atlantic Canada. This was precisely the coalition that had swept Brian Mulroney to power in 1984.

In the article, Harper and Flanagan noted the understanding that would need to occur for the parties to effectively co-operate:

---

[2] From the National Citizens Coalition website: www.morefreedom.org (accessed July 10, 2006).

[3] Johnson, *Stephen Harper*, 263.

> If co-operation [as opposed to a merger] is ever to work, the fragments of Canadian conservatism must recognize that each represents an authentic aspect of a larger conservative philosophy. Reformers will have to realize that there is something genuinely conservative in the Tory penchant for compromise and incrementalism. Tories will have to admit that compromise, to be honourable, must be guided by underlying principles, and that Reformers are not extremists for openly advocating smaller government, free markets, traditional values, and equality before law. And both will have to recognize that Quebec nationalism, while not in itself a conservative movement, appeals to the kind of voters who in other provinces support conservative parties.[4]

Harper was musing about the possibility of sustaining two or three conservative parties. Each would be regionally based, but all would come together to form a coalition government. Presumably, none of these parties would be national in scope or compete with one another in the same constituencies. On the one hand, this approach would enable the trio of interests to keep faith with the conservatism in their respective regions and make transparent the compromises that inevitably occur in a national government and in a country as diverse as Canada. The approach acknowledges the conflicts that are inevitable in a broadly based national party, and exposes the reality that there is not one cohesive national will. On the other hand, it would be hard for Canadians to understand how such an arrangement could work or would be good for the country. If nothing else, Harper's idea suggests that he was prepared to consider innovative and unprecedented approaches to overcome the conservative vote-splitting that had elected Liberal governments without so much as a fight. The messiness of a triad co-ordinating its efforts during a national election, through a coalition government, and including the

---

[4] Tom Flanagan and Stephen Harper, "Our Benign Dictatorship," *The Next City*, Winter, 1996/97.

thorny issue of selecting a leader and forming a cabinet, was probably enough of a headache to cause conservatives across the country
to seek a more simple arrangement than what Harper and Flanagan
were suggesting.

Their next suggestion: modified proportional representation.
Under such a system, lower-ranked parties would drop off the ballot until one party achieved a true majority of votes. It was easy to
see how a divided conservative vote would inevitably come together
under such a scenario, provided that conservatives didn't defect to
the Liberals when their first choice of conservative parties was
dropped. Of course, this would also serve to drive together the vote
from the left, and the conservatives would have to overcome a likely
Liberal–NDP alliance. But the main problem with the approach was
that it reduced the incentives for political parties, and Canadians
generally, to offer broad national leadership. Proportional representation is intrinsically divisive, possibly unworkable, and violates the
principles of confidence and consensus building that are fundamental to a parliamentary democracy.

IMMEDIATELY AFTER THE 1997 ELECTION, Harper took full
advantage of his freedom from the shackles of political correctness
in a commentary he co-wrote with Tom Flanagan for the *Calgary
Herald*. Harper critically dissected the view that resisting Quebec's
domination of federal politics was bad for Canadian unity. "For the
past 30 years, the Liberals and PCs . . . have used the fear of separatism . . . to control national politics. A succession of Prime
Ministers from Quebec . . . have built their careers on 'saving
Canada' . . . [using] the threat of separatism to justify their political
strategies."[5] This was essentially the view put forward by Peter
Brimelow in his 1986 book *The Patriot Game*. Harper pitted the aspirations of the West against the ambitions of Quebec-based
politicians, then suggested, "Reform has triumphed in the West, but

---

[5] Stephen Harper and Tom Flanagan, "On the pathway to power: With Liberals,
Conservatives, NDP and Lucien Bouchard lined up against them, Reformers appear to
be on the right side, the side of Canada," *Calgary Herald*, June 7, 1997, J6.

not elsewhere, because the West loses the most from the patriot game. The dynamic economies of Alberta and British Columbia disproportionately bear the cost of the regional transfers that are supposed to keep Quebec and Atlantic Canada happy."

Harper was impatient and frustrated when the West's legitimate calls for constitutional reform for an elected Senate were constantly thwarted by political elites who responded only to complaints from Quebec. Harper happily noted that the Reform party was vociferously attacked by Quebec sovereignists such as BQ leader Lucien Bouchard. If Reform was being targeted by Bouchard, suggested Harper, "Doesn't that mean that Reform is on the right side, the side of Canada?"

Unlike many other politicians and leading thinkers in Canada, Stephen Harper was prepared to take on Quebec sovereignists by not pandering to the rhetoric and demands for special status.

HARPER HARDLY LOOKED LIKE A prospective candidate for the leadership of a national political party when he penned an article for the *National Post* in December 2000.[6] He looked more like a provincial premier than a prime minister. Harper said, "If Ottawa giveth, then Ottawa can taketh away. This is just one more reason why Westerners, but Albertans in particular, need to think hard about their future in this country. After sober reflection, Albertans should decide that it is time to seek a new relationship with Canada."

Harper acknowledged the weak election campaign run by Stockwell Day and the Alliance in 2000, and suggested the reason for Chrétien's re-election was "a shrewd and sinister Liberal attack plan. The strategy—sometimes subtle, but sometimes blatant—was to pull up every prejudice about the West and every myth about Alberta that could be dredged." Harper suggested that the attack would be repeated, most likely successfully, "against any political movement perceived to have a Western, but especially an Alberta, identity."

---

[6] Stephen Harper, "Separation, Alberta-style: It is time to seek a new relationship with Canada," *National Post*, December 8, 2000, A18.

Harper mused about whether the Canadian Alliance had "hit a wall." In words that would later be used against him, Harper lamented the future of the nation: "Canada appears content to become a second-tier socialistic country, boasting ever more loudly about its economy and social services to mask its second-rate status, led by a second-world strongman [Chrétien] appropriately suited for the task. Albertans would be fatally ill-advised to view this situation as amusing or benign. Having hit a wall, the next logical step is not to bang our heads against it. It is to take the bricks and begin building another home; a stronger and much more autonomous Alberta. It is time to look at Quebec and to learn. What Albertans should take from this example is to become 'maîtres chez nous.' "

About a month later, Harper wrote an open letter, which quickly became known as the "firewall" letter, to Alberta premier Ralph Klein.[7] Many would understand the reference to "firewall" as a selfish impulse to seek to preserve Alberta's wealth for Albertans alone. But the word was a reference to computer technology and the systems designed to prevent unauthorized and harmful entry into a particular domain. In other words, Harper was trying to inoculate Alberta from a virus often delivered to provinces by the federal government.

Harper and six fellow signatories began the letter by suggesting that "the Chrétien government undertook a series of attacks not merely designed to defeat its partisan opponents, but to marginalize Alberta and Albertans within Canada's political system." The writers then proposed that Albertans "take greater charge of our own future. This means resuming control of the powers that we possess under the Constitution of Canada but that we have allowed the federal

[7] Stephen Harper, President, National Citizens' Coalition; Tom Flanagan, Professor of Political Science and former Director of Research, Reform Party of Canada; Ted Morton, Professor of Political Science and Alberta Senator-Elect; Rainer Knopff, Professor of Political Science; Andrew Crooks, Chairman, Canadian Taxpayers Federation; Ken Boessenkool, Former Policy Adviser to Stockwell Day, former Treasurer of Alberta, "Open letter to Ralph Klein," *National Post*, January 24, 2001, A14.

government to exercise." In other words, the letter writers were advocating measures that Alberta, or any province, could exercise under the constitution of Canada. The specific measures they suggested were: withdrawing from the Canada Pension Plan to create an Alberta Pension Plan; collecting revenues from personal income tax; creating an Alberta provincial police force in place of the RCMP; resuming provincial responsibility for health care policy (even if that meant penalties imposed under the Canada Health Act); and using a recent Supreme Court decision to force Senate reform onto the national agenda. They concluded by asking Premier Klein "to build firewalls around Alberta, to limit the extent to which an aggressive and hostile federal government can encroach upon legitimate provincial jurisdiction."

It is hard to imagine Harper thought he would be Canadian prime minister six years after advising Albertans they should build a more autonomous province by erecting a wall around Alberta's borders to protect it from federal intrusion into areas of provincial jurisdiction. Some might say he was, in fact, taking himself out of political contention by speaking his mind so freely. Harper was attacked for his views, but what could be so wrong about standing up to protect the allocation of constitutional powers delineated by the Fathers of Confederation? The ultimate solution for Harper was not to erect stronger borders around Alberta, however, but to offer Canadians a federal government that would respect provincial rights.

CHAPTER 9

TO THE DEATH, 1997–2003

A S THE TWO YOUNGER PLAYERS in the conservative drama were working hard and biding their time, the third was storming into Stornoway. Whatever exhilaration Preston Manning might have felt as he ascended to the office of Leader of the Opposition was quickly overshadowed by controversy, and the worst kind of controversy: the self-imposed variety.

Manning needed a place to live. And finding it became a test of the sincerity and commitment of Manning and his political movement. The choices were the $75-per-night budget hotel that had been Manning's home for the past four years, or 541 Acacia Drive, a $2-million mansion situated in posh Rockcliffe Park, just a few short kilometres from Parliament Hill. Known as Stornoway, this splendid mansion was faithfully maintained by the taxpayers of Canada and made available rent-free to the leader of Her Majesty's Loyal Opposition.

The previous occupant of Stornoway was Jean Chrétien, until the 1993 election, when he happily moved into the official residence of Canada's prime minister at 24 Sussex Drive. From 1993 to 1997, Stornoway stood empty because Bloc Québécois and Opposition leader Lucien Bouchard chose to live on the Quebec side of the border. This was a symbolic move on Bouchard's part, one that cleverly deflected the criticism that would have been heaped upon him for soaking up the perks of office of a country from which he wanted to separate. Bouchard gained a measure of respect for making such a consistent and principled gesture.

During the 1997 campaign, Manning ridiculed the prospect of moving into Stornoway: "We would suggest that maybe we would get a hold of it and use it as a bingo hall and apply the proceeds to the national debt."[1] However, once elected and faced with the choice, Manning looked at the issue somewhat differently. Not long after election day, Manning mused publicly that he would consider moving in, if the public wanted him to. In other words, he wanted to move in but did not want to take the political heat; he wanted others to encourage his flip-flop. However, many Reform MPs expressed their disgust with what they saw as a blatant repudiation of a symbolic promise, even if it was made in the heat of an election campaign. And Manning's political opponents, like Tory leader Jean Charest, were quick to point out the obvious: "It's become a joke; this whole idea that his caucus is pressuring him. I mean it's all very blatant and transparent and orchestrated and an example of his hypocrisy."[2]

Manning moved into Stornoway and managed to have his change of heart endorsed by the Reform caucus and the party's executive council. Despite the cover, the move hurt him politically, especially among Reform party members who had been expecting something different. It was an eye-opener to party members and a confirmation to Canadians that Manning had become a politician not unlike the leaders of the traditional parties.

The move into Stornoway was blatantly at odds with the populist image Manning had designed for himself. Could the man living in Stornoway be the same man who publicly shunned a government limousine and driver when he came to Parliament Hill in 1993? The Stornoway hypocrisy reminded people of the earlier controversy over an undisclosed and unreceipted $31,000 annual clothing allowance for Manning and his wife. The party that was supposed to

[1] As reported on CBC *The National*, June 17, 1997.
[2] Ibid.

be approachable and principled viewed these actions as elitist and self-serving. And to punctuate his about-face, after taking the heat for Stornoway, Manning decided to go whole hog and accepted the car and driver that came with the mansion.

CHAREST CAME INTO PARLIAMENT in 1997 as something of a hero. His party had been restored to official party status. He could book a meeting room on Parliament Hill, rather than a phone booth, for his caucus of MPs. And he no longer had to face jokes about his wife sleeping with half the Tory caucus.

But Charest had had enough of the misery and futility that came from a divided conservative movement and was determined to put an end to it. Soon after the election, Charest's staff began to prepare a plan for all-out war against Reform in what came to be known as the Keyser Soze strategy. (Soze was a fictional character in the 1995 movie *The Usual Suspects* whose ruthlessness—which led him to kill his wife and children to strike fear into the mob—was legendary.)

At the annual meeting of the party's national council in late February, Charest signalled a new strategy by taking on Manning's "politics of extremism." Charest told his council, "Preston Manning and the Reform party have misrepresented who and what they are to Canadians. We need to make our case to people who have voted Reform that they have been victims of this misrepresentation."[3] He refuted any suggestion that a merger between the parties was in the works: "Hell hasn't frozen over yet." Charest was preparing for battle.

The day after Charest made these remarks, the leader of the Quebec Liberal party, Daniel Johnson, resigned. The entire country, except for Quebec sovereignists, wanted Charest to take his place. Rarely in the history of Canadian politics has there been such a strong and resounding movement to draft a saviour into a position of leadership.

---

[3] Nahlah Ayed, "Charest brands Reform as enemy #1 [Annual meeting of national council]," Canadian Press, February 28, 1998.

It might seem odd that the leader of a national Conservative party would be asked to lead a provincial Liberal party. But in Quebec provincial politics there were two political forces: nationalist and federalist. Conservatives held the office of Quebec premier for twenty-five of the first thirty years after Confederation. The party ceased to be a force in the province at the turn of the twentieth century. The Union Nationale assumed the conservative mantle beginning in 1936 and alternated in government with the Liberals for the next forty years. In 1976, when the Parti Québécois came to power, everything changed. With a clear separatist option on the table, the federalist forces in Quebec coalesced under one party: the Liberal party.

The Liberal Party of Quebec was not necessarily left or right of centre; it was defined simply by its attachment to Canada. In other words, Charest could still be a conservative and lead the Quebec Liberal party. That point would be painfully evident to federal Liberals in the 2006 federal election campaign.

Charest took over the Quebec Liberal party on April 30, 1998. That meant that the leadership of a national political party was unexpectedly up for grabs. There is normally an extended period of jockeying among leadership hopefuls before such a job becomes available. In anticipation of a potential campaign, prospective candidates could usually be seen building networks of support, establishing an organization, securing financial commitments, and developing policy to define where they would take the party. For the most part, this testing of the waters would be done behind the scenes so as not to undermine the incumbent leader (although this was clearly not the case in the Liberal party throughout the 1990s, when Paul Martin was constantly sniping at Prime Minister Chrétien's heels). In 1998, the PC party had not anticipated, and was not prepared for, a leadership race. Losing Charest to Quebec was a blow, but one the party was prepared to accept graciously for the good of the country.

The race to replace him was wide open. Surprisingly, one candidate many senior party operatives thought would be the most attractive had not held a party membership in more than ten years.

In fact, he had done little but criticize the party for being unfocused, elitist, and unprincipled. That man was Stephen Harper.

Leading the charge to recruit Harper were two PC caucus members from the East: Jim Jones from Markham, Ontario, and John Herron from Fundy Royal, New Brunswick. These men took it upon themselves to act as emissaries for the PC party, and they visited Harper in Calgary to deliver a simple and clear message: he was the right man to unify the conservative cause in Canada. Gerry St. Germain, a former PC party president and Mulroney appointee to the Senate, also appealed to Harper to enter the race. Harper declined St. Germain's invitation, saying he couldn't see melding the two parties at that point. John Weissenberger was with Harper when he met with Jones and Herron: "Stephen refused to work actively against Preston. Had he been a more typical politician, and wanted leadership at any cost, he would have taken it."

Harper confirmed his decision with the press. "Because the country badly needs to build new bridges without burning down any more old ones, I have concluded that the idea of a candidacy by me for the Progressive Conservative leadership should not be attempted."[4] At the time, Peter MacKay was reported to be leery of Harper's seeking the Tory leadership, fearing it would be a disguised attempt by Reformers to "completely take over our party."[5] MacKay said whoever replaced Charest would have to be "of the mindset that we are not going to merge with the Reform Party."[6]

Weissenberger recalls that the admiration of PC party members for Harper didn't endure once he became Alliance leader in 2002: "Herron ended up being one of Stephen's most vociferous critics, calling him the Antichrist. I just have to roll my eyes because I was sitting in the room with him when he was trying to butter him up to get him to run for PC leader."

---

[4] Norma Greenaway, "The Tories' Great Right Hope," *Ottawa Citizen*, April 11, 1998, A5.

[5] Ibid.

[6] Dene Moore, "Manning details plan to unite right wing," Canadian Press, March 27, 1998.

Hugh Segal, who was later appointed to the Senate by Prime Minister Martin in 2005, was a more likely candidate for PC party leader in 1998. Several senior Mulroney cabinet ministers who had wanted Segal to run against Kim Campbell in 1993 would be there to support him again.[7] (Segal had declined in 1993, in part because he saw the virtue of electing Canada's first female prime minister.) While the draft-Segal movement had short legs in 1993, it planted the seed in Segal and the party that he was someone to consider next time around.

An unexpected entrant into the leadership race was David Orchard. A fourth-generation farmer from Borden, Saskatchewan, Orchard grew up just a few kilometres from the homestead of John Diefenbaker. His family farmed 1,800 acres of land without herbicides, pesticides, chemicals, or genetically modified organisms (GMOs). Why David Orchard would want to be leader of the PC party was a valid question. He had never held membership in the party. He campaigned and demonstrated against the Free Trade Agreement in 1988 through an organization he co-founded called Citizens Concerned about Free Trade. And he wrote a book in 1993, *The Fight for Canada: Four Centuries of Resistance to American Expansionism*, which included strong opposition to many of Mulroney's policies.

The book, Orchard maintained, was not intended to be a platform for entering politics. However, it struck Orchard as interesting that PC senator Heath MacQuarrie, who reviewed the book for the *Toronto Star*, remarked that all of Orchard's political heroes were Conservatives. Specifically, MacQuarrie was referring to Macdonald, Borden, and Diefenbaker—all strong nationalists who had opposed free trade with the United States. At the time, Orchard believed that

---

[7] Fearing that Campbell did not know the party and had limited experience in building a team or a coalition, and with Charest little known outside Quebec, ministers such as Michael Wilson, Bernard Valcourt, Bill McKnight, and Otto Jelinek worked the back rooms of the party to get Segal to enter the fray in 1993. McKnight told Segal that Charest could not win the convention and that Campbell could not win the country.

Senator MacQuarrie, an avid Red Tory, was feeling somewhat lonely in the party and was looking for kindred spirits.

Not a political partisan, Orchard had turned down offers to run for the Liberals and NDP in 1988. After he wrote an article about the deficiencies of the Meech Lake Constitutional Accord of 1987, he received a call from former prime minister Pierre Trudeau. This was the beginning of a long and close mentorship between the two. When Orchard told Trudeau of his interest in becoming involved with the PC party by offering policies that were diametrically opposed to current thinking, Trudeau replied, "It is an ingenious use of political reality, and it's historically correct, don't be ashamed of it." Trudeau was obviously taken with the talents of his political protégé and described the manuscript for Orchard's book as "a masterful treatment of history." Trudeau encouraged Orchard's activism, saying, "[You] could be the most popular man in Canada but without a political vehicle you could end up being a voice in the wilderness." Was the PC party the best home for Orchard's views? Trudeau said, "Your issues could be dealt with from the right, centre, or left. There is no obvious opening for you in the Liberal party with Mr. Chrétien or Mr. Martin." Mentioning Diefenbaker, Trudeau concluded, "The PC Party could be quite progressive."

Perhaps Orchard went with the PC party simply because there was an opening and an opportunity. Not only was the leadership up for grabs, but the party was relatively weak and in search of a new identity. "It was a home that had fallen apart. The party needed some reconstruction and we were prepared to do that," said Orchard adviser Marjaleena Repo. On the other hand, the Liberal party was a closed shop where gaining a membership form took monumental effort. What Orchard needed was a big-tent party: a place where he could disagree with others and still belong.

Orchard responded to the criticism from long-standing Tories who felt he didn't belong by saying he was the one who was most faithful to the party's roots. It was Brian Mulroney, argued Orchard, who had betrayed the legacy. "I had done my homework on the history of the party," said Orchard. "In 1983, only John Crosbie supported free trade. I was the one who was in the tradition." In addition to a Canadian nationalist, Orchard was a strong supporter of international law and the United Nations. He also opposed the Meech Lake and Charlottetown accords because of the possible weakening of the national government.

An equally surprising entrant to the race was former leader Joe Clark. Apparently, those who knew Clark best tried to talk him out of seeking the leadership. This included his wife, Maureen McTeer, his former political advisers, and staff members who had served him when he was party leader and minister of external affairs. But Clark was convinced he could win both his party and the country and was undeterred by those who told him his time had passed. Although he lived in Ottawa, he returned to his home province of Alberta on June 25, 1998, to announce his candidacy. Never shy about interjecting humour to make a point, Clark countered suggestions that he was yesterday's man by saying that in 1976 he was only "a little ahead of my time." Many commentators questioned why Clark would want to re-enter the fray and risk further damaging his already tarnished reputation as party leader. Surprisingly, Clark became the clear front-runner and enjoyed the support of a majority of caucus members, including Scott Brison.

Joining Clark, Orchard, and Segal in the race were Brian Pallister, a former cabinet minister from Manitoba, and Quebec lawyer Michel Fortier.

Clark enjoyed significant support from the Tory caucus. Peter MacKay was one of the few MPs who did not support him. Some in the media speculated that Elmer MacKay, who had long been a supporter of Brian Mulroney and a detractor of Joe Clark, spawned his son's support for Hugh Segal. Peter MacKay denied the connection; he was a teenager when Mulroney replaced Clark.

The leadership campaign captured limited public interest, although Clark was given credit for one of the more memorable quotes from the leadership debates when he labelled Orchard a tourist in the party. "He's here for the moment. He's a tourist in our party," Clark said. "I'm prepared to give him the courtesy we owe to a tourist but I don't want people to think that he defines the thinking of the party."[8]

The first ballot was held on October 24, 1998. Clark received 48.5 per cent support; Segal was second with 18.9 per cent; and Orchard was a respectable third with 16.3 per cent. As expected, Clark had emerged with an insurmountable lead, but not a majority. Orchard's result surprised many and was quite an accomplishment for a tourist.

Realizing that Clark would inevitably win, all candidates except David Orchard dropped out of the race. This forced a second ballot, which was held on November 14, three weeks after the first ballot. Orchard was well within his rights as a candidate to require a second ballot, but party officials thought it was an expensive exercise, an inconvenience to members, and meaningless to the outcome. Yet Orchard's support climbed to 22.5 per cent. Staying on the ballot enabled Orchard to boast (as he frequently did) that he finished second in the leadership race. Given that the second-place candidate had dropped out after the first ballot, Orchard's boast was dubious at best. Maureen McTeer described Orchard's decision to force a second ballot as "petty and mean . . . even those who had tolerated his anti-free-trade campaign were unforgiving in their criticism of him."[9]

Orchard took another view:

> Some people attacked me for having a second ballot, but I say why not? Look at how much money I brought in in terms of memberships and donations. The second ballot was fascinating in its own right to see where people would go. In fact, we increased our vote. We were in the public eye and the media spotlight was on us. I wanted to have some debates. Any publicity is better than none. Let's make an effort. Without effort nothing is done.

[8] "Clark dismisses foe of free trade as Tory 'tourist,'" *Toronto Star*, September 14, 1998, 1.

[9] Maureen McTeer, *In My Own Name: A Memoir* (Toronto: Random House, 2003), 280.

Joe Clark was determined to restore the PC party to past glory and had absolutely no appetite for electoral co-operation with the Reform party. He backed up his tough talk by leading the passage of an amendment to the PC party constitution that required the party to field candidates in every riding. This prevented local riding associations from co-operating with Reform party riding associations which might want to field a single or joint candidate. The amendment passed with 95 per cent support.

Preston Manning made several direct appeals to Joe Clark for co-operation: he wrote a letter, dated October 29, 1998, inviting Clark to attend the United Alternative convention, and he met with Clark at Clark's residence on Sunday, May 30, 1999. At the private meeting Clark told Manning he would be prepared to carry on an informal dialogue with small groups of people in a private setting. However, what Clark really wanted was for Reform to withdraw from the political arena and join the PCs, with Clark as leader.

In Edmonton in September 1999, Manning and Clark were keynote speakers at a conference called "Citizens' Empowerment in Government," co-hosted by PC House leader Peter MacKay and Reform member Ian McLelland. Those favouring a merger were hoping both sides would see how much the parties had in common. Manning was willing to identify areas of common interest and to explore methods of co-operation, but Clark saw the conference as an opportunity to bring Reformers into the Tory tent. Without immediate co-operation, Manning warned convention delegates, conservatives would have to wait two or three elections before they would have a shot at beating the Liberals. As it turned out, Manning wasn't far off in his prediction.

AFTER THE 1997 FEDERAL ELECTION CAMPAIGN, a dark reality began to sink in for Reform party strategists. In the early 1990s they had told themselves that 1997 would be the election they were going to win. Manning had said he was not in the race to build support slowly; they had to ride a wave that would take them right to power.

That never happened. There was the fatal article in the Reform party constitution looming over their heads that would end the experiment on November 1, 2000, when the party would become null and void.

It was clear to everyone who watched politics that the Reform party was conservative and had done little more than split votes with the Progressive Conservative Party and ensure Liberal victories. Since neither party wanted to dissolve, and because neither wanted to become a junior partner, other options were required.

Manning had some experience with creating political parties and energizing discontented troops. His idea should have come as no surprise: to form a new and more broadly supported political party. Manning took this idea—the United Alternative—to the Reform party convention in London, Ontario, in May 1998, where it was endorsed by 91 per cent of the delegates. They also endorsed Manning's leadership with a lofty 81 per cent support, an impressive number except that Manning was used to receiving ratings of 95 per cent or higher.

A convention was held in Ottawa on February 20, 1999, to discuss how a new party might work. Reform party members were asked in a mail-in ballot the following June if they wanted to continue with the United Alternative process. Less than half the members voted, and those who did gave the idea a lukewarm 60 per cent level of support.

Manning wanted to build a broader coalition. He was investing considerable effort to attract disaffected PC party members who were unhappy with Joe Clark, especially those from the provincial parties. John Weissenberger recalls: "This may be debated in the future by historians, but I don't think [Manning] was of the mind to co-operate with the PCs; nor did he want to do all he could to displace them. He was looking for a different strategy to move the whole thing forward."

The conservative parties were going nowhere but down in 1999. An Ekos poll in the fall showed the Liberals with the support of 53.3 per cent of decided voters; the Tories in second place with 16.6 per cent; and Reform in third place at 11.6 per cent.[10] The Liberals had substantial leads in every region in the country, including the West. Ekos concluded, "The PC Party, under Joe Clark, has emerged as the clear second choice for Canadians...although the gap with the Liberals is profound at 36 points. The Reform Party continues to falter [and] they have shown no success in transcending their position as a regional protest party." With talk of a United Alternative movement in the air, the Ekos analysis offered an ominous warning: "The UA movement has shown little in the way of results for Reform. Ironically, this Reform-led movement may ultimately point to a fatal flaw in the Reform Party itself. A stalled and declining Reform Party may suggest a return to the original UA: the PC Party of Canada. The preferred second choice of Reform is PC whereas the clear preferred second choice of PC supporters is Liberal."

The founding convention for what was ultimately called the Canadian Reform Conservative Alliance was held in Ottawa on January 29, 2000. The founders wisely declined to call the party the Canadian Reform Alliance Party, as some had suggested, realizing it would inevitably, if affectionately, be known as CRAP. At an overlapping convention, 75 per cent of Reform party members endorsed Manning's leadership. Manning's results were similar to those of the leaders in the traditional parties, but far lower than anything he had received to date. Manning's support among party members was in a steady trend of decline.

The choice of name was noteworthy: for the first time, Manning accepted the label "conservative." After arguing for more than a decade that Reform was a populist movement that appealed to the full spectrum of political voters—the right and the left—he accepted reality. He and his party were conservative.

A decision about the dissolution of the Reform Party, and the move to the Alliance, rested with Reform members. In a party-wide referendum, about two-thirds of the membership participated in the

---

[10] Ekos Research Associates Inc., "Federal Liberals riding high: Sovereignty movement dormant," October 14, 1989. The sample size was 4,647, which ensures the results are accurate within +/− 1.4 per cent, 19 times out of 20.

vote. Ninety-two per cent were in favour of joining with the Alliance party. Within days, Preston Manning submitted his resignation as leader of the defunct Reform party and announced his candidacy to lead the Canadian Alliance.

Most Reform party members assumed that Manning would win the leadership of the Alliance. "The attitude of the Manning people was that Preston was the party and the party was Preston," said John Weissenberger. As far as Weissenberger and Harper were concerned, this was an unhealthy situation, detrimental to any effort to institution-alize the party. What they sought was a principled Conservative party, one that would never be overly dependent on the ideas and personality of any one man. They could see how much Manning dominated Reform, a key reason both Harper and Weissenberger withdrew from party duties in 1997. Because Manning was expected to win, they saw no rea-son to return to an active role with the party in 2000. They passively, but openly, supported Tom Long for leader of the Alliance. Long had no experience as an elected politician, but he did have a reputation as a strong small-c conservative with a following among activists in his home province of Ontario. By not supporting Manning, Harper and Weissenberger were considered disloyal to the party. "Preston didn't appreciate that Stephen was not backing him 100 per cent," recalled Weissenberger. Preston's team "were still thinking in terms of Preston grabbing hold of the wave. Their focus was on win with Preston or the Alliance was done. To us, it was just not a logical way of thinking."

Others agreed with Harper and Weissenberger and thought the party was much bigger than its leader. In fact, they thought the party could be much bigger without Preston Manning.

ONE MAN IN CANADA who did not want to see Preston Manning continue in national politics was Brian Mulroney. In a rare appear-ance at a partisan event, Mulroney addressed the Tory faithful on June 9, 2000, and offered his most blunt assessment of Manning and Reform to date.[11]

---

[11] "Notes for an address..." (see chap. 7, n. 4).

The architect of today's disunity was Preston Manning. He did not say: "[Mulroney], I think you've strayed from conservative principles so I'll join you and help strengthen the right!" I would have welcomed both his constructive criticisms and him into the fold... After sixteen years of leftist damage by the Liberal government and only four years after Canada had its first conservative majority government in twenty-six years— he chose to launch a new party, split the vote, and give rise to the political fragmentation we know today... Imagine what we could have accomplished had he chosen to work with us, to help modify and improve our policies to make them even more effective for Canada. He could have emerged as a strong member of our leadership team. But we'll never know now, will we?

Mulroney reminded loyal Tories that they had faced division before from the ancestors of Reform:

By the way, there is nothing new in this Social Credit Reform group taking steps that damage the Conservatives and help the Liberals. John Diefenbaker's government was significantly weakened by the emergence of a Social Credit/Creditistes Alliance that split the conservative vote and facilitated the return to office of the Pearson Liberals. Result? One Prime Minister from Western Canada out. Joe Clark's government was defeated in the House on a budget designed to lower the deficit and contain the debt because the Social Credit/Creditistes abandoned the Conservatives and ensured the resurrection of the Trudeau Liberals [which gave the West the NEP, PGRT, and FIRA, in short order]. Result? A second Prime Minister from Western Canada out. So why should anyone have been surprised when the latest Social Credit progeny— Reform—was conceived to damage the Conservatives and help the Liberals back to government. They had been well trained in this dubious skill and played their roles to perfection.

Not inclined to reconcile, Mulroney cautioned PC supporters about being drawn into Manning's new United Alternative approach:

> Back then, he wasn't concerned with "uniting the right!" He wanted to lead something, anything. He was consumed with destroying a centrist and right-of-centre party whose policies in fact turned out to be so right for Canada that they have been followed to a T by the Chrétien government . . . Now our daring revolutionary—realizing that Reform is a spent force with no prospect of ever forming a national government and doing little except ensure power for the Liberals—has changed course: "Forget the negative things I've said about you for years," Mr. Manning says to the Conservatives, "Hey, I love you now. True, I've demonized your leaders, denigrated your policies and ridiculed your candidates in my implacable campaign to destroy your party, your reputation, and your legacy. But now, I've changed, I think you're great. Let me welcome you into my new party—it's called the Reform party in pantyhose—I'll be the leader, you'll be the followers, and we'll all be happy little campers together." Thank you, Mr. Manning, but no thanks. My only astonishment comes from the fact that some, not many, well-intentioned Progressive Conservatives are gullible enough to swallow this absurd message.

If there was an optimistic construction to Mulroney's thesis, it was to separate Manning from his followers and encourage the followers to return to their natural home, the Progressive Conservative Party, the only party that could win a national conservative government:

> I believe the overwhelming majority of Alliance members are good and decent people who want to change the present mediocre government. I share their view and encourage their ambition. I believe however that their goals can best be achieved within the broad national reach of a united

Progressive Conservative Party under the leadership of a Western Canadian who can win the entire country.

Brian Mulroney was officially and categorically opposed to any form of merger or co-operation with any party being led by Manning. As far as Mulroney was concerned, if there was a villain to the story, it was Preston Manning.

MOST CANADIANS THINK of Stockwell Day as an Albertan, but he was born in eastern Canada and grew up in Ontario, Quebec, and Atlantic Canada, in a family where politics were served at the dinner table. His father, Stockwell senior, held strong right-wing views and was active in the Social Credit Party.[12] In his first political campaign, the son worked as a volunteer for a Progressive Conservative candidate waging a valiant but hopeless battle in a Liberal stronghold in Quebec.

After living and working in various parts of Canada, Stockwell Day found a home in Alberta, working as an assistant pastor and school administrator at a Christian school. The Alberta government didn't know how to deal with Christian schools and independent education, so Day stepped in and helped form the Alberta Association of Independent Schools, which lobbied successfully for funding and regulatory reform on behalf of all Christian schools. This effort inspired Day to think that there might be a place for his skills in electoral politics.

He was elected to the Alberta legislature as a Progressive Conservative member for Red Deer North in 1986 and made it into Ralph Klein's cabinet as minister of labour in 1992. He subsequently took the portfolios of government House leader and social services, and in March 1997 he became Alberta treasurer.

Day considered the election of Ralph Klein as Alberta premier as a model of how politics should be fought and governments should be run. "In 1993 the Conservative Party in Alberta was about to

[12] The senior Stockwell Day ran as a Social Credit candidate in the 1972 election in a British Columbia riding against former Saskatchewan premier Tommy Douglas. He was badly trounced and finished fourth, receiving only 1,868 votes to Douglas's 25,483.

become extinct," according to Day. Klein put forward a strong small-c conservative platform and asked voters to "please trust us. This time, we will really do it." Day recalls it was a great time to be a Conservative if you wanted to make real change. "The reforms in our platform were so significant that we thought if we did what we said we were going to do, we wouldn't get re-elected," Day said. Oblivious to the polls, the Klein government was guided only by what it thought was right. Many of the key reforms were led by Stockwell Day. These included welfare reform, the restructuring of workers' compensation, the introduction of a single-rate tax, and debt elimination.

The economic news was generally good for Albertans, though nowhere near as good as it would become. Day recalled telling Ralph Klein, "Premier, if only oil would get to $24 a barrel and stay there this province would be in clover." By 2006, it would get to $60.

Being treasurer for Alberta was almost as good as being CFO for Tim Hortons, and it was a tough job for Day to leave, but a parade of people starting knocking on Day's door. "People were coming to me to say that Reform could not move ahead as a brand. Preston had done a great job, but would I consider responding to the call." He felt he had accomplished the key goals he had set for himself and was concerned about federal incursions into areas of provincial jurisdiction. "I thought federal intervention would continue and would hurt the country." The broadly based "draft Day" movement came equipped with polls that indicated he could win, as well as pledges of financial support to ensure that a campaign would not end up in debt. It didn't matter that Day had never been a member of the Reform party: he was a new and fresh face with all the credibility that came with being a successful provincial treasurer.

Day recalled that the campaign to beat Preston Manning was simple: "Just sell more memberships." His team knew Manning had much of the existing membership behind him, and that they would need to bring in a substantial number of new members to win. Selling memberships one at a time was not likely to get the job done. The winning strategy was to attract large groups of conservative-minded Canadians. While much would later be made of how Day recruited throngs of evangelical Christians to his side, which he did, Day said he spent as much time in secular colleges, beers halls, and dance halls as in places of worship. Day described his campaign as energetic, youthful, and broadly based. In most cases he won over supporters because of his approach to fiscal issues and by not being Preston Manning. The other part of Day's strategy was hard work: "We didn't sleep until it was won."

There is no question that Day was attractive to evangelical Christians, who were filling charismatic churches, especially in western Canada. Preston Manning also held Christian views, but he believed that free votes and voter-initiated referenda should rule supreme. Day's supporters thought their candidate would be more likely to govern with regard to his faith. Lloyd Mackey, who writes about faith and politics, observed, "To them [evangelical Christians], as well as to some of the more conservative Catholics, Manning was good but Stockwell Day was better and would take them further. Day had spent most of his Sundays in Pentecostal and charismatic churches, and many of their leaders, particularly in Alberta, saw him as Canada's great political hope. Briefly put, these people were able to muster the membership sales to make Day the leader of the Canadian Alliance."[13]

About three months before the Alliance leadership contest, the polls gave the federal Liberals a huge lead, with the Tories in second place, and Reform in third spot. Since the 1997 election, the governing Liberals had enjoyed an 18 per cent increase in support, while the Tories were down 6 per cent, and Reform was down 9 per cent.[14] The polls showed there was no effective opposition and no government in waiting. An Ekos poll offered the following conclusions: "Neither the Canadian Alliance phenomenon nor its

[13] Mackey, *The Pilgramage of Stephen Harper*, 90.

[14] Ekos Research Associates Inc., "Priorities and preferences in the post-budget environment: Part III: Preston Manning, Stockwell Day and the Party formerly known as Reform," March 30, 2000. The sample size of 1,208 respondents ensures accurate results within +/− 2.8 per cent, 19 times out of 20.

potential new savior Stockwell Day are registering much of an impact on the Canadian electorate." Ekos president Frank Graves went on to say, "Any hypothetical gain from Tory to Reform would be more than cancelled by a double gain to the Liberal Party of Canada." What Graves meant was that if the PC party disappeared, more of its vote would go to the Liberals than to the Alliance. However, the attention given to the unite-the-right movement in the pre-convention period was beginning to pay off for the Alliance party. By May 2000, Alliance climbed ahead of the Tories in the polls: 17 per cent to 11 per cent.[15]

The leadership selection process was "one member, one vote," with a true majority required to win. The first ballot was on June 24, 2000. Stockwell Day held the lead with 44 per cent support, followed by Preston Manning at 36 per cent. Tom Long, who had the support of Stephen Harper, carried 18 per cent support and was taken off the second ballot. Day recalled having all the momentum. "The night of the first ballot all the Tom Long people came to us and said 'great—we are with you.' It was not the faith crowd. We were feeling pretty good."

Day's exuberance was muted soon after the first ballot when Manning teamed up with Tom Long and then launched negative attacks. "It caught us off guard. Up until then, it had been a rigorous but civil campaign." It seemed peculiar that Tom Long would publicly endorse Manning when all of Long's supporters were streaming into the Day camp.

The second ballot was held on July 8. It gave Preston Manning the same 36 per cent support he had earned on the first ballot. That meant virtually all the Tom Long voters supported Stockwell Day. At the end of Manning's decade-long struggle in federal politics, all he could assemble in the leadership contest were forty thousand Canadians who would vote to sustain his leadership. Stockwell Day, who had been in the Alliance party mere months, was able to bring more than seventy thousand members to his side. Manning's appeal

---

[15] Ekos Research Associates Inc., "Update on political landscape," May 10, 2000.

was limited to mostly western Canadians who had stayed with him from the early 1990s. They were fed up with politics as usual in Ottawa and were attracted to the "common sense of the common man" approach that Manning had long been preaching. Day out-flanked Manning by changing the nature of the party's membership.

Manning was helped in his leadership bid by many of the original Reformers, as well as some new recruits. Interestingly, one individual given special attention in his autobiography is Belinda Stronach, whom Manning credited for her "unflagging support."[16]

WITH THE ELECTION OF STOCKWELL DAY as Alliance leader, there were two national political parties with leaders who did not have a seat in the House of Commons: Day for the Alliance and Clark for the Tories. The difference between the two was that by the summer of 2000 Stockwell Day had been in his job a matter of hours while Joe Clark had been Tory leader for almost two years. Clark had been under considerable pressure to force one of his twelve caucus members to resign so he could run in a by-election. Some in the party speculated that Clark resisted running because he was afraid he would lose the by-election. But Clark said he was prepared to wait until the general election; he had already been nominated as the PC candidate in the riding of Calgary Centre.

Hoping to get some of the media attention that was focused on the Alliance leadership vote, Clark issued a challenge to Stockwell Day. Some might have called it a duel. Clark challenged Day to run against him in a by-election in Calgary Centre. The sitting MP, Eric Lowther of the Alliance Party, would have to resign for the challenge to take effect. Clark hesitated when asked if he was putting his party on the line in a winner-take-all scenario. It was clear to most observers that a Clark defeat would destroy his leadership and most likely his party as well. To those who wanted the two parties to unite, Clark's proposal was a brilliant opportunity to end the division once and for all. The Tories had come a distant third in Calgary Centre in

---

[16] Manning, *Think Big*, 438.

1997, and the polls gave Alliance a huge lead in the summer of 2000. Clark's caucus colleagues expressed public support for the challenge, but it was a remarkably risky gambit. In effect, Clark was offering to place the existence of his party in the hands of the voters in one Alberta riding.

Day refused the offer and chose to run in a British Columbia by-election. "I was up for it. I liked the story line: first Preston; then Joe; then Chrétien. It was one, two, three. But the considered opinion among my advisers is that we needed to show we could win in another province. We would rather have run in Ontario but no seats were available." Most commentators agree with Day's initial instinctual assessment and remain curious why he chose to follow the advice of others. What persuaded Day to go along with his advisers was the belief that Clark was inherently weak, and that keeping him in place was the best strategy to overtake the PC party. Day offered this view of his decision:

> Clark was not seen among his own supporters as a white knight. We saw Clark as a liability to the PCs and thought it was just as good that he stay there. Had he lost then we would have to deal with a new rising star who could lead a resurgence. We always felt the PC core would remain. Rather than take the risk, we preferred to deal with a crusty entity that was not going to move ahead. We decided not to attack Clark, but would simply tell PCs why it was over and why we needed to move ahead. They were going to be a resistant rump and the only way to take them out was to crush them in an election.

The only real risk to Day and the Alliance in losing a Calgary by-election to Clark was that the NDP and Liberal forces might band with the Tories in a common front. However, running in B.C. made Day look as if he were changing teams just before the playoffs. It was hardly a bold or symbolic move: the B.C. riding he claimed had been won by the Alliance in 1997 with more than 53 per cent of the vote and a plurality of 12,329 over the second-place Liberal candidate.

Had Day wanted bragging rights he would have sought the Calgary Centre seat; or any seat east of the Manitoba border.

When all was said and done, Clark looked confident in his challenge to Day. He deflected some of the criticism he had received for not running in a by-election in the previous two years. But with Day about to enter the House of Commons through a B.C. by-election, Clark had little choice but to run in the safest seat he could find. Both Scott Brison and Peter MacKay offered their seats to enable Clark to run. Polling showed that Brison's Kings–Hants riding was the more winnable. (Peter MacKay's offer was noteworthy: his father, Elmer, had resigned his seat in Parliament in 1983 so that newly elected PC leader Brian Mulroney could enter the House of Commons through a by-election. Elmer MacKay reclaimed the seat in 1984 when Brian Mulroney chose to run in the Quebec riding of Manicouagan.)

The by-elections that brought Stockwell Day and Joe Clark into the House of Commons were held on September 11, 2000.[17] Day won easily: he ran unopposed by Liberals or Tories. There was no symbolism attached to winning a seat in another province, as his advisers had hoped. Clark faced an Alliance opponent who finished a distant third. It was not an entirely pleasant victory party for Clark, however. The by-election coincided with the defection of two of his Quebec caucus members, David Price and Diane St-Jacques, to the Liberals.

It was clear from the outset of Day's ascendancy to Opposition leader that the press were in no mood to give him a honeymoon. The day after his by-election victory, Day, dressed in a wetsuit, held a press conference on the shores of Okanagan Lake. Perhaps he intended a demonstration of youth and change, reminiscent of Jean Chrétien water-skiing before the 1993 election, or Pierre Trudeau doing flips from a diving board for the admiring and invited press. But the media ridiculed Day, saying his stunt made him look frivolous and clown-like. "We had to do things to break through. But

---

[17] Stockwell Day became the member from Okanagan–Coquihalla, British Columbia, and Joe Clark became the member for Kings–Hants, Nova Scotia.

nothing I did was going to get the approval of the national press. Can you imagine what they would do to Stephen Harper if he pirouetted behind the Queen?" said Day.

Stockwell Day took his seat across from Prime Minister Jean Chrétien in the House of Commons on September 19, 2000. He had been leader of the Opposition for little more than two months, and there had been an election three years earlier, but Day challenged the prime minister to call an election. It might have been no more serious than the new kid on the block challenging a bully to a schoolyard scrap: only after the words have been blurted out is the new kid left with the prospect of getting beaten to a pulp. Day rose to his feet in the House of Commons on September 25 and said:

> Will the Prime Minister, who disagrees with his Finance Minister on the high marginal rates of taxes and who now disagrees with his MPs, do one of two things? Will he either resign because he has no support over there or call an election based on his record of being the highest taxing leader in the G7 countries?[18]

Chrétien had been looking for an excuse to call an early election, and Day gave it to him gift-wrapped. Chrétien might have called the election within days of the challenge, but Pierre Trudeau's death on September 28, 2000, altered his timing.

As long as the Canadian Alliance and the Tories were splitting the conservative vote, Chrétien knew he was assured a victory. Winning a third consecutive majority would put Chrétien into the history books. It was a feat not even Trudeau had accomplished; in fact, Trudeau had not managed to win back-to-back majority governments. Chrétien could hardly be accused of political opportunism, since the official opposition had demanded the election.

Day thought challenging Chrétien was a wise strategic move: "We knew it was only a matter of days before the election was going

---

[18] Thirty-sixth Parliament, second Session, Edited Hansard, n. 117, Tuesday, September 25, 2000.

to be called. If there was going to be an election we wanted to define the ballot question and we wanted to have it on fiscal issues."

More important than winning a third term, a Chrétien victory would frustrate the ambitions of Paul Martin, who had been steadily undermining Chrétien as prime minister to the point of seeking a forced resignation. Martin could hardly plot an overthrow in the midst of an election campaign. A campaign win would enable Chrétien to lay legitimate claim to the throne for at least three more years. The 2000 election, which cost the country hundreds of millions of dollars, was in no small measure about the internal politics of the Liberal party and the competing egos of two men: Jean Chrétien and Paul Martin. Chrétien admitted as much to Stockwell Day not more than a year after the election. As Day recalled:

> When I flew down to ground zero[19] with the prime minister and other leaders, something we had to pressure the PM to do, he called me to the front of the plane. He said to me, "I called the 2000 election because Paul Martin was pushing me. And if he pushes me again I will call another election." His feeling towards Paul Martin was visceral; it was deep. I have never met a street fighter quite like him. He lives for that battle to leave people on their knees on the sidewalk.

The election call came on October 22, for a vote on November 27, 2000.

Just before the election was called, Day received an unexpected boost when Senator Gerry St. Germain joined the Alliance caucus. St. Germain had been elected as a Tory MP in 1984. He served as Prime Minister Mulroney's caucus chair until he was defeated in the general election of 1988. In 1989, he was elected president of the PC party, a post he held for six years. On June 23, 1993, St. Germain was summoned to the Senate on the recommendation of Prime

---

[19] Ground Zero refers to the site of the World Trade Center in New York. The buildings were levelled on September 11, 2001, by Al-Qaeda terrorists.

Minister Mulroney. To the dismay of his PC colleagues, particularly Mulroney, St. Germain defected to the Alliance caucus on October 18, 2000.[20] In the days before he made his decision to switch parties, St. Germain called Mulroney (they have not spoken since). "The conversation did not go well," recalled St. Germain. "He asked me to think it over. He wasn't pleased. He was preaching the virtues of Clark to me, a man with whom I had no rapport. I told him unless something is done, nothing is going to happen."

St. Germain had nothing but respect for Mulroney. The first thing a visitor sees when entering St. Germain's Senate office is a three-by-four-foot framed colour portrait of the former prime minister. But the man who caused St. Germain to make his bold decision was not Mulroney: "What drove me away from the PC party was Joe Clark. He saw the Alliance as the devil. There were certain things happening in caucus that were unreal and it had become very confrontational. Joe Clark might be one of the finer human beings you will ever meet, but as a political leader! Disaster." St. Germain thought it was time for something bold, something to shake up the standoff between Tories and Alliance. "I knew that somebody had to take drastic measures. There is a saying that I have lived by: the brave never live forever and the cautious never live at all. I could never see Joe Clark leading the troops back to where we are today." St. Germain's defection added important ammunition to Stockwell Day's contention, that Joe Clark and his Tory party were a spent force. Day was particularly impressed that St. Germain offered to resign his Senate seat should an Alliance government be able to convert the Senate from an appointed to an elected chamber.

Accepting St. Germain into the Alliance caucus required a vote of its members. In St. Germain's speech before the caucus vote, he said, "I am not going to relinquish any of my past statements. I think Brian Mulroney did great things for the country." This was not something Alliance members expected to hear. "But I see myself here for

---

[20] For a short period before Senator St. Germain joined the Alliance caucus, he sat as an independent in the Senate.

a reason. I don't hold any animosity to either side, but we [PC and Alliance] have to get together and make this thing work." The vote to welcome St. Germain was unanimous.

Once inside, St. Germain was surprised by what he saw: "They were far more interested in forming government than the Tories were at that point in time. They were more apt to put water in their wine and get on with it." This contrasted with what St. Germain saw in the Tory caucus: "The PCs saw themselves as the establishment and the Alliance as the renegades." The PC establishment was not happy about St. Germain's defection. "It was brutal," recalled St. Germain, "the worst thing I have ever gone through. My commitment to conservatism is deep. It was my commitment to conservatism that made me do what I did. It was in trouble. But I took a position. I took a lot of heat. I have no regrets."

The polls in 2000 were clearly favourable to the Liberals, who went into the campaign with support at 48 per cent, compared with the Alliance at 21 per cent, the Bloc at 10 per cent, and the NDP and the Tories pulling up the rear with 8 per cent support each.[21] Rarely had the Tory numbers been so low. While prospects for the Alliance were substantially higher than anything the Reform party had experienced, pollsters were warning that the Alliance had peaked. "Overall, the distinct demographic profile of the Manning-led Reform Party looks very similar to the Day-led CA constituency with support concentrated in western Canada (mainly Alberta among men). The surge enjoyed by the CA following the 'unite-the-right' and leadership proceedings appears to have plateaued and perhaps fallen back. Although Stockwell Day's recognition has been rising, there has been a steeper rise in the incidence of people who expressed low trust in Mr. Day."[22]

No one expected the government to be defeated. But with the Tories so far behind, Day might have been thinking this was his chance

---

[21] Manning, *Think Big*, 346.

[22] Ekos Research Associates Inc., "Ekos poll on the political landscape," October 12, 2000. There were 2,502 completed interviews from September 21 to October 7, 2000, with results valid +/− 2.0 percentage points 19 times out of 20.

to kill the PC party and end vote splitting once and for all. Tory leader Joe Clark had bravely decided to run in Calgary. A defeat in his home province would surely mean the end of his term as party leader. The survival of the PC party was still very much at stake in the 2000 election. The risk of a terminal defeat was much higher in 2000 than it had been when Jean Charest led the party into the 1997 campaign.

Chrétien's election strategy was easy to predict. The prime minister cast Day as an American-style social conservative out of touch with mainstream Canada. Stockwell Day's reluctance to campaign on Sunday, as well as a host of pro-family policies, reinforced the view that a Day government was going to be about more than lower taxes. However, for a time during the campaign, Day and the Alliance had momentum. "We went as high as 32 per cent in the polls," recalled Day. "That's when the Liberals resorted to fear tactics and name-calling, stuff that has no substance, but it sticks."

The media continued their efforts to make Stockwell look foolish, and ridiculed the Alliance platform, which called for citizen-led referenda on important national issues. CBC comedian Rick Mercer launched a petition to change Day's first name to Doris, after a 1950s ditzy blonde movie star.

In his first election as leader of the Tories since his stunning defeat as prime minister twenty years earlier, Joe Clark failed to generate much excitement—except in the televised leaders' debates, when he accused Prime Minister Chrétien of taking the country into an election because of his ego and his desire to keep leadership rival Paul Martin away from the top job. Otherwise, the PC party was widely ignored during the campaign. The party had no money, and many provincial teams that could otherwise be counted on for support were either sitting on their hands or helping Stockwell Day and the Alliance.

The outcome of the election, much like the previous two Liberal majority victories, was never in doubt. Chrétien was an easy and predictable winner. The Liberals took 172 seats, a gain of 17 from the 1997 campaign. The Canadian Alliance maintained Opposition status with 66 seats, a gain of 6. The NDP seat total plummeted from

21 to 13. The NDP did enough to stay alive at the margins, a place where they have rested in seemingly perpetual comfort.

The Progressive Conservatives stayed alive, but barely. From the 1997 campaign's 20 seats and 18.8 per cent of the vote, they went to 12 seats and a little more than 12 per cent. The Alliance attempt to wipe the Tories off the map failed. Even Joe Clark managed to win his seat in Alberta, by a comfortable 4,304 votes, in a province where the Alliance won 23 of 26 seats. There was solid evidence that Liberals voted for Joe Clark to help keep the family feud among conservatives alive. Clark's spouse, Maureen McTeer, describes an organized local effort by Liberals to elect Clark in Calgary Centre.[23] According to Jeff Clarke, the volunteer who ran Clark's tour in the campaign, "There was a rumour on the campaign that a deal was made with the Liberals. The Liberals felt Clark was their best tool and he proved that."

Had Clark lost, or had the Tories been reduced to fewer than 12 seats, the threshold for official party status, the party might well have died. What saved the Tories once again was the thin blue line of Tory support in Atlantic Canada, which delivered 9 of the party's 12 seats.

Entering the campaign, the Alliance had two primary goals: first, gain a substantial number of seats east of the Manitoba border, as many as 50; second, kill off the Tories to position itself for a stronger run next time out. It failed on both. The Tories survived, barely; and the Alliance managed to eke out 2 seats only in rural Ontario and no seats farther east.

Stockwell Day could claim victories on the battleground, but not in the outcome of the war. The Alliance vote, at 25.5 per cent, was more than double the Tory result. In the 1997 campaign the Reform party and PCs had been less than one percentage point apart, with neither party reaching 20 per cent of the popular vote. In this campaign the Alliance was more than 13 percentage points ahead. Yet, this was not enough for the Alliance party to let Stockwell Day keep his job as leader.

---

[23] McTeer, *In My Own Name*, 292.

It was not until the 2004 election that Day's electoral accomplishments as leader would be appropriately recognized. His 25.5 per cent support in 2000 compares extremely favourably with the 29.6 per cent support that Stephen Harper received in 2004 under a merged Conservative party. Day explained:

> The national media has invested so much personal invective against me that how could they then give me credit as somebody who could take the party into the next election. A senior columnist told me, "You had to know the national press corps was going to kill you because of your special conservative views. You have no idea how they talk about you, the things they say over beers and coffee because of your position on certain issues." When we watched the post-debate coverage, Daryl Bricker [of Angus Reid] reported that his rolling polls done throughout the debate had me winning four of five portions. But by the time the talking heads were on screen the only objective poll was never mentioned again.

Preston Manning, who thought he would have done better than Day, said: "Had I been able to hold on to the leadership we could have made our breakthrough in 2000. We had polling data that showed pretty good numbers for us and for the Alliance if I could have held on to [the leadership]."

Most people did not perceive the 2000 election as the first campaign for the Alliance party because they thought the switch from Reform to Alliance was simply a change in name. What was accomplished by turning Reform into the Canadian Alliance? Manning offered this view:

> We did get a fair number of conservatives [in the Alliance]. The heart of the thing was an alliance between the Harris conservatives and the western reformers. We got thinner as we got further east. The total mass and mix was quite bigger than Reform. We got people to accept our democratic processes.

But it was only partially successful, partly because when Stock got a hold of it he wasn't ready to be on the national stage and he didn't know how to handle his social conservative positions in that light. He was thrown into it very rapidly. And Joe Clark was still hanging around.

Conservatives, once again, were left to ponder the results. What if there had been one main opposition party fighting the Liberals, rather than two? Analysts were quick to superimpose the results of the 2000 campaign onto a combined Tory–Alliance scenario that assumed total retention of votes under the single party. There would have been a more forceful opposition, but Liberals would still have claimed the top prize. And the Liberals would still have won the popular vote (40.8 to 37.7), which was a wider gap than that of the 1997 campaign. The Liberals would also have more seats: 142 to 118.[24] Such an outcome would have placed the Liberal government in a minority position, but that was cold comfort to conservatives, who thought all they had to do to beat the Liberals was to join forces. Instead, these results showed that, to win, the conservative movement had to do much more than combine the parties.

Jean Chrétien and the Liberal party had won three successive majority governments "without even breaking a sweat."[25] To the detriment of the country, there was no effective opposition. Canadians heard little about the inadequacies of the Liberal administration because those on the opposition benches were more interested in fighting among themselves than in holding the government to account. The Liberals were playing in an arena where there was no competition.

WHILE CONSERVATIVES FOUGHT among themselves, Prime Minister Chrétien and Finance Minister Paul Martin had free rein to elimi-

---

[24] This was the conclusion of the election analysis from Simon Fraser University. See http://www.sfu.ca/~aheard/elections/index.htm (accessed July 10, 2006).
[25] This phrase was often used by the Right Honourable Brian Mulroney in speeches he delivered after the 2000 election.

nate the deficit by any manner they chose. An effective opposition, had it been in place, would have been able to make the case that eliminating the deficit had little to do with a judicious review of spending and much to do with raising taxes and diminishing the standard of living of every Canadian. An analysis of the government's finances from 1993 to 2000 revealed that there had been a $57.8-billion turnaround in government finances: from an inflation-adjusted $45.5-billion deficit to a $12.3-billion surplus.[26] What many Canadians did not fully appreciate is that $45.5 billion of that turnaround, some 70 per cent, was the result of higher taxes. The $18.3 billion in reduced spending came principally from three sources: transfers to provinces, National Defence, and payments to unemployed Canadians. Spending on actual federal government operations over this period increased by some $3 billion. As many commentators observed, Chrétien and Martin did not eliminate the deficit, they transferred it to the provinces.

Where the opposition should have been holding the government to account was the loss in value of the Canadian dollar. After peaking at US$0.8934 in 1991, the Canadian dollar began a steady fall and was only worth US$0.623 in November 2001. During Martin's tenure as finance minister, the dollar lost about one-quarter of its worth. Every time Canadians bought imported goods, they paid more. Every vacation outside Canada cost more. The Liberals contended that a weaker dollar was making the Canadian economy stronger because it was making Canadian exports less expensive. Brian Mulroney was one of the few to point out the fallacy of Liberal economics:

> Contrary to popular perception the declining dollar has not boosted competitiveness. Rather, it has undermined the incentive for Canadian companies to invest in expensive and usually imported new machinery thereby enhancing productivity, hurt

[26] "Measuring Progress: The State of Federal Government Finances, A Scorecard from the Canadian Institute of Chartered Accountants," April 1991. The author of this book was the principal author of the scorecard.

their ability to recruit top talent from abroad and reduced the
attractiveness of Canadian investments, leaving Canadian companies more vulnerable to takeovers at bargain prices. As a
result, Canada's competitiveness is in decline, from sixth place
in 1998 to eleventh in 2000. In consequence, the standard of
living of Canadians has been slipping relative to other countries. Even when measured by Purchasing Power Parity,
Canada's per capita GDP dropped from second in the world to
seventh in the last decade.[27]

With an ineffective opposition and no government in waiting,
elections had become meaningless. In short, democracy existed only
in name. The question remained, how long would this last? Canada
deserved better.

---

[27] Speech by Brian Mulroney to the PC Leadership Convention, June 10, 1983.

CHAPTER 10

HARPER TAKES THE ALLIANCE

NOT LONG AFTER THE NOVEMBER 2000 campaign, the knives came out in the Alliance party. After the disappointing election results and a steady stream of self-inflicted wounds, Stockwell Day lost the confidence of some key MPs, and they wanted him out. "People had such a built-in loyalty to Preston that they couldn't overcome it," said Day. He also admitted that a series of errors on his part contributed to his undoing. Usually such matters were sorted out in backroom machinations, but much of the rancour over Day's leadership took place in full public view. What transpired within the Alliance ranks for much of 2001 was nothing less than a farce.

Polls in early 2001 showed declining support for the Canadian Alliance, with Stockwell Day least trusted among the federal leaders. In April, deputy leader Deborah Grey and House leader Chuck Strahl resigned from caucus. Within months, thirteen of the most respected and experienced Alliance members left or were suspended from caucus. In July, Day faced a caucus-wide revolt that threatened to result in a caucus vote of non-confidence. Day learned what Brian Mulroney had always understood: "Without the support of caucus you have nothing."

The writing was on the wall, and Day knew it. He sounded a lot like Kim Campbell when he offered the view that he should have rebuilt the party with his own people rather than trying to win over those who did not support him on the leadership. "The mistake I made coming in was leaving all the Manning loyalists in place: in caucus and at party headquarters. In retrospect, that was not a wise move. It is not fair to expect people who didn't support you to be at your side when the going gets tough."

Facing open revolt is lethal to any leader. Day tried to hold off the dissidents. "The split-away group wanted me to step down, which was not a democratic response. When you are committed to democratic values you can't allow yourself to be overrun by what appears to be a lack of respect for democracy," Day said. In other words, it was up to party members, not caucus, to choose the party leader. Day had been leader for less than thirteen months. He had a choice to make. "Had I stepped down then, caucus would have disintegrated. The majority in caucus did not want me to step down. My supporters said fight it out, duke it out, and let's have a bloodbath. We will go after the dissidents in nomination meetings and we will have an all out war. I said no. Let's have a leadership race and that will carry us forward. It will settle things down and we will avoid tearing the party apart."

Right after the 2000 election, Day encouraged Alliance MPs to open up lines of communication with Tory MPs as a way to coordinate attacks on the government. A group of six Alliance MPs took these instructions a big step further and met with four Tory MPs, with the hopes of forming a partnership leading to a single conservative party.[1] A dinner meeting, a secret from Day but sanctioned by Joe Clark, took place in Ottawa at the swanky Rideau Club in late February 2001. Soon after news leaked of the dinner, Day said, "I am very encouraged by what is happening. No topic is being seen as verboten."[2] Clark offered a cautious statement about the talks: "From our point of view, the concept of merger is not on anybody's

---

[1] The Alliance MPs were Jay Hill, Gary Lunn, Chuck Strahl, Monte Solberg, Val Meredith, and John Williams. Representing the PC party were Bill Casey, Peter MacKay, Rick Borotsik, and Loyola Hearn.

[2] Sheldon Alberts and Joel-Denis Bellavance, "Tory-Alliance chat my idea, Day says," *National Post*, March 1, 2001, A6.

agenda. What will it lead to? From our point of view, we are interested in ensuring that the Liberal party doesn't get re-elected by default in the next election."[3] There were other signs of co-operation between the parties. Peter MacKay, one of the four Tory MPs meeting with Alliance members, travelled to Alberta to campaign for former Reform MP Ian McClelland, who was running in a provincial election.

Many of the participants at the February dinner met again in June 2001 to continue their discussions about co-operation. The meeting was hosted by Alliance MP John Williams in his Alberta riding of St. Albert, and progress was reported to be modest yet encouraging. "This is not going to come together like the big-bang theory. We don't want to move too quickly because we don't want one party to dominate," said Peter MacKay.[4] Vic Toews from the Alliance party said, "If one considers a baby's first step to be a small step, then it's a small step. But in the life of any parent, it's always an exciting time."

DISSIDENT ALLIANCE MPs went looking for a home in the summer of 2001. They gave themselves a name: the Democratic Representative Caucus (DRC). In August 2001, at Mont Tremblant, there were meetings between representatives of the DRC and the Progressive Conservative caucus to discuss methods of co-operation and alternate forms of organization. The Alliance party fought back by issuing an ultimatum to the dissidents to return to the fold or face expulsion. By early September three MPs returned home, but eight others formed a coalition with the Progressive Conservatives under the banner Progressive Conservative–Democratic–Representative Coalition. Leading the coalition was Joe Clark, flanked by former Alliance MPs Chuck Strahl as deputy leader and Deborah Grey as caucus chair. Their numbers were reduced to seven when Gary Lunn returned to the Alliance caucus in January 2002, as a sign of support for Stephen Harper.

---

[3] Ibid.

[4] Duncan Thorne, "No communique, but communication's fine: Trust is building, PC, Alliance MPs say after meetings," *Edmonton Journal*, June 21, 2001, A5.

Inevitably, the public meltdown affected the polls. By late summer 2001, the Alliance party had only single-digit support.[5] It had fallen 15.7 percentage points from the 2000 election, from 25.5 to 9.8, while the Tories had climbed 5.7 percentage points, from 12.2 to 17.9. The Liberals were also enjoying the show, and their support climbed from 40.9 per cent to 52.6 per cent. To its embarrassment, the Alliance was in third place in Alberta, behind the Liberals and the Tories.

In dismay, groups of conservatives began to organize themselves to urge the parties to reunite the conservative family. One such group, Expanding the Coalition: Working Group on Building a Strong Alternative, was formed in 2001 and co-chaired by Tory MP Rick Borotsik and the former national co-president of the Canadian Alliance, Ken Kalopsis. The group, which included more than a dozen luminaries from both parties, examined the pros and cons of a number of options for bringing the parties together.[6]

Stockwell Day promised to vacate the leadership of the Alliance party, and the race to replace him began to take shape. In December 2001, Stephen Harper and caucus members Diane Ablonczy and Grant Hill announced their candidacies. Taking a page out of the Joe Clark and Preston Manning history book, Stockwell Day resigned his leadership in December and became a leadership candidate in January. He might have learned from what happened to Clark in 1993 and to Manning in 2000 that returning as leader immediately after resigning seemed an impossible challenge (though Harper would later succeed). Day said, "If the members said they wanted a change so be it, but I felt I had to run to support the democratic principles of the party."

Ablonczy and Hill were both considered pro-merger candidates who remained close to Preston Manning. But Manning offered no help. "I didn't involve myself in the leadership," he said. Nonetheless,

---

[5] Ekos Research Associates Inc., "Confident Canadians ponder the future," August 31, 2001.

[6] Participants included Tories André Bachand and Rick Borotsik, both of whom refused to sit with the new Conservative caucus when the parties united in 2003.

he seemed prepared to concede that Harper should take over the party. "I had known for years, shortly after I hired Stephen, that he aspired to be leader. Stephen was never a follower. Leaders are rarely good followers."

Day clung to his leadership, but he was still focused on how to best unite the conservative family. The offer he made in 2001 to work with Joe Clark and the Tories was received with disdain and disrespect. "There were still some old Tories with deep imbedded venom over what happened in 1993," said Day, "but I have never seen the level of stubbornness that was in Joe Clark. At one point he sent over an emissary with an offer. He wanted us to join him, so long as he would remain leader. He suggested we try it for six months and then we would see. We fell off our chairs laughing." Day's response was to offer a merger and a leadership race. Clark was dismissive of anyone other than himself as leader.[7]

IN HIS FOUR YEARS as president of the National Citizen's Coalition, Stephen Harper had been spared much of the internal wrangling and discord in the Reform and Canadian Alliance parties. He watched as Reform failed to build any support beyond its traditional western base in the 1997 campaign; he bypassed the morphing of Reform into the Canadian Alliance in 1999–2000; and he kept his hands clean when Preston Manning lost the leadership to Stockwell Day. He watched Stockwell Day miss the best opportunity Alliance would ever likely get to defeat Jean Chrétien. Harper stayed on the sidelines when Stockwell Day self-destructed and the Alliance caucus effectively stripped him of his leadership. There was one question Harper had to answer for himself in 2001: was the Alliance party worth saving?

Harper was not quick to claim the throne as Alliance leader. In many ways he was a reluctant leader. Ultimately, however, Harper thought the party was worth one last effort: "If this party didn't

[7] Senator Gerry St. Germain also recalls that Clark was only prepared to consider merging with Alliance provided he would remain the leader. "He was never prepared to relinquish anything," said St. Germain.

exist, we'd need to create it. The party must not be allowed to implode. And if keeping the party alive requires me to run for the leadership, that's what I'll do. Because the party must survive."[8]

There were problems in the Alliance besides leadership. The party was deeply in debt, and donations had all but dried up.[9] Unlike many professional politicians, Harper was not a candidate waiting for an election to happen. There had to be a strong purpose and meaning to his candidacy, and he had every reason to be reluctant about seeking the Alliance leadership. On August 10, 2001, a fateful meeting took place in Calgary at the private 400 Club, attended by Stephen Harper, his brothers, Grant and Robert, Tom Flanagan, John Weissenberger, George Koch, and Mark Kihn. It was clear to those present that the Canadian Alliance was imploding under Day's leadership and that Joe Clark and the PCs were quickly picking up the pieces. Reflecting on the Alliance demise, however, was not the main item on the agenda: it was whether Harper should seek the leadership. They had to consider not only whether Stephen could win the race, but whether the party was worth saving. John Weissenberger, Reform party co-founder, said, "It was a pretty weighty decision, because it was very possible that we could put in a huge amount of effort and things could not be salvaged. We had to decide whether it was a realistic thing for Stephen to do, to salvage what could be salvaged. . . . We were trying to decide if this was worth doing."[10]

Perhaps the most persuasive argument that day was the fear that Joe Clark would end up as the voice of conservatism in Canada. There may also have been some pride in the room: everyone in attendance had invested years in the development of Reform and did not want to see their efforts go down the drain. If there was to be a battle to the death between the Tories and Alliance, these men thought Harper was the only person who could win. "If Stephen had not run as Alliance leader, it would have been a very tough go for the party. The stalwart Manning supporters were sitting with Joe Clark,"

---

[8] Johnson, *Stephen Harper*, 289.

[9] Ibid., 292.

[10] Duffy, "Stephen Harper," B4.

said Weissenberger. "Without Stephen, that would have been it for the Alliance."

By mid summer 2001, Harper officially indicated his intention to resign as president of the NCC, thereby signalling to Alliance members his interest in leading the party whenever the opportunity arose. At about the same time, Joe Clark and other PC caucus members were meeting with dissident Alliance members at Mont Tremblant to discuss co-operation among conservative-minded MPs. To Harper's dismay, this initiative was supported by Preston Manning. Manning's support further undermined the Alliance party's efforts to rebuild itself.

Harper's campaign for leadership did not start well, and he almost gave up in frustration. The problem was money, more specifically the lack of it. Without campaign offices or paid professional staff, a revamped campaign relied on high-powered volunteers to get the work done. Harper insisted that the campaign could not go into debt. The message sunk in as they charged $10 per head for party members to hear Harper speak. Party members clearly wanted Harper in the race and responded to a letter soliciting their support with donations of about $400,000, less than half of what was required to run Harper's leadership campaign.[11]

As campaign finances improved, so did the depth and quality of the effort. The main message to party members was this: "If you want to save the party from dying, vote Harper."

Tom Long was brought into the campaign to help build support in Ontario, but campaign insiders said he produced few results. When Harper heard that Ontario was in shambles, he vanished for three days. No one in the campaign knew where he was or what he was doing. A mid-campaign overhaul resulted, and Tom Flanagan was brought in as campaign manager. Instead of withdrawing in the face of adversity, Harper retrenched his team of core and trusted advisers. "He is not a control freak. When things are going well he is content to let them work," said Yaroslav Baran. "But Harper can be

---

[11] Johnson, *Stephen Harper*, 298.

very blunt, which some people find hard to take. He does not always exchange social pleasantries well. It's not that he intends to make people feel bad." When he was around people he knew, Harper could express himself more freely.

COMMENTATORS WOULD OFTEN compare an Alliance party under Harper to the Reform party under Preston Manning. In a press interview during the leadership campaign, without mentioning Manning by name, Harper articulated the basic differences in approach. "What we've got to do is turn this party into an institution. It's too often been viewed as a popular protest movement or a regional fragment or a leader-centric vehicle or a coalition thrown together for a single election. I think the way to address that is to show people that we are prepared to build a permanent professional political institution, one that they can dedicate their loyalty to on an ongoing basis."[12] Manning's vision of Reform had always been to ride a wave of popular discontent with the mainstream parties, win government, then realign the structure of political parties to be more consistent with the views of the common man. He was not institutional or purely devoted to conservatism, even if conservatism was the reality of his party's membership. Harper, in contrast, spoke of the need for the Alliance to provide a clear voice for conservatism in Canada: "He [Joe Clark] is intent as always on forming a second Liberal Party. And we want to form something different."

Harper won the one-member, one-vote contest on one ballot. But Stockwell Day remained a formidable opponent. While Harper initially concentrated on earning support from the long-standing Reform party members, Day remained deeply connected to the highly motivated and easily congregated evangelical Christian community. Harper was worried about what Day could produce on the ground and eventually invested in phone banks and technology that

---

[12] Kevin Michael Grace, "Getting back on track: The Canadian Alliance's newly elected leader, Stephen Harper, says his task now is to turn his party, often viewed as a regional protest movement, into an alternative government," *Montreal Gazette*, March 22, 2002, B3.

helped bring memberships in the door. "We took the leadership race very seriously. We took nothing for granted," recalled John Weissenberger.

Many party members had concluded that Stockwell Day had to go. But not because he was overly ambitious or antagonistic. Party staff member Tom Jarmyn said, "I will say this to the day I die, Stockwell Day is the nicest man I have ever met in politics. He is concerned about people and that engenders tremendous loyalty. He is a warm and kind person. People will walk through walls for Stockwell Day. But I told him he shouldn't run again for leader in 2002 because he had become a punchline."

Harper won the support of 48,561 members, who represented 55 per cent of the 88,228 votes cast. Day finished second with a respectable 37.5 per cent of the votes. The other leadership candidates, Diane Ablonzy and Grant Hill, favoured a merger with the Tories. Combined, they received only 7.5 per cent of the votes cast.

Had Day beat Harper, the hand of Joe Clark would have been strengthened considerably. The dissident Canadian Alliance members, in coalition with the Tories in the Democratic Representative Coalition, would have been loath to return to the Alliance under Day. The Alliance would have restricted itself to a largely western-based socially conservative perspective, with no realistic prospects of growth.

How would Harper's win affect a possible merger between the Alliance and Tory parties? The answer was anything but clear. If Day had won, the party might well have been weakened to the brink of death, making the merger a simple matter of picking up the pieces. The party might also have retained a resilient and religiously fervent core under Day, with views that were irreconcilable with the views of the Tory party. Day said, "Ultimately, the ballot question in the leadership was, who can get us out of this, and clearly most people thought it was Stephen, and he has proven them right."

After winning the leadership, Harper took stock. With the party almost $3 million in debt and support in the polls at around 10 per cent, the road to becoming prime minister was anything but clear.

THE ALLIANCE PARTY MATURED QUICKLY under Harper's leadership. It emerged from its populist roots—disgruntled westerners advocating economic and social policies that were out of touch with mainstream Canadians—and became a more focused, thoughtful, and intelligent conservative party. Stephen Harper had always been a policy wonk, and had been frustrated by the Reform policy development process in its early days.

Harper still had to deal with the unity of his party. In principal that meant bringing DRC members, including stalwarts Deborah Grey and Chuck Strahl, into his caucus. On March 28, 2002, Grey and Strahl, along with Ken Kalopsis, penned an open letter in the hopes of stirring a "fresh opportunity for reconciliation amongst democratic conservatives in Canada." While expressing hope that new leadership in the Alliance would be a positive step, they also referred to the very positive experience they had working with the Tories in the PC-DRC Coalition. "We have made new friends and respect has developed amongst good-willed people previously walled off from each other by the unfortunate constraints of bitter partisan rivalry," the open letter said. There were kind words for Senator Lowell Murray, and Joe Clark was singled out for praise: "Joe Clark has been constructive, open-minded and accommodating in encouraging recent foes to work constructively and respectfully with one another, and . . . without his encouragement the young coalition would likely not have come into existence nor been able to flourish." Strahl and Grey made three suggestions to promote reconciliation: a joint party task force on policy; a joint commission on developing a co-operative electoral strategy; and a working coalition in the House of Commons. Strahl and Grey advocated that Joe Clark and Stephen Harper sit down and co-operatively work out a plan to end the disunity and dysfunction that had plagued the conservative movement for more than a decade.

Not long thereafter, Stephen Harper reached out to Joe Clark, seeking a merger of the parties or some other form of agreement that would end vote splitting. Harper, who during the Alliance leadership race had suggested there would be no hope of co-operation so long as Clark was the Tory leader, had begun to rethink his position.

He told Alliance members at a party convention that he was open to proposals and that serious ideas would be submitted to party members for consideration. The lone meeting between Clark and Harper, on April 9, lasted only a few hours. Graham Fox, Clark's chief of staff, and Ray Speaker, a former Reform MP, also attended.

Clark came to the meeting with a written proposal on a range of issues dealing more with methods of co-operation than with a merger. Clark listened to what Harper had to say before concluding that what was on the table would have made his party the "junior partner" in a coalition. Apparently, Harper did not see equality between the sixty-six-member Alliance caucus and the twelve Tory MPs Clark represented. "Stephen was willing to deal with Joe, even on a regional split. But Joe would have none of it," said Weissenberger. Harper and Clark did not go deep enough to deal with the thorny issue of how a co-operative venture would be led. Some close to the discussion between Clark and Harper saw ambition as a stumbling block to progress and suggested that Harper was prepared to put his leadership on the line but Clark wasn't.

It would have been difficult for Clark to return to his caucus and tell them he agreed to a proposal that would give his side only one out of every six key positions in the Opposition (the same proportion as the number of MPs between the two caucuses). Clark suggested the thirty PC senators should be included in determining the size of his caucus.

Clark's hesitation about a merger did not place him fundamentally at odds with party members. Internal party polls showed about half wanted to combine with the Alliance, while the other half wanted to fight to the death. The split was widely known and could be exploited easily by Harper. Always the master tactician, Harper caught Clark flat-footed when he left the talks and proceeded immediately to the press gallery theatre, where he delivered his message that the country would have to wait for Clark to be replaced by some "future leader" before meaningful progress could be achieved.

A significant number of senior PC party members disagreed with Clark. PC senator David Angus began to change his views about co-operating with the Alliance: "I developed a very negative attitude towards Reform and Preston Manning following the 1993 election. But as I worked with some of their MPs on joint parliamentary committees it was clear to me that these were *our* people. I thought we should have been able to work with them." Having Manning out of the leader's chair helped: "He was a very destructive person. The premise of abandoning the ship was wrong; it was unjustified. He split the party and took away the disciples from the West." Mulroney held a similar view, and vowed that so long as he had influence there would be no merger or reconciliation between the parties while Preston Manning was in a position of influence.

With no prospect of a merger or reconciliation, all but one DRC member returned to the Alliance caucus on April 16, 2002. Only Inky Mark, the MP from Dauphin–Swan River–Marquette in Manitoba, remained independent. (He joined the Tories a few months later, on August 24, 2002.)

After the meeting with Joe Clark, Harper took his case directly to Progressive Conservatives in a column published in the *National Post* on May 1, 2002. The column advocated a three-phase approach. First was electoral co-operation, to deal with vote splitting. Second was establishing a coalition in the House of Commons. Third, and boldly expressed, was fully amalgamating the parties. Harper acknowledged the various strengths of the two parties and declared that the strategy of waiting until one wilted and died was tantamount to unending Liberal majorities.

While it may not have been his intent, he belittled the once great national Tory party by suggesting that its regional strength was limited to Atlantic Canada. It was difficult for Harper not to point to the relatively small Tory caucus and the need to dispose of the party's debt as evidence of the difficulties it faced. If he wanted a merger, offering faint praise was an unwise opening. Harper gave assurances that under a combined entity the important historical legacy of the Progressive Conservative party would be retained, and he offered a few complimentary passages about former prime minister Brian Mulroney. Yet there was a warning that the Tory legacy was in jeopardy: "My observation is that what many Progressive Conservatives value, far more than the causes which many of us share, is the preservation of your institution—the 'thin blue line' that links the party of Macdonald and Canadian Confederation to the majority governments of Brian Mulroney . . . . No matter how old and distinguished, a legacy cannot assure its own survival. Proof of this can be seen in Quebec, British Columbia and Saskatchewan, where the historic PC Party has all but vanished."

Harper couldn't resist taking a shot at anti-free-trade activist David Orchard. "Ironically, Mr. Mulroney's most lasting and worthwhile accomplishment—continental free trade—is more strongly attacked in your party than in any other. The growth of the David Orchard wing—a result of your last leadership race and the weakness of your current organization—is as much a threat to the Conservative legacy as any of your political opponents." This attempt to chide the Tories into submission showed a certain immaturity on Harper's part. Although it may have felt good to vent his feelings in the letter, it helped his cause not one iota.

WHEN HARPER TOOK OVER THE ALLIANCE leadership he brought with him more than the usual assortment of baggage. There was ample ammunition available to Harper's opponents to label this free-enterprise economist and president of a right-wing advocacy group as extreme and out of touch with mainstream Canadian values. In 2001, Harper had talked about building a firewall around Alberta ". . . to limit the extent to which an aggressive and hostile federal government can encroach upon legitimate provincial jurisdiction."[13] And earlier he had said, "Albertans should decide that it is time to seek a new relationship with Canada. . . . Having hit a wall, the next logical step is not to bang our heads against it. It is to take the bricks and begin building another home—a stronger and much more autonomous Alberta."[14]

---

[13] Harper, "Open Letter to Ralph Klein."

[14] Harper, "Separation, Alberta-style."

Commentators and opinion leaders might have excused tough talk from a right-wing think-tank president, but after he became leader they were eager to pounce on any statement that demonstrated the extremity of his views. It didn't take long.

On an east coast swing in May 2002, Harper said, "I think in Atlantic Canada, because of what happened in the decades following Confederation, there is a culture of defeat that we have to overcome. . . . Atlantic Canada's culture of defeat will be hard to overcome as long as Atlantic Canada is actually physically trailing the rest of the country."[15] He didn't stop there; the next day, he said, "There's unfortunately a view of too many people in Atlantic Canada that it's only through government favours that there's going to be economic progress, or that's what you look to . . . That kind of can't-do attitude is a problem in this country but it's obviously more serious in regions that have had have-not status for a long time . . . We have a program that says that Atlantic Canada can be as wealthy as any other region, but that needs to be pursued aggressively and we don't sit around waiting for favours."[16]

You have to give Harper credit for bravery. One might have expected such a comment to be made off the record to a bunch of frustrated western supporters; but Harper made his views known in full view in Atlantic Canada. Then he bragged about his boldness: "I've taken my position and frankly it's the same position that I took all through the [Alliance] leadership race. I delivered [speeches] everywhere I went, including in the Maritime provinces on several occasions, about the spirit of defeatism in the country and what drives it and how we have to address it."[17] Not satisfied with insulting Atlantic Canadians, Harper went after his western base: "I think in parts of the Prairies we are increasingly seeing similar views that

---

[15] "Harper says 'defeatist' attitude on East Coast needs changing," *The Telegram*, May 29, 2002, A8.

[16] "Harper plans to battle 'culture of defeatism' in Atlantic Canada," *The National*, CBC, May 30, 2002.

[17] Paul Wells, "Harper sticks to unpopular Atlantic stance," *National Post*, May 31, 2002, A8.

there is no hope, there is no way forward...generally the kind of can't-do attitude is a problem in this country but it's obviously more serious in regions that have had have-not status for a long time."[18]

Belittling the electorate is rarely a successful strategy. The Nova Scotia legislature, in a unanimous resolution, encouraged Harper to reflect upon the reality of achievement and optimism in the Atlantic region with his party's persistent string of defeats in most provinces. His political opponents began to string together Harper's comments. NDP leader Alexa McDonough, from Nova Scotia, said, "This is the real Stephen Harper who wanted to put up firewalls around Alberta to keep us nasty Eastern Canadians out because we're ne'er-do-wells and lazy bums."[19] Canadians had to wonder: who was the real Stephen Harper?

At the end of 2002, Harper had led his party for about nine months. Yet, when Canadians were asked who would make the best prime minister if Chrétien retired, only 2.3 per cent named Harper.[20] And that was down from the 3.1 per cent who gave him the nod in May, a little more than six months earlier. Paul Martin, on the other hand, was supported by 32.2 per cent of those surveyed. It was starting to look like the next campaign would resemble the 2000 election: no contest.

---

[18] Tonda MacCharles, "Eastern premiers blast Harper's 'defeatism'; But Alliance party leader stands by his remark," *Toronto Star*, May 30, 2002, A6.

[19] "Harper plans," *The National*, CBC, May 30, 2002.

[20] Ekos Research Associates Inc., "Federal political landscape and leadership," December 9, 2002, based on 1,205 completed interviews, accurate to within +/− 2.8 percentage points, 19 times out of 20.

CHAPTER 11

MACKAY TAKES THE PCS

T HE GOOD NEWS IS THAT I AM widely trusted and popular. The bad news is that we cannot translate those qualities into votes for the party."[1] This was how PC party leader Joe Clark described the political reality he faced when he announced his resignation on August 6, 2002. Clark confirmed to the national media what was already painfully obvious to anyone reading the polls: "For the party itself, the bad news is that [Progressive Conservatives] have not yet built a critical mass of Canadians who treat us as their first choice in an election."

Clark had translated bad news before. After a brief tenure in 1979 as Canada's youngest prime minister, Clark put his job on the line in 1983 because only *two-thirds* of the delegates at a national convention in Winnipeg endorsed his leadership. When Clark stepped down, the Tories were riding high in the polls. The country was fuming mad at Pierre Trudeau and the Liberal party. And it looked as if the Tories were poised for victory for the next election. But when the leadership vote was taken, Clark didn't want to take yes for an answer. Frustrated by the internal divisions within the party, Clark wanted to demonstrate his toughness by triggering a leadership contest. He didn't resign to leave the job; he resigned to reclaim it. But party members chose Brian Mulroney instead.

---

[1] Statement issued by the Right Honourable Joe Clark on August 6, 2002.

Clark came out of retirement in 1998 to reclaim the leadership he had voluntarily surrendered almost two decades earlier. The 2000 election would be his third as PC leader. He won a minority government in 1979 and promptly lost in 1980. Third time was not so lucky for Clark. The Tories won only 12 seats, the minimum threshold for official recognition as a party in the House of Commons.

Things weren't looking any better for Clark in August 2002. Despite his Alberta roots, Clark was unable to dent the grip the Canadian Alliance had on western conservatives. His party had anemic ratings in the polls. Canadians were having trouble finding anything in Clark to get excited about, and he had struck out in gaining any deal with the Alliance to end vote splitting. To top it off, a sledgehammer was about to land on Clark's head. The party's regular national convention, to be held in Edmonton in late August, would give delegates the opportunity to vote on Clark's leadership.

The leadership question was always asked of delegates at a convention after an election in which the party did not form a government. Party members would be asked: do you support Mr. Clark as leader of the party? Media reports speculated that Clark would receive more than the 50 per cent minimum to keep his job, but far less than the two-thirds support he received at the 1983 national convention where he had voluntarily resigned. Sean Durkan of the *Hill Times* suggested the result would be "a very embarrassing and damaging victory."[2] More important, Clark did not have the support of his caucus. During the summer of 2002, Greg Thompson, MP for New Brunswick Southwest, canvassed the caucus and found that Clark had the support of only a few members, notably Scott Brison and Peter MacKay. Thompson delivered the grim news to Clark in the form of an ultimatum: either step down as leader, or go to the convention, where his caucus would openly urge the delegates to vote for a leadership review. If there is one thing the leader of a political party needs, it's caucus. Brian

[2] Sean Durkin, "Joe's bold move might just work for Tories," *Hill Times*, August 12, 2002.

Mulroney's quip bears repeating: "Without the support of caucus, you have nothing."

So Clark had to face facts. He had kept the party from dying in 2000, but the party had lost about one-third of its seats under his leadership and had won in only 12 of 301 ridings. Clark decided to resign before a convention vote on his leadership to avoid rejection by party members.

While the leadership vote was off the convention agenda, co-operation with the Alliance was on. A contingent of delegates from Ottawa Centre placed a motion before the Edmonton convention seeking the removal of the "301" clause from party by-laws. The clause, endorsed by more than 95 per cent of delegates at a convention in 1999, required the party to run candidates in every riding. This prevented local riding associations from fielding joint candidates with the Alliance party to avoid vote splitting. Presumably, a mechanism would be found to determine which of the two parties had the better chance of winning a particular riding, and that party would get the nod to run a candidate. John Crosbie, a former cabinet minister in the Clark and Mulroney governments, spoke against the motion. Crosbie represented an Atlantic perspective, a region where vote splitting was not a factor. Western Canada was also somewhat immune, as Alliance losses there were usually not the result of having a Tory candidate on the ballot. Vote splitting occurred mostly in Ontario. Although the motion failed to achieve the required two-thirds support, almost half the delegates did vote in favour. "With the support we received at the convention," said Bill Pristanski, who had introduced the motion, "we put the issue back in play. Going into the 2003 leadership contest, the 301 clause was now a debatable subject within the party. It was an important first step in paving the way towards co-operation with the Alliance."

Alliance leader Stephen Harper took Clark's departure as an opportunity to open a new dialogue with the Tories. He suggested the parties come together to hold a joint leadership convention. While this might have appeared bold, it was hardly a risky proposition for Harper. The membership roll of the very activist Alliance party was thought to be double or triple that of the PCS. Such an imbalance would give Harper a huge advantage in a leadership race, and he would have coasted to an easy win over any Tory rival. No one in the Tory party took him seriously, and the race to replace Clark was on. The remaining eleven members of the PC caucus set out to choose an interim leader. Elsie Wayne, one of only two PCS elected in 1993, desperately wanted the job, but she faced stiff opposition. Although Wayne prevailed, consensus did not come easy that day.

EARLY SPECULATION ON candidates to replace Clark focused on three current or former provincial premiers. When Ralph Klein of Alberta and Mike Harris of Ontario immediately rejected the notion, attention swung to Bernard Lord of New Brunswick. Fluently bilingual, experienced in government, loyal to the party, and a proven winner, Lord seemed to be a good prospect in 2002. He had delivered an inspirational keynote address to the Edmonton policy convention, and later that day was mobbed in his hospitality suite by Tory delegates. No provincial premier had become prime minister of Canada. Perhaps Lord remembered this when he declined the invitation.

Almost every media pundit who handicapped the Tory leadership race made Peter MacKay the early favourite. Other potential candidates from the twelve-member caucus were Scott Brison from Nova Scotia and André Bachand from Quebec. Bachand entered the race but withdrew before the convention and threw his support to MacKay. From outside caucus, there were only two serious candidates: long-time party activist Jim Prentice and anti-free-trade crusader David Orchard.

MacKay had earned his way to front-runner status by virtue of his performance in Parliament and his ability to build strong and meaningful relationships with Tories in all parts of the country. It also helped that MacKay was connected to the Mulroney legacy by virtue of his father's role in the 1983 leadership contest and the nine years he served in Mulroney's cabinet. But Peter had earned his shot at the title. Within months of the 1997 campaign, journalists had begun to describe MacKay as a rising star: someone who could one day lead the party. In early 1998, the *Hill Times* had ranked him as a favourite up-and-coming politician. When Charest left for Quebec, there was considerable speculation about MacKay as a contender for the top job. But MacKay had quickly quashed the suggestion: "It's like putting the boxer in the ring too early, you don't want to get pummeled."[3] His father agreed, and even wondered in 2003 if running for the leadership was premature, if not audacious.

MacKay's charisma and accessibility made him something of a favourite with the media, and it was his performance in question period that made the media stand up and take notice. Respected CTV News host Mike Duffy could be overheard saying that MacKay was clearly the class of the field.

There are a few "automatics" that come with front-runner status. First, key party operatives jump onto the campaign team. Second, you raise more money than your opponents. And third, everyone else in the race gangs up against you.

A campaign team formed around MacKay in the early days after Clark's resignation. Leading the charge as campaign chair was Bill Pristanski, lobbyist with Prospectus Associates and a former executive assistant to Brian Mulroney. MacKay was also supported by his longtime assistant, Maureen Murphy-Makin, who was from his home province of Nova Scotia and who had worked in his father's office.

The support of Pristanski and other Mulroney loyalists, and of most of the PC senators and members of parliament, gave the impression that MacKay was the "establishment candidate." This was another way of saying he had the support of Brian Mulroney. As a consequence, Pristanski argued, Joe Clark and PC party headquarters were not inclined to do MacKay any favours. There was a longstanding feud between Mulroney and Clark, stemming back to 1976, when both ran for party leader. Clark blamed Mulroney for

---

[3] Beverley Ware, "MacKay says no to leadership bid," *Halifax Daily News*, March 24, 1998, 11.

much of the internal dissension that had plagued his first term as leader. Even with Mulroney out of office for almost a decade, and Clark's resignation in 2002, party members could still be identified by their loyalty to one of the two men. People inside party headquarters claim MacKay was always treated fairly and that Pristanski's complaints were simply smart politics, to refute the negative label of being the establishment candidate. If anyone had a legitimate accusation of bias and unfair treatment it was David Orchard, who never won any of the disputes he took to party staff.

Rick Morgan, a Quebecer and a former executive assistant to Brian Mulroney, was brought in to lead MacKay's campaign through stage one: electing delegates in each riding across Canada. Party stalwart John Laschinger was hired about three months before the convention to finish the job. "Lasch," as he was widely known, is perhaps Canada's only full-time political professional. Most campaign managers got hired because they had some history with a particular candidate; Laschinger was in a different category. He was frequently brought into campaigns and regions with which he had little familiarity. Strategically driven and a believer in the value of polling, Lasch focused on one goal: *winning*. He brought Mike Harris to the leadership of the Ontario PC party and steered Bernard Lord to victory as premier in New Brunswick. He had been campaign manager at two previous federal PC leadership conventions and was the party's national campaign manager in 2000. Lasch was also a student of politics: in 1992, with *Globe and Mail* columnist Jeffery Stevens, he co-authored the book *Leaders and Lesser Mortals: Backroom Politics in Canada*.

In addition to Pristanski and Laschinger, MacKay had Duncan Rayner, a man with encyclopedic knowledge of the party, its workers, and every riding in the country. Rayner had twice served as director of organization for the party and was working in Elsie Wayne's office when the opportunity to help MacKay arose. Every candidate had a Duncan Rayner: someone who could connect the campaign with provincial, regional, and local organizers, as well as individual delegates. Keeping track of the database of delegates, appropriately named the "black box," was database whiz and political operative Doug Earle.

MacKay had a network of supporters in almost every riding in Canada. Every Sunday evening for the three months before the convention, a national conference call was held with fifty or more volunteers leading the provincial and regional desks for MacKay. Nowhere was field organization more important than in the province of Quebec, where experienced and well-connected field operatives could resurrect moribund riding associations to deliver full slates of delegates for MacKay.

The other candidate from caucus was Scott Brison. Like Clark, Brison had been a Tory from birth. He had become the party's youth president, a stepping stone to fulfilling his lifelong ambition to be a parliamentarian. First elected to the House of Commons in 1997, the member from Kings–Hants, Nova Scotia, was known for his sharp wit, strong debating skills, entrepreneurial orientation, and economic policy expertise. He served as co-chairman of the Tory 2000 Policy Platform Committee, and in February 2001 he was elected vice-chairman of the prestigious House of Commons finance committee. Unlike most MPs, Brison enjoyed the fruits of outside employment, including a job he started in March 2000 as vice-president of investment banking at Yorkton Securities. Brison was a close confidant of Joe Clark, a connection that kept him plugged into party headquarters throughout the leadership race. Brison resigned his seat in 2000 to enable Clark to enter the House of Commons in a by-election. Only a few months after the by-election, a general election was called; Brison reclaimed his Nova Scotia seat, and Clark won in Calgary Centre. So close were Brison and Clark that they referred to themselves as the Batman and Robin of Kings–Hants. Clark officially claimed neutrality in the leadership race, but few believed that he was anything but committed to Brison.

Calgary lawyer and native land claims specialist Jim Prentice was the only Albertan in the race. Prentice was the elected treasurer of the party during the final years of the Mulroney government and had the unenviable task of dealing with bankers and donors immediately after the party's massive defeat in 1993. He was also one of the few westerners who had stayed loyal to the Tories during the rise of Preston Manning's Reform party.

It was not just because he was a westerner that Prentice was seen as the candidate most likely to co-operate with the Alliance. As the nominated PC candidate in the 2002 by-election for Calgary Southwest, the seat vacated by Preston Manning, Prentice withdrew when Alliance leader Stephen Harper became his party's candidate. This was partly a symbolic gesture, often accorded to a party leader who runs in a by-election. But it was more than that. In announcing his withdrawal from the by-election Prentice said, "My message to both parties today is simply this: let us lay down our arms. We are all conservatives. Let us focus upon those things which unite us . . . Let today be the last day we campaign against one another."[4] Withdrawing from the by-election was not easy for Prentice. He said, "For all the hours that had been put into winning the nomination and preparing for the campaign, it was a painful decision to make. But as a unity candidate, I felt I could not run against the man who was leading the party that was the other half of our family."

Except for a short period as a nominated by-election candidate, Prentice had no electoral experience. This was painfully evident at the beginning stages of the leadership campaign; Prentice seemed awkward and ill prepared at debates and party events. His performance dramatically improved as the campaign progressed, and he proved popular with party members who were willing to consider co-operation with the Alliance. However, in his speeches he would soft-pedal his leanings towards co-operation so as not to lose appeal with delegates who were dead set against anything to do with Stephen Harper and the descendents of the Reform party. Nonetheless, there were enough quips early in the campaign about being a "unity candidate" and "rebuilding the national conservative

---

4 Tom Maloney, "Tory steps aside for Harper: Unite-the-right supporter calls for end to vote splitting," *Ottawa Citizen*, March 31, 2002, A10.

coalition" to indicate that, among the legitimate candiates, he was the one most likely to lead a merger of the parties.

Anti-free-trade activist David Orchard had been a leadership candidate in 1998, when he won a respectable 16 per cent of the delegates on the first ballot. Orchard acknowledged those who said he came into the party "like a rock through a stained glass window." He ran as a Tory in the 2000 election in the Diefenbaker riding of Prince Albert, Saskatchewan, and finished in fourth place with a dismal 12 per cent of the vote. It was not much of a showing. Orchard thought of himself as a national leader, yet he suffered from a lack of support in his own community, even if he did outpoll other PC candidates in Saskatchewan. Nonetheless carrying the flag for the party in a general election demonstrated Orchard's commitment and loyalty to the party and to Joe Clark. It also showed that he could run under a platform that was not his own. Orchard said, "Some things I agreed with and some I disagreed with. Elizabeth May of the Sierra Club said we had the best platform of all political parties on the environment. In the policy convention we got a labelling law on GMOs and a review of all our trade agreements with respect to the environment. We got things that I was proud of. We lost more than we won, we accepted the losses, and we moved on. But I was always loyal." He said the 2000 campaign had not been without discomfort: "Mr. Laschinger [PC Party national campaign manager] wanted me to sign a document, which I felt went beyond the pale; something to the effect of a loyalty document. I told him I had paid my dues and was not going to sign the document." In 2003, Orchard continued his crusade as he once again offered his candidacy for party leader.

David Orchard was perhaps the most gracious, clear-headed, and consistent candidate in the race. He was quick on his feet and always had something substantial to say. But to many in the party, Orchard was a liability. Some called him a kook for his ardent nationalism and fervent opposition to the North American Free Trade Agreement. While Orchard likened himself to former Tory prime ministers Borden and Diefenbaker, he had to know his policies would not resonate with modern-day conservatives. Even the highly nationalist and socialist NDP, the party many Canadians thought would have been the logical home for Orchard, were no longer calling for the abrogation of the trade pact. By 2003, all political parties had accepted that free trade was good for the economy.

Orchard entered the race knowing he had no chance of winning. His goal was to make an impact and advance the nationalist causes he had talked about in his 1993 book, *The Fight for Canada*. The other leadership contestants used Orchard's presence in the race as a motivating factor. If loyal party members did not participate and recruit new members, warned the other candidates, Orchard might win, and the party would be in ruins. Orchard was the party's colourful and controversial contrarian who could claim support from such diverse people as country-and-western singer Stompin' Tom Connors and celebrated author Margaret Atwood. (It was hard to imagine the left-leaning Atwood finding anyone in the Tory party worth supporting.) Orchard was also supported by one of Canada's wealthiest industrialists. Frank Stronach, chairman of multi-billion-dollar auto parts supplier Magna Corporation, had amassed much of his fortune through trade with American markets. Curiously, Stronach gave Orchard $45,000 to launch his campaign. According to Orchard, he and Frank Stronach had a long-standing relationship based on a mutual opposition to free trade. While Stronach's daughter Belinda had been cozying up to conservatives over the past few years— including leaders from Reform, Alliance, and the PC parties—Frank was a Liberal. He ran unsuccessfully as the Liberal candidate in the 1988 election in the riding of York Mills, Ontario. Stronach's support for Orchard was a curiosity for many. It seemed reasonable to ask why a well-known Liberal was supporting an aspiring Tory leadership candidate who had no chance of winning.

MacKay maintained a civil relationship with Orchard throughout the leadership race. While there were clear disagreements on policy, the sparring between the two in debates was always friendly and respectful. "Of all the candidates, Orchard was the guy that was least vicious and visceral to me. He always presented himself in a respectful manner and we had a distant but very cordial relationship," said

MacKay, who had no difficulty being respectful while disagreeing with his opponents: "Orchard said some things that I thought were kind of kooky. I didn't think he was particularly conservative in many ways in terms of the approach he was advocating. But he was a legitimate person who brought a lot of new people into the party. There is no denying that he brought in people that would have never darkened the door of a Conservative convention. I had absolutely no malice towards him." Orchard appreciated MacKay's approach and told Bill Pristanski, "Of the candidates, Peter is the only one that talks about issues. The others are constantly attacking each other."

Many people in the MacKay camp wanted Orchard attacked. They thought of Orchard as a pariah in the party. "Bring Orchard down and the party will thank us for it," was the advice from some of MacKay's supporters at a national campaign meeting on April 13, 2003. But why would he do that? Orchard was never going to win. Why alienate someone who might ultimately become an important ally? Besides, it was not in Peter MacKay's character to pick a fight for no good reason.

In 1998, Joe Clark had labelled Orchard a "tourist" in the party. The quip was frequently repeated, even after Clark and Orchard developed a more respectful relationship. MacKay realized that for the sake of party unity it was best to treat all candidates with consideration and respect. It also seemed unwise for the fifth party in the House of Commons to alienate anyone who wanted to contribute time, money, and energy to its cause. Orchard was odd, but he was also harmless, unless, of course, candidates made a big deal over his presence and policies.

At the April 13 meeting in Ottawa, MacKay's only "in-person" national campaign meeting, both Pristanski and Laschinger pleaded with the thirty or so provincial and regional chairs to be respectful to all candidates. "We told them we needed second and third ballot support. That meant not doing anything to alienate any of the other candidates," said Pristanski. Laschinger directed the team not to bother running delegates in the home ridings of the other candidates. This command was promptly ignored, as the MacKay volunteers in the trenches preferred to win every battle, even at the risk of losing the war. "MacKay's team ran a very polarizing campaign," said Prentice. This suggested to Prentice that the prospects of any of the major combatants supporting MacKay on a second or subsequent ballot were low. And since MacKay and Orchard had waged the most and the toughest battles for delegates at the riding level, Prentice thought these two were the least likely to strike a deal at the convention.

Pristanski especially wanted the campaign team to be respectful of Orchard. "He is the only one in this race who can't win. There is absolutely nothing to be gained by taking Orchard down," Pristanski said. He reminded the team that if Prentice or Brison were on the final ballot, MacKay would need Orchard to win. Most of the campaign team found this upsetting and were incredulous. How could MacKay conceive of making a deal with Orchard and giving him credibility?

Pristanski recalled an earlier convention where a decision had to be made, to ensure the right candidates were on the final ballot. "In 1983, Marc Dorion was the youth chair for Mulroney in Quebec," said Pristanski, who in 1983 was a senior Mulroney organizer. "After the first ballot Dorion persuaded the entire contingent of Quebec Clark youth delegates to come to Mulroney. We told them to stay put. We knew we could beat Clark on the final ballot so there was nothing to be gained by angering his camp. More important, had Clark's numbers fallen, we might have ended up facing John Crosbie on the final ballot. We knew we would beat Clark but we weren't sure if we would win against Crosbie. We had to make sure Clark outlasted Crosbie, so we told Dorion to keep the Quebec Clark youth delegates voting for Clark until the time came." What was evident to Crosbie and Mulroney was not so clear to Clark. In her autobiography, Clark's wife, Maureen McTeer, described the scene where Newfoundland premier Brian Peckford asked Clark to withdraw before the third ballot and support Crosbie: "The number-three person on the ballot was asking the number-one candidate and current leader to fold up his tent and join his camp against the number-two contender. It might have made sense to the Crosbie team, but it made no sense to us at all. Our campaign team was shocked, but within seconds that turned to anger."[5] McTeer's anger escalated, and she was heard to say of Peckford, "Get this stupid bastard out of here." But it turned out he hadn't been so stupid: he had been right. Pristanski didn't want emotion and illogical thinking to cloud MacKay's strategy. He knew the only final ballot where MacKay was assured of victory was Orchard versus MacKay. In other words, keeping Orchard strong was in MacKay's interest.

There was little question that MacKay and Orchard were on opposite sides on most issues. MacKay was a strong supporter of free trade and free markets. As a former Crown prosecutor, he took a hard line on criminal justice issues and opposed the decriminalization of marijuana. These were positions one might expect from an older candidate, but not from an otherwise modern thirty-seven-year-old MP. MacKay might be seen as a Blue Tory and Orchard a Red Tory, but they shared a passion for protecting the environment. MacKay's mother was an environmentalist, as was his sister Mary. Mary looked like, talked like, and thought like many of the Orchard delegates, and moved freely in their midst throughout the convention. Given Orchard's clout, everyone at this convention went out of his or her way to look "green."

New Brunswick senator Noël Kinsella, a strong supporter of MacKay, had been a lifetime advocate for environmental and social justice issues. Unlike many Tories who treated Orchard scornfully, Kinsella had worked with Orchard on developing party policy, and they had become friends. Not many people in the Prentice and Brison camps had a similar relationship with Orchard, which would be to their detriment. Geoff Chutter, a two-time PC election candidate from B.C., was Jim Prentice's designated point man on David Orchard. Unfortunately for Prentice, Chutter had a much less familiar relationship with Orchard than did Kinsella. With the knowledge and consent of MacKay's senior campaign team, Kinsella kept in contact with Orchard throughout the leadership campaign. The bond of

---

[5] McTeer, *In My Own Name*, 156.

trust between Orchard and Kinsella would prove critical to the outcome of the convention.

Understanding the relationship between MacKay and Brison was more difficult. They were both from Nova Scotia and had come into Parliament together in 1997. On economic issues, Brison and MacKay were largely indistinguishable from one another. Although Brison liked to say he had bold new ideas, few could recall what any of them were. MacKay was into rough-and-tumble team sports like hockey and rugby, while Brison preferred the more solitary sport of long-distance running. One notable difference between them was that MacKay was straight and Brison was gay. Many speculated that Brison felt MacKay would be unsupportive of a gay man leading the party, although MacKay said it was a non-issue. To this day, MacKay does not understand why he and Brison were estranged.

The other key relationship in the campaign was between candidate and money. "If you want to know who is going to win, watch where the money goes," quipped John Laschinger. "Money always finds the winner." Fundraising for MacKay, which started out sluggishly because of poor organization and was of obvious concern to the candidate, became Laschinger's number-one priority. The official party list of donations larger than $200 reveals that MacKay raised $980,400, Prentice $427,350, Brison $315,975, and David Orchard $275,335. Among the more interesting donations to MacKay was an early $10,000 contribution from the Right Honourable Brian Mulroney and $100,000 from Magna International. Belinda Stronach arranged the latter donation. Belinda also raised funds for MacKay from her wide array of contacts. As noted, Magna hedged its bet, giving $45,000 to David Orchard and $20,000 to André Bachand (who dropped out before the convention). After the convention, the losing candidates tried to initiate controversy over the disclosure of financial contributors. Party officials confirmed that MacKay was the only candidate who provided all information required under the rules of the contest within the specified time frames.

MacKay needed money for more than campaign posters and buttons. Full-time staff had to be paid, and many delegates needed help with their convention costs. On average, a delegate's cost to register and attend the weekend convention would be about $1,500. While most paid their own way, delegates from the province of Quebec were given "special status," and were more likely to have their convention costs reimbursed by the campaign they support.

THE PARTY WANTED AN EXCITING convention and was worried that a one-member, one-vote system would be a dull affair. The party needed media interest. A number of bizarre and arcane rules were developed to stimulate drama and suspense. A delegated convention, with the inevitable deal-making among candidates, would provide the best television, but would also smack of a bygone era of undemocratic backroom politics. So the party ended up choosing a hybrid system. Party members elected delegates from their ridings to attend the convention, and for the first ballot these delegates were "locked in" to vote for the candidate they had declared as their preference at the delegate selection meeting. Each delegate was pre-approved by a particular candidate's team. The delegates who received the most votes at a local riding would be accredited to vote at the convention. To ensure that delegates honoured their declared intention, their first-ballot vote was cast automatically at the convention. The twist, and excitement, came from the second and subsequent ballots, where the elected delegates would be free to vote for whomever they chose. Only those who were ex-officio delegates—such as MPs, former MPs, and party officers—were free to choose a candidate for their first-ballot vote.

The system offered the advantage of preventing a candidate with 51 per cent of support in a particular riding from sweeping all the delegates. A candidate who received 25 per cent of the votes in a riding would effectively receive 25 per cent of first-ballot votes from delegates. This gave an incentive to all leadership candidates to sell party memberships in every riding, even in areas where their level of support was low. The rules gave candidates with minimal support a chance to win delegates and influence at the convention. "If we had any other set of rules we would have won on the first ballot," said

MacKay campaign chair Bill Pristanski. "The rules favoured the underdog in every way imaginable."

It wasn't just the delegate selection process that was complicated. The convention voting rules stipulated that any candidate receiving at least 5 per cent of the total vote on the first ballot would remain on the second ballot. Normally, the candidate who received the lowest number of votes on any ballot would be eliminated from subsequent ballots. But for this convention, there was no consequence to coming in last place, so long as the candidate had 5 per cent of the vote. This particular provision was adopted late in the process, and without consultation with all candidates. Many speculated that this bizarre rule was put in place by party officials to help Scott Brison, who was expected to be in last place on ballot one. Paul Lepsoe, who had been nominated as co-chair of the leadership selection committee before becoming MacKay's legal counsel, said, "The rules we ended up with were not what had originally been discussed." When asked if Joe Clark had a hand in changing the rules to support Brison, Lepsoe responded, "Given that there was a distinct 'anybody but Peter' movement, it's the only theory that I've seen that makes sense." The notion of a conspiracy can only be taken so far, however, because it was not until the Friday night speeches that the man destined to finish in last place on the first ballot, Craig Chandler, withdrew from the race.

There were other wild cards in the system. First, would the approximately five hundred ex-officio delegates (riding presidents, past candidates, senators, former MPs, party officials) come to the convention, and how would they vote? Second, would elected delegates invest the time and money to show up at the convention? And third, would candidates be able to hold their delegates on the second and subsequent ballots? Complicating the travel issue was the SARS crisis in the host city, Toronto, and delegate worries about health.[6]

---

[6] SARS (Severe Acute Respiratory Syndrome) is a severe form of pneumonia, spread mainly by close contact. There was an outbreak in Toronto and a number of other cities throughout the world in the spring of 2003. There were forty-four deaths and 375 infections attributed to SARS in the city of Toronto in 2003. See http://www.thestar.com/static/PDF/030926_sars_h4_h5.pdf (accessed July 10, 2006).

In well-established ridings, the key to a candidate's success was to secure the support of the leading local Tory volunteers. The stronger candidates had a network of provincial and regional chairs who recruited volunteers to sell memberships and identify potential delegates. In areas where the party was weak, riding associations might have lapsed, leaving no structure in place to organize a meeting and elect delegates. To resuscitate some of these ridings required only a handful of live bodies. Easy victories and many delegate spots were available to leadership contenders who were prepared to do basic organizational work.

Most of the moribund riding associations were in Quebec. MacKay's team was far better at organizing Quebec delegates than were the other teams, largely because of the skills of José Nicolas, Benoit Laroque, Dany Renaud, Denis Jolette, and Johanne Senecal, all longtime party operatives recruited into the MacKay team. The Quebec delegates were the liveliest at the convention. Arriving en masse in well-appointed buses, MacKay's jovial Quebec delegates were entertained en route by professional singers and musicians to keep them united and happy. Sometimes it's the little things that count.

Going into the convention, the published tally of elected delegates put MacKay out front with 42 per cent support. Orchard was comfortably in second place with 25 per cent, followed by Prentice at 15 per cent, and Brison in last place with 10 per cent of the delegates.

Since no candidate had a majority of delegates going into the convention, it was inevitable that deal-making would occur. MacKay needed the support of only one of his opponents to win, and it appeared that the other candidates required absolute unity to overcome MacKay's commanding lead.

In reality, only Brison and Prentice could have overcome MacKay. There was no scenario under which David Orchard could win the convention. Even if Brison or Prentice tried to persuade their delegates to support Orchard, they would not have succeeded. Prentice or Brison could win with a pact between themselves and Orchard. At least that was the way it was supposed to work. To John Laschinger, this was elementary convention politics: "When you need second-ballot support to win you can't make a deal with the front-runner. It was everybody against Peter."

Research and profiling revealed that Orchard's delegates had limited attachment to the party. As far as the convention was concerned, Orchard's delegates believed only in David Orchard. Perhaps like no other leadership convention in the history of the party, a candidate had near total command of his delegates. "Everyone knew that Orchard was going to move his delegates en masse. There was no question of leakage," said MacKay. In most leadership conventions, a candidate can take only two-thirds of his or her supporters to another camp, and no more. MacKay's delegate-tracking system told them that only 1 per cent of Orchard supporters were freethinkers. When Orchard came off the ballot he would deliver virtually 100 per cent of his delegates. MacKay's team, recognizing that Orchard could not win the convention, was curious about what would happen if Orchard did not instruct his delegates who to vote for when he was not on the ballot. Polling showed that one-quarter would not vote at all if Orchard was not on the ballot. The majority of the remainder indicated they would vote for fellow westerner Jim Prentice.

Orchard knew he could not win the convention. He went to Toronto with 25 per cent of the delegates and no prospects for second-ballot support. His first objective was to draw attention to himself and his issues. If everything went his way, he might end up controlling the outcome of the contest, with the ability to extract concessions from the eventual winner. For this to happen, none of the other candidates could throw their support to MacKay.

As the convention neared, candidates paid increasing attention to Orchard and went to great lengths to find common ground with their newfound friend. All of a sudden, being an organic prairie farmer and free-trade opponent was in vogue. Early in the campaign, Prentice was heard to say, "[Orchard] should be wondering why he is even in the party."[7] Geoff Chutter immediately took Prentice aside

---

[7] Barbara Yaffe, "Maverick Tory shakes up Tory race again," *Vancouver Sun*, January 25, 2003, A22.

and told him to tone it down. In the days before the convention, Prentice spokesperson Jason Hatcher argued that his candidate was not too "right wing" for Orchard, and that the two men had much in common on a range of policies dealing with the environment, aboriginal Canadians, and social policy.[8] Prentice went further. "I support looking at ideas," he said, referring to a review of the free-trade agreement.[9] Brison also reached out to Orchard delegates with words of praise. "We've heard arguments that David Orchard is not a true Conservative. I don't buy that. Our party attracts people with values and ideas on building a better country. David is one of those people."[10] Prentice did his best to signal a willingness to warm up to Orchard's desire for a review of the FTA without saying more than would alarm his supporters. "To the extent that what Mr. Orchard is talking about is strengthening our capacity to trade with the Americans and to make sure it's in a fair way and it's in a way that suits us as Canadians, then I support having a look at ideas. The NAFTA agreement is 10 years old at this point and I think we've seen from the U.S. farm bill and some other examples of protectionism that there are issues that we need to sit down and talk about."[11] While neither Brison nor Prentice was repudiating free trade, each was clearly signalling an opening to something Orchard was seeking: a review of the impact of NAFTA. Both Brison and Prentice called Orchard before the convention to request a meeting, although no meetings took place. Prentice also approached every Orchard delegate individually by way of a personalized letter to emphasize their shared views on many issues, as well as their common western roots. Geoff Chutter spoke with Orchard's key strategists, who said they wanted a quid pro quo deal. "They would support us provided we

[8] Norma Greenaway, "Wooing the new Tory kingmaker," *Ottawa Citizen*, May 18, 2003.
[9] Norma Greenaway, "Orchard wild card in race: Underdogs woo Sask. farmer in hopes of staging upset," *Saskatoon StarPhoenix*, May 30, 2003, B6.
[10] Ibid.
[11] Brian Laghi, "Tories court Orchard's support from all sides; Maverick leadership candidate sought by others for his 25% of delegate votes," *Globe and Mail*, May 30, 2003, A7.

would agree to support Orchard if we fell off the ballot." No deal, was the answer.

MacKay's team was mindful of Orchard as a potential king-maker. "I always knew that Orchard was going to be the key," said MacKay's campaign manager, John Laschinger. "He had 25 per cent of the delegates and was going to decide the contest on the final ballot." At the convention, Laschinger had lunch with Grant Orchard, David's brother. Lasch learned that what Orchard wanted most from the convention was to have an impact and be heard. "We gained the insight that David Orchard wanted nothing for himself. Everything was going to be based on principle," said Laschinger.

After the delegate selection process was complete, the campaign teams focused on making sure their supporters made it to Toronto for the convention. In the weeks before the convention, delegate trackers paid daily attention to the list of delegates who had not yet paid the registration fee. The usual limiting factor was money. Without financial help, many would not make it to the convention to vote. For John Laschinger, the question was how many of these cash-strapped delegates did he have to bring to the convention to win. Laschinger was clearly committed to this process and used his personal credit card to ensure MacKay delegates got registered. He would be reimbursed by donations that had been pledged, but he knew the budget was limited and he didn't want the campaign to end in a deficit. Lasch thought MacKay did not need to win on the first ballot and that by bringing two-thirds of the MacKay delegates to Toronto, both financial and operational objectives would be met. This assumed the other candidates would bring in less than the two-thirds ratio.

As delegate registration drew to a close, it was clear that Laschinger's assumptions were wrong. The other candidates had delivered close to eighty per cent of their delegates. "Had we been able to raise an additional $100,000 and brought all our delegates to Toronto, we would have won on the first ballot," said campaign chair Bill Pristanski. "After the registration numbers came in, we knew we needed help to win. We couldn't do it on our own."

The MacKay campaign was strong on the people side of the organization, but there were some weaknesses in the delegate-tracking system. Said assistant director of organization Duncan Rayner, "The weakest element of our campaign was our floor plan. We didn't have adequate insight into what the non-MacKay delegates were going to do once they got to the floor of the convention and other candidates dropped off. We also did a miserable job keeping track of the automatic delegates." There were other glaring organizational weaknesses, said Rayner: "We did not have a buddy system to bring delegates over. We figured we needed about 45 per cent support on the first ballot and the other candidates would concede a MacKay win was inevitable. But otherwise, we had no Plan B if we were significantly below 45 per cent and all the other candidates ganged up against us."

There was little doubt at the convention that a gang-up against MacKay was in the works. Early in the campaign, Rayner saw indications of trouble if MacKay did not come close to winning on the first ballot. At a campaign event at the University of Ottawa, workers from the Brison and Prentice campaigns acted as if there were a partnership in the works. Rayner ran into Dale Palmeter, Brison's campaign manager, who told him, "I will never be in a party with Peter MacKay." Apparently Brison felt a lingering resentment towards MacKay for the media attention MacKay had received in the House of Commons, some of which Brison thought was rightfully his. A few weeks before the convention, another MacKay campaign worker, Terrance Oakey, met a Prentice organizer, who said MacKay's strong lead in delegate selections was meaningless and that a deal had already been made with Brison, and that Orchard was on-board. Prentice denied he had any formal agreement with Brison, then added, "We were friendly with the Brison campaign and had a pretty good feeling that they would come to us when the time came." Rayner relayed this intelligence to both Rick Morgan and John Laschinger. "They told me no candidate can bring more than 50 per cent of their delegates with them when they endorse another candidate," said Rayner.

Doug Earle, the man who kept the "black box" of delegate profiles, established a rating system of one to five to indicate likely attachment to MacKay. Information would be fed to Earle from three sources: organizers in the field; phone polling; and convention observations. He shared his numbers with only one person, John Laschinger. Earle acknowledged that the tracking of "automatic" delegates was weak; otherwise, the quality of the data was good.

THE CONVENTION SHOWDOWN began on Thursday, May 29, 2003, with a tribute to retiring leader Joe Clark. It was a modest and respectful affair, but not what the delegates had come to see.

Jeff Clarke, a former Mulroney special assistant who also ran a tour for Joe Clark in the 2000 election, was brought in to lead MacKay through the convention. "I was at Peter's side for every step of convention weekend," said Clarke. "My job was to keep Peter confident and to make sure everything we did was consistent with our strategy. I also made sure Peter projected well." Clarke was MacKay's virtual sounding board for everything that happened that weekend.

Also by MacKay's side was his girlfriend, Lisa Merrithew. The Merrithew name was well known in Conservative circles. Gerry Merrithew, Lisa's father, was a twelve-year veteran of the New Brunswick legislature and had been a two-term MP and cabinet minister for Brian Mulroney. His daughter had been active in the PC party from her youth; she had been engaged in partisan politics much longer than had MacKay. When Lisa told her father of her budding romance with MacKay, he responded that he had raised his daughter to become an MP not date one. A communications consultant, Merrithew came to the convention feeling frustrated because the communications support around MacKay was not producing clear and coherent messages.[12] She also sensed that the convention strategy had minimal depth and lacked contingency plans to deal with a full range of voting scenarios. It seemed to Merrithew, and

[12] At the time of writing, Lisa Merrithew was deputy chief of staff to the premier of New Brunswick, responsible for communications.

also to MacKay, that the strategy of combining a commanding first-ballot lead with leakage from candidates was risky and simplistic. It was the sort of strategy, Merrithew feared, that would result in the need to make last-minute decisions in a moment of crisis.

Thursday night visits to hospitality suites normally led to delegates sleeping in on Friday morning, resting up for the hectic weekend ahead. But this Friday convention morning was different. The convention floor was packed, and the air was electric: former prime minister Brian Mulroney was about to deliver his keynote address. In this party, Mulroney was, and still is, magic.

Mulroney delivered a speech that was both defensive and self-critical. He acknowledged his personal unpopularity, particularly at the end of his mandate, but reminded delegates that his accomplishments were enduring and of significant benefit to Canada.

On this day, Mulroney wanted to address not just his overall record, but the very specific measures he had undertaken as prime minister to respond to regional frustration from the West. The measures he cited included free trade, ending the National Energy Program, abolishing the Petroleum Gas Revenue Tax, and replacing the Foreign Investment Review Agency with Investment Canada. After setting the record straight, and with a strong rebuke aimed at Preston Manning and the Reform party, Mulroney told delegates it was time to "turn the page." What he meant was that it was time to reunite the conservative coalition and co-operate with Stephen Harper to put an end to Liberal rule in Canada.

The closer MacKay got to becoming leader, the more he realized he would one day have to co-operate with Stephen Harper and reunite conservatives. In the debates and speeches leading up to the convention, MacKay often said, "It is time to reunite the conservative family." He urged Alliance members to "come home," but few had ever responded to such a plea. To some his plea seemed arrogant, especially to Alliance party members younger than thirty who had never joined the PC party. All they knew of politics was their experience with the Reform or Alliance. They had no other home.

The first big test for the candidates was the Friday night speeches. Short of a disaster, convention speeches usually have no impact on early balloting. But in a brokered convention with multiple ballots, the momentum and energy a candidate achieves in a plenary speech can have a profound influence on the more independent-minded delegates. This influence can be critical when a delegate's first-choice candidate is dropped from the ballot. Most observers gave the nod for the best speeches of the night to Prentice and Brison, both of whom delivered inspired and passionate addresses, away from the podium but within sight of the teleprompter. Content was of less importance than form, although Prentice went out of his way to appeal to the anti-Alliance Orchard delegates by affirming that the PC party was here to stay. MacKay used most of his speech to attack the Liberals, rather than articulating his vision for Canada. His was a safe "front-runner" speech designed to help bring some of the ex-officio delegates to his side. The problem for MacKay was that many delegates from the other camps viewed him as strong on organization but weak on policy. Many were looking for him to show he was serious about policy, which he did not do.

Orchard used his speech to deliver a lecture on Canadian history. It would have been informative and interesting in a classroom, but it was out of place at a leadership convention. Indeed, as Orchard was wrapping up his speech he came up against the time limit, and the power to his microphone was awkwardly cut off in mid-sentence.

Craig Chandler gave a nasty discourse, during which he withdrew from the race to avoid impending embarrassment and to potentially reduce his financial burden. Chandler chastised MacKay for not supporting a merger with the Alliance and for his reluctance to support a socially conservative agenda. He paid tribute to his preferred candidate, Jim Prentice. This was a man, declared Chandler, he could follow. Prentice was initially delighted by the turn of events, but cringed when he realized that he had just been endorsed by the most intolerant and extreme candidate in the race. It was hard to imagine Craig Chandler on the same side of any issue as David Orchard or

Scott Brison. Chandler had no delegates to offer, while Orchard had more than six hundred supporters, and Brison had more than four hundred. Prentice was expecting Chandler's support, but was taken aback by his methods. "What Chandler said and the way he said it was very surprising. No one expected or appreciated it." Orchard later recalled that Chandler's move to Prentice was significant: "He was openly advocating a merger and that was his reason for going to Prentice. There was a clear sense that that was the way things would go with Mr. Prentice." It may have come late, but Prentice went to great pains the next morning to distance himself from Chandler. Even though Chandler was a bit player, his ranting was unpleasant for MacKay. MacKay did not realize at the time that losing Chandler would help him win the convention.

The voting on Saturday began late and proceeded slowly. Delegates waited impatiently to vote and waited even longer to hear results. The delays gave the television networks little choice but to give the party more time on national television than was deserved or intended. Coverage, which had been expected to wrap up before the 6:00 p.m. newscasts, was kept alive well into the early evening. Many thought it was a good strategy for the party to gain visibility; others saw it as a demonstration of the party's incompetence.

Before the first-ballot results were read to the convention, Pristanski went to Orchard's bleachers. He told Orchard how upset MacKay was with the party for cutting off Orchard's speech mid-sentence. "David," said Pristanski, "the people who are running this convention, the Joe Clark people, showed enormous disrespect. Everyone knew you were wrapping up your speech and they should have let you finish." It was a good way for Pristanski to start the conversation, but it wasn't what the visit was for. Pristanski told Orchard to expect that Brison would support Prentice. Appealing to Orchard's sense of fairness, Pristanski said, "They are going to try and gang up and steal this thing." Pristanski suggested that if Brison moved, Orchard and MacKay should meet to see if they could find common ground. Orchard agreed, cellphone numbers were exchanged, and the meeting location was established: Orchard's Crowne Plaza hotel suite.

The first ballot put MacKay in first place with 41.0 per cent support. David Orchard followed with 24.3 per cent; Jim Prentice was third at 18.2 per cent: and Scott Brison was last with 13.4 per cent. The key revelation from the first ballot was that Brison and Prentice had more support from the ex-officio or automatic delegates than expected. "So much for being the establishment candidate," said MacKay. This should not have been a surprise. Brison, who did not have nearly as strong an organization in the ridings as did MacKay, spent considerable time courting the approximately five hundred automatic delegates. And for all the organizational strengths of the MacKay campaign, this was one area where the team underachieved.

The math at this point was simple. MacKay needed to attract 235 more delegates. Conversely, 234 delegates was all the other candidates could lose from their pool of 1,549 votes, or MacKay would win. MacKay could win with support from any one of the other candidates. They could all be kingmakers.

For the MacKay team the numbers were a disappointment. The team had expected to deliver another bus from Quebec and had expected the support of more automatic delegates. To win without making a deal with another candidate, MacKay strategists thought they needed 45 per cent on the first ballot. After falling short of that mark, they turned their attention to the other candidates.

After any ballot at a leadership convention, all eyes are on the lower-ranked candidates. In this case, the attention was on Scott Brison. Would he take himself out of the contest and support another candidate? Had he dropped out and instructed his delegates to support MacKay, the convention would have been over.

A few of the youth-for-MacKay sought to encourage Brison supporters their way. Completely unknown to MacKay, they concocted a scheme early that morning to create the impression that Brison could not hold his delegates. With some ill-gotten Brison T-shirts, they sat themselves in the Brison bleachers for the reading of the first ballot. Soon after the results were read, they rose en masse and proceeded slowly but deliberately across the convention floor towards MacKay. It was a juvenile stunt that was quickly exposed as a fraud.

Brison immediately saw what was happening and responded by sending a terse note to MacKay demanding an apology and the return of his T-shirts. "It sounded like a wild allegation to me," said MacKay. He started to write a strong note back to Brison, denying knowledge of the incident, when Jeff Clarke interceded. "I told Peter he should chill out. There was nothing to be gained and so the note went back in his pocket." The result of the incident was to further exacerbate the tensions between the Brison and MacKay camps. Not a good move for team MacKay.

All candidates received more than 5 per cent support, and Brison declined to drop out. The second ballot was identical to the first except that elected delegates were free to vote for whomever they wanted. This freedom was not without consequence, and it provided a small but interesting shift. First, a few delegates went home: there were sixty-three fewer votes cast on the second ballot than on the first. MacKay retained a commanding lead, with 39.7 per cent of the delegates, but had lost sixty-two votes. David Orchard and Jim Prentice also lost votes, but their ranking of second and third place did not change. The only candidate with momentum on the second ballot was Scott Brison. He picked up thirty-two votes and finished only *three votes* behind Jim Prentice. Nonetheless, Brison was still in last place and so was dropped from the third ballot. Brison could only wonder, "What if?" Had he eclipsed Prentice and then persuaded Orchard to come to his side, the convention could have been his. There were many reports that some Brison supporters had not bothered to vote on the second ballot because they thought their candidate was going to lose.

The MacKay team knew that Brison was going to pick up votes on the second ballot, and had predicted he would be tied with Prentice. "Brison had delegates that ran as MacKay supporters because they knew it was the only way they would get elected in their riding," said Pristanski. "They deceived their riding association members and us. But we had it all figured out by the time we got to the convention. They were going to move to Brison on ballot two and there was nothing we could do to stop them."

MacKay's team was hoping for a tie between Brison and Prentice. Had they tied, both would have been eliminated, and MacKay would have won with 75 per cent of the vote on the third ballot. No deals would have been necessary.

Although he lost some votes, it wasn't all bad news for MacKay. The chances of Brison doing a deal with Orchard were far higher than with Prentice. Orchard thought Prentice was the candidate closest to the Alliance, an anathema to Orchard. "On some of the issues Brison and I were closer than with Prentice," Orchard revealed. "With Brison I had no sense of him being prepared to merge the party with the Alliance, and he would have been more on an equal footing with MacKay. Probably my rapport with Brison had been the best. I knew some of Brison's key people, like Libby Burnham, and I would have given a fair amount of weight to their views." Had Brison, rather than Prentice, come in third, MacKay would have been in a tough spot. It is conceivable that the three votes separating the third- and fourth-place candidates on the second ballot changed the outcome of the convention. Of course, this assumes that the Prentice delegates would have moved en masse to Brison, which was anything but certain. MacKay delegate-tracking indicated the Prentice delegates were more favourable to MacKay than were the Brison delegates. Had the MacKay camp been highly confident they could win on a final ballot against Brison, without making any deals based on leakage from Prentice, it would have been a clever strategy to have a small number of MacKay delegates vote for Brison on the second ballot to take Prentice out of the race. Prentice strategist Geoff Chutter believes MacKay's team made such an attempt. "Jim was the only one who could beat MacKay. John Laschinger had some of his delegates support Brison in the early ballots to try and take Prentice out. I suppose all is fair in love and political conventions." Laschinger denied the allegation.

Going into the convention, Brison and Prentice had to tell one another each would support the other in his time of need. The only issue was whether the survivor on this reality show could persuade

Orchard to join his tribe to make MacKay the loser. It wouldn't help if Orchard dropped out and declared himself neutral. If Orchard delegates went home, the combination of Prentice–Brison votes did not stack up to the MacKay total. Against that backdrop, there was not much Orchard could ask for that Prentice or Brison would not be prepared to give.

Out of the third ballot, and with MacKay so far ahead, Brison must have contemplated what was best for the party. Nova Scotia premier John Hamm pleaded with Brison to move to MacKay, calling it unconscionable for him not to support a fellow Nova Scotian.

Horrified that David Orchard might become the kingmaker of the convention, Joe Clark also beseeched Brison to go to MacKay. Although the retiring leader was officially neutral in the race, the presence of his wife and daughter in the Brison bleachers, not to mention Clark's history of taking over Brison's seat in 2000, were good indications that Clark was an influential Brison supporter. In addition, Clark was displeased with the Prentice campaign. When MacKay and Brison delegates spoke about Prentice not being in the House of Commons, Prentice spokesperson Ken Hughes had told the media that Clark would "do the right thing" and resign his seat for Prentice. There had been no discussions about this matter with Clark, who was on the record stating he wanted to finish his term as an MP.

Brison called MacKay. It was a short conversation. "He said he was going to Prentice. I was not surprised," said MacKay. "He had been churlish and small throughout the campaign, attacking me personally while cozying up to Prentice at every opportunity." Many from Atlantic Canada who had seen Brison and MacKay together would have predicted the outcome. "Those who thought Brison would come over were simply nuts," said Lisa Merrithew. A month before the convention Brison had publicly and unequivocally declared his distaste for MacKay: "Peter has flip-flopped on a range of issues over the last several weeks and months. For those people who left the PC party because they didn't know what we stood for or didn't believe we stood for anything, Peter, with his poll-mongering pragmatism, is not going to attract them back."[13] Rick Morgan conceded that a fundamental weakness of the convention plan was that the senior people plotting strategy did not understand the personal relationship that existed between MacKay and Brison. It is revealing that Lisa Merrithew seemed to know before the convention that Brison was not going to support MacKay, while those who laid out convention strategy had banked on the opposite. That MacKay and Brison never met or spoke before the convention was a strong indication that the two would never make a deal on voting day.

Before the convention, rank-and-file members would have bristled at an outcome in which the new leader would be beholden to Orchard. Brison had to know that going to Prentice would make Orchard the kingmaker. After he was gone from the ballot, Brison desperately wanted Orchard to support Prentice.

Orchard said Prentice was willing to give him everything he wanted. But Orchard was reluctant to strike a deal with the man who came from the heartland of Alliance country. He also objected to supporting a candidate who came to the convention with only 15 per cent support. "I am a democrat," Orchard told Pristanski, suggesting that this would make it unpalatable for him to support Prentice. Even though MacKay was in a much stronger and more legitimate position to negotiate than was Prentice, Orchard thought it was more honourable to deal with the front-runner than with the man who was in third place after two ballots. Orchard told Pristanski, "We [MacKay and Orchard] came to this convention with 65 per cent of the delegates and it would be wrong for either Prentice or Brison to walk away as leader." Orchard might well have been thinking of the difficulties Joe Clark had leading the party in 1976 after having garnered only 11.7 per cent of the delegates on the first ballot.

MacKay knew that not all of Brison's delegates would follow him to Prentice. John Herron, a caucus member from New Brunswick,

<hr>

[13] Sheldon Alberts, "Foes may unite to block MacKay on second ballot," *National Post*, May 1, 2003, A8.

and Rick Byers, the party's candidate from Oakville, moved swiftly
to MacKay's bleachers. Herron had been under a lot of pressure
from people in his region to support MacKay. His riding was adjacent to the home of Gerry Merrithew, Lisa's father. Herron told his
supporters that he would stick with Brison, a former college room-
mate, only on the first ballot. After the first ballot John and Beth
Herron made their move to MacKay, although Brison was still on
the ballot. Herron later told reporters that although he was in
MacKay's bleachers before the second-ballot results were released,
he had voted for Brison on ballot two. It seems odd that he would
not have stayed by Brison's side at least until the second-ballot
results were announced. These votes, plus a handful of others, could
have made the difference between Brison finishing third or in last
place on the second ballot. The Herron move left Brison perplexed.
"I certainly don't mind being double-crossed. Triple-crossed
becomes a little bit irritating," said Brison of the Herron clan. "But
in any case, John's John. At the end of the day, leadership races are
good for a number of reasons. They galvanize people and you learn
about people."[14]

Bill Pristanski was hoping that Byers, a former assistant to
Michael Wilson, would help persuade Brison to move to MacKay.
He told Byers a story to whisper in Brison's ear: "In the 1983 leadership, Michael Wilson was in Mulroney's box thirty seconds after
the results of the first ballot were read and he became Minister of
Finance. David Crombie huddled with his advisers for thirty minutes
and he became Minister for Indian and Northern Affairs."

With third-ballot voting underway, MacKay knew he would not
gain enough freethinking Brison delegates to win. There was also the
worry that, because of the delays in voting and the multiple ballots,
some of MacKay's Toronto delegates might tire and head home.

Delegate-tracking predicted that on ballot three, Prentice would
be in second place with Orchard falling to third. Consequently,

---

[14] Bill Curry and Sheldon Alberts, with files from Robert Fife, "MacKay tackles Tory
divisions," *National Post*, June 2, 2003, A1.

Orchard would be off the ballot, leaving a showdown between MacKay and Prentice. Fearing a deal between Prentice and Orchard, two of MacKay's key campaign workers who knew the delegate numbers best, Duncan Rayner and Terrance Oakey, thought the convention was lost. The young MP assistants started to speculate about their next career.

After the second ballot Orchard's cellphone was the most popular one at the convention, and his bleachers the most active. Orchard says he was approached by two delegates who claimed to have negotiating authority on behalf of Jim Prentice. They were Barry Cline from Ontario and Geoff Chutter from British Columbia. Orchard told Chutter it was confusing and frustrating to be approached by multiple spokespersons. Prentice said only Chutter was empowered. "The clearest thing we did was to establish a single point of contact with Orchard. For a multiplicity of reasons, no one other than Chutter had any authority to negotiate with Orchard on behalf of my campaign." Cline, originally a Brison delegate, claims he asked and received Prentice's permission to speak with Orchard on his behalf.

Orchard contends that Prentice's emissary (or emissaries) offered the free trade review, the clean-up of head office staff, and other policy planks for his support. "The negotiations did not get to the point of discussing a no-merger-with-the-Alliance clause," said Orchard. Chutter and Prentice recalled the discussions with Orchard differently. Prentice said he agreed to a review of the FTA, that there would be changes in staffing at party headquarters, but the sticking point related to co-operation with the Alliance: "Nothing about 301 was discussed. And it was never in writing. There was no request that it be in writing." Chutter, who said he was by Orchard's side when the results of the first and second ballots were read out, recalls that very little was said about the relationship between the Alliance and PC parties in his discussions with Orchard, and that he rejected any notion of Orchard being involved in staffing decision at party headquarters. "Our campaign manager warned us that for all we knew he would nominate Maude Barlow as national director," said Chutter. What is not in dispute is that Prentice was prepared to make a deal with Orchard at the convention and, at a minimum, offered up a review of NAFTA to gain Orchard's support.

The dominant issue to Orchard was no merger with the Alliance. As much as Prentice's convention remarks indicated he was opposed to a merger, Orchard doubted his sincerity. There were enough people around Prentice who thought a merger was a good idea to make Orchard uneasy, plus there was the Chandler incident. Had Orchard searched press clippings for the previous twelve months, he would have exposed a pro-merger history. Because Prentice could not win the leadership as a "unity candidate," he kept his views to himself during the campaign. Long after the leadership race, Orchard remarked, "It is very interesting that Prentice claims he was a unity candidate at the 2003 leadership, when he said nothing of the sort during the campaign."

Orchard could see that Senator Noël Kinsella had entered his bleachers, with Bill Pristanski not far behind. Orchard and Kinsella had enjoyed many conversations about free trade over the years. Unlike other members of the Tory caucus, Kinsella thought Orchard would be a welcome addition to the PC front benches. In short, Orchard and Kinsella trusted one another. Kinsella knew this would be an important encounter. "I was convinced Peter needed a deal. We had our elbows out and we were playing the game to win." When Kinsella got close to Orchard he could see a number of Prentice people milling about. "I told David that he and Peter should meet," said Kinsella. Orchard responded somewhat favourably, asking what they should meet about. Kinsella laid out the conditions that would become the basis of the MacKay–Orchard agreement: free trade review and no merger. Orchard added his concern for policies on sustainable development and the need to clean up some of the practices at party headquarters. Kinsella saw nothing problematic in the proposals. Kinsella had just participated in a Senate committee hearing on the impact of free trade and saw nothing wrong with a review led by a group of Tory MPs. "I will talk to Peter and call you back," he told Orchard.

Orchard was receptive to dealing with Kinsella. "He was very clear, very specific, and got right down to brass tacks. The Prentice campaign seemed like amateur hour by comparison. They had to keep going back to check on what they could do and what they couldn't."

"Orchard said he wants to talk to us," Kinsella told MacKay. Jeff Clarke overheard Kinsella's explanation to MacKay of what Orchard was looking for. "I was surprised," recalled Clarke. "No one thought, going into the convention, that Orchard was for sale." Clarke cautioned MacKay and asked incredulously, "Do we really want to think about this, Peter?" Orchard had been expecting to deal with MacKay, but MacKay seemed surprised to be dealing with Orchard. "I don't know, Jeff," said MacKay. "I suppose it can't hurt for us to talk and listen." Kinsella knew there was going to be a deal, and that it could just as easily have been with Prentice as with MacKay. "Prentice was prepared to give Orchard everything but the kitchen sink," said Kinsella. There was no time to waste—an agreement with Orchard needed to be locked down quickly, before Prentice made Orchard an offer he couldn't refuse. The next time Orchard's phone rang it was Kinsella. In something of an overstatement, to help conclude matters, Kinsella told Orchard, "We have an agreement."

All efforts were made to keep the Orchard–MacKay meeting a secret. Jeff Clarke led the small cadre of MacKay's senior team members to Orchard's suite by walking outside the convention site along Front Street to Orchard's hotel. They avoided the notice of most delegates, who were congregating in the enclosed convention space and on the walkway between the convention floor and the hotel. Orchard was less discreet and recalls that Prentice's emissaries were running along beside him while he was returning to his suite to meet MacKay.

THE FACE-TO-FACE MEETING between MacKay and Orchard took place at 7:00 p.m. in Orchard's Crowne Plaza hotel suite. Joining MacKay were adviser Senator Kinsella and supporter Fred Doucet. Orchard was joined by his long-time adviser Marjaleena Repo and his brother Grant. A few others from both camps waited in the hallway outside the hotel room, including, by happenstance, New Brunswick MP Greg Thompson.

Orchard had written his conditions on a sheet of paper:

Agreement between David Orchard and Peter MacKay
1. *No merger, talks, or joint candidates w Alliance, maintain 301.*
2. *Review of FTA/NAFTA—blue ribbon commission—with DO choice of chair. Rest of members to be jointly agreed upon.*
3. *Clean up head office including a change of national director with consultation, and some of DO's people working at head office.*
4. *Commitment to make environmental protection front and centre, incl sustainable agriculture, forestry, including reducing pollution through rail.*

MacKay reviewed the document, nodded agreement, and quickly made some changes.

First, he struck out the word "talks" under point one. He knew from his days with the DRC, as well as previous efforts with Reform party members, that it was important to have an open dialogue with the other opposition parties. "We had to be able to move forward with the Alliance so I insisted in the deal with David that 'talks' be permitted," said MacKay. Orchard agreed, although he later claimed the talks were only intended to cover procedural matters and certainly not a merger. Of course the agreement itself said "no merger," so MacKay was in rough water if he thought permission for "talks" could be taken very far. MacKay recalls not worrying at the time about the merger condition. "When I made the deal," said MacKay, "it was inconceivable that a merger between the parties was even in the cards. It was in our constitution that we had to run 301 candidates so this was only confirming party policy. I had no authority to ratify a merger with the Alliance on my own in any event. That would take the approval of two-thirds of the entire membership."

Second, MacKay made the choice of chair of the blue-ribbon commission subject to his agreement. MacKay knew there was no possibility the party's position on free trade was going to change, but he didn't want the blue-ribbon commission to become a circus because Orchard picked an extremist as its chair.

Third, MacKay put a time frame around the changes in head office personnel. It was clear that Orchard had in his sights David Scrymgeour, a man he wanted replaced as PC national director.

Senator Kinsella sensed that MacKay had some discomfort over signing an agreement with Orchard. MacKay had not expected to be facing this decision and had precious little time to think it through. Before signing, MacKay left the room to discuss the conditions with his key advisers. Laschinger told MacKay the deal was "trouble," but then said, "It's the right thing to do. You can't win without it, so let's get on with it." Jeff Clarke was opposed. He did not object to the specific content of the agreement, rather he opposed giving Orchard so much influence over the party and over MacKay. Like many in MacKay's camp, Clarke thought MacKay could win without dealing with Orchard. But those with access to the pre-convention research, such as Pristanski and Laschinger, thought otherwise. They felt it was not just a risk, but would mean certain defeat, to go into the final ballot with Orchard and Prentice on the same side. Laschinger knew that with only 40 per cent support after two ballots, MacKay had no choice but to deal with Orchard if he wanted to win. Even though MacKay and Prentice were 15 percentage points apart on the third ballot, they may as well have been tied. The margin for victory rested with Orchard. Like Prentice, MacKay realized he needed Orchard to win. There was no other scenario that worked.

In the hallway Pristanski asked MacKay three questions. First, would Prentice accept the same deal? "Absolutely," was MacKay's reply. Second, who is better able to lead this party and put the pieces back together, MacKay or Prentice? MacKay didn't have to answer that question. Third, can you sell this deal back to your supporters? The answer from MacKay was yes, but no one had thought about how, or what should be said about the agreement.

It was clear to MacKay that there was nothing earth-shattering in the content of the agreement:

> I signed that deal thinking there was no way between now and the next election that we were going to bring these parties

together. First of all there didn't seem to be the will within the party membership, and I picked that up quite strongly during the campaign. Now, in retrospect, anybody could see that it had to happen. But that wasn't the atmosphere leading up to and in the aftermath of the leadership convention. We weren't breaking any new ground.

Jeff Clarke was very uneasy about making any sort of deal with Orchard. "I never thought it would sell. I grabbed a piece of paper and rolled it up to pretend it was a microphone. I shoved in front of Peter's face and shouted, 'Have you made a deal? What sort of deal did you make with the guy who is anti–free trade?' as if we were in a media scrum. It was a pointed question but I wanted to let Peter know he was going to be under attack and he better be ready to answer some questions." Clarke remembered the air being filled with stunned silence. The silence should have been a signal to senior MacKay advisers that it was time to find a quiet room and work out a communications plan. It was easy to predict that, with news of the deal, the convention floor and the media would simultaneously erupt. To say the deal would produce shock waves was an understatement. There was no talk of messaging or a communications plan around the deal; MacKay simply re-entered the room and signed the agreement.

There was a sense that the signing of the agreement was of historic significance, and photos were taken to commemorate the event. Pictures could also be evidence in case someone tried to deny what had taken place. While some would later say this was a "nefarious backroom deal," it was probably the most public agreement ever struck at a political convention. Leadership campaign veteran Bill Pristanski remarked how it was likely the first deal ever struck at a convention that did not include a request from the losing candidate for money to cover campaign debts plus a position of power in the party or government. It was also unique in that the agreement was in writing for all to see, with photographs to mark the occasion.

Meanwhile, the Prentice campaign went into panic mode. They were desperate for a deal and confident that they could give Orchard more than anything MacKay would put on the table. While MacKay sat in Orchard's suite, Orchard's cellphone rang. It was Scott Brison calling from Jim Prentice's hotel suite. "I have Jim here with me," said Brison. Prentice was by his side, anxiously waiting to speak with Orchard. "Yes, I know," someone heard Orchard say. "I understand you would agree, but I am here talking right now with Peter. It's too late. I'll call you back." Orchard jotted down Brison's cellphone number on the agreement he had just signed with MacKay.

MacKay signed the agreement, and his campaign chair, Bill Pristanski, called Brian Mulroney to bring him up to date. "I told Brian what had happened and asked his advice on how the agreement might be sold," said Pristanski. Mulroney replied, "Don't worry. A deal between MacKay and Orchard to review the NAFTA was hardly going to jeopardize the trade in goods and services across North America." Mulroney reassured Pristanski that MacKay had done the right thing. "I think the point of going to a convention was to win," Mulroney said. Pristanski asked Mulroney to contribute a few lines to MacKay's acceptance speech to ensure the free trade review would not become problematic.

Mulroney discussed strategy with Bill Fox, a MacKay supporter and former Mulroney communications director, and then dictated his suggestions to Fox, who wrote them on the back of a shredded MacKay campaign poster. Mulroney suggested words to the effect that, "no deal is perfect and can always be improved." It was a far cry from implying that the commission's mandate was to abrogate NAFTA. Orchard took no exception to the remarks: he was happy simply to have the trade agreement exposed to scrutiny.

When the agreement was signed the third-ballot results had yet to be announced. Both MacKay and Orchard thought the delegates should hear the tally before the two men embraced on the convention floor. They arranged to return to their bleachers without giving any indication that a deal had been struck.

MacKay returned to his box and briefly met with his closest advisers to explain what had just transpired. Those he spoke with included caucus members who had supported him all along, plus

John Herron, who came over from Brison after the first ballot. MacKay recalled, "I huddled with my caucus colleagues who were in the box: Inky Mark, Norm Doyle, Loyola Hearn, Bill Casey, and John Herron, and a number of PC senators. They were all there. I took them through the four points that were in the agreement. I said we can agree to all of these things; they all said, 'Absolutely, do it.' "

Looking for reassurance, MacKay asked Senator Angus, "Would Brian [Mulroney] have done the deal with Orchard?" Angus replied, "Of course he would have." However, at the time Angus didn't know the contents of the deal or that it was in writing, factors that might have changed his response to MacKay's question.

Meanwhile, Pristanski was desperate to alert the campaign spinners, who were providing media commentary for MacKay. Pristanski wanted to minimize the significance of the deal and did not want the spinners to appear surprised or alarmed by what had happened. Before a meeting with the spinners could be arranged, the reading of the third ballot got underway. No one knew what the agreement said, and no one knew what to say in MacKay's defence. "The mistake we made is we lost control of the timing of the convention," said Jeff Clarke. "After we made the deal with Orchard we should not have gone back to the convention floor until we were totally ready. We weren't ready. The spinning hadn't occurred and we were caught flat-footed without a message of what the deal was really about."

The third-ballot results confirmed what the MacKay team had expected. Peter picked up 110 votes, almost one-third of Brison's delegates, mostly from Atlantic Canada. That left MacKay 126 votes short of a majority. Prentice had leapt over Orchard into second place, picking up 295 of Brison's 463 second-ballot delegates. But with 761 delegates, Prentice was still 20 percentage points short of what he needed for a win. Orchard's supporters remained intact, and he was held to just below 25 per cent. However, with the Orchard agreement in place there was no longer any doubt that MacKay would win the convention.

Those in the party who hoped a delegated convention would produce drama and excitement could not possibly have imagined the stunning scene about to unfold before the nation on live television. News anchors excitedly watched David Orchard and Peter MacKay make their way towards one another. Before the convention, most commentators thought a deal like this was impossible. First, Orchard had so little in common with the other candidates it was hard to imagine he could embrace any of his opponents. Second, Orchard was supposed to be immune to compromise or the seedy underside of politics marked by backroom deals. He was not thought to be a deal-making kind of politician. Third, it was hard for commentators to imagine that either MacKay or Prentice would give Orchard the prestige of being the kingmaker. Fourth, could a legitimate Tory turn his back on the Mulroney legacy and cozy up to an anti-free-trade crusader? The unexpected always makes for better television. With the convention delegates and the national media sorting through the third-ballot numbers, MacKay and Orchard began their walk to one another to signal that the outcome of the convention had been determined. Because the Prentice bleacher was between the MacKay and Orchard encampments, Jim Prentice had the best seat in the house to witness the act that would seal his fate.

Only a handful of people in MacKay's bleachers knew what was about to happen. MacKay's official agent, Doug McLarty, looked worried, thinking that Orchard was making his way to Prentice. Seeing his anxiety, John Laschinger leaned over and told him, "Don't worry. What do you think I have been doing for the last four hours?"

MacKay thought Orchard's delegates would unquestionably follow their candidate in lockstep, but there were surprising indications of trouble. When Orchard told his supporters he wanted them to vote for MacKay on the fourth ballot, he faced howls of protest. "It was a tumultuous meeting . . . some people were sobbing . . . some would have rather I just walk out. My delegates said, 'We fought [MacKay] in the trenches and he will betray us.' I made the case as strong as I could. I told them I signed this deal with Peter and we have to take people at face value." Most of Orchard's delegates were from the West, and had some affinity with Prentice. The letter from Prentice to all Orchard delegates was also a factor. "He put a lot of energy into courting my delegates," said Orchard. Geoff Chutter remained in Orchard's bleachers and witnessed considerable distress. "There was so much animosity towards MacKay that Orchard's delegates were dumbfounded. They responded as if they had just been asked to vote for the devil." Ultimately, MacKay addressed Orchard's delegates to provide some much-needed reassurance. To make sure he delivered his vote to MacKay, Orchard placed organizers at the front of the line where delegates went to cast their final ballot. To leave no doubt, just before Orchard delegates reached the voting booth, they were pulled aside and told what David Orchard wanted them to do. "We delivered the vote," said Marjaleena Repo, Orchard's campaign manager.

As MacKay and Orchard walked past the Prentice section of the bleachers, a loud, repetitive, and spontaneous chant could be heard. "Brison and Prentice stood up in their sections and shouted, 'Integrity, Integrity.' It was ridiculous," said Marjaleena Repo. "We had just been dealing with these people and they had been pounding us, saying, 'Whatever you want.' My cellphone was full with their desperate messages." Of course, Prentice's delegates who joined in the chant didn't know the truth of the matter. "This idea that Prentice was not in negotiation was pure fantasy," said Orchard.

Repo ensured that the truth about Brison and Prentice seeking an agreement with Orchard was made plain and clear in a strongly worded letter published in the *Globe and Mail* under the title "The Prentice Canard":

> Prentice rejected nothing and it was his team of negotiators who breathlessly pursued David Orchard to the very end. I should know as I was, as Orchard's senior advisor and negotiator, at the receiving end of urgent phone calls from the Prentice team and was present when Scott Brison, on behalf of Jim Prentice, reached David Orchard's cell phone at the very moment when the agreement between Orchard and MacKay was being signed. As proof of this final fervent attempt to get

Orchard's support is the phone number for Brison that Orchard scribbled in haste on the actual document that was to be signed.[15]

The results of the final ballot were a foregone conclusion, with MacKay winning 64.8 per cent of the votes cast. Although 132 fewer delegates voted on the fourth ballot, Jim Prentice still managed to increase his vote total by 75. These votes had to have come from either Orchard or MacKay delegates, more likely the latter. Paul Lepsoe, MacKay's chief legal adviser, was one of the delegates who switched to Prentice on ballot four out of protest. Lepsoe thought MacKay should have been prepared to ensure that a deal with Orchard was avoidable. "Peter should have worked the Brison and Orchard delegates before the convention to make sure they would move to him if Prentice and Orchard struck a deal," Lepsoe said. But MacKay did the deal with Orchard and didn't lose very many of his delegates. It was doubtful that MacKay could have done anything before or at the convention to stop Prentice from winning had he secured an agreement with Orchard. Had Orchard gone to Prentice, MacKay would have needed votes from 17 per cent of Prentice's third-ballot supporters to win. It was a very unlikely outcome. There was only one man who could have realistically taken away Orchard's power at the convention, and that was Scott Brison. By choosing to support Prentice, Brison handed the keys of the convention to David Orchard.

When the victory speech was over and the hoopla had subsided, MacKay walked through a throng of delegates on the convention floor. "Some youth delegates had said some very unpleasant things to Peter about the Orchard deal and he was bothered by it," recalled Jeff Clarke. "We knew we had a battle." MacKay, Lisa Merrithew, and Clarke made their way to MacKay's suite. "It became abundantly clear that Lisa was not happy," Clarke said. "In fact, she was very frustrated. She thought the Orchard deal was an albatross, saying you

---

[15] Marjaleena Repo, "The Prentice Canard," letter to the editor, *Globe and Mail*, January 7, 2004.

can't put 'lipstick on a pig and make it look good.' She was also upset that she was left out of the decision-making process. This was not the exhilarating and joyous moment that they had been hoping for." MacKay acknowledged that it had been a mistake not to have Merrithew with him when the pivotal decision was made to negotiate with Orchard: "Lisa had been a tremendous source of support and gave very sound tactical advice. I deeply regret that I had not included her more fully in the final decisions. I also know her skills in communications could have been put to better use in the aftermath of what then ensued."

Long before the convention, MacKay had assembled a transition team to take him through the brief period from candidate to leader. Led by Bill Pristanski, the team included Rick Morgan, Maureen Murphy-Makin, Denis Jolette, and José Nicolas. Graham Fox, who represented the former leader, was also included in the discussions. The team, code named "hockey pool," had a plan and strategy that had not anticipated the Orchard deal, which had since become priority number one. So the team met late on the night of the leadership vote to make the requisite adjustments, giving MacKay time early the next morning to brief the media and his caucus about why the Orchard deal was "of no great consequence." However, they underestimated the extent of the difficulty of moving beyond the Orchard agreement.

THE BIG NEWS FROM THE CONVENTION was not who won. Everyone in the media had expected a MacKay victory. It was how he did it. Newspaper headlines vilifying MacKay were stark and plentiful. Mulroney biographer and *Montreal Gazette* columnist L. Ian MacDonald wrote under the headline "A dumb, stupid deal: Peter MacKay's signed pact with David Orchard is reason to question the new Tory leader's integrity and judgment."[16] The criticism in his home province was equally strong. "MacKay's ambition outweighs principles: Nova Scotian's deal with rival turned the Tory leadership

---

[16] L. Ian MacDonald, "A dumb, stupid deal," *Montreal Gazette*, June 4, 2003, A27.

into a tarnished prize," screamed the headline in the Halifax *Daily News.*[17] In MacKay's first week as leader he faced nothing but accounts that he was "Wounded"[18] and "Bereft of leadership, judgment."[19]

The MacKay–Orchard deal reached such epic proportions that some editors and columnists were describing its essence in folkloric terms. It was, some suggested, "A Faustian Bargain."[20] The phrase invoked the popular tale in which the learned German gentleman Faust, in his quest for material things, made a pact with the Devil. The Devil offered to serve him for a period of time, but at the cost of his soul. Joe Clark's former chief of staff Goldy Hyder, in his live colour commentary for CBC television, called the MacKay–Orchard agreement a "deal with the Devil." It was not that Hyder was inclined to give MacKay rough treatment; this was his gut on-air reaction to something about which he had received no warning. He was not the only commentator who could be seen leaning over his broadcast booth wondering what should be said about the deal. One commentator who asked MacKay's director of operations, Rick Morgan, for approved lines was told, "Everyone is overreacting. Don't say a damn thing." Morgan had not seen the agreement and did not even know it was in writing. In effect, MacKay's spokespeople were flying blind.

To this day, MacKay expresses frustration that such a transparent agreement could conjure up Faustian references. "While Orchard held views and positions I disagreed with, he was not an evil or unprincipled individual," said MacKay. "The story line did not make sense. I went into the convention as the front-runner and I made a practical decision based on the reality I faced. I didn't go to the convention to lose. It was either make the deal or watch everything go up in smoke."

Things were not easy for MacKay in the press or with certain party members. But, had Prentice won by dealing with Orchard, it

---

[17] Charles Moore, "MacKay's ambition," *Halifax Daily News,* June 6, 2003, 20.

[18] Garfield Mullins, "Wounded," *Cornwall Standard-Freeholder,* June 7, 2003.

[19] "Bereft of leadership," *Montreal Gazette,* June 4, 2003, A26.

[20] "A Faustian bargain," *National Post,* June 3, 2003, A17.

would have been much worse. "The party would have completely imploded and disintegrated," said Duncan Rayner, a key MacKay planner and former director of organization for the party. "Prentice was not in caucus and didn't have a national network of support. We would never have recovered as a party."

Columnists anxious to have only one Conservative party were pleased with the MacKay–Orchard deal, even though its contents precluded a merger. They saw the agreement as the Tory version of political suicide.[21] A weakened MacKay and PC party, it was suggested, made Stephen Harper and the Alliance the only credible alternative to the Liberals.

A week after the convention concluded, however, a few columnists began to see the MacKay–Orchard agreement in a different light. Some cast MacKay's decision as coalition building, somewhat akin to what Sir John A. Macdonald might have done.[22] They pointed out that the very origins of the country involved political deal-making and consensus-building with vastly different political and regional interests. Others liked the unexpected leadership qualities in MacKay. Rick Salutin of the *Globe and Mail* offered this assessment: "It revealed the hitherto bland, risk-averse new leader, choice of the dull old party brass, as having a mild touch of ruthlessness (I'm not ready to go to Faustian), which can be attractive—or useful—in a politician."[23] Convention delegate and on-air news analyst Annie Perrault saw something in MacKay she did not expect: "He showed me he had what it took to win. I hadn't seen that in a Tory leader since Brian Mulroney. I was impressed." And former Alliance leader Stockwell Day offered qualified support to MacKay: "People have to make tough decisions in politics and he showed that he could do it. He took the hit and moved along very well."

---

[21] Diane Francis, "The destructive Mr. MacKay: New Tory leader's western stance is suicidal," *Financial Post*, June 5, 2003, 3.

[22] Arthur Milnes, *Kingston Whig-Standard*, "MacKay wants to follow lead of first PM," June 6, 2003, 10.

[23] Rick Salutin, "History is what happened this morning," *Globe and Mail*, June 6, 2003, A17.

But the overall perception was decidedly negative, and MacKay was stung by the criticism. The morning after winning the leadership, after less than two hours of sleep, MacKay faced the largest media scrum of his life. "It was like trying to swim in a shark tank," MacKay remembered. "It was an unbelievable feeding frenzy and I was not prepared for the savage and accusatory tone of the questions." He did his best to explain the reality of the agreement, but with limited success. "The die had been cast in the hours after news of the agreement broke and we were unprepared to respond, although we certainly tried."

A blue-ribbon panel of conservatives, MacKay argued, was hardly going to imperil the Free Trade Agreement or result in a change in party policy. In his acceptance speech on the night of the vote, MacKay went to some lengths to praise the virtues of free trade in words suggested by Brian Mulroney. He made light of the merger restrictions, stating they were a simple restatement of party policy. MacKay was incredulous: "You would think this was the first agreement ever struck by a candidate at a leadership convention in Canadian political history." Even Orchard downplayed the reach and authority of the blue-ribbon commission he asked for in his agreement with MacKay during the convention. "My objective was to let people know what is in the agreement . . . that it is about more than trade . . . it's about energy reserves, foreign corporations overturning our environmental laws. I wanted the document better understood."

MacKay was right to remind reporters of the history of such matters. Agreements among candidates at delegated conventions were prominent in every Tory leadership since John Diefenbaker won on the first ballot in 1956. In many ways, his deal was tame by past standards. In the MacKay–Orchard deal there was no promise of money, no cabinet post at stake, and no clandestine pact to withhold a deep, dark secret. Rae Murphy of the *Winnipeg Free Press* sided with MacKay: "It is even more surprising that federal Tory leader Peter MacKay would be criticized for making a deal with Orchard to win his support. Deals among competitors and party power brokers and activists are part of the process of determining policy. Watching deals made and deals unraveled is what made Tory conventions the great spectator sport they once were. It is hard then to understand the hyper-ventilating about MacKay's 'deal with the devil,' or 'Faustian bargain.' If the devil himself was a delegate and controlled a block of votes that he needed, MacKay would still need to deal. But it was only Orchard and he is already back on the farm growing organic vegetables."[24] The reference to Orchard underscored the reality that he was in a place where he could do MacKay little harm.

In the midst of the firestorm MacKay wanted to release the agreement to the press but held back. "I didn't feel comfortable making it public until I had discussed it with my entire caucus. They needed to hear it from me and not through the press." And there was another twist. "The original document had Brison's cellphone number on it and I wanted it blanked out so he wouldn't be drawn into the aftermath. I did that to protect him and to show good faith," said MacKay. His campaign team and other advisers were split on releasing the agreement. Graham Fox had wanted the text of the agreement released immediately after it was signed.

The press knew there was a written agreement. Making them wait to see a copy made matters worse, as speculation about its content kept the story in the press. (Speculation is almost always worse than reality.) Within forty-eight hours the text of the document was published in newspapers and on the Web. It may be the only agreement between candidates at a political convention that has been made public. Bill Pristanski conceded that the delay in making the agreement public made the story much bigger than it needed to be.

What MacKay found most difficult through this ordeal was that his character was under attack. "I had established a principled reputation throughout my career as a Crown prosecutor and as House leader in the House of Commons. Having my reputation savaged and assailed was uncomfortable in the extreme. People said it was shameless naked ambition, that I was a political cutthroat. Acts of

---

[24] Rae Murphy, "What's the big deal?," *Winnipeg Free Press*, June 11, 2003.

unbelievable treachery were being attributed to me. It was stunning and completely misplaced when you looked at the substance of the agreement. No one wanted to analyze what I had done. They simply wanted to attack me personally," said MacKay.

In mounting his defence, MacKay stuck with the cold, hard facts and reiterated his intention to honour his agreement with Orchard. What he really wanted to say was that Orchard got nothing special from the deal, that the most the blue-ribbon panel could produce were recommendations, that it was not up to MacKay to decide if there would be a merger, and that only the party members could ratify a merger. But such a clear statement would have made MacKay seem disingenuous and Orchard naïve. Instead, MacKay took whatever abuse was sent his way. "We did not communicate it well," MacKay lamented. "We thought the firestorm would calm down after a few days, but it never did."

While the MacKay–Orchard deal was unexpected and perhaps a little unseemly, the attack by the media seemed disproportionate. This deal was trivial compared with Jean Chrétien's telling the voters of Canada in 1993 that he was going to scrap the GST and abrogate the free trade agreement, only to do a dramatic flip-flop once elected. Or what about Pierre Trudeau ridiculing Robert Stanfield for his position on wage and price controls in the 1974 election, only to implement them as prime minister in 1975. These bold and manipulative moves by Chrétien and Trudeau involved billions of dollars and a broken trust with voters, yet they were considered an accepted part of the cut and thrust of politics. Why, wondered MacKay, was he being held to such a ridiculous standard?

Wherever MacKay went that summer, he was hounded by questions about the Orchard deal—from the media, his supporters, and party members. Few people understood that, had he not made the deal with Orchard, MacKay would have lost the convention. People assumed he won the convention because he was the only candidate prepared to give Orchard what he wanted. Prentice was credited for being a man of principle because he did not deal with Orchard. MacKay never believed it for a moment: "There is no question whatsoever in my mind that this deal would have been accepted by either Brison or Prentice. I just didn't want to broadcast that fact because it would have done nothing to promote party unity." Orchard didn't hesitate to set the record straight with the press: "I can tell you that there's a story that's appeared several times about the notion that Jim Prentice did not negotiate with me or refused my conditions, and I can tell you that is patently false. Prentice was negotiating with me right along and so was Brison, and Prentice was offering the free trade review panel and the cleanup of head office and all of this, so I just want to make that crystal clear that that is not correct. In fact, I was receiving urgent phone calls from him right as we were writing up our agreement between MacKay and myself."[25]

Unlike MacKay, Orchard came out of the convention looking like a winner: "You won the convention," former Liberal prime minister John Turner told Orchard. "When the delegates come out of a convention and a candidate's policies and what he stands for are known across the country, that's very rare. People know exactly what you stand for. That almost never happens. David, you won the convention."

MacKay had clearly underestimated the challenge of overcoming the taint of the Orchard deal. "I was in a rebuilding mode," he affirmed. "In fact, I spent more time reaching out to Scott Brison, Jim Prentice, David Orchard, and their supporters than I did to my own team. I even made Brison policy chair for the election campaign. I attended events in his riding, left him as finance critic at his request, and donated money to help pay off his election debt. When we released a copy of the agreement with Orchard we whited out Brison's cellphone number so he wouldn't get dragged into any of the mess. What I didn't know at the time was that Brison had already checked out of the party. I was told he was spending time that summer with Paul Martin on his farm in the Eastern Townships of Quebec and he had even talked to Martin from the convention in

---

[25] Bill Curry, "MacKay talks 'ongoing,' Orchard says," *National Post*, August 21, 2003, A4.

June. So I suppose many of my efforts were never going to be productive." MacKay graciously gave Joe Clark all the time he wanted to vacate the leader's office and listened carefully to the advice Clark offered. It was clear to MacKay that he was not Clark's first choice to head the party, but he nonetheless gave Clark every respect normally accorded to a retiring leader.

MacKay had every intention of honouring the deal with Orchard. He spent time that summer putting together the blue-ribbon commission, and he and Orchard agreed on a chair. Their first choice, former finance minister Michael Wilson, agreed to lead the commission but had to withdraw over a conflict. Orchard suggested PC caucus member Bill Casey, and MacKay readily agreed. Also to serve on the panel was Bob Blair, a former president of billion-dollar Canadian energy company Nova Corporation. Senator Kinsella, who shepherded the agreement between MacKay and Orchard, was also named to the panel. A few meetings of the panel occurred before it was overtaken by events. Changes were made at party headquarters, with Denis Jolette brought in as the new national director.

MacKay and Orchard met for lunch in the middle of the summer to discuss the constructive developments that had taken place since the convention. MacKay's chief of staff, Rick Morgan, had regular phone conversations with Orchard to bring him up to date on issues. If there were any delays in moving forward with the provisions of the agreement, they were caused by Orchard, who went missing for much of the summer. This was just as well for MacKay, because having Orchard in front of the press would have inevitably triggered more stories about the infamous agreement. MacKay tried to counter his critics by showing that David Orchard was not a devil and that every condition of the agreement was non-threatening. Orchard was intent on supporting MacKay, just as he had supported Clark after the 1998 leadership contest.

MacKay hoped that winning the leadership would be exhilarating and energizing. In the few quiet moments he had after the convention, he realized he had lost a lot of political capital and faced more of an uphill battle than he ever anticipated. It did not help that Brison and Prentice did nothing to support MacKay's leadership.

But Paul Martin and the Liberal party could not have been happier. The convention agreement guaranteed a continuation of the vote splitting on the right, and MacKay would begin his term as leader deeply wounded by the so-called Faustian bargain. As Jean Chrétien had been blessed by the arrival of Preston Manning, Paul Martin had David Orchard to thank for keeping the conservative movement in disarray. David Orchard could almost have been a Liberal plant. But David Orchard had run for the Tory leadership on two occasions, and as a Tory in the 2000 election. He couldn't possibly be a Liberal, could he?[26]

---

[26] David Orchard joined the Liberal party in January 2006.

CHAPTER 12

THE MERGER

POLITICAL LEADERS ARE OFTEN judged by their first one hundred days. Without the levers of government, and burdened by flak over the Orchard deal, there was little Peter MacKay could have been expected to accomplish that summer. Yet, within one hundred days of being elected leader, MacKay had set in motion the process that would ultimately result in the loss of his leadership and the dissolution of his party.

This should have been an enjoyable period for MacKay. It wasn't. He might have expected to bask in the glory of victory while he prepared for the fall session of Parliament, but instead he faced mostly criticism. As Chantal Hébert of the *Toronto Star* explained, "When [MacKay] signed his pre-nuptial contract with Orchard, the new Tory leader bargained away his honeymoon."[1] He was not the first newly elected Tory leader to have a rough start. When Joe Clark won the leadership in February 1976, everybody asked, "Joe Who?" As a headline, the question echoed across the country and expressed the astonishment that a virtual unknown could win the leadership of a national political party after starting with only 12 per cent support and coming in third of eleven on the first ballot.

---

[1] Chantal Hébert, "The fallout from MacKay's win," *Toronto Star*, June 4, 2003, A23.

While the number-one problem for MacKay was the Orchard agreement, party finances were also an issue. Despite a substantial reduction in debt over the past three years, the party still owed $4 million, and donors had grown weary of supporting two conservative parties that had no chance of defeating the Liberals.

Despite the bad press, the polling data for MacKay and the Tories were encouraging. Post-convention, the Tories under MacKay remained comfortably ahead of the Harper-led Alliance—16.7 per cent to 11.2 per cent—although both parties were dwarfed by the whopping 54.0 per cent Liberal support.[2] Alliance and the PCs were tied in Alberta; the Tories were ahead in all other parts of the country except British Columbia. The Alliance had only 8 per cent support in Ontario. Even more encouraging to Tories was that they were the second choice of most voters, indicating opportunity for growth. The Tories enjoyed a two-to-one margin over the Alliance in second-choice support. While the Orchard deal dominated the post-convention media coverage, it appeared not to have hurt MacKay in the polls, as he rated a score very similar to Harper on the issue of trust.

A more ominous conclusion from the polls, for both MacKay and Harper, was the stranglehold a Martin-led Liberal party had on the electorate. And that was before he became Liberal leader.

In the battle of the parties of the right, Ekos president Frank Graves gave the PC party the decided edge. "What you have is a reduced core of loyal Canadian Alliance voters who really have very little room to pick up additional support and no sign of being able to capture the public's attention. The Tories, on the other hand, are now looked at as the only party besides the Liberals who could credibly be seen as forming a national government."

Two weeks after being elected leader, Peter MacKay attended the annual press gallery dinner, an unrepentantly humorous evening where speeches are judged by the quality of the self-deprecation. MacKay began his remarks by saying, "I am sorry if I have to leave

---

[2] Ekos Research Associates Inc., "The Canadian political scene," July 17, 2003, based on a random sample of 1,501 telephone interviews conducted between June 19 and July 9, 2003, results accurate +/− 2.5 percentage points 19 times out of 20.

early. I told David Orchard I would be in by eleven." The audience roared approval. MacKay showed he had not lost his sense of humour. The CBC's Larry Zolf offered this assessment of MacKay's performance:

> The real star of the evening was new Conservative leader Peter MacKay. His speech was funny, and all at his own expense. Said MacKay: "I've been called treacherous, stupid, venal, lazy... and that's only by the Tories." MacKay spoke of "NAFTA, Shmafta." Then he referred to his famous refusal to register his gun. Said MacKay: "I finally registered my gun. I couldn't go into a shotgun wedding with David Orchard unless I had my own gun with me." MacKay got an added laugh when he referred to his gallery speech as "my honeymoon." It was a honeymoon, indeed. Laughing at himself, MacKay offered to send Elsie Wayne, the homophobic Tory MP, to be a marshal at Toronto's Gay Pride parade. He got a huge standing ovation from the crowd. My politicos called MacKay's speech a turning point: he was the real winner, politically, of the evening. After this speech, no one will be laughing at MacKay. My politicos said he'll do well in the next election.[3]

This was perhaps the first indication that MacKay had a communications plan for the Orchard agreement. "What was done at the dinner wasn't based on anybody's strategic advice. It was just having fun and keeping it all in perspective," said MacKay, although his girlfriend, Lisa Merrithew, provided some of the lines. MacKay called the evening an attempt at "self-preservation." Even David Orchard took MacKay's comments in good humour.

HARPER AND HIS ADVISERS had anticipated a MacKay win. Over the spring Harper and MacKay advisers would cross paths, hinting to

[3] Larry Zolf, CBC News Viewpoint, "The Parliamentary Press Gallery Dinner," June 17, 2003. See http://www.cbc.ca/news/viewpoint/vp_zolf/20030617.html (accessed July 10, 2006).

each other that soon they would "need to talk." What that meant in concrete terms was unspoken, but there was a sense that a change in leadership would bring a new era of co-operation. Harper and the entire Alliance team were particularly glad that Joe Clark would be taken out of the equation. Harper sent some of his senior advisers to the Tory leadership convention with the explicit purpose of signalling to MacKay that Harper was ready to dialogue.

Since taking over the Alliance leadership, Harper had become convinced that a deal with the Tories was not only desirable, but essential. One event a few weeks before the Tory leadership convention sealed this conviction. Harper had been leader of the Alliance for more than a year and had invested much of his time trying to build support in voter-rich Ontario. An important test of his progress would be plain to see in a by-election in Perth–Middlesex on May 12, 2003.

Citing poor health, Liberal John Richardson had resigned his Perth–Middlesex seat in 2002, about six months before the by-election was called. The rambling southwestern Ontario constituency was ideal territory for the Alliance. It was rural, and heavily influenced by local farmers who were angry with the Liberal government about the firearms registry. It was just about as perfect a storm as could be imagined for the Alliance, and an ideal opportunity for Harper to demonstrate he could overpower the Tories in Ontario. To top it off, the Tories were effectively leaderless: Joe Clark had announced his resignation some nine months earlier, and the convention to choose his successor was still weeks away.

The Alliance knew full well how a by-election could change party fortunes. Reform had gained enormous credibility from having won the 1989 by-election in Beaver River, Alberta. Harper signalled the importance of this by-election by visiting the riding on numerous occasions to drum up support for his candidate, long-time resident and local businesswoman Marian Meinen.

The results were Harper's worst nightmare: Alliance lost, and the Tories won. Tory Gary Schellenberger bested his Liberal opponent, Brian Innes, by 1,001 votes. The Alliance candidate came in a distant third, only 697 votes ahead of the fourth-place NDP candidate. The Tory vote was almost double that of the Alliance. And the Alliance received 4,385 fewer votes than they had garnered in the 2000 general election.

More than any poll or optimistic forecast, the Perth–Middlesex by-election left a deep scar on the Alliance psyche. It was a humiliating defeat in what should have been one of the most winnable seats in Ontario. If Alliance couldn't win seats in Ontario, it couldn't win government. "Stephen made the decision he had to merge with the Tories after the Perth–Middlesex by-election," said Tom Jarmyn, a political adviser from Harper's staff. There was only one answer to the Ontario question: an Alliance-PC merger. Harper was reminded of that fact in the House of Commons in June 2003, when newly elected Tory leader Peter MacKay, with Schellenberger on his arm, walked past Harper en route to introduce his newest member to the Speaker.

IT WOULD HAVE BEEN EASY FOR HARPER to conclude that the MacKay–Orchard agreement precluded any meaningful liaison with the Tories. And Harper did what he could to use the agreement to split the Tory party and undermine MacKay's leadership. A weakened Tory party, he thought, would ultimately bring the rank-and-file Tories to their senses, and then to the Alliance fold.

In the days after the convention, Harper could not resist ridiculing the Tories for moving to the left of the political spectrum. Harper went so far as to refer to the Tories as the new "socialist" party of Canada. Speaking through the media to Canadian conservatives, Harper expressed shock and bewilderment: "I think [PC party members] would rather see a conservative alternative—a party that works with the Canadian Alliance—not a party that works with the socialists. Mr. Orchard in the picture is obviously a complication and a difficulty."[4] While addressing Alliance supporters, Harper was clearly speaking to members of the PC party when he said, " The

---

[4] "MacKay's deal harms unite-the-right drive: Harper," *Saskatoon StarPhoenix*, June 4, 2003, A9.

choice for Tories is no longer the status quo. The choice is a coalition with the Canadian Alliance or a coalition with the Orchardistas."[5] The term "Orchardistas" evoked the memory of the Sandinista National Liberation Front that ruled Nicaragua from 1979 to 1990 and was Harper's way of saying the Tories had gone "radical" and "socialist."

Having Orchard in the mix was both an opportunity and a hardship for Harper. On the one hand, Harper could use the agreement to undermine the Tories. On the other hand, the agreement diminished Harper's hope that he and MacKay would find a way to end vote splitting before the next election.[6] "We felt David Orchard and his people did not really fit inside the PC party," said Jarmyn. Nonetheless, there was a sense in the Alliance brain trust that it would take another election before a merger would be possible: "We looked at the next election as the *primary* to determine which of the conservative parties would carry the banner," Jarmyn explained.[7]

In the summer of 2003, most commentators seemed to accept that a deal between the Alliance and PC parties was not going to happen. Chantal Hébert of the *Toronto Star* wrote, "[MacKay] . . . probably sold out Stephen Harper's best chance of changing the course of the next federal election. The weekend events leave the Alliance Leader all dressed up for a serious negotiation with the Tories with nowhere to go, and with no real consolation prize in sight . . . . But even if MacKay really wanted to make a deal— something that has not always been clear since the convention—the ambiguous nature of his victory would be bound to tie his hands."[8]

---

[5] Johnson, *Stephen Harper*, 328.

[6] Allan Thompson, "Orchard deal an obstacle to uniting the right: Harper," *Toronto Star*, June 4, 2003, A8.

[7] In this context, "primary" refers to a runoff election in which two candidates or entities from the same party square off against one another to determine who will take on an inevitable opponent. The term is often used to describe the process by which American political parties choose their candidates to run for president.

[8] Hébert, "The fallout from MacKay's win."

MacKay gave every indication, in the days after the convention, that he would not deal with the Alliance, and he defended his agreement with Orchard. Reminding reporters that he had never been an advocate of an institutional merger, MacKay said, "In the next federal election, the Progressive Conservative Party will present 301 candidates."[9]

Despite the rhetoric, there were surprising, although faint, indications from the two leaders that a merger was possible before the next election. Harper said he was still willing to co-operate with the Tories, but his appeal was directed to rank-and-file members rather than to leadership. MacKay was more direct and spoke of his plans to appoint a "special adviser" who would serve as his counsel on how best to build a national conservative coalition. He also suggested that nothing in his agreement with Orchard precluded talks with anyone who was interested in uniting conservative voters. Perhaps he was leaving himself open to other options when he said, "Until I hear otherwise, I believe the formula is within the existing structure of the Progressive Conservative Party of Canada."[10] At the time, few people appreciated the extent of MacKay's openness.

MacKay made his next move in a speech to party supporters at a luncheon meeting of the Confederation Club in mid-June, where he reportedly offered an "open hand" to Stephen Harper: "I said the door is open for discussions. I'm not only open; I'm enthusiastic about having discussions with Mr. Harper."[11] Harper quickly responded: "I am encouraged by Peter's remarks today and his openness to discussing a common cause." MacKay was careful not to raise expectations and tried to calm those in the party who opposed any sort of institutional merger: "Given the histories, standings, and prospects of our two parties, I believe we must first find common cause and common goals and establish trust before setting out a

[9] "MacKay's deal, *Saskatoon StarPhoenix*."
[10] Sheldon Alberts, "Harper won't discuss strategy with MacKay: 'Shocked' by Orchard deal," *National Post*, June 3, 2003, A6.
[11] Norma Greenaway, "MacKay straddles unite the right fence," CanWest News Service, June 19, 2003.

common electoral strategy. The first steps are important. Let's take the time to make sure they are the right ones."

Before the June leadership convention, rank-and-file PC party members might have expected that Brian Mulroney, the only Conservative who could compare electoral records with Sir John A. Macdonald, would be angry with MacKay for hinting at co-operation with the Reform-Alliance gang, which had split Mulroney's coalition. However, Mulroney staked out new ground in his convention speech. He reminded delegates of the damage done by Preston Manning and the Reform party, then concluded that it was time to end the civil war:

> At the very moment the centre-right was gaining effectiveness in Canada, Mr. Manning chose to launch a new party, split the vote and give rise to the political fragmentation we know today. In the process he has given the Liberals an extraordinarily generous gift sufficiently munificent that a government so demonstrably mediocre as our present one can contemplate a 4th term without breaking a sweat. As Mr. Chrétien says every night before falling asleep, 'merci beaucoup, Preston.' That is a little recent history. *But let us now turn the page.*[12]

Mulroney described what *turning the page* implied for the leader who would be chosen the following day:

> I have said that the next Conservative leader must be open and magnanimous about opportunities to co-operate and build a winning coalition with other like-minded Canadians. In order to build a national alternative government that Canadians will accept, we must listen carefully to all potential allies and act selflessly in Canada's interest.[13]

---

[12] "Notes for an address." (see chap. 4, n. 55).
[13] Ibid.

Putting Canada first meant seeking an honourable truce that would reunite conservative forces and put an end to otherwise interminable Liberal rule.

Mulroney was not suggesting that PC forces should surrender. Mulroney spoke proudly of the legacy that could be claimed by those who had built and sustained the PC party:

> . . . regional political movements have come and gone throughout our history. They have swept, sputtered and eventually collapsed because they failed to articulate a broad, generous and inclusive vision of Canada and all her people. Regional rancour is no substitute for nation building and Canadians know this instinctively. The Conservative party founded Canada 135 years ago. It today constitutes government in 5 provinces representing almost 65 per cent of Canada's GDP; forms the official opposition in 2 others; is represented in the House of Commons by members of Parliament from 7 provinces; forms the official opposition in the Senate of Canada; comes second in almost every national public opinion poll in Canada—and the Conservative Party which founded our country 135 years ago will be here and fighting for Canada 135 years from today.

The speech Mulroney delivered at the convention was among his most important since leaving office and very likely changed the dynamics that divided the Alliance and PC parties.[14] And it was vintage Mulroney. Even the media, who had long treated Mulroney as a virtual punching bag, were talking about how much they missed him on the national scene.

And so the scene was set. Let the negotiations begin.

THE FIRST FACE-TO-FACE ENCOUNTER between Harper and MacKay occurred without notice or warning. It was late June, only a

---

[14] There is no more meaningful indication of the importance Mulroney attached to the speech than that he went to Toronto at about the same time as he was notified that his son Nicholas had been in an accident at school and had broken both arms.

few weeks after MacKay won the leadership. MacKay approached Harper in the lobby of the House of Commons in plain view of other members. He told Harper that he had just instructed PC party legal counsel to drop a lawsuit Joe Clark had launched against the Alliance in May 2000.[15] MacKay said to Harper, "You and I have to talk." Harper was taken aback—pleasantly so—and immediately accepted the offer.

Beyond the Bay Street types, who were shutting down the financial tap to the Tory and Alliance parties until a merger was done, other leading figures were telling Harper and MacKay what had to be done. No one was more willing to encourage this process than Belinda Stronach, president and chief executive officer of Magna International. She was convinced, she said, that for the sake of democracy and the end of Liberal rule the two conservative parties had to unite.

Stronach was well placed to help. She had been a financial supporter of both parties and had the ear of both leaders. Her donations and fundraising for Peter MacKay contributed significantly to his ability to win the leadership. She had supported Preston Manning and was friendly with Brian Mulroney. As head of a billion-dollar company, she had the administrative, logistical, and financial resources at her disposal to help facilitate meetings between the parties. In terms of raw power, she was someone whose phone calls were returned.

Harper and MacKay met on June 26, 2003, just north of Toronto, in an old house that was used by Magna International for off-site meetings. The meeting was top secret, which meant that only a handful of people knew about it. Even MacKay's senior staff were kept out of the loop. There was no formal agenda. On the table was a discussion about a process by which an agreement on co-operation might be struck. Both leaders agreed to appoint senior representatives to initiate "talks" between the parties. Originally the representatives were to be called "sherpas." (The term was com-

---

[15] The lawsuit was over the use of the word "Conservative" by the Alliance party. Officially they were known as the Canadian Reform Conservative Alliance Party.

monly used in government circles to describe people who do the actual work at international meetings, preparing agreements to be signed by heads of state.) The Alliance team didn't like the term: to them sherpas were expert guides who assisted climbers in the Himalayan Mountains. They suggested "eminent persons," who ultimately became known as "emissaries."

The emissaries were to meet over the course of the summer and report back to their leaders on what they thought could be achieved in the short term. Three ground rules were established for the emissary process. First, the emissaries would be free to explore any and all options. Second, the initiative was to be kept strictly secret. Finally, during the period of secret negotiations, public statements by party leaders and their representatives would refrain from any negative comments about each other.

At the outset, both Harper and MacKay were hoping the talks would lead to co-operation in the House of Commons and perhaps a way to deal with vote splitting in the next election. Harper was on record advocating an institutional merger, but he didn't expect that could be achieved in the short term. MacKay knew the conservative family would eventually reunite, but a merger was not in his thinking in June 2003. Both Harper and MacKay thought the emissary process was an important first step in what would become a multiyear process.

When MacKay reported the results of the planning meeting to his senior staff, they were taken aback. "Peter was way ahead of us on initiating discussions with Harper," said MacKay chief of staff Rick Morgan. "We were hesitant and cautious at first."

MacKay considered a number of emissaries at the outset of the process. Former Alberta premier Peter Lougheed came to mind, as did former PC leadership candidate Hugh Segal. Both were highly respected in the party and were experienced negotiators. They represented different parts of Canada and would be powerful forces in persuading party members that whatever agreement was worked out would be in the party's best interests. Both would be seen as strong defenders of the party's interests and sufficiently independent of MacKay to offer objective advice. MacKay called Lougheed and Segal to get their views on the Alliance and what they thought could be achieved in the short term. Lougheed replied that he didn't think he was the right person for the job because of his provincial outlook. He also said he wasn't ready to welcome the Alliance into the Tory fold. After speaking with Lougheed and Segal, MacKay thought of two other individuals to lead the process: Bill Davis and Don Mazankowski.

Bill Davis had been premier of Ontario and Don Mazankowski, from Vegreville, Alberta, had been a revered deputy prime minister in Mulroney's administration. The two had iconic status in the party and in the country. They also had stellar reputations for integrity and honesty. They did not come easily to the task, however: MacKay and others had to persuade them to accept.

Mazankowski had seen many of his colleagues go down to humiliating defeat at the hands of the Reform party in 1993 and felt bitter towards those who he felt had broken up a family compact. He saw little difference between Alliance and Reform, or between Manning and Harper. Like many western PC cabinet ministers, Mazankowski had underestimated Manning in the late 1980s. He was not comfortable with the idea of sitting across a table negotiating with the Reform-Alliance team as equals. It took Peter MacKay, Elmer MacKay, Michael Wilson, Bill Davis, and a number of PC senators to persuade Mazankowski to go to the negotiating table. Brian Mulroney called from Spain to make sure Mazankowski was on the PC negotiating team. Mazankowski knew in his heart that if the Liberals were ever to be defeated, the parties would have to be brought back together. Ultimately, the goal of a conservative government was more powerful than any resentment Mazankowski felt towards Reform-Alliance. Mazankowski might not have accepted the role had it not been for a chance encounter with Alliance senator Gerry St. Germain in a Winnipeg airport in early August. St. Germain remembers a conversation that went something like this:

St. Germain:	Maz, I hear they've asked you to negotiate this thing. Are you going to do it?
Mazankowski:	I don't think so.
St. G:	I can't believe you're not. Do you know that they're prepared to call it the Conservative Party of Canada?
M:	Oh, they'll never do that.
St. G:	Believe me. I know what they're thinking and this is a given.
M:	Oh, they can't do that.

Mazankowski recalls the thought process he went through before becoming an emissary. "I didn't get caught up in efforts to co-operate over the years. I wasn't thinking merger until I heard the Alliance was ready to name it the Conservative Party of Canada. That's really what I wanted. If it had been the Conservative Alliance or the Conservative Reform Party, I don't think I would have been there. The Conservative Party of Canada, CPC, that was very important to me."

Bill Davis was a Red Tory from Ontario's Big Blue PC Machine. He had rarely, if ever, said a good word about Preston Manning or Stephen Harper and did not identify with their policies. He was one of the premiers who had led the patriation of the constitution with Trudeau in 1981 and was a strong believer in official bilingualism, a policy that was not uniformly popular in the Alliance party. "Davis had serious doubts about the prospects of reintegrating the party," said MacKay. "But he also knew about the value of a united Conservative party in Ontario, which is where we were hitting the wall time and time again with vote splitting."

MacKay understood that caucus support would be critical to the acceptance of any agreement. Even though he had agreed with Harper that there would be only two emissaries from each side, MacKay was uncomfortable that his caucus would not be directly represented. Loyola Hearn was a wise counsel and a trusted confidant to MacKay, and could help bring caucus on side with an agreement. Hearn was the representative from St. John's West,

Newfoundland, and like all Atlantic Canadians, had cause to suspect Harper, who had chastised easterners for a culture of dependency and defeatism. Hearn had quipped to Deborah Grey, then an Alliance MP: "There were not enough Alliance members in Newfoundland to row a dory."[16] Hearn was a calm and gentle man, but had the passion and power of persuasion one might expect from a Newfoundlander. "People knew that Loyola was his own man and wouldn't accept any guff from the Alliance. He had the demeanor and credibility that would be required to navigate the tricky waters that lay ahead," said MacKay.

Harper's emissaries were Gerry St. Germain, Ray Speaker, and Scott Reid. Senator St. Germain, the most controversial of the three, was also the most persuasive. He was the only Alliance emissary who had been active in the PC party. His duties as a PC included one term as a PC member of parliament, its caucus chair, party president, and senator. On October 18, 2000, St. Germain became the only senator in the Alliance caucus. He was well qualified to be an emissary. He knew the PC party and its key players well. In 1998, he tried to persuade Stephen Harper to run as Tory leader. He had also initiated and chaired secret meetings between Tory and Alliance MPs and senators between 2001 and 2003. None of his efforts at reconciliation was easy. "I was leading the pack but I would rather not say who was coming to my meetings. They are really good friends of mine and they are the only ones that I have."

After Preston Manning, Ray Speaker was the closest thing the Alliance had to an elder statesman. A farmer from Enchant, Alberta, and a member of the Order of Canada (2001), Speaker had served in the Alberta Social Credit cabinet of Ernest Manning and the Progressive Conservative cabinet of Don Getty, had been leader of the Representative Party of Alberta, and was a founder of the Reform party. In 1993, he was elected to the House of Commons under the Reform banner. In 1999, Prime Minister Chrétien appointed Speaker a member of the Security Intelligence Review

---

[16] Story told by Deborah Grey on Cable Public Affairs Channel on February 6, 2006.

Committee (SIRC), an agency that provides Parliament and the Canadian public with an external review of the Canadian Security Intelligence Service (CSIS). Reform staff member Tom Jarmyn offered this assessment of Speaker: "Ray had a lot of credibility in the Reform party. He was a calming influence and had extremely good judgment."

Scott Reid was added as an emissary after MacKay advised Harper that he had added Loyola Hearn to the PC team. Reid was an Alliance MP from Lanark–Frontenac–Lennox and Addington, near Ottawa. He had a reputation for his knowledge of constitutional matters and was not known to make compromises. Harper appointed Reid as an emissary because he was a trusted adviser and because Reid was opposed to a merger. "Having Scott at the table helped us determine how the party might react to a merger proposal. He was an honest reflection of the populist traditions that might not have identified with the PC party," said Jarmyn.

The six emissaries constituted an interesting mixture. Some on the PC side hoped that Senator St. Germain would be anxious to ingratiate himself with his former colleagues and restore his relationship with Mulroney. Reid, on the other hand, was young and brash, and did not show any indications of intimidation or deference to the Tory icons.

MacKay and the PC emissaries held their first planning meeting on August 3 via conference call. Most of the discussion revolved around goals and objectives. The initial goal was to build an atmosphere of trust and goodwill; the ultimate goal for the PC team was to "recreate the Conservative party." Mazankowski's notes from the meeting reflect his admiration for MacKay and the approach he took to the negotiations: "I was impressed with MacKay. He made it very clear that this was being done in the interests of the country and the democratic welfare of the nation. He said that if he got beheaded in the process that was a small price to pay for what needed to be done."

A second conference call was held on August 16. There had been rumblings that the Alliance side was going to "smother" PC forces. Mazankowski sought to minimize the negativity and public outbursts by occasionally speaking with Alliance caucus members, including Monte Solberg, who told Mazankowski that Harper had come 180 degrees and wanted a deal with the pcs. Solberg also said the entire Alliance caucus was committed to ending the division in the conservative movement and wanted to end vote splitting.

THE FIRST EMISSARY MEETING, organized by Rick Morgan, was held on August 21 at the Glenerin Inn, a twenty-nine-room country-house hotel located near the Toronto airport. The meeting room was booked under the name John Macdonald, the first leader of Canada's Conservative party.

The meeting was historic and emotional for Don Mazankowski. "It wasn't easy for me to walk into that room and start negotiating because of the old wounds and what they did in splitting the party. But I was also excited and enthused by the fact that we could restore the Conservative Party of Canada."

While all options were open for discussion, Mazankowski suggested, and all emissaries agreed, that the one-party option should be the first priority. The rationale was that a single party would represent the best opportunity to defeat the Liberals in the next election.

A new party would need a name. It took little time and no debate to choose the name "Conservative Party of Canada." Dropping the "Progressive" moniker would be viewed by exuberant Red Tories as evidence that the new party would be positioned further to the right of the political spectrum than had the pc party. (Such an assumption ignored the fact that the term "progressive" had been adopted in 1942, when the party chose as its leader Manitoba's former Progressive Party premier John Bracken. Historically the Progressive Party was a closer cousin to Reform than it was to the Red Tories.) It seemed to matter much less to Harper's emissaries that the words "Reform" or "Alliance" were nowhere to be seen. The new name was hardly a concession on Harper's part. He always wanted to be part of a single principled Conservative party. Recognizing that some pc supporters would feel slighted by the change in name, the "first principles" of the new party included a statement that the party would follow "progressive" social policies.

For the PC emissaries, the most encouraging development from that first meeting was an agreement that the new party would follow the aims and principles embedded in the constitution of the Progressive Conservative Party of Canada. The founding principles of the new Conservative Party of Canada were lifted virtually verbatim from the PC party constitution—the same words, in the same order.

Only three clauses were added:

1. A belief that English and French have equality of status and equal rights and privileges as to their use in all institutions of the Parliament and Government of Canada;
2. A belief that all Canadians should have reasonable access to quality health care regardless of their ability to pay;
3. A belief that the greatest potential for achieving social and economic objectives is under a global trading regime that is free and fair.

That the party should commit itself to free and fair trade is hardly earth-shattering, although it may have been an attempt by the Alliance side to remind all concerned of MacKay's flirtation with David Orchard. Adding clauses about public health care and bilingualism were clear victories for Red Tories.

What is stunning is that the aims and principles in the new constitution would contain virtually none of the elements fundamental to the Reform party constitution drafted by Preston Manning. There was no Triple-E Senate; there were no protections for the family unit; no references to democratic inclusiveness, such as referenda; no assemblies or recall; no requirement that allegiance to a constituent would supersede party obligation; no requirement for balanced budgets; and no reference to more positive relations with the United States.

The first meeting went much better than any of the PC emissaries had predicted. MacKay, who was vacationing in Greece with Lisa

Merrithew at the time, recalls hearing from Mazankowski after the first meeting: "The emissaries came back and said they are willing to give us everything. We kept thinking this is too good. He [Mazankowski] said the Alliance put stuff forward and they would capitulate before we even had a chance to finish our arguments. He said there wasn't a single proposal that was made that was not immediately accepted." The Tory emissaries had prepared themselves for a tough negotiation; the first meeting was anything but.

In many ways, the progress was more than MacKay had bargained for. He expected slow and steady progress from his emissaries—not a breakthrough. "Peter got nervous after the first emissary meeting. Then he began to see the possibility of what could be built and he started believing," said Morgan.

The arrangement between the parties was clearly predicated on an equal partnership. The relationship that existed between the PC party and its provincial counterparts was enshrined, and that enshrinement included a prohibition against forming any new provincial Conservative parties. To ensure the new party did not revert to the roots of any one of the pre-merger entities, a commitment was made to build a "national force that reaches out to all Canadians, not just like-minded conservatives."

If the founding principles of the new Conservative Party of Canada were any indication, the new entity was going to look and feel a lot like the former Progressive Conservative Party. Stephen Harper had no quarrel with how the PCs defined themselves on paper. In the months after the merger, Harper told a staff member that he had never liked the Reform or Alliance constitutions and always preferred the construction and content of the PC party aims and principles. Harper knew the Reform party constitution was not the product of a bottom-up populist outreach; rather, it was a Preston Manning creation, written hastily by one man in an afternoon at a political convention.

The PC emissaries were surprised at how well the negotiations were going because they had limited insight into what the Alliance team really wanted. When all was said and done, Stephen Harper had few firm conditions. Because the PCs had a constitution that reflected conservative values, Harper saw little point in debating the constitution. "We didn't give them anything that we didn't already believe in," said Harper staff member Tom Jarmyn. All this leads to a question: Why break away from the PC party in the first place?

As negotiations progressed, the leaders became more directive about where they thought the talks should go. Harper gave his emissary team a prescriptive fourteen-point plan. The plan included a proposal for a new name for the party and provided details on a leadership selection process. Otherwise the proposal offered only transitional and mechanical measures. Curiously, Harper said nothing about policy, principles, or building a sustainable coalition. The fourteen points were:

1. The new party shall be called the "Conservative Party," although a longer more inclusive name is possible.
2. The new party will assume all the assets and liabilities of the merged parties.
3. The CA and PC leaders will be responsible for obtaining approvals from their respective parties by October 10, 2003.
4. The PC and Alliance parties shall each appoint eleven members to an interim governing body with equal representation from each province.
5. The interim governing body will address responsibilities with Elections Canada, draft a constitution, establish riding associations and oversee candidate nominations.
6. The new party will establish a trust capable of raising money and retire the debt of the PC Party. This entity will be the predecessor of the Conservative Fund.
7. The Conservative Party Parliamentary Caucus will be immediately established.
8. The Conservative Party caucus will immediately elect an interim leader by secret ballot, and draft a statement of principles and policies by December 31, 2003.
9. The interim leader, who cannot be a candidate in the leadership

race, will serve as Leader of the Opposition in the House of Commons and be responsible for election preparations.

10. The CA and PC parties will each name two individuals to a leadership election organizing committee.

11. The leadership vote shall be conducted by mail-in ballot on the basis of one-member one-vote. The membership cut-off shall be November 17, 2003. The first ballot shall be completed by December 17, 2003. Any runoff ballot shall be completed by January 7, 2003.

12. The founding convention of the Conservative Party shall be held in Ottawa on February 19–21, 2004.

13. The founding convention shall be responsible for the amendment and adoption of a constitution and a statement of principles and policies.

14. Where possible, the selection of CA and PC candidates shall be grandfathered to the Conservative Party, and further CA and PC nomination meetings shall immediately cease.

Peter MacKay gave his emissaries far fewer detailed instructions. His five points spoke mostly to the core values that he believed needed to be represented in a new party:

1. An equal partnership between the PC and CA parties, especially with regard to leadership selection.

2. A partnership with provincial PC parties.

3. Reach out to all Canadians, including other like-minded conservatives, in building the membership of the party.

4. The party must follow the principles as outlined in the PC Party constitution.

5. The result should be an effective alternative to the governing Liberals and a political force nationally—in every region of the country.

Inevitably, news of the talks leaked to the media. The source of the leaks has never been identified, but based on his conversations with various journalists MacKay believes it came from the Alliance camp. In a newspaper story under the headline "Merger leak angers Tories: MacKay says talks with Alliance will continue, despite breach of trust," MacKay said, "Whether it's a personal relationship, professional or whether it's politics, when you have a breakdown in your belief of sincerity from the other side it has a very negative impact. It undermines, it eats away at your own confidence of what you're trying to accomplish."[17] Sources close to the story suggest the leaks came from Alliance MP John Reynolds and Senator St. Germain, although St. Germain denies involvement. "They just about blew the whole thing with the leaks," said MacKay, who suggested that the half-truths and incomplete information might have made his caucus and party officials unnecessarily anxious and uncontrollable. However, given the coincidence that the CBC was holding a conference in the same hotel and at the same time the negotiations were underway, it is amazing that both sides kept the negotiation secret as long as they did.

MacKay was aware that Harper had a two-stream strategy in the works. While negotiating in good faith with the Tories, Alliance was simultaneously preparing an aggressive and possibly brutal advertising campaign for the fall. "They were not coming back to Parliament to take on the Liberals, they were coming back to try and bury us," MacKay said. St. Germain confirmed that a war was in the offing: "The contingency plan was to go at it as aggressively as we could and try and tear each other apart."

After the talks became public, MacKay issued a news release confirming the discussions. He reiterated the five core values he had communicated to his emissaries and offered his commitment that any firm proposals "would have to be considered by my party's caucus and membership."[18] MacKay was careful to keep expectations low. "It was more sensitive for us because we were trying to keep the talks quiet. We knew the negotiations might get

---

[17] Bruce Cheadle, "Merger leak angers Tories: MacKay says talks with Alliance will continue, despite breach of trust," *Halifax Daily News*, September 19, 2003, 10.

[18] A statement by Peter MacKay, leader of the Progressive Conservative Party of Canada, on co-operation with the Canadian Alliance, September 18, 2003.

sidetracked if party members were given incomplete or erroneous information. It made sense to provide details if and when we had a deal," MacKay said.

Most in the media gave Harper credit for kick-starting the merger discussions, although Harper declined comment because discussions were "ongoing." One of Harper's MPs was at greater liberty to speak and anonymously offered some tough talk to the press: "It is a very serious offer. Brian Mulroney wants it to happen, and so do a lot of other Tories. Peter MacKay has been told, if you don't do it, you will bring the party down like Kim Campbell did."[19] Only later would the Tories discover how the Alliance side knew Mulroney wanted it to happen: Mulroney was speaking with the PC team, and also with Stronach and Harper. He wanted the merger to happen.

Leadership candidate David Orchard happened to be in Ottawa the day news of the talks leaked. "I was assured by Rick Morgan [MacKay's chief of staff] that these talks were simply about how the parties can co-operate in the House of Commons and that I had nothing to worry about," Orchard said. Morgan contended that he was less specific than Orchard claims, although clearly Morgan was trying to finesse Orchard. Morgan wanted to temporarily neutralize Orchard for two reasons. First, if a merger did not happen MacKay could claim "no harm no foul" on the Orchard agreement. Second, Morgan wanted to keep Orchard quiet while the negotiations were underway. If MacKay was going to have any chance of winning the leadership of the new party, he would need to render Orchard a non-factor. Many key people knew Orchard well enough to believe he would have been willing to play ball had he been told the truth about the discussions and treated with greater respect. Instead, MacKay was left with an ugly aftermath: he had to deal with Orchard's accusations of betrayal and deceit.

---

[19] Robert Fife, "Harper offers Conservatives full merger by spring: Secret meetings held," *National Post*, September 18, 2003, A1.

MacKay was in a far more difficult position with his caucus than he was with Orchard. He said, "Like any sensitive negotiation, it could not be run by committee. I was concerned about a leak. While Loyola Hearn was there to represent caucus, it was gut-wrenching for me not to include everyone else. I could hardly tell Orchard what I was not ready to tell my caucus."

A few days after Orchard's trip to Ottawa, an important call came in to his Saskatchewan office:

"My boss wants to speak to your boss," said the caller.

"Who is your boss?" came the reply.

"The prime minister of Canada."

Orchard confirmed the call was legitimate and that Jean Chrétien was on the line, and the purpose of the call was quickly made clear. Chrétien said, "In the House of Commons, when I told MacKay 'you are the man who put the knife in the back of David Orchard,' I just want to make sure I got it right. He did stab you in the back?" (Chrétien's retort in the House of Commons had come in response to MacKay's accusations of Liberal corruption.) Chrétien added, "Imagine me defending you [Orchard] after you demonstrated against me for free trade."

THE SECOND MEETING WAS organized by PC party staff and was held on September 22–23. The six emissaries were joined by CA lawyer and political staffer Tom Jarmyn, MacKay chief of staff Rick Morgan, PC party national director Denis Jolette, and Belinda Stronach.

Stronach had been an active supporter and fundraiser for MacKay in his bid for the Tory leadership, and she had a history with the Reform and Alliance parties. The Tory contingent had its own view about which side Stronach was on. "It was clear that she wanted a merger of the parties, but we had no trust that we could confide in her," said MacKay. "It seemed to us she was much closer to the Alliance side of the table."

Rick Morgan was always suspicious of Stronach's claims of neutrality. "It was Harper's team that were always pushing her as a facilitator. She also seemed to know what proposals the Alliance side

were going to make next. I think the Alliance team felt Stronach had
some influence over Brian Mulroney. We did not trust Stronach and
I believe the Alliance team used her for its own purposes." It was
beginning to look as if Stronach was either a double agent or spy—
anything but neutral. It also seemed odd to the Tory emissaries that
she announced she had absolutely no aspirations to lead the new
party when no one had bothered to ask her the question.

Of her own accord, Stronach drew up minutes from the meeting;
her notes suggested there was agreement on every issue except for
what was to be resolved at a third meeting, scheduled for September
29. She noted that the PC emissaries were expected to present
detailed written proposals on the outstanding issues before the next
meeting. Alliance emissaries clearly thought they had the makings of
a deal. They reported to Harper that a deal was close and would be
finalized at the September 29 meeting. However, the PC emissaries
still thought substantial issues needed to be resolved, most significantly, leadership selection. While the Alliance side was looking for
written proposals from the Tory emissaries, none was forthcoming.
"Everything we gave them was leaked," said Mazankowski, "so we
were reluctant to do that."

The emissaries talked by conference call on September 26. This
did not go well. When it became clear to the Alliance emissaries that
the agreement would not be ready for signing on September 29, they
reacted very negatively. In a letter delivered to Stephen Harper dated
September 28, 2003, Scott Reid wrote:

> During the course of the 14:30 call, it became apparent that the
> only substantive agreement between the two groups of emis-
> saries was that we should look at forming a new party called the
> "Conservative Party of Canada." Even those relatively uncontro-
> versial elements of your proposal that we were certain we had
> agreement upon were suddenly the source of disagreement or
> hesitation. As mentioned on several occasions, we have not
> received a specific counterproposal or statement of position
> (despite many requests) from the PCs and beyond the statements

above, we cannot give any guidance with respect to their position on these issues. The emissaries had contemplated meeting on Monday to sign off on the agreement, but given that there is no such agreement and no proposal from the PC emissaries, we have advised them yet again that we will not be attending any such meeting. We did, however, encourage them to make use of their time on September 29th to formulate a comprehensive, coherent and workable proposal. Only then, can we accomplish the mandate that you gave to us in June of this year.

Senator St. Germain was worried that the Tory side might be going through the motions without any real commitment to the merger process. He said: "As much as they knew it had to happen, their enthusiasm was fairly low. Nothing concrete was developing in the negotiations so we put down in writing what we wanted. But nothing was coming from them. We weren't sure if they really wanted a deal because they didn't want to show us their cards."

When no written proposals came from the PC side before the scheduled meeting on the twenty-ninth, Harper made the decision that the Alliance emissaries should not go to the meeting. If this was brinkmanship, it was coming fairly early in the negotiating process. MacKay chose to call the bluff. "We were at the negotiating table. They would have to explain their absence."

When Belinda Stronach heard that the Alliance side had broken off talks, she called St. Germain at home the night before the meeting. "Put your boots on," was Stronach's opening line. "I will have my driver pick you up at the airport." St. Germain was already uncomfortable with the decision not to show up for the meeting. "My feeling was that if we didn't show up we would lose by default. The PC side was going to the meeting and would be able to claim they weren't the ones holding things up. So I called Harper and he reluctantly agreed that I should go." St. Germain rushed to the airport and caught the red-eye to Toronto with no time to spare. "When I showed up the next morning Mazinkowski was shocked," St. Germain recalled. "Maz said, 'What are you doing here?' I told him failure is not an option. The whole country is depending on us, otherwise the Liberals will be there for five hundred years."

Both sides were again talking, but there was still no comprehensive deal.

ON SEPTEMBER 29, Harper wrote to members of his caucus and the Alliance National Council to report on talks with the PC party. He outlined the steps he had taken to advance the process:

> The essence of the proposal was to create a new national party to be called the "Conservative Party." I indicated I would be prepared to take this proposal to our membership for a vote. I asked Mr. MacKay to respond to the proposal. Mr. MacKay did not respond to the proposal in terms of an acceptance in principle, a clear rejection or a counter proposal. Instead he asked that we re-activate the emissaries process. My preference remained for a reply. After a number of discussions it was finally agreed that our representatives would meet again on September 22.... The September 22 meeting ended on September 23 with my representatives reporting to me they believed they had an agreement in principle. They had agreed to compile and finalize their findings by conference call on September 26 and, with their leaders' consent, to sign the agreement in principle in person on September 29. The agreement would then go to our membership for a decision.... At this point, I do not know whether Mr. MacKay personally supports the formation of the new "Conservative Party of Canada," let alone how he believes it could be done within the current timeframe. I have asked, again, for Mr. MacKay's clear commitment and workable counter proposal. If I receive that, we shall proceed. I continue to believe that moving forward on this would be in the best interests of our membership and the Canadian people. I also contend that a coalition between our two parties is better for the PC Party than continuing the deal with David Orchard. Please feel free to share this information.

I would appreciate any guidance you or our grassroots membership may have on this matter.[20]

The issue, in all its nuances, was now in full media play. Harper and his Alliance emissaries were trying to portray MacKay and the PC representatives as indecisive, disorganized, unprepared, and confused. They suggested that deadlines had not been met and that supposed agreements had been thwarted. Harper took a personal shot at MacKay, citing the contentious agreement between MacKay and Orchard as the best Plan B the Tories could muster.

MacKay and his emissaries replied to the Alliance leaks on September 30 with a full media briefing. The PC party press release suggested Stephen Harper was at fault:

MacKay said it was deeply regrettable that the talks with the Canadian Alliance had come to such an abrupt halt. He added that significant progress had been made since the emissaries first met on August 21. While not closing the door on further talks, he said he had to be realistic and take into account the obvious reticence of the Canadian Alliance to resume discussions.[21]

The accompanying twelve-page PC emissary report, prepared by Denis Jolette, was complete, professional, and articulate. "I was focused and inspired," said Jolette.

> Our overall objective in accepting the role as emissaries for the Progressive Conservative Party was to find common ground with the Canadian Alliance with the aim of providing Canadians with a united, national, and competitive alternative to the Liberal government.... we advanced options for consideration by the CA emissaries that would never jeopardize basic values that Canadians hold in common and compromise a vision for a diverse and moderate party... we were disappointed to learn

[20] Memo from Stephen Harper to members of the Canadian Alliance Parliamentary Caucus and National Council, September 29, 2003.
[21] Progressive Conservative Party of Canada, "MacKay realistic, but holds door open for further talks with Alliance," press release, September 30, 2003.

that the meeting of September 29 would not be held when Mr. Stephen Harper, the Leader of the CA, stated in a press conference on September 26 that "there's no further meeting agreed to" and "we're at the point where we've exhausted the process".... We would like to report that substantial progress had been achieved on fundamental issues. These achievements, in our perspective, were meaningful and signified to us that the goal of a unified national Conservative Party was within reach and that the two parties were closer than ever before to finding common ground.[22]

The report described the twelve areas in which agreement was achieved and the two issues that were considered contentious. The first contentious issue was the leadership selection process. The second was an Alliance proposal that incumbent MPs be grandfathered as candidates for the next election, which meant existing MPs would not have to face a vote of constituency members to determine who would be the party's candidate in the next election.

MacKay brought Mazankowski into a PC caucus meeting to explain the progress that had been made and the issues that remained unresolved. "It was a rough meeting," recalled MacKay. Mazankowski concurred: "When I took the package to the caucus it was not a slam dunk. I remember what Senator Pat Carney said when she saw the wholesale adoption of the PC constitution. She said, 'I can live with this. No problem at all.' But others were very angry, belligerent, and very offensive. Others were opposed, but not as vicious. It was not a pleasant time." Despite the meeting, Mazankowski's eagerness for a united Conservative party and his belief that that's what party members wanted sustained his enthusiasm. It helped that wherever Mazankowski went—in airports or on the street—people would come up to offer support and encouragement.

---

[22] Emissaries for the Progressive Conservative Party of Canada, "A report concerning our discussion on a potential partnership with the Canadian Alliance," submitted to Peter MacKay, leader, Progressive Conservative Party of Canada, September 29, 2003.

The emissary report, along with MacKay's statements to the media, persuaded Harper that the PC team was serious and prepared to deal. "As soon as MacKay sat down in front of the national press gallery and said he was committed, this deal was done," said Tom Jarmyn.

The tone of Scott Reid's next letter, written to Don Mazinkowski on October 3, was decidedly different from the tone of his earlier letter to Harper:

> I have reviewed your report with my colleagues and it appears that there is a sound basis for further discussions and a compromise that could lead to our final recommendations to our leader with respect to an agreement in principle . . . it appears there is only one serious issue to be resolved—leadership selection.[23]

MOST MERGERS BEGIN WITH A DUE diligence process designed to expose any hidden secrets or sins the parties might bring with them into the new entity. Rumours of Tory debt were so legendary that some Reformers thought a better merger strategy might be to let their conservative cousins die in bankruptcy.[24] Stephen Harper mentioned the need to raise funds to retire the debt of the PC party in his fourteen-point merger plan. However, there was a surprise for everyone when the books were finally opened up. For the three years up to and including 2003, the Tories had recorded consecutive surpluses totalling $6.1 million.[25] In the same period,

---

[23] Scott Reid MP, emissary, Canadian Alliance, to Don Mazankowski, emissary, PC party, October 3, 2003.

[24] Recent books that describe the merger take this position. In his book on Harper, William Johnson states, "The proposal had some attractive features for Tories. They had a substantial debt and the Alliance was now debt-free," (Johnson, *Stephen Harper*, 332). Similarly, in *Rescuing Canada's Right*, Tasha Kheiriddin and Adam Daifallah state, "The PC party was in debt and Bay Street backers were fed up with funding the Tories losing efforts." (Kleiriddin and Daifallah, 37).

[25] The PC party surplus included a $4.2-million contribution in 2001 from the collapse of the Bracken House Trust.

the Alliance party had recorded deficits of $2.5 million. At the time of the merger, both parties had bank debt of $4 million, although the PC debt was effectively of lower value since it was interest free and payable over the following six years. In addition to the bank debt, the Alliance party carried loans from its constituency associations of another $2 million. Because the Alliance books had much higher cash and other working capital balances, Alliance maintained a slightly stronger financial position than did the Tories, but not by much.

THERE WAS STILL ONLY ONE thorny issue in the merger of the Alliance and PC parties—leadership selection.[26]

The Alliance party wanted a one-member, one-vote system. Under this system, the leader would be chosen by a majority of votes cast. There may have been some flexibility around the mechanics of the vote, such as whether it was a mail-in vote, a vote cast in a ballot box, or whether the ballot would be preferential.[27] But absent technical issues, one-member, one-vote was democratic religion for Harper and the Alliance.

MacKay wanted a leadership-selection system that gave equal weight to each constituency in Canada. Under this system, each constituency—whether it had ten, one hundred, or one thousand members—would get the same number of votes to elect the leader. The system might seem unfair and disproportionate, but MacKay argued that it was fundamental to building a truly national party and entirely consistent with how governments are elected in Canada. Under MacKay's "equal-weight system," leadership candidates would be forced to establish networks and members in every region and riding in Canada.

---

[26] The main issue was leadership selection. Establishing the principle of the equality of ridings was also significant for the election of delegates to policy conventions, electing the executive body, and making constitutional amendments.

[27] Under a preferential ballot, members vote only once and rank all the candidates. As the last-place candidate is dropped from the list, the votes are retabulated. The process continues until a clear majority winner is determined.

The positions advocated by the Alliance and PC leaders were not devoid of self-interest. A one-member, one-vote system would naturally favour a western-based leader like Stephen Harper, whose party membership and activism were traditionally strong. At the time of the negotiations, there were about 83,000 Alliance members and only 48,000 PC members. If the memberships of both parties were allocated to individual constituencies under an equal-weight system, the numeric superiority of the Alliance membership would be substantially diminished.

In some Quebec ridings, the membership rolls of the Alliance party were non-existent, and Tory membership numbers were anemically low. Someone vying to be leader of the new Conservative party would quickly discover that one of Alberta's twenty-eight ridings might have more members than did the entire province of Quebec with its seventy-five ridings. While not a Quebecer, MacKay had a strong political network east of the Ontario border that would need to be strong to give him any chance of winning the leadership of the new party. A one-member, one-vote system guaranteed Harper the leadership. Under a weighted system, MacKay would have a fighting chance. But self-interest was not MacKay's primary motivation. Pristanski recalls a meeting with MacKay, the emissaries, Morgan, and Jolette and making the point that if MacKay was to lead the new party, the equal-weight leadership formula was essential. MacKay surprised the group by interjecting that he would not necessarily be a candidate in such a leadership campaign. He maintained that the equal-weight formula was a necessary founding principle for the new united party. He said that for the party to be successful, any hint of regionalism had to be eliminated. "Regionalism is the root cause of how we got ourselves in perpetual opposition. We must found a truly national party where every region of the country is fairly represented. The leadership-selection formula must reflect the way we elect the House of Commons. No riding gets half a member. No riding will be shortchanged in this new party." After the meeting, Pristanski remembered discussing with Morgan how MacKay had so quickly gained the mantra of a strong party leader and how he was clearly in charge of the negotiating team. "Maz had his foot on the gas pedal, Davis had his foot on the brakes, and Loyola was cheering us all on. But Peter was clearly in charge and was guided by fundamental beliefs and principles," said Pristanski.

The emissaries tried and failed to reach an agreement on the leadership-selection process. It was the only area of contention and the only issue over which voices were raised at the negotiating table. There are differing accounts of heated exchanges between Don Mazankowski and Scott Reid: one says they were simply stating strongly held positions; another says Reid showed disrespect. Mazankowski recalls Reid as a partisan and a technician: "The rest of us left our partisanship at the door as we tried to work though the issues. Reid had more difficulty with that. He would inject extraneous issues that would complicate the process while we were trying to get fundamental agreement on basic objectives and principles."

Part of the brilliance of the emissary process was that it would be a test to see if those on the far right of the conservative movement could get along and agree with those on the far left. Bill Davis was a Red Tory; Don Mazankowski, Loyola Hearn, and Ray Speaker were moderates; and Scott Reid and Gerry St. Germain were Blue Tories. Bill Davis, a man of great wisdom and wit, would occasionally tell the emissaries that if the Conservative party wasn't big enough to accommodate all conservatives then it didn't have any hope of winning the country. This was an important reminder to all emissaries of the reasons compromise was necessary. Ultimately, it was up to the leaders to negotiate face to face to resolve the leadership-selection issue.

ON OCTOBER 8 HARPER revealed the full extent of his desperation to get a deal with MacKay. Without any pre-arrangements, Harper followed MacKay to the Ottawa airport. MacKay and Rick Morgan were catching a flight to Toronto to attend a Tory fundraiser at the Woodbine race track. Harper, who was seated in the first-class section, exited the aircraft first. MacKay saw Harper when they were both off the plane and asked, "Are you stalking me?" Ignoring the quip, Harper replied, "We really should talk." MacKay's reply was, "I am willing to talk."

Seeing that Harper's press secretary, Carolyn Stewart-Olsen, and his assistant, Ray Novak, were also on the flight, Morgan was suspicious that a trap was being set. Harper's staff suggested the leaders should meet at the Sheraton Hotel, and Morgan sent a staff member to scout the location, only to find reporters milling about waiting to catch MacKay and Harper for a photograph and a few questions. Morgan concluded that Harper's staff had tipped off the press in the hopes of discomfiting MacKay. At the last minute, Morgan had Ian Anderson book a suite at another hotel under the name John A. Macdonald. This was supposed to be a private and secret meeting. Belinda Stronach, forewarned by Harper's staff, appeared at the second hotel. Earlier Stronach had called Brian Mulroney to tell him of the meeting and to look for some support and instructions. Mulroney, surprised that Stronach was interceding in the negotiations, called Morgan to tell him of the call and what he had heard.

MacKay and Harper met alone while Morgan and Stronach waited in the hallway. Harper suggested various compromises on the leadership-selection issue, but MacKay stood firm. Harper, known for his steady stare, looked directly at MacKay to gauge his resolve. MacKay stared right back and without flinching said, "This is my stepping-off point. The party will respect the equality of ridings or there will be no merger." Harper did not say yes or no.

The brinkmanship displayed by Harper in September and October was based on his pressing need to achieve a merger before the next election. MacKay was less focused on the next election and more concerned with the next generation. "We never bought into the Paul Martin timeline and the need to rush through a merger," said Rick Morgan. "We knew we were contemplating one of the most important mergers in the history of Canada and we wanted to get it right." The process was more than a simple rearrangement of ownership; the process could potentially restore meaningful democracy to Canada.

Just before Thanksgiving weekend Harper spoke with MacKay and offered to accept the equality of ridings, but with a formula that would be determined only at the party's founding policy convention. Again MacKay said no. Both leaders decided to take the long weekend to reflect.

Besides leadership selection, Harper was holding out on a clause that would have grandfathered sitting Alliance MPs as the Conservative party candidates in the next election. That meant whoever was organizing in a riding from the PC party would have to step aside. Bill Pristanski and Rick Morgan had lunch on October 10 and thought MacKay might get the leadership-selection terms he wanted if he gave in to Harper's demand for the grandfather clause. Pristanski called MacKay to urge him to compromise but was promptly rebuffed. "I am not giving the Alliance anything more than I have already," replied MacKay, who was thinking of people like Gord Keller, his nominated candidate in the riding of Dewdney–Alouette, British Columbia. Under Harper's plan, Keller would have been forced to relinquish his hard-won nomination to the sitting Alliance MP, Grant McNally. MacKay thought this was unfair and undemocratic. Sensing MacKay would not budge, and believing that his leader was on the right course, Pristanski called a few of his Alliance friends and asked them to alert Harper that he would have to accept what was on the table or there would be no deal.[28]

MacKay spent a comfortable Thanksgiving weekend at his Nova Scotia home. The line in the sand had been clearly drawn, and MacKay, convinced that he had offered Harper the best deal possible for the country and for conservatives, was at peace with himself.

Harper had the more difficult task over the Thanksgiving weekend—either accept MacKay's vision for a national party, or fight the next election against another conservative party. Harper sized up the risks and went through his analysis.

---

[28] Those who were reported to have contacted Harper included former leadership candidate Tony Clement, Alberta strategist Rod Love, Toronto lawyer Bob Dechert, and Alberta premier Ralph Klein.

"Stephen had the longer-term view in mind," said John Weissenberger. "It was better to get a deal than to get a deal that was good for us. It was a calculated risk to accept the PC party rules." That didn't mean Harper thought the equal-weight leadership-selection process was a good idea. He still doesn't. "You should want to remove the opportunity for non-democratic manipulation," said Weissenberger.

In his admiring and well-researched biography of Stephen Harper, William Johnson gushes praise onto Harper for being principled, inflexible, and clear-headed. Yet when it came to the governance of the new Conservative party, Johnson wrote, Harper demonstrated a different persona: "Harper may have the image of an inflexible, ideologically driven politician; he was proving to be the opposite in these negotiations where he, rather than the Tories, made all the compromises."[29]

MACKAY DID NOT FEEL PRESSURED to compromise. He was comfortable driving a hard bargain. The pressure came only when it looked as if Harper was ready to let him have everything he had asked for. MacKay said,

> Since the convention, my life was made miserable from all sides. My own loyalists were furious with me for having done this Shakespearean tragedy. They thought I had poisoned the chalice and that this would preclude me from unifying the party in any way, shape or form. Then as things progressed, and the quiet discussions with the Alliance leaked out, the old Red Tory element, some of whom were with me, were incensed that I would even entertain talks of doing this. Then you had the Orchard faction that was screaming blue bloody murder for any thought of talking with Alliance. Added to that were the people who were close to me, including my father and girlfriend, who were saying, "What the hell are you doing?"

---

[29] Johnson, *Stephen Harper*, 332.

MacKay discussed what he should do with Brian Mulroney. The advice he received was to overlook the criticism and "bring the family back together." Whenever MacKay felt hesitant about moving forward with the negotiations, Mulroney was there with encouragement and support. Mulroney also reviewed some of the draft documents that were being discussed and offered comment.

Others in the party were critical of MacKay's willingness to discuss merger with the Alliance. The critics included Senator Lowell Murray and former leader Joe Clark, who saw Reform and Alliance as mortal enemies. MacKay recalled:

> There were a few strains in the PC party. There was the pure of heart: the PCs that said, "Never surrender—Damn it all, we are the true bloods. Our DNA goes back to John A.: not those Alliance guys. They are the ones that have caused the problem." And I understood that. I had a lot of that myself with animosity, although it was emotionally based. In the world of politics that is all nice and it's very sentimental and it's heady thought. But at the end of the day, it doesn't address the realities.

MacKay wanted to get past the emotional baggage the party had been carrying since 1993 and to focus more clearly on what was right for Canada:

> The emotional response wasn't clear thinking or strategic political thinking. The political theory and nuance was understandable, but at the end of the day, it was really about getting it done. As much as I think of myself as a Progressive Conservative I am also a practical conservative, a pragmatic conservative. This civil war, that then turned into the cold war among conservatives, has got to end.

Despite the bruising his party had taken over the years, and despite his competitive spirit, MacKay concluded that the nucleus of the PC and Alliance parties had enough in common that they could work in common cause in government:

> I thought, we can fight this out, but I had also spent enough time in the trenches at that point in my political career, and enough time quietly getting to know Reformers like Monte Solberg, Gary Lunn, and John Williams. I had participated in all efforts to co-operate, including the DRC experience. Through all of this my conclusion was we were really not that different.

MacKay knew what had to be done, but he wondered if he could bring his party with him:

> There were also people like my father, like [Don] Mazankowski, like [Bill] Davis, like my girlfriend, Lisa, whose very existence in politics was defined within the PC party, and they had suffered from this breakaway party. People very close to me were dead set against this and I understood why. People like Davis and Mazinkowski expressed grave reservations, but they came around after they saw the deal we were able to achieve.

MacKay knew in his mind that a merger was inevitable. That didn't diminish the pressure he was under as time for a decision drew near:

> The pressure was at times staggering. As I look back on it now, the thought of handing away my leadership just wasn't in my mind. I wanted to ensure the outcome was something I could live with. I was thinking about how we could do this properly and cement the foundation back together for the long run; not for a quick fix. We had to do this right so it wouldn't fall apart or leave a sour taste in everybody's mouth.

The fateful telephone call from Harper came in the early morning of Tuesday, October 14. Both men were in their constituency offices, Harper in a Calgary strip mall and MacKay in a New Glasgow strip mall. The other key people on the line were the lawyers, Paul Lepsoe for the PCS and Tom Jarmyn for the Alliance. The leaders proceeded clause by clause in a sombre and businesslike manner.

As they arrived at the section of the document that dealt with leadership selection, Harper paused. "I have been thinking a lot about this. We have made a lot of progress," said Harper. "This is a very historic decision," MacKay replied. Signalling that he was accepting all MacKay's conditions, Harper said, "We should do this."

In the end, Harper had given everything MacKay could have asked for. Harper had a blank cheque from his caucus to negotiate a deal and he ultimately sought only two conditions. First, the parties had to merge; and second, there had to be a leadership contest. This was a far cry from what Harper had offered Joe Clark in 2002. (In a way, this better deal validated Clark's decision to break away from talks with Harper.) Effectively, MacKay could have imposed whatever terms he wanted, and that's exactly what he did. But he still had a decision to make. While he knew a better deal would not be possible, the enormity of the decision gave him pause. Was this the right thing to do for his party? Was this the right thing to do for Canada? And he had other personal questions to face. Was he prepared to give up his leadership six months after it had been won? Was he prepared to face the ridicule that would come his way over breaking his agreement with David Orchard? Would he be a candidate for the leadership of a new Conservative Party of Canada?

It was not long before all doubt left his mind: "It was one of those rare moments of total clarity, like a ringing in the air. It was one of those few moments in your life, I suppose like when you are standing at the altar or your first child is born, a defining moment, when everything seems clear," MacKay said.

The leaders had agreed. It was left to the lawyers to work into the night and put it all down on paper. MacKay and Harper made their way back to Ottawa, and the agreement in principle was signed on Wednesday, October 15, 2003. Far from a glittering affair and media spectacle, the signing took place at Alliance party headquarters at

THE MERGER   319

10:30 in the evening. It almost didn't happen because the elevator carrying Stephen Harper and his staff to the signing ceremony got stuck between floors. The parties that had been divided for two decades would have to wait another ten minutes for the elevator to come back into service. MacKay arrived at the meeting on crutches, having been injured in a Thanksgiving weekend rugby match.

STEPHEN HARPER WAS DOWNRIGHT gleeful when he announced the merger of the parties to the press on October 16. The painfully reserved and often emotionless Harper declared: "I could hardly sleep last night. It is like Christmas morning. Our swords will henceforth be pointed at the Liberals, not at each other." Sensing that many members of his party would receive the news with mixed feelings, the usually jocular and energetic MacKay was more reserved: "This is something that, when I began in June to pursue, quite frankly I didn't think it would go this far, this fast." MacKay asked party members to "join us in this historic initiative."[30] MacKay told the press it was a tough decision to make, but what he signed was "not only an agreement in principle, it is a principled agreement."[31] Former prime minister Brian Mulroney offered immediate support for the agreement and suggested it was something the Liberals should fear. Speaking from Berlin, Mulroney said:

> [Martin] has been speaking about the democratic deficit in Canada and the greatest democratic deficit has come from the divided opposition. If you split the conservative vote two or three ways, then you're going to elect Liberals 10 times out of 10, which might be fun for the Liberals but eventually it is not very good for the country. The Liberals certainly didn't go out

---

[30] Canadian Press "Political parties join forces: Merger between Tories, Alliance first step in long process to make inroads against Liberals," *Charlottetown Guardian*, October 17, 2003. A1.

[31] Sean Gordon, with files from Bill Curry and Robert Fife, "Our swords will point at Liberals," *National Post*, October 17, 2003, A1.

of their way for me to be elected. I think in the interests of democracy, this is an important turning point.[32]

With the agreement done, the next deadline to meet was December 12, 2003: the date when the ratification of the agreement by party members must be completed, or the agreement would be null and void. The heavy lifting was far from over.

---

[32] Susan Delacourt, "Unified party good for democracy Mulroney; Not eager to see Liberal 'fun' continue, Says Martin should welcome change," *Toronto Star*, October 17, 2003, A7.

CHAPTER 13

RATIFICATION

T
HE LEADERS OF THE PC PARTY and the Alliance
agree to take steps to achieve the support of their
respective parties for this agreement as expeditiously
as possible. This process is to be completed by December 12,
2003."[1]

From the time the Agreement in Principle was signed on October
15, 2003, clause 11 left the leaders only eight short weeks to have
the agreement ratified. This would be more than enough time for
Harper, because his party was already an enthusiastic supporter. But
MacKay had to deal with the "pure of heart" PCs, the party members
who were loath to have anything to do with the Alliance. MacKay had
a battle on his hands.

The tight timeline for ratification was dictated by the coming
election, almost certain to be called for spring 2004. There was only
a handful of months to ratify the agreement, merge the two organizations, consolidate the finances, hold a leadership contest,
reconstitute 308 riding associations, nominate 308 candidates, develop
an election strategy, and design a platform. There was no margin for
any error in the timeline.

---

[1] Agreement in Principle on the Establishment of the Conservative Party of Canada,
Clause 11, October 15, 2003.

The Martin Liberals had done everything possible so they could call an election by April 1, 2004. To do this, they violated the usual terms of electoral laws.[2] If ratification did not occur by the December 12 deadline, it would have been impossible to reschedule a vote and hold a leadership contest before the next election.

The Alliance party had the benefit of merger experience, and the party constitution was structured to allow a one-member, one-vote mail-in ballot to decide such questions. All the party needed for the merger was the support of a simple majority of votes cast. Alliance adviser and lawyer Tom Jarmyn contended that Harper could have ratified the agreement without a vote of the membership because it was consistent with the objects of the corporation. That interpretation would have been politically unpopular and was never used.

According to the constitution of the PC party, ratification required the support of not less than two-thirds of party members. How this was to be done, and whether the two-thirds support could be achieved, were matters of considerable uncertainty. The party had just gone through a leadership-selection process in which none of the legitimate candidates had argued in favour of a merger. In fact, the only pro-merger candidate, Craig Chandler, had been treated with derision at the convention. At a 1999 convention, the party had overwhelmingly voted to prevent local riding associations from co-operating with the Alliance. Many senior members of the party were vehemently opposed to a merger and were trying to rouse rank-and-file members to reject it. The approximately 25 per cent of the party membership that was faithful to David Orchard would most certainly vote against the deal. Even if only a small portion of the non-Orchard party members voted against it, the deal was dead.

---

[2] According to PC legal counsel Paul Lepsoe, the Election Boundaries Adjustment Act had just come into force. While there is usually a one-year period after passing the Act to allow political parties and their local constituencies to reorganize, the Liberal government had substantially reduced the normal waiting period. Liberals were anxious to go to the polls under the new boundaries, which provided more seats in vote-rich and Liberal-friendly Ontario.

The PC party had a history of delegated conventions. But with only weeks to organize—coupled with the prohibitive cost of holding a national convention—the party's management committee quickly settled on a "virtual convention" as the only practical method. Voting centres would be set up across the country on Saturday, December 6, where delegates representing all 308 ridings would debate and vote via conference call. But first the party needed a system to elect delegates.

For the 2003 leadership convention, delegates had been chosen under a hybrid system, which gave each riding the same number of delegates regardless of the number of party members in the constituency. Delegates were determined on a proportionate basis such that if 25 per cent of constituency members voted for a particular candidate, that candidate would receive 25 per cent of the delegate spots. This was a new system designed to provide a more freewheeling and exciting convention. But the party had more experience with another system. Traditionally, prospective delegates who received the most votes in a constituency contest were elected to attend a convention. Under this system, controlling 51 per cent of a riding membership meant winning 100 per cent of delegates. Those who wanted the agreement ratified were attracted to the traditional system: a vote of 51 per cent support at the riding level could deliver an overwhelming number of delegates in favour of the agreement to the virtual convention. Taken to an extreme, a simple majority win at delegate-selection meetings could be turned into a unanimous show of support when the vote was called on the merger.

Paul Lepsoe, an expert in the party's constitution and Canadian election law, contended that the traditional voting system was in accordance with PC party bylaws. He also pointed out that elected delegates could not control the outcome by themselves, and that they represented only two-thirds of those eligible to vote. The other third were ex-officio delegates: those eligible to vote at conventions by virtue of their status as former MPs, senators, party officers, defeated candidates, and riding presidents.

David Orchard and others argued that the rules for the vote were biased and unfair. A group of people used this argument in an injunction filed in opposition to the merger. Lepsoe countered that the procedures followed a long-standing tradition in the party and did not break any new ground. Whatever the tradition, rules helped exaggerate the strength of an affirmative vote.

The forces opposed to the merger began to speak out. Senator Marjory LeBreton, a staunch Mulroney loyalist and one of the few remaining Tories who could speak of working for John Diefenbaker, said:

> I was reluctant to support the merger. I didn't like the way we weren't told the truth in caucus about what was happening and was worried what the end result would be; that it might be seen as an Alliance takeover. I was under pressure from Lowell Murray to sign a petition opposing the merger, which I refused to do. I had to step back and look at this objectively and have a long chat with myself to sort out what I really believed. I was worried about the survival of the PC party, especially under the rules of the new Election Act. I debated the issue many times with Brian Mulroney.

It took more than heavy-duty persuasion from Mulroney for LeBreton to support the merger. Mulroney would make many calls to many people before the ratification vote to help ensure it would pass the two-thirds threshold.

Other senators were more difficult to persuade. PC Senator Lowell Murray lamented, "It didn't have to be this way. Canadian Alliance and Progressive Conservative MPs could have created joint panels to try to find common ground on some of the most divisive issues, such as social policy and bilingualism. If they succeeded, the creation of a unified party would be stamped with principle, integrity and political credibility."[3] Murray suggested that the

---

[3] Lowell Murray, "Tories: Block the deal before it's too late," *Globe and Mail*, October 23, 2003, A21.

merger was done in haste before a new election financing law came into effect: "The paymasters will have to stuff their money into this and other political trusts before Dec. 31 when a new federal law takes effect, outlawing corporate political donations. This is the real explanation for the big rush to create and fund a new party that has no policy, no leader, and no discernible body of support."[4] Murray criticized Harper and MacKay because the nineteen founding principles in the agreement "give motherhood a bad name." Of course Murray's analysis ignored the fact that these principles were lifted word for word from the party that had honoured him at the ripe old age of forty-three with a place in the Senate.[5]

Two days after Murray's commentary appeared in the *Globe and Mail*, Peter MacKay penned his own *National Post* op-ed piece under the headline "Canada needs a viable conservative alternative."[6] MacKay wrote of the need for a single conservative voice to defeat the Liberals, and of the extended history of talks between the Alliance and PC parties, including the efforts of Joe Clark, who led the PC–Democratic Representative Coalition in the House of Commons.

Almost immediately after the agreement was signed, MacKay began a cross-country tour to drum up support. He had reason to be confident. The party conducted a poll through John Laschinger's Northstar Research, which indicated a strong majority of members were ready to move past the differences that had divided the movement for more than a decade. The poll helped shape the message MacKay took to the party: "The split in the conservative family [that] has given the Liberals a free pass in election after election has to end. Just give us a fighting chance." He proudly told party members that the agreement "respected our history and accomplishments."[7] At a

---

[4] Senator Murray's statement was technically incorrect. At the time, corporate donations were limited to $1,000 and individual donations to $5,000 per year.

[5] Lowell Murray was appointed to the Senate by Joe Clark on September 13, 1979.

[6] Peter MacKay, "Canada needs a viable conservative alternative," *National Post*, October 25, 2003, A17.

[7] Taken from speaking notes for Peter MacKay, supplied to the author by Denis Jolette.

regular fall meeting of the PC Canada Fund, board members did something they rarely do: they took a vote. They wanted to go on record to offer their support to MacKay, which they did unanimously.[8] MacKay sought and received the endorsement for the merger from his caucus, the party's executive, and the party's national council.

MacKay was frequently asked to reconcile the position he had taken during the leadership race of not being the merger candidate, with the agreement he took to party members. The Orchard deal, which was available for all to see on various websites, was a written reminder of what MacKay told party delegates in May. MacKay responded to these questions carefully and deliberately:

> I have always talked about the need to build a broad, national alternative. Frankly, when we started down this road, I really didn't think we would get to this point, but I did believe it was worth a try. I initiated the emissary process with an open mind, and put complete faith in the process and the emissaries themselves. The bottom line is that the Party membership will have the final word on the agreement.[9]

MacKay could not totally escape his personal dilemma, however. As much as he tried to say that the Orchard agreement contemplated "talks" with the Alliance, the deal hung around his neck like the proverbial albatross. Even though it would be party members, and not MacKay, who would decide the outcome, he had still led the process that produced the agreement after he had promised Orchard there would be no merger. But to MacKay, the magnitude of the merger made the agreement between MacKay and Orchard inconsequential. "I had more scorn heaped on me for signing the agreement than I did for breaking it," said MacKay. This was a rare admission, on MacKay's part, that he did, in fact, break his agreement with Orchard.

---

[8] Among those on the PC Canada Fund Board at the time, and voting in favour of the motion, was Scott Brison.

[9] Speaking notes, Peter MacKay. (see chap. 13 n. 7)

MacKay tried to counter the suspicion that he had intended all along to break the deal with Orchard and that he had orchestrated a plot to lead the party into a merger:

> I wasn't trying to play him . . . I felt I had a fairly accurate vantage point on the likelihood of a merger taking place before the next election and I never imagined it could happen. And what was the expiry date on the agreement . . . Was I saying it would never happen? I don't think so . . . I went in there with every intention of keeping those conditions because I really didn't think it could happen. I specifically said there has to be talks, even for the purposes of getting along in Parliament. I didn't think it was going to play out this quickly. Throughout the whole leadership process, on the floor of the convention, I didn't think it was going to be possible for the next election, never."[10]

While most party members seemed to care little about the MacKay–Orchard deal, the press added it as an uncomfortable footnote to most stories about the ratification vote. MacKay saw the constant press references to the Orchard deal as Liberal media bias fed by disgruntled Red Tories:

> The Liberal media sure as hell didn't want this merger to happen. This was Paul Martin's worst nightmare and he certainly didn't anticipate this was going to happen. We put a massive stick in the spokes of the Liberal juggernaut. The day after the merger Paul Martin started down a slippery slope. He had banked on having the same winning conditions that Jean Chrétien experienced. Chrétien would never have won three (maybe even not one) majority governments had there been a united conservative party in the country.

---

[10] Sean Gordon, "MacKay harbours no regrets for merger: Appears poised for leadership run," *Calgary Herald*, December 26, 2003, A11.

Joe Clark and others in the twelve-member PC caucus spoke out against the deal. "I think this will, by its very nature, be a narrower party than the PC Party has been," Clark said.[11] Deputy leader André Bachand, who supported MacKay for the leadership, criticized his leader for abandoning Quebec by hooking up with Harper and the Alliance. John Herron of New Brunswick, who had once tried to persuade Stephen Harper to run for PC leader, also voted against the deal. None of the three would ever sit in the caucus of the new Conservative party. Rick Borotsik of Manitoba, who also opposed the agreement, stayed in the Conservative caucus, but did not run in the 2004 election and openly supported the Liberal candidates in his home province.

MacKay was concerned about every PC member who did not support the merger, but he was particularly distressed that André Bachand was not on side. MacKay could only wonder at the influence Bachand would have had: "As our only member from Quebec, Bachand would have been a giant in the party. He was also a good friend who turned away at a critical moment."

Scott Brison was another matter altogether. Before the agreement in principle was signed, and soon after the existence of the merger talks had been leaked to the press, Brison had teamed up with Peter White, a long-time business colleague of Conrad Black, and with Reform-Alliance supporter Ken Kalopsis, to pen a *National Post* commentary in support of a merger.[12]

> Canadians deserve a competitive conservative alternative to the Liberal Party. The current dialogue between the Progressive Conservative Party of Canada and the Canadian Alliance could be a positive step towards building that alternative. But if some form of union of our parties is to succeed, it must be based on a common set of basic values and principles.

---

[11] Bill Curry and Sean Gordon, "Unite the right dissenters condemn deal," CanWest News Service, October 16, 2003.

[12] Scott Brison, Peter G. White, and Ken Kalopsis, "A charter for a political alternative," *National Post*, September 26, 2003.

They stated that a new party must:

> ...maintain and improve our national system of publicly funded health care. We must also allow those in need of care to deal directly with health-care professionals, and acknowledge the important contributions that the private sector can make in improving the delivery of services;
>
> ....[ensure] honesty, fairness, transparency, and frugality from our governments;
>
> ...not tolerate budgetary deficits, or excessive public spending, and...must commit to a national debt repayment program;
>
> ...[allow] Members of Parliament to be free to follow their own beliefs [on matters of personal conscience] while remaining accountable to their constituents;
>
> ...replace Canada's failed regional economic development programs and corporate welfare with an innovative tax-driven approach. We believe that the market can pick winners better than bureaucrats and politicians;
>
> ...If there are no fundamental differences of principle or policy dividing our two parties, there is no good reason why the parties should not co-operate in the interests of all Canadians. We believe they must.

At about the same time Brison was advocating a merger, the *Hill Times* reported a rumour that Scott Brison was getting ready to jump ship to the Liberals: "Mr. Brison apparently met with some of Paul Martin's advisors last week on the Hill to discuss crossing the floor over to the Libs. A well-placed Grit source told Mr. Francoli [of the *Hill Times*] that it was the popular Mr. Brison who sought out the meeting. Word is there was talk of a possible Cabinet position for the bright and openly gay Mr. Brison."[13]

The following week, the *Hill Times* reported that Brison "remains deeply committed to his [PC] party and that he supports all efforts to

---

[13] Sean Durkan, "Heard on the Hill," *Hill Times*, October 13, 2003.

create a single Conservative Party 'that is centrist, socially moderate, fiscally conservative.'"[14] Brison "flatly rejected that any meeting [with the Liberals] took place." But Liberal party sources insisted that it was Mr. Brison who initiated the contact.[15] Brison denied the rumours and said, "I will be working in favour of the deal, since I'm strongly supportive of the role for a fiscally conservative, socially centrist party." If Brison was trying to sound clear and decisive, it wasn't working.[16] He was quickly becoming one of the most inconsistent and confusing politicians in Canada.

Brison attended the ratification vote in his home province of Nova Scotia and asked permission to address the nation's delegates. After arrangements were made for him to speak, Brison changed his mind. A former Nova Scotia party president, John MacDonnell, had his eye on Brison when the show of hands was called for and noticed that Brison's arm moved cautiously as he voted for the merger. Brison voted yes on December 6. He crossed the floor and became a Liberal on December 11.

Using all his political acumen to predict what lay ahead, Brison boasted, "I don't think Canada has ever had a Prime Minister as well prepared for the job as Paul Martin. And I am absolutely enthusiastic about the prospects of a Canada under his leadership."[17] His repudiation of the new Conservative party he voted to create a few days earlier was absolute and unequivocal: "I want to work in a party that I can support without reservation, a party fuelled by bold ideas, not rigid ideologies." Martin heaped praise on Brison and called him a "very good friend." The reference to friendship was evidence that

---

[14] Paco Francoli, "Tory MP Brison denies he's in Liberal talks with Martin's team," *Hill Times*, October 20, 2003.

[15] Ibid.

[16] Marjaleena Repo, campaign manager for David Orchard, was somewhat leery of Brison because he was "hard and fast as a free market, free trade person." Yet when Brison announced his defection to the Liberal party, he was critical of Conservatives because they followed a rigid ideology.

[17] Mark Kennedy, "Another blow for new party as Tory MP defects to Liberals," *Edmonton Journal*, December 11, 2003, A6.

Martin and Brison had been close for a considerable period of time before his record-setting post-ratification conversion. Peter MacKay said the defection helped clarify a few things in his mind: "I would rather know where people are and be able to see them in front of me on the opposition bench than have them sneak up behind me. I think there is an element of personal vindictiveness behind this. Bitterness aimed either at me or people around me."[18] MacKay said he was not entirely surprised by Brison's move: "He told me the day after the leadership convention that he spoke with Paul Martin." This suggested to MacKay that the legwork preceding Brison's defection began soon after his defeat at the Tory convention.

Brison was appointed parliamentary secretary to the prime minister with a special emphasis on Canada–U.S. relations. Anne Dawson, the chief political correspondent for the *National Post*, reported grumblings in the Liberal party over a fundraiser to help Brison pay off his Conservative leadership campaign debts.[19] "There was always speculation on Parliament Hill Mr. Brison, who lost the Tory leadership race to Peter MacKay last June, had received a guarantee he would either get a cabinet post or get his campaign debt paid off as payback for crossing the floor," wrote Dawson. An angry Liberal, Shelia Copps, was quoted to say, "Just imagine how many Liberals across the country are trying to raise money for their campaigns. The party itself has been in substantial debt and to be raising money to pay off the leadership debt of another party is absurd." When confronted with the story, Brison backtracked more than once. "Mr. Brison . . . initially told CanWest News Service he was invited to attend a Liberal fundraising event at the University Club of Toronto next Thursday as an opportunity to meet Liberal lawyers and businesspeople, but said he was uncertain if the money was going to his campaign debt. This despite the fact that those attending the event were asked to make their cheques payable to the 'Scott Brison Campaign'," reported

---

[18] Ibid.

[19] Anne Dawson, "Grits assailed for Brison funding," *National Post*, January 17, 2004, A2.

Dawson. Then he acknowledged the original intention of the event was to pay off his debt. On further reflection, Brison said it would be inappropriate to accept the money to pay off his debts. "I don't like the optics of that. It's not a huge amount of money anyway. I would much rather pay it off myself," he said. Brison then offered the proceeds from the event to the Paul Martin's Seniors Society, an endowment fund sponsored by the March of Dimes which conducts medical research on polio."[20] It is unlikely this was what the organizers of the fundraiser had in mind when they first conceived the event.

Conservatives were also upset with Brison over his financial dealings with the local PC Kings–Hants riding association. Brison continued to fundraise from Conservatives when he ought to have known his days with the party were numbered. He also had a cheque written to himself from his Conservative riding association for more than $4,000 just days before crossing the floor. The payment was not supported by receipts. Brison offered no explanation as to why a cheque dated, July 31, was not cashed until December 11, the day of the floor crossing.[21]

IN THE FIGHT TO RATIFY THE AGREEMENT, MacKay had only eight of twelve PC members clearly on his side—and that included himself and Brison. That worked out to two-thirds in favour and one-third opposed, precisely the minimum threshold for ratification. MacKay also had to deal rather directly with David Orchard.

MacKay knew he had no chance of winning over Orchard or any of his supporters. His strategy was to make sure his deal with Orchard, and whatever opposition Orchard could muster, would be effectively countered. "I have honoured my commitments to Mr. Orchard," said MacKay. David Orchard thought otherwise:

---

[20] This paragraph is based largely on Anne Dawson's article "Grits assailed for Brison funding."

[21] "Brison says handling of $4,000 cheque donated to him was above board," Canadian Press, Apr 15, 2005.

I spoke with Peter MacKay this morning [October 16, 2003] and he offered to send me a copy of the agreement that he had signed. I told him it was a complete and utter betrayal of our agreement; but more importantly that it was a betrayal of the PC Party of Canada, its constitution and its history. It's incomprehensible to me that a new leader would campaign in a leadership race across the country pledging that he was not a merger candidate in front of forums across Canada, then obtained the leadership on the basis of a written document pledging not to merge the PC Party and to respect its constitution and within days, after winning the leadership, set in the process to dissolve the Progressive Conservative Party. What he has done, in my view, is a breach of the trust of every member of our party. This new creature, this so-called Conservative Party of Canada, if it goes forward, will be an illegitimate creation conceived in deception and born in betrayal.[22]

MacKay spoke of his responsibility as party leader, which extended beyond David Orchard's or even Peter MacKay's best interests:

> The talks conducted over the past two months have produced recommendations that are going to the full membership of our party for their consideration and approval. My main responsibility as Leader of the PC Party is to promote the aims and principles of the party. These principles are at the heart of the recommendations contained in the agreement. This question can't be decided unilaterally by Mr. Orchard, by me, or by Mr. Harper. It must be decided and will be decided in a democratic process that involves every member of our party.[23]

---

[22] F. Abbas Rana, "Strategists say two-plus-two will equal more than four," *Hill Times*, October 20, 2003.

[23] Speaking notes, Peter MacKay (see chap. 13 n. 7).

Orchard spokeswoman Marjaleena Repo called the deal a "coup d'état" and suggested that Alliance members would join the PC party to overwhelm the membership and vote to ratify the deal. "We're 40,000 and they're 100,000. There's no way we could win."[24] (Repo's numbers were wrong; there were about 83,000 Alliance members to about 48,000 Tories.[25]) The worry that Alliance members would take out memberships in the PC party to solidify a "takeover" turned out to be wrong. After the merger an analysis of crossover membership revealed that relatively few people were members of both parties.[26] Orchard was worried about Alliance members swamping the PC party, but there was nothing stopping him from signing up thousands of new members to help defeat the merger. He had every reason to do so, as he would lose influence in a much larger Conservative party.

Orchard's next step was to declare the proposed merger null and void in the courts. He and twenty-three other applicants filed an application with the Ontario Superior Court of Justice on November 20, 2003. The application sought a declaration of the court that the proposed merger, as well as the voting procedures, violated the constitution of the PC party. The application also sought a declaration that Peter MacKay was in violation of his written agreement with Orchard and that damages be determined. The latter part of the application was subsequently withdrawn.

The affidavit sworn by Orchard argued that the merger was inconsistent with party history and the positions taken by its leaders and leadership candidates over the years. It zeroed in on Peter MacKay and the agreement signed at the leadership convention five months earlier. The affidavit noted that in the written agreement the word "talks" had been crossed out by MacKay because "Mr. MacKay

---

[24] Bill Curry and Sean Gordon, "Unite the right dissenters condemn deal," CanWest News Service, October 16, 2003.

[25] These numbers were provided by Tom Jarmyn. He was responsible for merging the lists of party members from the Alliance and PC parties.

[26] The analysis was done by Tom Jarmyn. He indicated there were fewer than 2,000 crossover memberships.

indicated that he wished to be free to talk with other parties concerning day-to-day matters in the House of Commons, to which I readily agreed. Mr. MacKay expressly agreed that this did not in any way detract from the remaining, very clear, provisions of the agreement."[27] The affidavit described a meeting between Orchard and MacKay's chief of staff, Rick Morgan, on September 19, 2003, when Orchard was reassured that "no merger was being contemplated and that the talks being reported in the media at the time were simply explorations about co-operation between the two parties in the House of Commons." This reassurance is difficult to reconcile with the fact that emissaries had met on at least three occasions, and substantial progress had been made on an agreement.

Orchard also pointed to what he considered unfair rules for the ratification vote: ". . . it is important to understand that this does not mean that two-thirds of the party's members must be in support of the resolution in order that it be passed. . . .In the result, in each constituency where a bare majority of members support the resolution, all of the elected delegates from that constituency will vote in favour of the resolution . . . 51 per cent of the membership could translate into, and appear as, overwhelming support at the delegate level."

The PC party did not take the court case lightly and realized it needed to find a legal precedent to counter Orchard's claims or it might lose. The party's lawyers were able to argue that a political party in Canada is a sophisticated entity that is governed and regulated by statute. Paul Lepsoe said, "The PC party was not a stamp club in which members could raise disputes amongst themselves as if there was an underlying matrix of contracts amongst the membership." Lepsoe's argument was persuasive and countered Orchard's contention that, as a member, he had specific rights to override the powers of the executive.

The matter was heard before Mr. Justice J. Juriansz on Thursday, December 4, two days before the scheduled Saturday vote. The

---

[27] David Orchard, affidavit submitted November 20, 2003, 10, filed with Application, Ontario Superior Court of Justice, Court file 03-CV-259202CMI.

336   FULL CIRCLE

ruling came down the next day. Justice Juriansz began by noting the obvious: that the applicants were party members who were opposed to the merger and that the courts were reluctant to "get involved in supervising the internal affairs of voluntary associations. However, courts do recognize that membership in a voluntary association can give individuals important social rights that are worthy of some protection." The judge was ". . . satisfied that the situation is sufficiently developed to give rise to an actual dispute between the parties. Both sides have important interests at stake [and] . . . this dispute arises in extraordinary circumstances not contemplated by its Constitution."

Mr. Justice Juriansz declared that the specific provisions of the Canada Elections Act, found in Sections 400 to 403 regarding the merger of political parties, provide sufficient clarity and scope to permit the merger of the Canadian Alliance and PC parties with the attendant transfer of assets into the merged entity. The Chief Electoral Officer, it was ruled, can validate a merger when the application is certified by the party leaders and accompanied by a resolution from each of the merging parties approving the proposed merger. The application from Orchard et al. was dismissed in its entirety, and counsel was invited to make an appointment to address the issue of costs.

THE RESULT OF THE ALLIANCE mail-in vote was announced on Friday, December 4. Stephen Harper buoyantly reported that of the 53,315 mail-in ballots, 95.9 per cent were in favour of the merger. Harper called the agreement to merge with the PC party "the beginning of a new era in Canadian politics" and said it was a great time to be a conservative. The Alliance vote was stronger than most observers anticipated, but there was little drama attached to an outcome where only 51 per cent was required for ratification.

The Tory vote was another matter. It was held the following day and took place at twenty-seven hubs across the country. Delegates to the virtual convention, both for and against the motion, were selected at each site. Memorable speeches were delivered by the likes of former finance minister Michael Wilson in support of the merger and former leader Joe Clark in opposition. If an applause meter from the speeches had been used to determine the outcome, ratification was going to pass with flying colours. The actual vote was done via a show of hands rather than a secret ballot. The final tally was 2,234 delegates in favour and 247 opposed: slightly over 90 per cent support. It was a much better result than MacKay had anticipated. Afterwards, MacKay humorously accused his staff of misleading him into thinking the results would be much closer to keep him motivated so he would ensure that every last vote was won.

After the vote was announced MacKay delivered an election-style speech: "With this overwhelming vote, we have just become Paul Martin's worst nightmare." Soon after that, Harry Forestall of the CBC pressed MacKay with a question: "Why bother to win a leadership only to give it away a few months later?" The reply that popped into MacKay's head at that moment was eloquent and simple: "Because I put the country first."

THE LOGISTICAL WORK TO MERGE the parties was just beginning, and there was obviously no time to waste. It might seem ambitious to try to get the new party registered a week after the ratification vote, let alone the following day. But this is precisely what happened.

While the PC and Alliance legal advisers might say it is speculation, any reasonable observer would conclude that the haste to formalize the merger with Canada's Chief Electoral Officer was done to thwart the efforts of those who might want to file an injunction against the result. In what might be a stunning revelation to those who think bureaucrats are lazy and do not work overtime, the Chief Electoral Officer agreed to meet the legal team of the Alliance and PC parties on Sunday, December 7, the day after the PC vote and a day before the courts opened for business. Full credit is due to those who thought this through and to the bureaucrats for coming in on a Sunday to receive party representatives Paul Lepsoe and Tom Jarmyn.

There was a subsequent legal application filed by the Honourable Sinclair Stevens claiming that the Chief Electoral Officer should have waited thirty days to approve the merger of the parties. While there may have been a technical violation, no court that has heard the matter has seen fit to unwind the merger.[28]

The party had to deal with one other legal challenge. David Orchard claimed he was owed $72,000 from the Progressive Conservative Party. This was his share of donations his campaign collected, which were funnelled through the party's bank account so a tax receipt could be issued. The procedure was well within the rules and was used by all leadership candidates. Normally, the funds flowed back to the candidate on a forty-eight-hour turnaround. However, when Orchard launched his legal challenge to the merger, the flow of money to his campaign stopped. Orchard needed legal intervention to persuade the party that the amount in question should be paid in full. Before the party issued a cheque, it wanted assurances that Orchard would launch no other lawsuits—including any lawsuits he might initiate against Peter MacKay related to the agreement that was signed at the convention. It took a judge's ruling in early 2006 to sort out the scope of the legal release. By May 2006, the funds had yet to be released to Orchard. The final dispute was over interest on money owed. The Conservative party told Orchard he would have to sue if he wanted interest.

WHILE PARTY MEMBERS MIGHT have thought that joining forces would give them a fighting chance in the next election, the polls indicated otherwise. The headline in the *Globe and Mail* on December 5 told the sad story for conservatives: "Layton's NDP inching past conservatives, poll indicates." The results showed 43 per cent for the Liberals, 15 per cent for the NDP, 14 per cent for the Progressive Conservatives, and 10 per cent for the Canadian Alliance.[29] Given these results, the best a perfect combination of Conservative support could yield was something in the order of 25 per cent.

---

[28] On April 27, 2006, the Supreme Court of Canada issued a response to an application in which it declined to hear the case of the Honourable Sinclair Stevens v. Conservative Party of Canada (F.C.) (31281), with costs.

[29] For Ipsos Reid poll, see: http://www.ipsos-na.com/news/ pressrelease.cfm?id=1988 (accessed July 7, 2006).

The country's response to the merged party was underwhelming, to say the least. The first poll conducted after the merger showed that the new party had the support of only 21 per cent of Canadians. The Liberals, on the other hand, had increased their support from a pre-merger poll by 5 percentage points to 48 per cent.[30] There was much work ahead for Conservatives to prove they deserved to be trusted.

While the last official act of the civil war in Canada's conservative family officially ended on December 7, 2003, in the offices of Canada's Chief Electoral Officer, the fight for the heart and soul of this new party was about to begin. What Don Mazankowski had called a "vicious circle" had been closed. But the real test of the merger was winning over the Canadian people and defeating the Liberals. The merger was not an end in itself: real success was forming government.

The first test would be over leadership. The second would be the election. The Conservative Party had not come full circle: not just yet.

---

[30] Poll conducted on behalf of *Globe and Mail* and CTV; see: www.ipsos-na.com/news/pressrelease.cfm?id=1996 (accessed July 10, 2006).

CHAPTER 14

FULL CIRCLE, ACT I

D URING THE TWENTIETH CENTURY Liberals held office seven out of every ten days. An enviable record. In fact, Liberals are so good at winning elections they are known as Canada's natural governing party.

The Conservative electoral record, when united, has not been good, and when divided it has been abysmal. Anyone who thought the merger would cure all the Conservative ills grossly underestimated the challenges the party faced in 2004.

At the time of the merger, the polls indicated that Canadians were not ready to give the new party their confidence. The reaction was not unprecedented. Only a handful of Conservative leaders—Macdonald, Borden, Bennett, Diefenbaker, and Mulroney, the country's most successful Conservative prime ministers—had risen to the challenge of winning majority government. Conservatives would need to demonstrate many of the characteristics of these five leaders if they hoped to emulate their success.

Among the many challenges, five were at the top. First, the party had to be united and still embrace the full spectrum of conservatives. Second, the party had to build a broad national coalition, with appeal across all regions of Canada, including French and English Canada. Third, it needed moderate policies that would draw support from mainstream Canada. Fourth, it had to isolate and possibly expel any extreme elements. Finally, it needed visionary and inspiring leadership.

IN THE MEANTIME, the party needed someone to take the reins for the three-month period leading up to the March 20, 2004, leadership vote. Choosing an interim leader fell to Peter MacKay and Stephen Harper, and provided the two with an opportunity to mend fences and build bridges among the various pre-merger conservative factions.

Representing the common sentiment among the opposition and the press—that the merger was merely an Alliance takeover—the conservatives who felt the most uncertain or displaced in the new party were the PCs. Wanting to reach out to them, Harper and MacKay agreed on Joe Clark as interim leader. While it may have been easy for MacKay to endorse Clark, it was a far more significant gesture for Harper to make in favour of a former opponent. The symbolic act was an early and bold indication of the willingness of both former leaders to heal past wounds. Bringing Clark on side would be a signal to a wide swath of Red Tories that there was a place of respect for them in this new party. It was good politics.

Putting Clark in charge was something Brian Mulroney would have done. Mulroney would have identified the competing factions in the party and crafted a bold gesture to build unity, precisely as he had done in 1983 when he affirmed Erik Nielsen as his first choice for deputy leader just after Nielsen announced that Mulroney was not *his* first choice for party leader.

Accepting the interim leadership might have been a fitting and even glorious end to Clark's career in Parliament. Given the very favourable agreement negotiated by MacKay in 2003 for the PCs, Clark could have claimed vindication for refusing Harper's more strict conditions some eighteen months earlier. Clark might also have been able to use the position to influence the party's direction, strategy, and platform for the upcoming 2004 election.

However, despite Clark's previous efforts to merge the parties under his leadership, and his earlier willingness to bring DRC members into the PC caucus, the two-time PC leader could not bear the thought of joining the Conservative Party of Canada. Clark's immediate, strident, and vehement opposition to the merger was indication enough that he would not accept the position. "I don't believe in this new party as I see it now," he said. "I may be proven wrong in time, but I don't intend to add my reputation to a venture that on the evidence I see now is not something I would like to see governing the country."[1] He added, "[It's] not like a death in the family. It's the family dying. The party to which I had an obligation has been taken out of existence. This is a terrible time for me."[2] *Montreal Gazette* columnist L. Ian MacDonald wrote: "Poor Joe Clark. He never misses a chance to miss a chance."[3]

The position of interim leader went to PC senator John Lynch-Staunton, a somewhat ironic choice given the Alliance party's staunch opposition to an unelected Senate. To balance the ticket, the position of interim leader in the House of Commons was given to Alliance MP Grant Hill.

Joe Clark, John Herron, and Scott Brison resigned from the Tory caucus immediately after the merger was ratified. Because Parliament would not convene until after the Christmas break, their departures caused the number of PC caucus members to dip below the threshold for official party recognition in the House of Commons. Consequently, the party risked losing its research budget until the Speaker recognized the new party in the House of Commons. Throwing a number of PC staff members out of work just before the Christmas break because of a transitional issue did not seem right. To preserve full party status and foster goodwill among the two camps, four Alliance members "crossed the aisle" on December 12 and joined the PC party.[4]

On January 14, 2004, Keith Martin, who had been elected as a Reform MP from British Columbia in 1993 and 1997 and as a

---

[1] Sean Gordon, "Clark leads Tory defections: 'Terrible time for me,' says former PM," *Calgary Herald*, December 9, 2003, A59.

[2] Ibid.

[3] L. Ian MacDonald, "The new Conservatives won't miss Joe Clark," *Ottawa Citizen*, December 11, 2003, A19.

[4] Those who made the switch were all from Alberta. They were Monte Solberg, James Rajotte, Deepak Obhrai, and Grant Hill.

Canadian Alliance member in 2000, began sitting as an independent MP. He ran and was elected as a Liberal in the 2004 general election. The switching went both ways. John Bryden, elected as a Liberal MP on three occasions from Ancaster, Ontario, crossed the floor and joined the Conservatives on February 25, 2004.

IN A 2003 YEAR-END INTERVIEW from his Parliament Hill office, Peter MacKay summed up his year and mused about the prospects of entering the race to lead the new party. He spoke of fatigue as he reflected on the year-long struggle to win the PC leadership, negotiate an agreement with the Alliance, and secure ratification from party members. "It's a bit like running five back-to-back triathlons. You get to the finish line and somebody says 'all right, here's a glass of water, go out there again.' I think the toll has been more on my political capital as opposed to my own constitution. I'm not physically tired...but I feel it. This has been an incredibly intense, condensed, and forced period in my life."[5]

MacKay's most senior political adviser, Rick Morgan, did not agree that MacKay's political capital had been damaged, but thought instead that the fallout from the Orchard agreement was overblown and of no enduring consequence. During the ratification process, Morgan and Maureen Murphy-Makin, MacKay's long-time assistant, could see that Harper was able to devote a lot of time to the leadership race while MacKay was still embroiled in a fight to get the merger passed. Throughout the process, the two had been laying the organizational and strategic foundation to prepare for a MacKay run at the leadership of the new party. They were convinced MacKay would sweep Atlantic Canada and Quebec, and win enough support in Ontario to beat Harper. Bill Pristanski, chair of MacKay's successful 2003 PC leadership campaign, shared their views, and was convinced that MacKay would win the leadership because "his support was spread more evenly across the country and, at the time, he was a better campaigner than Harper."

---

[5] Gordon, "MacKay harbours no regrets for merger."

Ideally, they wanted MacKay to declare immediately after the ratification vote. They suggested the PC caucus Christmas Party——the last of its kind—which would be held on Parliament Hill on December 8 as an ideal venue for the announcement. But in mid-December, MacKay was still assessing his options. "It was a very painful process," recalled Morgan. "The delay and uncertainty also made it difficult for others from the PC side to enter the race in a timely manner."

Political columnist Don Martin named Stephen Harper 2003 "politician of the year," The column handicapped MacKay's prospects for the leadership: "There is, one could argue, legitimate competition for top honours from MacKay, who sacrificed more and had to push harder to make the deal a reality as the lesser of the two party leaders. But the selling of his soul in the Orchard deal and the almost instantaneous U-turn on the anti-merger terms precludes him from consideration."[6] Don Martin agreed with MacKay that he would be "damaged goods" until history was able to vindicate him.

Brian Mulroney indicated privately at the time that the delay and financial cost of a leadership campaign would distract from the greater goal of winning the next election. He thought the party would be better equipped to fight the Liberals if a leader was appointed, rather than elected. Presumably, he meant either MacKay or Harper. Selecting rather than electing a leader would look undemocratic. A clause allowing for the appointment of a leader should have been included in the merger agreement, so that such an appointment would be legitimate. Another strategic option would have been for Mulroney and a large number of key figures from the Alliance and PC sides to endorse a leadership team. An overwhelming display of support would have rendered a leadership contest the equivalent of a coronation and spared the cost and inevitable infighting of a leadership vote. The thinking was that, given the relative strength of the party membership and the size of the Alliance caucus, no one other

---

[6] Don Martin, "Canada's politician of 2003: It's Stephen Harper," *Victoria Times Colonist*, December 26, 2003, A20.

than Stephen Harper could have emerged as the anointed leader. In the end, the idea of bypassing a leadership convention was one of the few areas where Mulroney's opinion was disregarded.

Meanwhile, Peter MacKay's family members were urging him to sit out the leadership race. They sensed that it would be better to let the Orchard deal blow over completely before running again. There was also the issue of money. MacKay was not a gifted fundraiser; he was uncomfortable approaching prospective donors, and his efforts were clumsy at best. He did not like to ask for money. In addition, MacKay's most important donor and fundraiser from his last leadership campaign, Belinda Stronach, was poised to become a candidate for the leadership. MacKay's 2003 leadership chair, Bill Pristanski, thought the money would come. "I think his fatigue, rather than worry about raising money for a campaign, was the main reason he didn't run. Peter was exhausted after the leadership, merger negotiations, and ratification."

For much of the previous year, MacKay had listened and accepted the advice of his staff and campaign team. They helped him win the leadership, but he wasn't always comfortable with the predicaments he had been forced to face. Ultimately, the risks of launching another national leadership campaign within seven months of his last run were too great, and his fatigue was too strong. MacKay made a personal choice and decided to take a pass. Rather than be a candidate, he took on the role of caucus policy chair and laid the groundwork for the election platform.

But MacKay still wanted a credible candidate from the PC side of the family to enter the leadership race. Just before Christmas, MacKay visited New Brunswick premier Bernard Lord. MacKay offered his full support to Lord, and encouraged him to seek the leadership. Lord's government was in a precarious position, with only a razor-thin majority, Lord had no obvious successor and, had he left, the Tory government in the province almost certainly would have fallen. Lord declined, and pledged his support to MacKay. MacKay was no longer interested in running, and his hopes for a strong PC candidate never materialized.

WITH THE MERGER RATIFIED and the Christmas season behind him, Stephen Harper surprised no one when he announced his candidacy for the leadership on January 12, 2004. His core campaign team was similar to the group he had assembled to win the 2002 Alliance leadership. The ever-present Tom Flanagan led the effort. Other notables included MPs Scott Reid, Rob Anders, James Rajotte, James Moore, and Jim Abbott. Ken Boosenkool took the lead on policy, with Yaroslav Baran on communications. Carolyn Stewart Olsen handled media, and Mark Kihn, Eric Hughes, and Devin Iverson were responsible for organization and campaign systems. John Weissenberger provided his steady hand and his deep knowledge of Harper to the campaign team. Although there were more foot soldiers in the 2004 leadership campaign team, the nucleus included only about a dozen key Harper loyalists who worked flat out from the beginning to the end of the campaign. The big difference from Harper's 2002 Alliance bid was that this campaign was run out of Ottawa rather than Calgary.

Harper was ready to welcome support from all conservative factions, but he was clearly most comfortable with the Reform-Alliance side of the house. He didn't, at least initially, want to be called a Tory. "It's actually not a label I love," said Harper. "I am more comfortable with a more populist tradition of conservatism. Toryism has the historical context of hierarchy and elitism and is a different kind of political philosophy. It's not my favourite term, but we're probably stuck with it."[7]

A number of people in the PC party thought the best way to build party unity and achieve a complete merger was to support a candidate from "the other side." One of the first on board with Harper was 1998 PC leadership candidate Michel Fortier. His endorsement was also symbolic: it demonstrated that Harper had friends in Quebec. Another key convert was Michael Coates, a man with a lifetime of experience and commitment to the PC party. In 1998, Coates had been one of many who sought a reconciliation of conservative forces

---

[7] Various websites include this quote from Harper, which was attributed to the *Hamilton Spectator*, January 24, 2004. See: www.bcpolitics.ca/left_harperstand.htm (accessed July 10, 2006).

by encouraging Stephen Harper to run for leader of the PC party. Coates was on the PC Canada Fund when Peter MacKay and Stephen Harper signed the agreement to merge the parties and thought it was important for ". . . senior people in the PC Party to support candidates from our sister party." Others who felt the same way and would join Fortier and Coates included MacKay's former chief of staff, Rick Morgan, former PC national director Denis Jolette, and PC party treasurer Brian Mitchell. Greg Thompson was the only sitting PC member of parliament who supported Harper. Each PC convert brought in a variety of volunteers and donors, all designed to show that the new Conservative party under Harper's leadership could represent the full spectrum of Conservatives. "What we wanted to show was that it was not a takeover and that the merger was a success," said Rick Morgan. Most of these people came of their own volition. They were not recruited by Harper, who had yet to feel comfortable enough in the new party to reach out to former PC supporters and invite them to his team.

In any late-November CFL game, it is the ground game that wins. So too in any political leadership contest. It matters little who is most popular with the general public, who has the best ideas and policies, gets the most media exposure, or delivers the most passionate speech. In leadership races, the candidate who persuades the most people to buy a party membership and then turn out to cast a ballot on selection day wins. In terms of a ground game, Stephen Harper began the campaign with a huge advantage over his prospective opponents. First, he had recently and decisively won the Alliance leadership. Second, he was well known and widely supported by the Alliance rank and file, who held nearly a two-to-one margin in party membership. Third, he was unlikely to face any Alliance opponents. Fourth, he had a sophisticated fundraising and direct-mail system, a huge advantage in a short campaign. And finally, the size and demographics of the combined party memberships made it difficult for any single special-interest group to dominate and take over the party.

But Harper was not without some obvious and significant weaknesses. He began with virtually no organization in Quebec, a province that would account for roughly 25 per cent of the votes. Some of his past statements had made him unpopular in Atlantic Canada. And he had an image as a right-wing ideologue, which would cost him support outside western Canada.

When he stood to announce his leadership bid, Harper was more inclined to highlight the PC forces who were by his side than the fifty Alliance MPs who were already in the stable. The PC recruits included campaign co-chair Michael Fortier and Ontario PC MPPs John Baird and Bob Runciman. Like many Harris Tories, these two MPPs were closer to the Reform-Alliance side than to their namesake party. But that didn't stop Baird from recognizing Harper's attractiveness to those in the center of the political spectrum. "I think Stephen's got a lot of appeal, he wants a big-tent party that can appeal to Red Tories, the more conservative Tories, to everyone in the party...I'm excited about Stephen's chances."[8]

Setting his expectations low and staking out his ground as the underdog, Harper said, "I warn you that I am no Paul Martin. I have not been packaged by an empire of pollsters and media managers. I have not been groomed by the experts and the influential."[9] Reinforcing what he saw as another key advantage, Harper added "I don't stand for patronage because I don't owe anybody anything."[10]

The day Harper entered the race, PC leadership candidate Jim Prentice announced he would not be a candidate, citing the financial burden of raising money for two leadership campaigns in the same year. Having a fellow westerner out of the race was a boost to the Harper campaign.

The next day, Peter MacKay confirmed he would not enter the race. "The achievements of the past several months have been significant, but I also recognize they have come at some cost. My frank

[8] Sean Gordon, "Harper says, 'I'm no Paul Martin': Enters new party's leadership race as Prentice bows out," *National Post*, January 13, 2004, A1.
[9] Ibid.
[10] Ibid.

assessment is that this is not my time."[11] The reference to "cost" would seem to include both his political and financial capital.

Former Ontario health minister Tony Clement jumped into the race on January 15. Clement's strategy was to capture much of his home province vote and present a safe alternative to those who thought the new party needed a leader not burdened by past PC–Reform–Alliance battles. A seasoned provincial politician, Clement offered some things none of his opponents could: practical experience with the levers of government and a solid international track record, thanks to his leadership during the SARS crisis. Nevertheless, his candidacy would not generate much passion or enthusiasm.

IN THE FALL OF 2003, speculation began to build that Belinda Stronach would be a candidate to lead the party she helped found. Not much about Stronach had been reported in the press while the merger negotiations were underway; then, soon after the deal was done, media reports began to use words such as "initiated" and "mastermind" to describe her contribution. Sources in a Canadian Press story credited Stronach as "the spark that generated key talks between Alliance leader Stephen Harper and Tory leader Peter MacKay."[12] Stronach made herself conspicuously available to confirm her seemingly selfless and noble role in the merger: "This is in my capacity as a citizen, as a Canadian, and my concern for the needs for checks and balances in our political process . . . I feel that it's important that we have strong parties so we can debate policies . . . so we can once again create policies and debate policies which are good for Canada and which make for a stronger Canada."[13]

Those close to the merger talks gave Stronach limited credit. According to Denis Jolette, the Tory national director who attended the emissary meetings, Stronach's contribution to vision, content,

---

[11] David Heyman and Maria Canton, "Shallow war chest quashes MacKay's leadership bid: Quebec MP quits, another to join Grits," *Calgary Herald*, January 14, 2004, A5.

[12] Louise Elliott, "Top CEO was spark that ignited merger," *Ottawa Citizen*, October 17, 2003, A5.

[13] Ibid.

and strategy was virtually nil. "What she wanted was a deal at all costs and [she] didn't seem to care about the content." Alliance representatives agreed: "I don't think she was substantively involved. She was not very experienced in the practical side of political parties," said Harper staff member Tom Jarmyn. Rick Morgan agreed: "She did not understand party politics. Although she was well intentioned, her interventions were often a distraction." But she had been a source of encouragement to some of the emissaries and could justifiably claim to have played a role in the merger.

Stronach found celebrity status as a political strategist behind the creation of the new Conservative Party of Canada. Her ambition now took her in a new direction. Initially, she denied any interest in elected office. When she was on Parliament Hill in late November 2003 to present awards to the winners of a Magna-sponsored Canada-wide essay contest on what university students would do if they were prime minister of Canada, Stronach was adamant that she would not seek the leadership. "That's a definitive no. That's a no. That's a no."[14]

Stronach's reservations about becoming a leadership candidate evaporated over the next two months. On January 20, she stepped before the national media to announce she was running for the Conservative leadership to help Canada build a "bigger economic pie." Commentators would use this clumsy metaphor, as superficial as it was succinct, to ridicule her lack of policy depth and political experience. Stronach espoused very loose, non-threatening, and unfocused high-level economic policies. Unless a person despised entrepreneurs and wealth creation, Stronach's motherhood statements about economic development were hard to criticize. Where she did distinguish herself from her peers was in the area of social policy. A moderate, she staked out ground on social policies that would put her at odds with the socially conservative views commonplace in the Alliance, including support for same-sex marriage. And

---

[14] Bruce Cheadle, "Magna CEO Belinda Stronach deftly denies political aspirations," Canadian Press, November 20, 2003.

as if to ensure there was no confusion, her campaign hastened to add she was pro-choice.

Correctly sensing an inability to dislodge Harper in his home turf, Stronach targeted those on the PC side of the merger, something she would not have been able to do had Peter MacKay been in the race. Stronach told PC national director Denis Jolette that she would not have run had MacKay been a candidate. She was successful in winning support from the PC side, but that support seemed to lack depth and enthusiasm. Senator Marjory LeBreton expressed a widely held sentiment: "I voted for Belinda because she was a woman and was bringing new blood into the party. It was also in response to not wanting the merger to appear as a takeover. But I was never overly impressed with her."

And there was a flaw in Stronach's strategy; there weren't enough PC votes to give her a win. Even if Stronach swept the PC vote, she would finish a distant second. To win, Stronach needed to broaden her base and bring tens of thousands of new members into the party.

Stronach's personal wealth and access to the Magna International supplier list gave her campaign an overwhelming advantage in financial resources. The contrast between the fundraising operations and success of Stronach and those of Harper and Clement was stark. The list of donors contributing more than $200 to the Harper campaign filled thirty-eight pages and totalled $1,356,789. Stronach's list fit on only eleven pages and totalled $5,356,168. Donors whose surname was Harper contributed $3,525 to Stephen's campaign, while Stronach gave $3,950,000 to her own campaign. Clements raised $826,807 in donations. (Given new election laws, Stronach's campaign might be the last of its kind in Canada where personal wealth could have such a substantial impact. In this regard, Stronach's political entry was well timed.)

With such a huge financial disparity, Stronach was able to out-manoeuvre her opponents on several fronts. She could hire seasoned political strategists and field organizers, even though she had no political roots or connections. She used the most sophisticated phone banks to recruit members. Thanks to in-depth polling of party members, her campaign could regularly tap into what members were thinking. But nowhere was money more influential to the outcome than in the province of Quebec. A derelict Quebec riding association with a handful of members was every bit as important as an Alberta riding association with five thousand members. Peter MacKay recognized this and had done well with his paid Quebec organizers in the previous PC leadership campaign. Stronach recognized it as well, and thanks to her campaign's deep pockets she was able to buy virtually the entire MacKay team plus many other Quebec organizers.

Stronach was a natural for Quebec Conservatives. She had the glamour, money, sex appeal, and the liberal social views that Quebecers seem to love. There was only one problem: she could barely speak a word of French. Stronach would need to sweep Quebec for any chance of winning the leadership; it would be interesting to see how her language deficiency would play out.

Meanwhile, Stephen Harper was fashioning a Quebec strategy of his own. Although bilingual, Harper was not well understood in the province. At best Quebecers knew him as an opponent of Meech Lake, and at worst as someone who did not believe that Quebec was a distinct society. A few remembered him as one of the architects behind the Clarity Act. However, when some soft Quebec nationalists dug deeper into Harper's writings, they found common ground in his overall approach to provincial rights. Harper often spoke of resisting federal incursions into areas of provincial jurisdiction, and of allowing provinces to manage in the areas of language and culture. Harper needed someone who would look beyond the headlines that portrayed him as anti-Quebec. He found that man in Action démocratique du Québec leader Mario Dumont. Dumont's political network offered discrete but indispensable support and helped Harper's team recruit valuable memberships in many rural Quebec ridings.

Heading Stronach's campaign team was John Laschinger, the man who had propelled MacKay to the PC leadership. Geoff Norquay took charge of communications, and Guy Giorno handled policy. Prominent Alberta strategist Rod Love took a senior role on

Stronach's advisory team. Stronach also enjoyed the quiet support of Preston Manning, a man who knew Harper well. In fact, Stronach's campaign members used their financial muscle to vacuum up every political operative they could get their hands on.

Stronach's involvement in the leadership campaign sparked considerable curiosity from the media and the general public. Even western Canada was not immune. A normal Calgary Chamber of Commerce luncheon might attract 150 people with a good speaker, but when Belinda Stronach came to town, the luncheon was a sell-out, with more than eight hundred people paying to check her out.

John Laschinger was a master political strategist, and his candidates almost always won. Even when they came in second, they were usually perceived as winners because they exceeded the expectations he carefully established at the front end of every campaign. Laschinger followed his formula with Stronach. In her maiden speech she signalled that she would be making mistakes during the campaign. With expectations low, she impressed even seasoned politicians with her political debut. "For her first leap into the shark pool, she swam not badly," said Stockwell Day, someone who knew first-hand about media scrutiny. But winning admiration and winning votes are not the same thing. Stockwell Day may have admired Stronach, but he voted for Stephen Harper and encouraged anyone who would listen to do so as well.

John Laschinger had a lot of ground to cover so his candidate would be taken seriously by a skeptical media, who saw Stronach as lacking depth, vision, and knowledge. In his book *Lesser Mortals,* Laschinger recounted the antics of a wealthy political novice campaigning for leadership of the PC party in 1983. Peter Pocklington was drumming up support in P.E.I. when he came face to face with some tough questions. As many a politician had done before him when stumped, Pocklington said:

"That was a very good question. What's your name?"

"My name is Jim Lee," came the response.

"And what do you do in Prince Edward Island, Jim?" asked Pocklington.

"I'm the premier."

Clearly, Laschinger would not let that happen to his candidate. To win, however, Stronach would have to do much more than exceed expectations: she would have to look as if she could lead the party and the country. But could her handlers make up for Stronach's weak grasp of issues and political inexperience? "The biggest concern I had," said her communication director, Geoff Norquay, "and I don't say this disparagingly, is that she was somewhat unformed as a political animal." Given her subsequent defection to the Liberal party, "unformed" seems like an understatement. However, those close to Stronach did not question her beliefs in 2004. "While she represented the progressive wing of the party, I didn't doubt that she was still a conservative," said Norquay.

What Stronach lacked in experience she compensated for with enthusiasm, money, energy, and hard work. Said Norquay, "She was a delight to work with and was very focused. She was also a hard worker. She did not act like an heiress in that campaign: she worked her butt off." To support his assessment, Norquay offered this anecdote: "The first time I met her, I briefed her for a trip to Atlantic Canada. Recognizing the best media exposure was the early morning CBC radio show, with some trepidation I suggested that she be ready to be on-air at 6:45 a.m. She replied, 'I get up at 5:00 a.m. every morning for exercise: set it up.'"

The last time Conservatives had elected a female leader they went from 169 seats to 2, and the patient almost died on the operating table. Senator David Angus had watched that debacle, but he thought Stronach was strong enough and interesting enough to overcome that legacy. "In 2003, I thought the party was ready for a woman leader. I thought it would be a fun campaign." But as the campaign evolved, Angus came to a different view. "I believed she was bilingual, which she obviously wasn't. She was not properly prepared. She wasn't ready."

Meanwhile, something unexpected was happening during the leadership campaign: Conservatives began to register as a significant electoral threat to Paul Martin. While no one suggested Paul

Martin's tenure as prime minister was being seriously challenged, the February polls hinted that a majority Liberal government was far from certain.[15] "This is the steepest and most rapid decline in Liberal Party of Canada fortunes in contemporary political history," commented Ekos pollster Frank Graves. The main reason for the decline in Liberal support was the sponsorship scandal, but the emergence of a united conservative movement was a major contributing factor to rising Tory support. Graves commented that the Liberal decline was "more than a blip" because a leaderless Conservative party without policies had already borne some political fruit. The poll was not good news for Liberals, although the results showed them comfortably in the lead with 41.8 per cent support, about 1 percentage point ahead of the 2000 election. The Conservative party, at 31.9 per cent support, was 5.8 percentage points lower than the combined PC-Alliance vote in 2000, but much higher than the 25.5 per cent the Alliance had received. The difference between 31.9 and 25.5 per cent could be the difference between a minority and a majority Liberal government. The NDP appeared to have benefited most from the merger on the right: Red Tories seemed to have bypassed the Liberal party altogether and moved further to the left. Equally troubling for Liberals was the relatively small number of voters who thought of them as their second choice; this suggested there was little room for growth.

In the leadership race, the February poll showed that Belinda Stronach had slightly more appeal than Stephen Harper among voters. Of those polled, 46 per cent said they would never vote Conservative with Harper as leader, while slightly less, 43 per cent, would never vote for a Stronach-led party. Interesting, perhaps, but that poll was taken with the Canadian public, and not with the party members who were likely to vote for a new Conservative leader on March 20. If Stronach had substantially outpolled Harper in public opinion, party

---

[15] Ekos Research Associates Inc. Data are based on telephone interviews conducted February 23–25, 2004 with a random sample of 1,020 Canadians aged eighteen and older. A sample of this size provides a margin of error of +/− 3.1 percentage points, 19 times out of 20.

members who wanted to win above all else might have given Stronach a second look, but a 3 per cent difference was not that persuasive.

In the very early stages of the race, amid the glitz and media domination she achieved, it looked as if Stronach might have a decent chance of winning. Columnist Don Martin had noted the effects of Belindamania:

> The former Magna International executive has become an overnight sensation in her quest for the reunited right's leadership, wowing some of the most grizzled veterans of political trench warfare with her script-sticking oratorical skills, and ability to pay outrageous retainers for their services.... Stronach has grabbed three times the front-page space of her two rivals combined after six days in the race. She attracts huge crowds, has bought and unleashed an organizational blitzkrieg which has left the other camps reeling and turns down more media interviews per day than her attention-starved rivals get in a week. Impossible as it may have seemed at her launch in Aurora, Ont., a week ago, the 37-year-old has become a serious leadership contender and winning this thing no longer unleashes the snort of derision it probably should.[16]

Yet Martin added a critical proviso to Stronach's apparent winability: "Her ability to think fast on her feet has not been proven. And her flimsy grasp of important issues is complicated by having so little time to master the files."[17] Martin provided a few colourful quips from unnamed Tories, including: "She can sing all the hymns, but doesn't know the meaning of the words." John Weissenberger agreed: "She had the nuts and bolts of a leadership campaign but she simply could not perform at the same level as Stephen and Tony."

Unlike other competitors Harper faced, Stronach was a real political wild card. Not until the final days of the campaign did

---

[16] Don Martin, "Stronach wowing 'em," *Regina LeaderPost*, January 28, 2004, B7.
[17] Ibid.

Harper have a clear sense of what Stronach and her financial resources might produce. Her campaign team tried every technique imaginable—direct mail, telemarketing, house parties—to bring new members into the party. The membership base was approaching an impressive two hundred thousand, but Stronach's team was running out of momentum and time.

Had Stronach come far enough in such a short period of time? Polls during the final weeks of the campaign provided the answer: Harper had the leadership locked up. John Laschinger, Stronach's campaign manager, seemed to confirm that his candidate was going to lose when he urged the party to delay the vote because of technical irregularities in the registration process. Such a request would never have been made had Stronach been in the lead.

The voting proceeded as scheduled on March 20, 2004. Deep bank accounts, progressive social policies, and media glitz had helped Stronach overcome linguistic limitations: she won 61 per cent of the Quebec vote. But she needed closer to 90 per cent in Quebec to threaten Harper. With the help of Mario Dumont's Action démocratique du Québec, Harper won a surprising 33 per cent of Quebec's vote. As expected, Stronach won a majority of the vote in Atlantic Canada, but not by much. Despite previous negative remarks about Atlantic Canadians, Harper attracted 35 per cent of the vote. There were no surprises in the West, where Harper won handily. In the end, it all boiled down to Ontario. Stronach and Clement, both from Ontario, expected to fare well. But Harper won decisively there too, with 57 per cent of Ontario votes, compared to Stronach at 27 per cent and Clement at 16 per cent.

Stronach's multimillion-dollar investment to recruit at least one hundred thousand new members into the Conservative Party of Canada—about three hundred in every federal riding—had failed. Columnist and future Stronach biographer Don Martin quipped, "In the end, it could not be bought."[18]

---

[18] Don Martin, "He earned his victory," *Calgary Herald*, March 21, 2004, A1.

There was no need for a preferential ballot to determine the winner. Despite the best efforts of party organizers to create some suspense and stretch out media coverage, Harper was announced as the overwhelming first-ballot winner with 55.5 per cent; Stronach had 35.5 per cent; and Clement had 9.5 per cent.

TONY CLEMENT HAD BANKED his leadership campaign on the premise that Stephen Harper would not be able to unify the troops. Harper had his chance to prove Clement wrong.

At his first caucus meeting as leader, Harper began by speaking of the need to draw together the various strands of a broad conservative coalition. He pointed out that both Preston Manning and Brian Mulroney were part of the party's heritage and added that he was leading the party of Sir John A. Macdonald and Sir George Etienne Cartier. Harper's point: that this party's lineage dated back to the earliest days of Confederation, and not to December 7, 2003, the date it was registered with the Chief Electoral Officer of Canada. Tories in the room breathed a sigh of relief: they could still call themselves Tories.

Harper, the intellectual, showed himself to be an able leader and politician. He demonstrated an unexpected sensitivity to different points of view and charmed caucus members who had been hesitant about the merger. Senator Marjory LeBreton is a case in point. "I was not a fan of Stephen Harper. He won me over in caucus. He listened to what everyone said and considered all points of view. He was calm and cool-headed. He worked hard to build consensus and allowed free votes. There was no nonsense and no overblown rhetoric. He made sure neither of the pre-merger parties dominated; to the point where both sides could complain of being taken over. And he was also very decisive."

In building his new coalition, Harper appeared to care little whether someone was a supporter or detractor, a former PC or CA. Soon after he won the leadership, for example, Harper called Senator David Angus. "He indicated that he wasn't concerned that I didn't support him in the leadership. He said, 'I want your input and I need you in the Senate.' He was totally focused."

Harper's efforts to unite the party were not universally successful. Joe Clark chose to spend his last day as a parliamentarian by
burning his remaining bridges to Canada's conservative movement.
With an election call imminent, Clark ruminated on CTV's *Question
Period* that "The issue is going to be which leader is better, which
leader is worse, and I think the question is a very tough one...I
would be extremely worried about Mr. Harper. I personally would
prefer to go with the devil we know. I'm that concerned about the
imprint of Stephen Harper."[19] While Clark would encourage voters
to base their voting choice on strength of local candidates, equating
Harper with the devil was a terminal act that would prevent Clark
from having influence or involvement with the new Tory party.

Clark suggested that supporters of Brian Mulroney should be
alarmed: "I've seen nothing in the Stephen Harper–led party that on
issues like human rights, issues like the environment, issues like
bilingualism, issues like the nature of the country, this is anything like
the governments that either Mr. Mulroney or I led."[20] Clark's words
pointed to another example of the difference between former
rivals Clark and Mulroney. Speaking in New Brunswick the day before
Clark's outburst, Mulroney had heaped praise on Harper and the
"moderate, successful Conservative party" he was leading.[21]

Even reluctant converts to the merger were outraged by Clark's
comments. Marjory LeBreton called them "quite an inglorious end
to a great career. I guess he's calling all of us moderates who stayed
at the table stupid...I think there are a lot of Joe Clark supporters
who are going to be appalled by this."[22] But not all, as it turned out.
A few MPs left the PC caucus with Clark, as well as four PC senators

---

[19] Sean Gordon, "PM less scary than Harper, Joe Clark says," *Ottawa Citizen*, April 26,
2004, A3.

[20] Sean Gordon, "Tory Clark endorses Martin: Politician states case after Mulroney
backs party's new leader," *Victoria Times–Colonist*, April 26, 2004, A3.

[21] Mary Gordon, "Clark backs Martin; 'Devil we know' likely a better choice than
Harper for PM. Ex-Tory leader says he's supporting best riding candidates," *Toronto
Star*, April 26, 2004, A1.

[22] Ibid.

remained loyal: Mira Spivak, Norman Atkins, Lowell Murray, and William Doody. Murray and Doody were the last remaining Senate appointees from Clark's short-lived 1979 government.

HARPER KNEW HE DID NOT have much time to draw the party together. An election was looming, and that gave him very little time to demonstrate that he led a moderate, inclusive national party that was sensitive to all factions in the caucus and all regions of the country. It also gave him precious little time to build a campaign team. "We expected the election to be called any day after the leadership contest," said Michael Coates. "In effect we were in a hurry-up offence. We went with the same organization and team that won Harper the leadership."

As it turned out, Harper had about two months after the leadership victory before Paul Martin asked that the writ be dropped, on May 24, for an election on June 28. The new party would have preferred more time to get ready. In the span of a few months it had merged two statutory entities—each with its own staff, information systems, legal structure, and accounting records. It had to reconstitute 308 constituencies—no easy task given the challenge of merging local associations with distinct executives. The party also had to hold 308 candidate nomination meetings: another beast, because there were already a PC and an Alliance candidate in most ridings. "It was a vast amount of work, making it all the more difficult to prepare for the general election," said Weissenberger.

The 2004 election would be the first time the Liberals faced a unified Conservative party since they lost to Brian Mulroney in the free trade vote of 1988.[23] In the past three elections, Liberals had to do little more than show up to win successive majorities, and in some respects they had become lazy and arrogant. Paul Martin had not yet faced real competition; the only battles he had fought were within, in his party. According to John Weissenberger, it was inevitable that Martin's hubris would get the better of him.

---

[23] The Reform party ran 72 candidates and received 275,000 votes, but it elected no members. The case can be made that by taking conservative votes Reform helped elect a few NDP members in British Columbia in some close races.

Martin's advisers were ruthless and reckless in the way they behaved towards their internal opponents. They exiled anyone who could have been a potential rival to Martin, to the extent of overthrowing riding associations of ministers, like Herb Dhaliwal, who opposed him. Knowing that these guys are not novices at this, the only thing I can conclude from that behaviour is that they must have looked at the political landscape in 2002 and figured there is no way that the opposition is ever going to get together and be a threat. They thought they could do whatever the heck they wanted within their own party. They could destroy internal opponents as viciously as they wanted and there would be no consequences. If you look at it objectively, the odds were on their side. No one thought Conservatives would get their act together and be a viable alternative. They thought they could be bullies and get away with it. Chrétien didn't ostracize his rivals. But when Martin's guys had the opportunity they did everybody in with the long knives.

One of the most important tests Harper would face in the 2004 election was the nationally televised leaders' debates. An election equivalent to going undefeated over an entire CFL football season and then losing the Grey Cup, screw up the debates and it doesn't matter if a party leader does everything else perfectly. Harper's debate team consisted mostly of former Progressive Conservatives. Michael Coates led debate preparation, with behind-the-scenes support from Lynne Maheux, Ken Boosenkool, Bruce Carson, and Philippe Gervais. In the mock debates, former PC treasurer Brian Mitchell played Jack Layton, Walter Robinson from the Canadian Taxpayer's Federation was Paul Martin, and Richard Décarie was Gilles Duceppe. In the actual debates, the open-mike system predictably resulted in a shouting match. Nonetheless, Coates was pleased with the outcome. "Harper won because he was more polite. He did not want to be seen as being harsh. What he wanted to project was that he was an agent of safe moderate change."

Ekos pollster Frank Graves's impartial view was that Harper had done little to bring support to his new party. The demographic data showed that Harper was doing best with what Graves called "grumpies," which meant he appealed mostly to old men. Of more concern to Conservative strategists was the significant advantage Martin had over Harper on the issue of leadership. Martin outranked Harper even on the dimension of honesty, a stunning result given the flak Martin and the Liberals were taking daily over the sponsorship scandal. The problem, it seemed, was that persistent prompting from Liberals had convinced many Canadians that Harper had a hidden agenda for Canada.

But this problem may have been partially the Conservatives' own doing. There was a harshness to the Conservative campaign, and harshness was something they desperately needed to avoid if they hoped to show Harper's softer side and portray him as an agent of moderate and safe change. The forty-six-page election platform came with the ornery title "Demanding Better." The document was reminiscent of the old saw "We're mad as hell and we aren't going to take it anymore." The preface noted, "Canadians have had enough." It was time, the platform suggested, to demand better accountability, stronger economic performance, improved heath care, safer communities, and meaningful national security.

> After ten years of Liberal failure to deliver, to *demand better* means to demand a change in government. Only the Conservative Party led by Stephen Harper offers the vision for change and the will to do things differently in Ottawa. Demand better. Vote Conservative.

The platform included a reduction in the tax rate on middle-income Canadians of more than 25 per cent, and a $2,000-per-child deduction for all dependent children younger than sixteen. There was also a pledge to hold a free vote in the House of Commons on the issue of same-sex marriage. There was no slash-and-burn tax-fighter mentality; the platform included increases in both spending and revenue over the projections of the current Liberal administration.

But the platform was as interesting for what it did not contain. Nothing in the document referred specifically to the needs and interests of Quebecers. There was nothing about regional economic development, other than to say that regional considerations would not be a factor in determining how funds would be allocated by federal granting councils. There was nothing about hot-button issues near and dear to the former Alliance side, such as abortion or capital punishment, except the free vote on the issue of same-sex marriage. There was a pledge to increase the size of Canada's armed forces to eighty thousand troops, but there was no mention of Canada joining the war in Iraq, something Harper had vocally supported in the past.

Page 16 of the platform carried the peculiar heading "We will protect our children by eliminating legal loopholes for child pornography." It was a marker that would get the party into serious trouble when, towards the end of the campaign, the Tory war room produced a press release under the overblown headline "Paul Martin supports child pornography?" After an hour's reflection, the war room admitted its goof and recalled the press release, changing the headline to: "Today, Martin says he's against child pornography. But his voting record proves otherwise." No Canadian would ever believe Paul Martin supported child pornography, and the outrageous press release put Harper on the defensive. Harper, whose decisiveness can occasionally get him into trouble, refused Martin's heartfelt demand for an apology by saying, "I'm not going to, in any way, give the Liberal Party any break on its record on child pornography. It is disgraceful."[24] Voters were left to answer their own question about the meaning of the overblown Tory rhetoric; if Conservatives thought Paul Martin supported child pornography, what sort of draconian plan did Harper and his band of social conservatives hold for Canada?

[24] Sandra Cordon, "Campaign turns ugly: Conservatives allege, then retract claim Prime Minister Martin favours child porn," *Charlottetown Guardian*, June 19, 2004, A4.

Even among the Conservative caucus there were few who defended Harper. "The press release about Martin and child pornography was over the top," said Senator Marjory LeBreton.

When the writ was dropped in late May, the Liberals enjoyed a comfortable 8 to 10 percentage point lead in the polls. By the end of the first week in June, however, the Tories were showing a slight lead. That was enough to ratchet up public and media scrutiny of Stephen Harper and his band of candidates. Despite Harper's calm and measured public persona throughout the campaign, the media pounced on any gaffe or misstep that might reveal Harper as a wolf in sheep's clothing. In this, the media and the Liberal party were aligned. "It was a pro Paul Martin media that were hostile to Stephen Harper," recalled LeBreton. "They enabled the Liberals to raise the so-called hidden agenda. It also didn't help that we had a few MPs and candidates who were outspoken." LeBreton was referring to remarks by three sitting Conservative MPs that helped Martin and the media reinforce the view that Harper and his party were socially conservative and intolerant. MP Scott Reid spoke out against Canada's official bilingual policy early in the campaign, costing him his job as the critic for official languages. Cheryl Gallant got into hot water for comparing abortion to the beheading of an American in Iraq. And Rob Merrifield's recommendation for third-party counselling before a woman could terminate a pregnancy challenged Harper's stated position that he had no intention of impinging on a woman's right to choose.

In an effort to limit damage caused by outspoken candidates, Harper had imposed restrictions on his candidates. But the need for restrictions only fuelled suspicion about the radical nature of Harper's team. Attempts to muzzle candidates drew headlines, for example, "Tory candidates sign gag order, document shows."[25] The article referred to a document all Conservative candidates were required to sign, pledging that they agreed "not to publicly criticize any other colleague, the Leader or the Party."

---

[25] Anne Dawson, "Tory candidates sign gag order, document shows," CanWest News Service, June 10, 2004.

Conservative candidates were not the only ones making Canadians wonder where a Conservative government would take the country on social issues. Early in the campaign, Harper said that as a matter of principle MPs would be free to introduce private member's bills on any issue, including abortion and capital punishment. "Any private member can table a bill and any bill can be voted on. That is absolutely the case today. I will not be making free votes and private members' legislation more difficult than it is already." Harper was saying that a Conservative government would not initiate or sponsor such legislation in its first term, but there was sufficient ambiguity to create a lot of unanswered questions in the minds of voters. Was Harper sincere or was he simply being cagey? And he qualified his commitment to a first term. Were voters wrong to conclude that Harper was setting aside an issue because it was politically expedient to do so?

There was one area where Harper did not want to tread: the Canada Health Act and its provisions for universal public access to health care. Harper promised an increase in public funding, a reduction in wait times, and a series of performance and accountability measures that would strengthen the public system. So it was not helpful when Alberta PC premier Ralph Klein mused on June 16 that his pending Alberta health-care reforms, due to be announced two days after the federal election, might violate the Canada Health Act. Paul Martin accepted this gift, then called Stephen Harper Klein's "silent partner" in a "hidden agenda" for the "dismantling of our health-care program." Klein's remarks had no impact in the West, where Conservatives were strong. But the prospect of major health-care reforms struck fear in the minds of voters elsewhere.

Harper's pledge of free votes in Parliament on social issues, coupled with media amplification of every extreme and intolerant statement by one of his candidates, made it easy for Paul Martin to accuse him of having a hidden agenda. The Liberals could find nothing in the Conservative platform that was scary or extreme. But thanks to loose lips they were able to cobble together a number of television ads that portrayed Harper as a leader who was more comfortable in George Bush's America than in Canada.

From day one the Conservative strategy was to front-load the release of the platform so that voters would have the chance to see for themselves that the ideas were practical, reasonable, and manageable. This, Conservatives hoped, would clearly show there was nothing to fear from a Stephen Harper government. According to Geoff Norquay, there was a huge problem with the approach. With every plank in the platform released so early in the campaign, Norquay said, "The script ended." There was little Harper could offer that would control the agenda and make news as the campaign progressed. Consequently, as the stumping wound down, the media focused on the inflammatory statements from radical members of the party.

In the final week of the campaign, as some pollsters were projecting a Conservative victory, more controversy struck. Randy White, long-time Reform and Alliance MP and co-chair of the Conservative election-readiness committee, was interviewed about an unreleased documentary. He said, "If the Charter of Rights and Freedoms is going to be used as a crutch to carry forward what social libertarians want, then there's got to be for us conservatives out there a way to put checks and balances in there. So the notwithstanding clause...should be used, and I would think not just for the definition of marriage."[26] White had provided an explosive opportunity for the Liberal war room. With media and Liberal prompting, Canadians were left to wonder how the Conservatives might use the notwithstanding clause. White did what he could to distance himself from his party: "These were my own personal opinions. They are not the leader's views, and they are not the views of the party." But Harper was again put on the defensive, and he responded decisively. Referring to the freedom of MPs to speak their minds and reflect the views of their constituents, Harper said, "In our party that's allowed. In terms of what Mr. White or somebody else may have said about a controversial issue, frankly this is unimportant. It is a smokescreen,

---

[26] Sean Gordon with files from Anne Dawson, "MP's views are his own, Harper says," *National Post*, June 26, 2004, A6.

it is a smear tactic by the Liberal party."[27] Harper's defence of White's right to free speech did little to calm the nerves of uncertain voters.

Despite all the missteps and controversy, it appeared that Stephen Harper and the Conservative party might win. Almost every key national pollster had data that showed the parties in a dead heat in the last week of the campaign. The election was up for grabs. Liberals were in full panic mode and incited fear among the electors that a Harper government would jeopardize a woman's right to choose and that Canada would be plunged head first into every imaginable American conflict, including Iraq. The scare tactics were aimed at voters leaning to Harper, and also at those on the left of the political spectrum who might be frightened enough to shift support from the NDP to the Liberals to ward off a Harper government.

While Martin was sounding the alarm, Harper began to make statements about transitioning into the role of prime minister. It was enough to cause Canadian voters to do precisely what the Liberal ads suggested: "think twice." When Harper chose to spend the final days of the campaign in the West, with boasts of how Alberta was about to take its rightful place in the halls of power, Ontario got a bad case of cold feet. Harper's return to Alberta was damaging and pointless: he already had the province won. He should have been in Ontario where Conservative momentum was sliding. Laschinger could feel the loss of momentum. "We lost election day by 200 votes but won the advance poll by 1,000 when things were going well."

AT THE OUTSET OF THE CAMPAIGN, Conservatives would have been ecstatic to hold the Martin Liberals to a minority government. After they began to believe the hype, election night was a deep disappointment.

With 135 seats, the Liberals were down 37 members. Conservatives won 99 seats, an increase of 21 from the combined PC and Canadian Alliance total from 2000. The Bloc Québécois won 54,

---

[27] Ibid.

up 16, mainly because Quebecers were punishing the Liberals over the sponsorship scandal. The NDP maintained official party status with 19 seats, an increase of 6. Chuck Cadman was the lone independent MP elected. Cadman had been a Reform, then an Alliance MP for the suburban Vancouver riding of Surrey North, but lost the Conservative party nomination for the 2004 campaign. The voters seemed to like Chuck more then they liked any party.

If a united Conservative party was designed to end vote splitting, particularly in Ontario, then the merger was a raging success. From 2 Ontario Alliance seats in 2000, Stephen Harper's Conservatives came in with 24 of Ontario's 106 seats, a net gain of 22 seats in Ontario. The gain was offset by a net decrease of 3 seats in the rest of the country. The party was down seats in four provinces—Nova Scotia, New Brunswick, Quebec, and British Columbia—with only modest gains in Alberta and Saskatchewan. The party held the clear majority of seats in the West, but won only 7 of 32 seats in Atlantic Canada and was shut out in Quebec's 75 ridings. It was hardly an unfamiliar ending: 31 out of a possible 213 seats east of the Manitoba border.

That's not all: the popular vote for the Tories, at 29.6 per cent, was a far cry from the combined PC and Alliance vote in the 2000 campaign, at 37.7 per cent. The Alliance party on its own had polled 25.5 per cent in 2000. If one assumed that most of the Alliance voters from 2000 would stay with the Conservative party under Stephen Harper, one might conclude that a majority of the PC supporters went to other parties in 2004. Anchoring the relatively poor popular vote was the 8.8 per cent vote in Quebec, well below the combined 11.8 per cent of the PC-Alliance vote in 2000.

The biggest surprise of the campaign was the strength of the Green Party. Although they elected no members, the Greens garnered 582,247 votes nationwide (4.3 per cent of votes cast), a tenfold increase from the 1997 campaign. The Liberals ended up 7.3 percentage points ahead of the Conservatives, winning their minority with only 36.7 per cent support. This was down from 40.8 per cent in 1997 and 38.5 per cent with which they had won majorities in 1997 and in 2000.

Conservatives needed to remind themselves how far they had come. "We went into the campaign hoping for 85 seats," war room communications specialist Yaroslav Baran pointed out. "We thought we would be doing well to hold the Liberals to a minority government. We hoped to weather the Martin storm so that we would have a few years to build the Party and market Stephen to voters." Conservative strategist and CPAC panelist Bill Pristanski agreed.[28] "Harper did a remarkable job as leader. Six months earlier the pundits had been musing that Martin would win the largest majority in Canadian history. We now had time to re-group and learn from our mistakes."

Reporters couldn't help but wonder about the impact those controversial statements by Conservative candidates might have had on the outcome. One reporter asked Baran about how outspoken candidates might get dealt with next time around. "Our goal is not to stop every outrageous statement that candidates make and we won't duct tape our candidates. That [outspoken candidates] will happen in our party the same way yahoos appear in every party. Where we want to be is a place where it doesn't matter what any one candidate might say on any given day because it only matters what Stephen Harper says. He leads the party and that's it. If you want to know where we stand, just ask Stephen Harper."

When the dust settled, the Conservative party could claim progress on only a few of the top challenges. It did not have appeal across all regions of Canada and was a non-factor in Quebec. It did not seem that the party was reaching out to build a broad national coalition. There was nothing extreme in the official party platform, yet some of the more radical candidates were drawing far too much attention, and that attention worked against the moderate and mainstream campaign Harper was trying to lead. Yes, Harper's leadership was clear and decisive at times, but near the end of the campaign he faltered and looked more like a regional than a national leader.

---

[28] CPAC is the Cable Public Affairs Channel.

But one area where Harper and the party scored well was with party unity. The core group of Canadians who call themselves Conservatives was relatively small, but with a national campaign behind them they were firmly behind their party and its leader. They had transformed what many thought would be a Liberal landslide into a minority government. Harper and the Conservative Party of Canada would live to fight another day.

CHAPTER 15

FULL CIRCLE, ACT II

THE MORNING AFTER THE 2004 ELECTION, reporters were clamouring for a scrum with Harper. They wanted to know his assessment of the campaign and what it meant to his future in politics. But Harper was in no mood for interviews. He had come close to becoming prime minister, only to have it slip away in the final week of the campaign. Harper turned inward. He did not fume and explode; he became quiet, sullen, and reclusive. He had, to use an expression his staff coined, "gone dark."

He had done this before. In the middle of the 2002 Alliance leadership race, for example, he disappeared from sight after he discovered his Ontario campaign team had mislead him about its activities and accomplishments. The length of his "dark" episodes varied. Some lasted for days and some were brief, as when he would suddenly and inexplicably turn away in the middle of a conversation for no apparent reason. Weissenberger believed that what some people called "dark" might be deep thinking and analysis. "There was some frustration because it looked like there might be an opening in the middle of that campaign to make a breakthrough. When it didn't happen there was some frustration. Stephen did not experience any great funk."

Frustration or funk, Harper's staff members understood that this was not a time for him to be speaking to the press. They hatched a plan so he could leave Calgary unnoticed the morning after the election. But an industrious press pinned Harper down at the Calgary airport. Asked about his future in politics, Harper spontaneously responded, "I'm going to take a little bit of time with my family, obviously I'm already talking to people across the country."[1] It was much more than anyone expected he would divulge. The story the day after the election was not that Paul Martin had been stopped in his tracks and held to a minority; it was whether Stephen Harper would stay on as Conservative leader to fight another day.

Harper's comment about assessing his options overshadowed everything he said that day about the progress the party had made and the fact that the Liberal government, for the first time since the 1988 election, was going to face real opposition in the House of Commons. Harper's staff urged him to clarify his remarks and confirm he would redouble his efforts to defeat the Liberals next time out. But Harper was in no mood to retract or clarify anything. The flip side of his decisiveness was stubbornness, and Harper was not one who easily changed his mind or admitted error.

Although he did not speak about it publicly until after he became prime minister, one of Harper's advisers about his political future was Brian Mulroney. In 2006, Harper said, "Although we first met many, many years ago, I have only come to know Brian Mulroney personally over the past 3 years."[2] It was not something Harper dare say while campaigning: it was too risky. No one knew for sure what the impact would be on the Conservatives' election prospects. After Harper won the leadership, Mulroney had become a highly discreet but indispensable member of his strategic team. Harper noted, "When one assumes the sometimes lonely role as national Conservative leader and more importantly as Conservative prime minister, there are precious few voices of experience to whom one can turn."[3]

---

[1] Sean Gordon, "Harper to ponder his future as leader: Recriminations were swift," *National Post*, June 30, 2004, A4.

[2] Speaking remarks by Prime Minister Harper on the occasion of Brian Mulroney being awarded the distinction of Canada's Greenest Prime Minister by *Corporate Knights* magazine at the Chateau Laurier Hotel, Ottawa, April 20, 2006.

[3] Ibid.

Mulroney had registered some of the lowest approval ratings of any prime minister in English Canada near the end of his second term, so he was equipped to help Harper work through the inevitable low moments he would encounter. According to John Weissenberger, the conversations between Mulroney and Harper began while Harper was Alliance leader and intensified around the time of the merger. This surprised most PC loyalists, and those in the Alliance party, too, many of whom became active in politics because of their angry perceptions of how Mulroney's government responded to concerns from the West. Harper's openness to discuss politics with Mulroney while Alliance leader was not something Preston Manning would have done.

Mulroney had both affection and admiration for Harper and would have encouraged him to continue to lead the Conservative charge. Mulroney also advised Harper on what it took to win. The question Mulroney put to Harper was whether he wanted to be Leader of the Opposition or prime minister of Canada. Mulroney set an example for Harper to follow: build a national coalition of conservatives that were moderate in policy and tone; ditch any far-right policies; and avoid any hot-button social issues. The other key to success was Quebec. While conventional thinking in 2005 was that Conservatives could not win in Quebec, Mulroney thought otherwise, and encouraged Harper to build bridges.

After he gathered his thoughts and worked through the understandable disappointment and dark moments after the 2004 campaign, Harper recommitted himself to one goal: becoming prime minister. Marjory LeBreton recalled Harper telling his caucus that he would not have stayed on as party leader if he didn't think he could win the next election. Based on his track record, the statement was more than just political bravado. In 1993, when Harper lost faith in the Reform campaign team, he withdrew from the national campaign and concentrated on his own riding. In 1997, sensing Reform was going nowhere electorally, Harper resigned his seat and went to the National Citizens Coalition.

Harper took Mulroney's advice and decided to make a serious investment in Quebec. After the 2004 election, Josée Verner became one of Harper's most important Quebec operatives. She was Harper's most successful Quebec candidate in 2004. She finished ahead of the Liberal candidate and lost to the BQ victor by only 3,281 votes in her Quebec City riding of Louis-Saint-Laurent. She had been a staff member for Quebec premier Robert Bourassa and a member of the Action démocratique du Québec, and she helped build a political network and provide much-needed credibility for Harper in Quebec. In a decision that may be unprecedented in Conservative politics, Harper named the unelected Verner to his shadow cabinet and invited her to attend caucus meetings. He also appointed her chair of the Quebec Conservative caucus. (The latter post was largely symbolic, because the Quebec caucus at the time included only Verner and Conservative senators David Angus and Pierre Claude Nolin.)

By the fall of 2004, the polls showed a slight strengthening for the Liberals from the June election results. The Liberals, at 37.2 per cent support, enjoyed a 10.4 percentage point lead over the Conservatives, who had dropped by 2.8 percentage points.[4] Clearly, Harper would have to shake things up if he was going to defeat Martin. The 2004 election had come on the heels of the merger and a leadership contest. For the next election Harper and the party would have an opportunity to prepare.

Right after the 2004 campaign, Harper initiated an exhaustive and comprehensive post-mortem in which no facet of the campaign and no ego were spared, including his own. "Harper led the post-mortem," said Norquay. "He wanted to know what went right and what went wrong. It was brutally frank, with himself and everyone else. The advertising, the speech writing, the fact that the script ended three weeks before election day leaving nothing else to say." Harper wanted to know what Conservatives would have to do to win. He intended to run a different campaign next time: a winning

---

[4] Ekos Research Associates Inc. Data are based on telephone interviews conducted October 13–17, 2004 with a random sample of 1,237 Canadians aged eighteen and older. A sample of this size provides a margin of error of +/– 2.8 percentage points, 19 times out of 20.

campaign, a campaign that was more thoughtful, professional, methodical, and strategic in every facet of electioneering.

Not everything Harper did to build his new team was initially judged successful. In a speech delivered in Quebec City on October 15, 2004, Harper endorsed the views of Action démocratique du Québec leader Mario Dumont, that Quebec should be allowed to change its name and have its own constitution. Harper also told his Quebec audience that a future Conservative government would consider Belgium as a model for developing community-based linguistic institutions.

> In Belgium, for example, federal authority has been divided, not just with geographically based regions, but also with linguistic communities as well. I want my party to consider how this model could be adapted to Canada. Rather than devolving more authority to provinces in areas like cultural affairs and international relations, perhaps the federal government, working with the provinces and particularly with Quebec, could establish francophone and anglophone community institutions for jurisdictions in areas like the CRTC and the CBC, or the Francophonie, the Commonwealth and UNESCO.[5]

The Belgium speech was noteworthy for a number of reasons. It was the first time Harper spoke directly to Quebecers about language and culture. Before, Harper had written about the equality of provinces; in this speech he acknowledged that Quebecers were different and deserved special recognition. Harper had taken Mulroney's advice and was intent on adding a Quebec contingent to his coalition. That included establishing formal and visible links to Quebec politicians and bringing the likes of Mario Dumont and the Action démocratique supporters who had been so critical to his leadership success out of the shadows.

---

[5] Anne Dawson, "Harper backs ADQ on autonomy," *Montreal Gazette*, October 19, 2004, A12.

Commentators were quick to ridicule Harper's efforts. L. Ian MacDonald, a leading Quebec federalist and close confidant to Brian Mulroney, wrote in the *Montreal Gazette* editorial pages:

> Stephen Harper came dangerously close yesterday to being a Belgian joke, the European equivalent of the old Newfie joke. What's Blue and floats in the Ottawa River? Leaders who suggest modelling Canadian federalism on the Belgian experience. Whose really dumb idea was that? And who persuaded Harper there would be no problem in going along with Mario Dumont's suggestion of styling this province as the autonomous state of Quebec? It would have no more effect, Harper shrugged, than a U.S. state calling itself the Commonwealth of Massachusetts. Technically and intellectually, he's quite right. Politically, he's dead and dangerously wrong.[6]

Macdonald's stinging editorial implied that Mario Dumont, rather than Brian Mulroney, was consulted on the content for the Belgium speech. Although elements of Harper's speech and ideas were successfully resurrected in the 2006 election, little was heard of Belgium.

A COMMON REFRAIN FROM Liberal spin doctors in the 2004 election was that Stephen Harper had a hidden and scary agenda for Canada. Liberal fear-mongers had guns being pointed at Canadians and women fretting about losing the right to choose an abortion if Stephen Harper became prime minister. The Liberals pointed to the fact that, in its haste to unite, the Conservative party had yet to hold its first policy conference. Without clear direction from party members, Liberals argued, Stephen Harper had carte blanche to implement whatever scary idea came into his head. Those who understood party politics recognized this as a ridiculous proposition,

---

[6] L. Ian MacDonald, "The Belgian waffle," *Montreal Gazette*, October 20, 2004, A31.

but the idea may have helped persuade voters that the Conservatives were not ready to govern. Conservatives like Marjory LeBreton willingly and enthusiastically accepted the challenge. "After the 2004 election, the merger was still a work in progress. There was a desire by voters to defeat the Liberals but it was too soon for us. We still needed to sort out who we were and what we stood for." LeBreton and her party were prepared to be judged by the positions adopted by party members at its first policy conference, to be held in Montreal on March 17–19, 2005.

Montreal was chosen as the host city to reinforce in the minds of Quebecers and the national media that the Conservative party was committed to winning seats in *la belle province*. Showing a presence in Quebec was important, but more important was demonstrating that the party had a moderate and inclusive view of Canada. The press would be searching for indications of maturity and asking if the party had the discipline and moderation required to win the next election. The conference would also be a test of Stephen Harper's leadership.

Although the party was looking to build a bigger tent, not everyone was invited inside. "After the merger some from both the PC and Alliance side asked me to renew. Some even wanted me to run for the leadership," said David Orchard. "So I renewed my membership and paid the observer fee to attend the policy convention." When party headquarters reviewed the list of attendees, Orchard's name stood out like an organic prairie weed. The party's national director, Ian Brodie, called Orchard two days before the convention: "You are not welcome. We are refunding your money and are not allowing you in," he told Orchard. Comedian Rick Mercer suggested that Orchard do a television skit in which he was being rejected at the registration desk. A serious fellow, Orchard demurred.

The opening night of the convention was designed to demonstrate that the new party represented all regions of the country. Deputy leader and Nova Scotian Peter MacKay, who chaired the caucus committee that put together the policy document delegates would debate, led off the proceedings. Other speakers included Josée Verner representing Quebec and Rahim Jaffer from the West.

The final speaker of the evening, Ontario PC leader John Tory, had to withdraw because of a by-election in his riding.

Belinda Stronach, trade critic and at the time MacKay's girl-friend, believed that as the runner-up in the leadership race and a leading moderate voice in caucus she should stand in for Tory as the Ontario speaker for the evening. Instead, Harper and the organizing committee chose former provincial cabinet minister and key Harper supporter John Baird. It was a wise choice in one respect: Baird admitted later that partway through his speech to the cheering throng of delegates, he decided he would seek the federal nomina-tion in his Ottawa West riding.

Stronach was disappointed not getting the nod to be keynote speaker, but made her mark on the party's founding convention in another way. One of the most talked-about events of the convention was the "Cool Blue" party she hosted at the Hotel Godin. Reported to have cost $86,000, the event featured blue lights, glowing blue ice cubes in martinis, complementary wine, and Canadian music legend Tom Cochrane. The glitz of the party put a whole new view on what it looked like to be a Conservative. With Stronach and her money on the scene, it was cool to be Tory.

The delegates and the press came to the convention for more serious business. They wanted to know if Harper's Conservative party had gone mainstream, or if the more socially conservative views from the Alliance would prevail in the merged party. The lit-mus test was the issue of abortion. In the workshops, as expected, delegates made motions on abortion that went against Harper's stated views. Harper had consistently maintained that the party should not adopt policy on issues of conscience. Rather, members of Parliament should have a free vote on such questions. The delegates supported Harper's position, although by only the narrowest of mar-gins: 55 per cent to 45 per cent. Had that vote gone the other way, the Conservatives would have carried a millstone around their necks that would have almost certainly defeated them in the next election. Social conservatives were disappointed with the result, but nonethe-less were prepared to stay with the party.

The next test of maturity was party unity. More specifically, had the rift that had divided the movement for the past decade been bridged, or would the past continue to hamper the party's ability to present Canadians with a clear and united option for government? The media could easily have canvassed delegates to find signs of acrimony and tension, but that wasn't necessary. The state of party unity was visibly and emotionally tested over the issue of the equality of ridings. Scott Reid, one of Harper's emissaries in the merger discussions, took the lead on two proposed constitutional amendments. The first was to amend the party's by-laws to allow a one-member, one-vote system for electing the leader. The second would link the number of delegates a constituency could send to a convention with the number of party members.

Taking a firm and impassioned stand in opposition to the amendments was deputy leader Peter MacKay. With the ink barely dry on the seventeen-month-old party constitution, MacKay was outraged that such a fundamental provision of the agreement he had signed was up for discussion. Indignant and angry, MacKay, who as caucus policy chair had used most of his pre-convention efforts on policy and platform development, now told delegates he would never have agreed to merge had the equality-of-ridings provision not been included. MacKay lectured convention delegates: "This is about ensuring that every region of the country has an opportunity to build this party, to demonstrate to the country that we respect every region equally. This was a decision I felt impacted on our ability to present ourselves to the country as ready to govern."[7] MacKay defended the intensity of his outburst, telling the press, "I was upset. I am not denying that. And I was emotional about it because I was very involved in the bringing together of these parties and one of the things we insisted upon was the equality of ridings, and we made concessions to get there . . . I am not apologizing one little bit. I felt strongly about it. I may have been intemperate, but that was a result of the passion I was feeling."

---

[7] Ian Bailey, "Boos greet controversial delegate-selection amendment," CanWest News Service, March 20, 2005.

When Scott Reid addressed the 2,200 delegates with his motions, MacKay had the convention on his side. Reid took the brunt of the rejection, and some boos, but he was not alone in thinking the motion was a good idea. Harper was not directly involved in the fracas and made no statements about it to the media, but he clearly believed the motions had merit. One senior party official overheard him say, "I have no problem with the motion proposed by Scott." That Harper did not support riding equality was not news: he had conceded to MacKay only with reluctance in the merger negotiations. But it was newsworthy that senior people in the party were prepared to revisit a fundamental aspect of the agreement so soon after it was negotiated and ratified.

Reid's amendment was easily justified. The MacKay–Harper agreement stipulated that the party's first convention would be used to review the constitution. The agreement further stated that the first convention would be based on the equality of ridings, and said nothing about subsequent conventions. More specifically, section six of the merger agreement stipulated that "the system used to elect the *first* leader need not be used for later leadership elections and the membership of the Conservative Party of Canada could select an alternative method of electing future leaders." One of the drafters of the MacKay–Harper agreement believed that delegates at the party convention had an obligation to consider the leadership-selection process. Tom Jarmyn, Harper's lead in the merger discussions, said, "The wording in the agreement meant there was a positive obligation on the party at the convention to adopt a new model. The words in the agreement are plain and obvious." In response to the boos, Reid defended himself: "There was always the understanding that this would be something that could be amended at a future date. There was never anything written that said this was an unamendable provision in any part of it."[8] Paul Lepsoe, moderator of the session that debated Reid's motions,

---

[8] Ibid.

said, "It was not part of an us versus them battle. Most delegates who supported the motion did so because they fundamentally believed it was right and democratic."

John Weissenberger believed Reid's proposal was fair and reasonable. Stipulating that a riding association needed to have at least a minimal number of members to gain a full slate of delegates would have gone a long way to reducing the potential for electoral manipulation and abuse. The minimal number was one hundred, at a time when the average complement of members in an association was more than five hundred. Weissenberger could recall the days when some Quebec riding associations with only a handful of members could easily be taken over by a few "instant Tories" who were not necessarily dedicated to the principles of the party. Scott Reid's motions made it out of the workshop, but by the time they got to the plenary session they were dead in the water. "It was symbolism that carried the day, rather than rational compromise," said Weissenberger.

Whether Harper put Reid up to it is not known for certain, although Reid said he did not, a position confirmed by convention moderator Paul Lepsoe. In the end, Harper ceded to MacKay's conviction and sent a signal through his spokesman that the motion should be defeated. It was too early in the new party to be revisiting issues that had been negotiated and agreed upon a year earlier. "It would have been as if we placed a motion on the floor to change the name of the party to the Progressive Conservative Party of Canada," said Denis Jolette. "People would have thought us a bit crazy. Likewise, we didn't think it was right to start changing a fundamental part of the deal we just negotiated. It was just too early for this. Why risk dividing the party?"

After affirming moderate social policies and retaining the MacKay formula for leadership selection, the new Conservative party was looking increasingly like the old Progressive Conservative party. Vestiges of the populist Reform party, such as voter-initiated recall and referenda, were hard to find at the policy convention.

"They stripped the party of its Reform populism," says Faron Ellis, an Alberta political scientist and author of a book on Reform titled *Limits of Participation*.[9]

Party unity and moderate social policies were critical to a successful convention. So was clear and strong leadership. Despite having fumbled a lead towards the end of the 2004 election, Harper received an impressive 84 per cent support from the delegates for his leadership. There was no question that the party was prepared to support him into another election. Harper's keynote speech covered all the bases. He attacked the Liberals for providing government that was good only for advertising firms and Liberal cronies. He scored easy points by chastising Martin for needlessly undermining Canada's relationship with the United States. But mainly, he set the course for the party to be moderate and centrist on policy issues. The only socially conservative issue Harper was prepared to discuss was a promise to defend the traditional definition of marriage. Yet even on this, he told delegates that there was room for diverging views in the party and that he would treat everyone respectfully.

Harper had been talking about building bridges and coalitions from the time he was elected leader of the Canadian Alliance. Structurally, this began with the merger of the parties, but Harper also wanted to bring as many elements of the small-c conservative movement back to the party as possible. Economic and social conservatives could be rather distinct groups; Harper needed to apply careful judgment and soft diplomacy. He also wanted to attract scores of new Canadians, and he thought that speaking to traditional family values, such as the traditional definition of marriage, would attract many of Canada's ethnic groups. In taking this position, Harper ran the risk of dividing the social conservatives and Red Tories in his caucus.

In his caucus, Harper encouraged dialogue among those with diverging social views. In the fall of 2003 Harper had been asked

[9] Norma Greenaway, "The Conservative de-Reformation," *Ottawa Citizen*, April 22, 2006, B4.

how he would reconcile the openly gay PC Scott Brison with Larry Spence, the Alliance MP who said he would not be opposed to laws that would make homosexuality a crime. Harper had replied that he would make them seatmates in the House of Commons. That's precisely what he did with the evangelical Stockwell Day and the more liberally minded Belinda Stronach. Harper's approach to irreconcilable views was to encourage dialogue but to keep everyone together in the same party.

Nothing "scary" came from the Montreal convention. On the contrary, it was clear that Harper led a united party with a moderate platform endorsed by the party membership. Liberals hoping to demonize Harper in the next election should have taken note: fearmongering would be a tougher sell next time around.

Intent on demonstrating his commitment to the policy positions adopted in Montreal, Harper chose to affirm his newfound moderation on April 29, 2005, in a luncheon speech sponsored by the Fraser Institute, an organization committed to market solutions for public policy problems. He began his speech by saying, "Today, I will say some things some of you in the Fraser Institute may not want to hear." Maintaining that he was open to new ideas from the Fraser Institute, Harper said recent suggestions from former Ontario premier Mike Harris and Reform Party founder Preston Manning to reform the Canada Health Act were "non-starters." Leaving behind his economic past, Harper then said, directly and somewhat confrontationally: "If this represents a departure from the market norms that guide much of the public policy thinking of this Institute, then so be it . . . The ability to pay cannot control access to necessary medical services for ordinary Canadians, and it will not in a national Conservative government."

THE LATE SPRING OF 2005 was beginning to look like the "perfect storm" for Conservatives. They had mustered enough votes in the House of Commons to defeat the Martin government, and support for Conservatives in the polls had reached record levels. Conservatives were buoyed by a 26-point turnaround in popular support, rebounding from a 15-point deficit to the Liberals in early February to an

11-point lead in April.[10] An Ekos poll pegged Tory support at 36.2 per cent, compared with only 25.0 per cent for the Liberals. The changing fortunes were largely attributed to the release of shocking testimony at the Gomery inquiry about systemic abuses of the public treasury by the Liberal party, as well as illegal and fraudulent activity by some advertising executives and Liberal party insiders. By a margin of two to one, Canadians believed Prime Minster Martin should be held accountable for the sponsorship mess. Ekos president Frank Graves cautioned Liberals that there would be no easy recovery from this slide. "We have seen other spikes in the past which have proven to be temporary...The current situation, however, seems to be qualitatively different, with a good old-fashioned scandal apparently tied more directly to a wing of the federal Party."

Just as the Opposition parties were about to defeat the government on a vote of non-confidence in mid-May, however, a political bomb went off in Ottawa. Belinda Stronach crossed the floor to the Liberal benches.

The defection of Belinda Stronach from Conservative opposition trade critic to Liberal Minister of Human Resources and Parliamentary Reform was an important test for Stephen Harper and the conservative coalition he was trying to build. Was Stronach's defection evidence that the party was not relevant to mainstream and moderate Canadians? Would the defection reinforce Liberal fear-mongering that Stephen Harper had a hidden agenda? Would Stronach reveal any secrets about the dark side of the Conservative party? And what about her relationship with Conservative deputy leader Peter MacKay?

The political apprenticeship of Belinda Stronach has no precedent. While it is not unusual for an experienced business executive to enter politics after a distinguished career, Stronach hardly fit that description. Being CEO of a billion-dollar auto parts manufacturer

---

[10] Ekos Research Associates Inc. Data based on telephone interviews conducted April 7–9, 2005 with a random sample of 1,125 Canadians aged eighteen and older. A sample of this size provides a margin of error of +/– 2.9 percentage points, 19 times out of 20.

looks impressive on a résumé, but the position was bestowed by birthright: her dad gave her the job. There is no clear evidence that her contribution to Magna's success was positive, negative, or neutral. She had no academic record to speak of, having dropped out of York University after less than one year of study. During her predictably rapid rise through the executive offices of Magna, Stronach had shown an interest in conservative politics. In 2000, she supported Preston Manning in the Alliance leadership race. In 2003, she was Peter MacKay's most munificent donor and fundraiser. Later that summer, she used her Alliance and PC connections to urge the parties to merge. Most of this activity was behind the scenes and high-level. The most important attribute she brought to politics was money. With money came power and access. The missing ingredients were experience, knowledge, and content.

Stronach clearly had a keen interest in becoming a political operative, but it is reasonable to ask whether she ever was a Conservative. Her ever-dominant father, Frank, had been the Liberal candidate in 1988 in the riding of York Mills, Ontario. Although Frank Stronach lost that election by almost 7,000 votes to Tory candidate and municipal politician John Cole, he seemed never to lose touch with his Liberal friends. Dennis Mills, a former Liberal MP, became a Magna Corporation vice-president. Former Ontario Liberal premier David Peterson and defeated Liberal cabinet minister Doug Young sat on the board of Tesma, a Magna subsidiary in Cape Breton, Nova Scotia.

Frank Stronach the Liberal and Belinda Stronach the Conservative: a useful partnership that covered the political bases. However, some in the media questioned Belinda's Conservative credentials well before she crossed the floor in 2005. A few months before the party's spring policy convention in Montreal, Judi McLeod of the Canada Free Press wrote: "[The] media missed out on a Stronach story that would likely matter most to rank and file Canadian Conservatives: A Liberal opportunist with money was taking on the Conservative Party from the top...How this Liberal found a home in the fledgling Conservative Party remains an unwritten story to this day."[11] Suggesting an element of conspiracy, McLeod labelled Belinda a modern-day Mata Hari. A week later, McLeod ratcheted up the story. "Can there really be any serious doubt that blondie Belinda is a Liberal, dispatched by the Liberals as the sugar and spice wrecking hammer against the advancement of a vulnerable new Conservative Party of Canada? Liberals capable of big tent invasion is hardly a new concept."[12] A year earlier, when Belinda was running for the Conservative leadership, a Canada Free Press article had appeared under the headline, "Belinda—she's just another liberal."[13]

Whatever bona fides Stronach had gained in the Conservative party, they did not come from her support of the Conservative–Alliance merger or her premature run for the leadership of the party in the spring of 2004. If there was victory to be claimed in the leadership contest, it was only that she exceeded the expectations of the media, who thought she would fall flat on her face. While her knowledge of the issues was superficial at best, she proved a capable student of John Laschinger by sticking to her well-rehearsed script. The real credibility Stronach had as a Conservative came from her willingness to grind it out in the June 2004 election. Once again, Stronach followed Laschinger's advice and doggedly ran a door-to-door, constituency-driven campaign, which she won by only 689 votes over Liberal Martha Hall Findlay. Thereafter, she was warmly welcomed into the Conservative caucus, assigned a good seat in the House of Commons, and placed in the shadow cabinet as the critic for international trade.

Outside the world of politics, the international media was taking note of Belinda Stronach's personal wealth and rising national influence. Most notable was *Forbes Magazine*, which in August 2004 named Stronach to its list of the world's one hundred most powerful

---

[11] Judi McLeod, "Belinda Bedazzled: Love bug misses 'plant' in Conservative Party," Canadafreepress.com, January 29, 2005.

[12] Judi McLeod, "Devil's ditty introduces Belinda," Canadafreepress.com, February 9, 2004.

[13] Arthur Weinreb, "Belinda—she's just another liberal," Canadafreepress.com, February 2, 2004.

women. Even mainstream Canada appeared to be fascinated with Stronach, and Yahoo! Canada reported that she had been one of the year's most popular Internet search requests. The auto parts heiress was starting to impress even the Parliament Hill skeptics.

In early January 2005, news reports began to circulate about a romance between the twice-divorced Stronach and Peter MacKay.[14] MacKay seemed more willing to speak of the romance than Stronach: "Suffice it to say, I'm very happy and quite smitten. Belinda is just a terrific person and we're getting along famously."

Stronach found some happiness with MacKay, but the same could not be said for her professional relationship with Harper. The rift between the two extended far beyond Stronach's well-publicized views on abortion and gay marriage. Their disagreements on social issues were not fatal because Harper believed such issues should be settled by free votes in the House of Commons. Consequently, Stronach enjoyed the comfort of being able to hold her views from inside the Tory caucus. Nonetheless, it rankled Harper that Stronach seemed inordinately pleased whenever she was given the opportunity to distinguish herself from her leader and others in the Tory caucus.

The real problem, hidden not far below the surface, was leadership. In short, Stephen Harper was leader and she was not. Harper did not appreciate being undermined by the freewheeling Stronach, and Stronach did not like being disciplined for being ambitious and a Harper contrarian.

One of the first indications of serious trouble came in March 2005 when a senior Conservative party source leaked information to the *Toronto Star* that Stronach owed about $350,000 to the party from her failed 2004 leadership campaign.[15] It was not unusual that the party and a leadership candidate would be in dispute over such

---

[14] Stronach divorced her first husband, Magna executive Donald Walker, in 1995. She divorced her second husband, Johann Olav Koss, in 2003. Koss, from Norway, was an Olympic Gold medallist in speed skating.

[15] Tonda MacCharles, "Stronach, party fighting; Her campaign owes $350,000, sources say Conservatives challenging her expense report," *Toronto Star*, March 24, 2004, A8.

matters, but it was shocking that a paid party staff member would try to make Stronach look bad in the press.

The same month, at the policy convention in Montreal, Stronach had expected to deliver a keynote address. This would not be unusual for someone who had just placed second in the leadership contest. But party officials were prepared to give Stronach only a minor role: introducing Ontario MPP and future Harper cabinet minister John Baird. Stronach turned down what she considered to be a "bit part" and fumed that she was not given the starring role to which she felt entitled. It was evident to many delegates at the convention that Stronach was acting as if the leadership race was still on.

Stronach certainly had effective moments as trade critic, particularly when criticizing Liberals for their inept support of Canadian beef farmers, who were suffering from severely restricted access to the American market because of the mad cow crisis. "Someone has to defend the interests of hard-working, suffering Canadian farmers," said Stronach. "If Paul Martin won't get the job done because he is too distracted by his political misfortune to govern, we will step up to the plate."[16] The next day, after receiving good press for advancing an issue of importance to hard-working Canadian farmers, Stronach was written up in the gossip pages for having dinner with former U.S. president Bill Clinton and actor Jack Nicholson. Conservative MPs did not know what to make of their colleague. Was she the farmer's best friend or an international celebrity jet-setter?

After the 2004 election, William Johnson requested an interview with Stronach for his upcoming biography on Harper. Johnson spoke with one of Stronach's staff who agreed to the interview provided she was not asked questions about Harper and his leadership. This was because, the staffer explained, Stronach did not think that Harper was the right person to build the party and move it forward. Making this statement to a journalist was tantamount to open revolt.[17]

---

[16] "Conservatives seek legal standing in U.S. mad cow case," Canadian Press, *Charlottetown Guardian*, April 22, 2005, A13.

[17] This anecdote was provided to the author by John Weissenberger.

On May 16, the day before Stronach joined Martin's cabinet, the *Hill Times* published an article that exposed Stronach's continuing leadership objectives. The article quoted a staff member close to Stronach:

> "She has her eyes on the leadership of the party and she also wants to become the Prime Minister if possible. Do you think she came to Ottawa just to be one of the 308 MPs? Do you think she's traveling across the country, helping people raise funds, giving media interviews just to be another MP? No, no, no. It's all about the next leadership. She's new in politics and she does-n't want to stay in politics for a long time. And for her to be the next leader [of the party], she needs political and media advice on a daily basis. She can't afford to make mistakes."[18]

One of Stronach's key confidantes, in her run for the leadership and after, had been Conservative senator David Angus. Former chairman of the PC Canada Fund and long-time friend and supporter of Brian Mulroney, Angus provided Stronach with the political memory the neophyte MP so desperately needed. Angus recalled taking a shine to Stronach after she lost the leadership. "I thought Belinda was a key player in our party. She represented a softer, more progressive side to the party. She was a contemporary woman. She had a lot of style and pizzazz and she knew how to have fun. We love that in Quebec." Stronach confided to Angus that she was unhappy with how Harper treated her. She confided that she thought she was not being accepted in the party. "She had a real problem with Harper and said he was no good as a leader," said Angus.

The proverbial straw that broke the camel's back was an article Stronach co-wrote for the editorial pages of the *Globe and Mail*. Harper's office had initially approved the article, but Harper staffer

---

18 F. Abbas Rana, "The man behind MP Stronach: Belinda Stronach, who has big lead-ership aspirations, may be a rookie, but she carries the workload of a Cabinet Minister, so says her high-profile advisor and seasoned political veteran Mark Entwistle," *Hill Times*, May 16, 2005, 1.

Bruce Carson later called the *Globe* to retract the submission. A distressed Stronach approached Angus with a request: Would he consider talking to the leader on her behalf? To Angus, this was an indication Stronach was still willing to work co-operatively with Harper and the party.

Angus requested a meeting, and he and Harper met shortly thereafter. Angus began the meeting with, "This will only take five minutes." "David," came the reply, "take whatever time you need." Angus said he was there to talk about Belinda. With that one sentence the conversation came to an abrupt end. "David, she is not there for us." Angus asked, "What do you mean? She was great at the Montreal convention and she represents a dimension to the Party that is badly needed in Quebec." Harper was not moved. "That's your view, David, but she is just not there for us and she is not on my radar screen." There was nothing more for Angus to say. The case was closed.

Angus had supported Stronach for the leadership. Later he reflected on Harper's dismissive response to him, and to Stronach generally. "It was clear that Harper felt Stronach was a complete loose cannon and was always offside. She was always freelancing her own stuff. But it was a mistake on my part to support her as leader for our party. In hindsight, it appears I was mistaken. Harper's judgment on Belinda was better than mine."

Stronach took her concerns about Harper's leadership to the Ontario caucus, hoping to win support and make new friends. But she achieved the opposite. A heated exchange ensued, in which Stronach was admonished by her colleagues. She had isolated herself: the caucus was solidly behind Harper even if she was not.

Next, Stronach suggested that Harper's plan to defeat the government before certain parts of the spring 2005 budget were passed might be a mistake. Caucus disunity about the budget and about a vote of confidence in the government could hardly be tolerated. On May 7, Brian Laghi wrote an insightful article for the *Globe and Mail* that examined the two sides of Belinda Stronach: political rookie and savvy operator. Laghi wrote: "With an increasingly large presence in the Conservative Party, and a newly expanded team to advise her,

Belinda Stronach is being seen in a different light these days. Savvy retail politician is one characterization MPs are using. Thorn in the side is another."[19] Laghi quoted one long-time Tory and senior campaigner who suggested Stronach was choosing issues and moments with leadership ambitions in mind: "She knows exactly what she's doing . . . She's beginning to take a series of policy decisions on the youth wing, on equal marriage and that kind of stuff, which sets her apart from others. Anybody who thinks she ran just to be an MP or a cabinet minister is very mistaken." And an unnamed MP suggested that Stronach had been speaking out of turn more than should be accepted. "I think it was a real mistake in a lot of ways. It demonstrated some political immaturity. To feel you have to put this out in public, no matter the cost to the party. It hurt the party, and secondly, it hurt her."

Still, other than the Laghi article, there was nothing in the popular media to suggest a bombshell was about to go off in Ottawa.

By chance, on Thursday, May 12, Stronach ran into former Liberal premier of Ontario David Peterson at an event honouring former Ontario PC premier William Davis.[20] Stronach told Peterson of her unhappiness about a range of issues. Peterson took the conversation seriously enough to speak with Stronach again the following day. Before the close of business on Friday, Tim Murphy, Prime Minister Paul Martin's chief of staff, was brought into the loop, on the condition of absolute secrecy. Murphy briefed the prime minister. After a weekend of discussion and negotiations, Peterson travelled to Ottawa on Monday, May 16, where he met Stronach and Murphy at the Chateau Laurier at 4:00 in the afternoon, and a deal was finalized. Stronach would cross the floor and enter cabinet as Minister for Human Resources and Skills Development, and Minister for Democratic Renewal. The second portfolio would make her responsible for the government's response to recommendations from the Gomery inquiry.

---

[19] Brian Laghi, "Political rookie or savvy operator?" *Globe and Mail*, May 7, 2005, A1.

[20] Much of the content for this paragraph is drawn from Mark Kennedy, "Chance meeting leads to political blockbuster for Stronach," *Ottawa Citizen*, May 18, 2005, A1.

When Martin was informed of the deal at 6:30 p.m., he invited Stronach to dinner at his Sussex Drive residence. In between cutting her deal and consummating it with the prime minister at 24 Sussex, Stronach met MacKay at Zoe's, the Chateau Laurier Hotel lounge named for the wife of Sir Wilfrid Laurier. They finished dinner at about 8:00 p.m., Stronach rose from the table, said she had a meeting to attend, and kissed MacKay goodbye. As she left Zoe's, Stronach saw Jeff Clarke, a friend of MacKay's, and engaged in some nervous conversation. Clarke sensed something was peculiar in the conversation and went to MacKay to inquire if anything was wrong. MacKay and Clarke were puzzled by Stronach's demeanour and sensed something was up.

It was close to midnight when Stronach returned to the Chateau Laurier suite where MacKay waited. Evasive at first, she eventually told him where she had been and what she intended to do in the morning. A shaken MacKay outlined for Stronach, a political newcomer, how this decision would permanently destroy her credibility. At first, Stronach responded with the talking points she had been given by Tim Murphy, which she was to say at the press conference in the morning. However, these were all positive lines. She had heard nothing but encouragement from Liberals and her father in the past five days, and had given little thought to the personal and political downside, which included the end of her relationship with MacKay.

Stronach thought that withholding the knowledge of her discussions with Liberals from her boyfriend and failing to involve him in this life-altering decision would have no impact on their relationship. After MacKay started to pack his things, it became more of a two-way conversation.

From which of her Conservative friends did she obtain advice? MacKay pressed Stronach. Over her short political career she had regularly turned to Brian Mulroney, Don Mazankowski, Bill Davis, and Elmer MacKay for counsel. But none of them had been asked their opinion. There was every indication that her decision was not thought out from all sides.

By 4:00 in the morning, Stronach concluded she had made a mistake. She called Mark Entwistle, her communications adviser, to tell him to call everything off, that she was not going through with it. She made arrangements to meet Entwistle before her scheduled breakfast with Murphy and Peterson, to undo what she had begun. Both Peterson and Murphy were at the Chateau Laurier that evening to make sure they were available to respond in a moment of crisis.

With two hours of sleep, after promising MacKay she would not defect, Stronach left for breakfast. When she returned to her Chateau Laurier suite at about 8:00 a.m. she had her BlackBerry in her hand and her father was on the line. Her father, a former Liberal candidate, was deeply involved in her decision. She told MacKay it was too late, that she couldn't stop what she had started. The press release had been drafted and a press conference arranged. The word from anxious Liberal negotiators was that the deal was "closed." They had already spoken with Martha Hall Findlay about standing down as the Liberal candidate in Newmarket Aurora, and there was no turning back. MacKay pointed out that nothing mattered until she walked into the press theatre to make the announcement; that she was still in control. Then she handed MacKay her BlackBerry and asked him to speak with her father. It was a short conversation.

MacKay offered to arrange meetings and work with Stronach and Harper to try to patch up their differences. MacKay was unaware of similar efforts made by Senator Angus. But Stronach was firmly committed.

MacKay called his father, and Brian Mulroney, and then Stephen Harper to warn them of the calamity that was about to strike. Mulroney reassured MacKay that he had done nothing wrong; that it was not his fault. That was something MacKay desperately needed to hear. Harper went to MacKay's office to offer his support. Harper's first concern was for MacKay's well-being. It was an encounter that would help the two men understand and appreciate one another.

About fifteen minutes before she entered the parliamentary press gallery theatre with the prime minister to announce her decision, Stronach called Harper to give him the news.

At the announcement, Paul Martin remarked, "[She] and I have agreed that she fits more comfortably, can serve more appropriately and can contribute more substantially as a member of the government caucus... But I am particularly proud to have her join us at this important time. The significance of her decision is not that it necessarily alters the outcome of Thursday's vote—indeed we still do not know whether the budget will pass." The prime minister delivered this line with all seriousness, but the press gallery uncharacteristically erupted in laughter, knowing that the wily Martin had just negotiated a reprieve from a confidence vote that would have defeated his government. Martin concluded his remarks by calling Stronach "gutsy" and declaring that he was "proud to have Belinda Stronach as part of my team."[21]

Stronach's statement was designed to portray her decision as one based on deep principle and concern for the welfare of the nation. "The political crisis affecting Canada is too risky and dangerous for blind partisanship. I watch and listen and feel that the interests of individuals or parties are often placed above the national interests. The country must come first." Her carefully scripted, condescending remarks about the Conservative party—"Over time, the Conservative Party will mature and grow"—were surely aimed at Harper. There was a more direct attack on Harper: "I've been uncomfortable for some time with the direction the leader of the Conservative Party has been taking... I do not believe the party leader is truly sensitive to the needs of each part of the country and how big and complicated Canada really is." Perhaps she was thinking of Peter MacKay when she said, "There are many good and talented folks that I have a great deal of respect for in the Conservative Party." It was cold comfort to MacKay.

One reason Stronach gave for switching parties was her concern that Conservatives were aligning themselves with the Bloc Québécois to defeat the government. "The result," she warned, "will be to stack the deck in favour of separatism and the possibility of a

---

[21] Despite Martin's expressed admiration for Stronach, he took it upon himself to ridicule and discomfort his newest cabinet minister at the 2005 fall press gallery dinner. In his remarks, which were often meant to be humorous exaggerations of political events and circumstances, Martin cast Stronach as a ditzy, inarticulate, prepubescent schoolgirl as she pondered her decision to cross the floor to the Liberals. "He made her look like a pawn and a fool," said Peter MacKay.

Conservative government beholden to the separatists. After agonizing soul-searching, I just cannot support such a large risk with my country." It seemed to matter little that it was the Liberal party, under Jean Chrétien, which had weakened the federalist voice in Quebec through the sponsorship scandal. And she was unable to articulate what was so peculiar about the BQ and Conservative parties standing up together in opposition to corruption and scandal. In fact, it was a good sign for federalists that the BQ was prepared to work co-operatively with another party to hold a corrupt government accountable. It was a federal election that was being called for, not a referendum on Quebec sovereignty.

The reporters almost did not know where to start. They asked why she told Peter MacKay of her plans only after she had made her deal with Martin. Those questions were likely the most uncomfortable to answer. "With respect to Peter and myself, those are private discussions," Stronach said. "I have a great deal of respect for Peter MacKay, the contribution that he made to bring the parties together, that he makes within the Conservative Party to bring forward more moderate, mainstream policies." MacKay was not of a mind at the time to respond to Stronach's comment, but his leader offered a statement in his defence. "I think Peter is taking this pretty hard, as you could imagine," said Harper. "If she has such a high opinion of Peter MacKay, I would venture today after my discussion with him, she has an awfully tough way of conveying that to him."

Harper took his own shot at Stronach, saying he was not surprised by the defection, which he attributed to Stronach's unsatisfied leadership ambitions, which "weren't in the cards" in the Conservative party. When a reporter asked him about the complex reasons Stronach had offered for her decision, Harper replied, "I've never noticed complexity to be Belinda's strong point."

Most Conservatives were outraged by Stronach's action, and a few of them used sexist and demeaning language to describe her. But she also received sympathy from some in the party who knew her well. John Laschinger, Stronach's campaign manager for the leadership and for the 2004 election, said, "Harper had only himself to blame for Belinda's departure. Harper treated her badly and he pushed her out of the party."

Stockwell Day thought Stronach acted impetuously. "I sat beside her every day in the House. I could tell she was not happy. But I think her move was not well thought out. She was impatient and badly advised." Day, who witnessed much of the contact between Harper and Stronach, refutes the contention of bad behaviour between the two. "Stephen always respected her. It was other people who fanned the flames of her discontent."

Geoff Norquay, who had run communications for Stronach's leadership campaign, thought her lack of experience in partisan politics contributed to her many rash decisions. He said, "There was a lack of understanding on her part of the discipline required to exercise message coherence and control. When you are in opposition, you are not a free agent." Tom Jarmyn, who had worked with Stronach during the emissary process, said he could only understand Stronach through her "crass ambitions."

MacKay did what he had done many times before when faced with a personal crisis. He went home to Nova Scotia. As fellow Nova Scotia MP Gerald Keedy told the press, "An afternoon in Atlantic Canada is better than a week on a shrink's couch."[22]

The press camped out near the MacKay farm to see if the jilted deputy leader would grant an interview. Eventually, MacKay emerged from the garden, where he had been sharing a private moment with his father, wearing rubber boots and accompanied by Jack, the family dog. The loyalty of the family pooch became part of the story. The CBC's Tom Murphy grilled an unprepared and exhausted MacKay for nearly nine minutes. Containing his emotions, MacKay spoke in hushed tones, barely above a whisper:

> I'm moving on—I have a lot of people around me who are very supportive . . . I came home to heal and think a little bit . . . my head is clear . . . my heart is banged up but that will heal . . . I

---

[22] Liane George, "Peter and Belinda: The Whole Story," *Maclean's*, May 31, 2005, 26.

was like everybody. I was shocked. I didn't see it coming. I had no idea...I knew she was unhappy, but I certainly didn't see this as the outcome...She was unhappy for a few weeks I suppose...The personal side of this is separate...This too shall pass...I am not going to be critical of her. I wish her the best. I really do. I have a lot of affection for her family, her kids in particular...I spent a lot of time with her and her children over the last number of months. It hurts...She did what she had to do...I wish her happiness. Everybody has been through this at one point or another in their lives. We have to suck it up...that's the Canadian way, that's the conservative way."

MacKay wanted to demonstrate that the reasons for Stronach's defection were misguided and misplaced:

It's not true. We are not aligning ourselves with the Bloc... that's nonsense...The problem in Quebec is directly attributed to the actions of the Liberal party who have been corrupt...who have through criminal means tried to buy people and simultaneously reward their own party for political gain. This is what has given rise to separatism. Nothing that the Conservative party under Stephen Harper has done. It is perverse to suggest otherwise. For the Liberals to remain in office, that to me is the biggest threat to national unity, not only in Quebec but in the West.

The moderate views are alive and well...we saw that in Montreal, in the policy positions we have taken. I feel very comfortable in this party...It is a party I helped build with others, including Mr. Harper, including Ms. Stronach...any suggestion that this party is not inclusive and open and moderate and national in its scope is completely false. It is an attempt to damage the good work of so many Canadians that have been a part of this exercise.

MacKay wanted to show that he would not be deterred from serving his constituents and the Conservative party:

> I am committed to continuing serving in the Parliament of Canada, to work for my constituents here in Central Nova and do that work through the Conservative Party of Canada under Stephen Harper's leadership. I will continue to work hard . . . I still believe you put the country first . . . sometimes you just need to put your head down and keep going and that's what I intend to do . . . We are committed to forming government . . . This is just a very minor setback that will not affect our goals or our eventual return to government . . . [although] there were hundreds of thousands of people in this party who are affected . . . I hope people's faith will not be shaken by what's taken place.

Elmer MacKay expressed confidence in his son and said Peter had been "bushwhacked," something that was likely to happen more than once in his life. Almost no one was critical of MacKay. Even David Orchard, the man who said he had been betrayed by MacKay, would offer no comment. All MacKay would say of his relationship with Stronach was, "It was a private and painful part of my life that I have put behind me."

WITH STRONACH'S DEFECTION, and with independent MP Chuck Cadman siding with the government, the confidence vote held on May 19, 2005, ended in a tie. Liberal MP and Speaker of the House Peter Milliken cast the deciding vote for the government. Belinda Stronach had changed the course of political history and allowed Paul Martin's government to live another day.

Stronach's defection was certainly a boost for Paul Martin's short-term popularity. A few weeks after the Stronach defection, an Ekos poll provided nothing but bad news for Conservatives: Stephen Harper was rated as the least trusted among the three national leaders; more Canadians supported Stronach's defection to the Liberals than were opposed to it; a large majority of Canadians said they did not want an immediate election; Conservatives ranked behind the NDP and the Liberals as the second choice for voters; and finally, Conservatives had dropped 7.9 percentage points in just one month and were at a level below that of the 2004 election. The Liberals were in front with 34.7 per cent, compared with 28.3 per cent for Conservatives. "Despite an auspicious political climate, the Conservatives have not only failed to advance but have retreated to their core constituency in recent weeks," said Ekos president Frank Graves. "All this paints a considerably darker picture of Conservative prospects than appeared a month ago." If there was even a hint of good news it was that Liberal support in Quebec had plummeted to 20 per cent, while Conservatives, at 13 per cent, were showing some signs of life in that province.[23]

The damage to Harper and the party was short-lived. It would have been a different story had Stronach been able to convince other Conservative MPs to follow her lead. Instead, an outraged party rallied behind Harper, and Stronach's justifications for her actions proved to be as solid as her commitment to conservative principles. There was some bitterness in the party, particularly among those who had supported her for leader, but most in caucus thought it was better than if she had left during an election, when the damage could have been irreversible. And, because it shored up the Liberals for the no-confidence vote, the defection gave Harper and his party more time to prepare for the next election.

The polls were no better in the fall. Nonetheless, Harper sustained his commitment to defeat the government and force an election. With revelations of the sponsorship scandal no longer fresh in the minds of Canadians, Liberals were holding a lead of nearly 10 percentage points (38.7 per cent to 29.4 per cent) over the Conservatives in November 2005. Frank Graves sensed momentum on the Liberal side. "Although the election campaign could

---

[23] Ekos Research Associates Inc. Data are based on 1,704 interviews with a national random sample of Canadians eighteen years of age and older. Conducted between May 13–17, 2005, valid within +/– 2.4 percentage points, 19 times out of 20.

substantially alter the balance between the parties, from their position now, the Liberals can begin to dream about recovering the majority they lost in the 2004 election."[24] The Liberal party held commanding leads in B.C. and Ontario. And Harper's Conservatives were 21 percentage points behind the Liberals in Quebec. There was nothing in the polls to encourage Harper. He knew that two election defeats would mean the end of his political career, particularly if the Liberals scooped up a majority.

Harper had spent the past summer on a cross-country "barbecue tour" that had yet to yield any positive results. The tour had been an attempt to get Harper closer to voters and soften his image as a stiff intellectual who lacked emotion and warmth, a chance for him to listen more than talk. The press ridiculed the effort. Media training consultant Barry McLoughlin said, "Rather than a summer barbecue tour, I'd like to see him tour world capitals and let's see him meeting Tony Blair, let's see him meeting the UN Secretary General and all these people...I haven't seen many photos of him meeting with premiers, with mayors of cities."[25] One particularly memorable photo from that summer tour, splashed across the front pages of virtually every newspaper in the country, showed Harper at the Calgary Stampede dressed in a cowboy hat, string tie, and poorly fitted leather vest, looking very uncomfortable. One headline proclaimed, "More Gobsmacked than *Gunsmoke*." Harper responded by poking fun at himself. "My dad would have said, 'To me, you look like a cowboy, but I'm not sure to a cowboy you look like a cowboy.'"

Senator Marjory Lebreton thought the media underestimated the value of what Harper learned that summer. "The national press gallery and the elite missed the real story of what happened in the 2005 summer barbecue circuit. They panned what Harper was

[24] Ekos Research Associates Inc. Data based on telephone interviews conducted November 22–24, 2005 with a random sample of 802 Canadians aged eighteen and older. A sample of this size provides a margin of error of +/− 3.5 percentage points, 19 times out of 20.
[25] F. Abbas Rana, "Harper should give BBQ circuit a break: McLoughlin," *Hill Times*, August 8, 2005, 1.

doing. So did some in the party. But he learned how to be a retail politician that summer, which was of enormous value when the election came." So what if the photos aren't suitable for fashion magazines, the senator added. "He is not a photo op kind of politician. He finds them phony and trivial."

IN THE FALL OF 2005, Harper put himself and his party in a state of perpetual election readiness. The brutal 2004 post-mortem had produced new strategies and tactics designed to make it difficult for Martin or the media to cast Harper as "scary" or a man with a "hidden agenda." A key element of the new strategy was to control the agenda by getting the media and voters talking about Conservative issues and policies of the day. That meant speaking less of Liberal failures and more about Conservative ideas. It meant releasing a new promise virtually every day of the campaign to give the media something of substance to report about Harper. Campaign events would be held early in the morning to get a lead in media coverage and put Martin in a defensive and reactive position. The tour would also stay out of Alberta and would not visit the same riding more than once, no matter what. Most important, the platform would be so detailed, so specific and comprehensive that no one could possibly fear something was being hidden. In fact, many of the promises did not speak of change but of maintaining the programs and policies the Liberal government had recently implemented.

Harper decided to build a national coalition, just as Mulroney had done to win in 1984. He was prepared to set aside his economist instincts about policy in favour of what—within the bounds of centre-right conservative thinking—would make him prime minister. In other words, Harper had acquired the will to win. According to his colleague and friend of two decades John Weissenberger, Harper had concluded, "Half a loaf is better than no loaf. And, that's the way we were going to proceed."

The party platform was ready. The day-by-day election script was drafted. Conservatives had held the party's founding convention, and the campaign team was broadened. There was a realistic strategy in place to address Quebec. Harper and the party had learned from previous mistakes: there would be no candidate outbursts, and Harper would stay out of Alberta until election day.

The Liberals were intent on rerunning the 2004 campaign. They would replay the fear card that had saved them from the abyss last time out. The Martin team, virtually unchanged from the 2004 campaign, was again unwilling to invite experienced Chrétien supporters into the inner circle, which left them gloating whenever Martin faltered.

Harper needed a push to get the campaign started.

On November 1, Mr. Justice John Gomery issued his first report on the sponsorship scandal, titled *Who is Responsible?*[26] In his preface, Judge Gomery stated:

> The report that follows chronicles a depressing story of multiple failures to plan a government program appropriately and to control waste—a story of greed, venality and misconduct both in government and advertising and communications agencies, all of which contributed to the loss and misuse of huge amounts of money at the expense of Canadian taxpayers. They are outraged and have valid reasons for their anger.

Gomery's language was concise and his conclusions were clear. His report offered numerous conclusions that Conservatives could lift as campaign themes and slogans. Many of the major findings stuck directly to the Liberal government of Jean Chrétien and to the Liberal Party of Canada: ". . . a complex web of financial transactions . . . involving kickbacks and illegal contributions to a political party in the context of the Sponsorship Program; certain agencies carrying on their payrolls individuals in effect, working on Liberal Party matters; the refusal of Ministers, senior officials in the Prime Minister's Office and public servants to acknowledge their responsibility for the problems of mismanagement that occurred."

Harper's political instincts told him that with this damning report an election must be called sooner rather than later. Martin

---

[26] See: www.gomery.ca/en/phase1report/summary/index.asp (accessed July 11, 2006).

had pledged to have an election within thirty days of the final report, scheduled for February 1, 2006, but by then this first report would be virtually forgotten. As well, the final report would be prescriptive, and Martin could endorse it in an attempt to put the Liberal sponsorship scandal behind him. Harper wanted the election called immediately, to maximize the impact of Judge Gomery's first report. There were allegations of criminal misconduct by persons close to the Liberal party; Harper asserted that the government had lost its moral authority to govern.

To precipitate an election, Harper needed to defeat the government on a motion of non-confidence. With support for the Liberals in Quebec at historically low levels, the Bloc Québécois was eager to support a Conservative motion. The NDP was more difficult to pin down.

In early November, party leader Jack Layton said the NDP would prop up the government only if the Liberals met his demand to curb the privatization of health care. Layton had had his way with Martin once before, when he extracted significant changes to the 2005 budget in exchange for NDP support on a confidence vote. The cost for NDP votes was $4.5 billion in new spending for affordable housing, post-secondary education, the environment, and foreign aid. The deal also included cancelling proposed corporate income tax cuts, although Finance Minister Ralph Goodale backtracked, claiming he said he would reintroduce these measures at a later date. With the NDP proving that its support of the scandal-plagued Liberal government could be bought, Harper was reluctant to make a motion that Layton could once again use as leverage.

Martin seemed to like his political chances better in the fall than in the spring, and he rejected Layton's demands. This put Layton where Harper wanted him: on the record calling for an election. Harper and Duceppe, recalling the spring budget deal with Martin, put the onus on Layton to make the first move. Like other opposition leaders, Layton did not want to be seen triggering an election over the Christmas period. On November 13, after a long afternoon of bargaining, the three opposition party leaders reached a compromise. They announced that if Martin did not agree to dissolve Parliament in January for a February vote, they would trigger an election themselves.

Stephen Harper introduced and Jack Layton seconded the fateful motion on November 24: "That this House has lost confidence in the government." Four days later, the motion passed by a vote of 171 to 133. The next day, Martin visited the Governor General, and the election date was set for January 23, 2006. The eight-week campaign would be the longest in twenty-one years. Liberal strategists thought a lengthy campaign would make it more difficult for Harper to muzzle some of the more right-wing members of the Conservative party (an early indication that the Liberals would run the 2006 campaign the same way they had run the 2004 campaign). But Conservatives were more disciplined and better prepared than in 2004. One Conservative spokesperson remarked, tongue in cheek, that perhaps Belinda Stronach would reveal Harper's "scary" secret plan. "Surely, as a member of Harper's shadow cabinet, and someone briefed on campaign strategy and policy development, she would have kept a copy of the so-called hidden agenda that the Liberals kept talking about."

THE MOST COMPELLING EVIDENCE of Harper's commitment to win in 2006 was his platform. Election platforms often derive from elaborate, multi-faceted, national grassroots, consultative processes. But the Conservative platform for the 2006 election was the work of two men only: policy adviser Bruce Carson and Stephen Harper. "It was a back and forth process between the two," said Geoff Norquay. "The original version of the platform was loaded with what I call 'words of comfort.' But over the summer of 2005 Stephen went through it and struck out all the flowery language for the simple reason that it raises more questions than it answers. A platform can't be all things to all people." As the architect of the platform, Harper would also have the advantage of "knowing the document cold." Norquay also noted that the platform achieved a perfect amalgamation of the pre-merger parties. "All of the flame-thrower preambles were Alliance, and all of the policy bullets were PC."

Even Preston Manning declared Harper's platform tame by Reform standards:

Notwithstanding, Stephen's personal interest in policy is a lot deeper level than is reflected in the platform; that platform was designed to send one message, and it was not particularly their position on taxes or anything. It was to send a message that we are a safe choice. There is not a wild idea in there. In fact this may strike you as placid and pretty tame but that was the principle objective, I believe, of that platform and the way they rolled it out. Because the biggest thing they were trying to counter from 2004 was that somehow they were scary or had some ideas that were wild and woolly. From that standpoint it was eminently successful.

Brian Mulroney could only recoil at the thought of Preston Manning being converted from a principled, hard-right ideologue to a political strategist with affection for the political centre. If Manning endorsed a move to the centre, he would be repudiating his entire political philosophy. Stephen Harper's 2006 election platform, unlike the Reform platforms of the 1990s, contained nothing Mulroney would not have endorsed wholeheartedly. To Mulroney, the party being led by Stephen Harper was, for all intents and purposes, indistinguishable from the party Mulroney had led in 1984.

The specifics of the 2006 platform are in sharp contrast to the much harsher and more narrowly cast platform of 2004. Even the title, "Stand up for Canada," was more positive and inspiring than "Demanding Better." To ensure there would no confusing what Harper did and did not stand for, the crisp forty-six-page document featured more than four hundred bulleted policy positions.

While the 2004 platform said nothing about regional economic development "Standing up for Canada" spoke of maintaining current funding levels for "regional development agencies, like ACOA, WED, FedNor and CED-Q."[27] It also pledged to "Develop, together with northerners, both Aboriginal and non-Aboriginal, a northern

---

[27] ACOA is the Atlantic Canada Opportunities Agency; WED is Western Economic Diversification; FedNor champions northern and rural southern Ontario's economic diversification; and CED-Q is Canada Economic Development for Quebec.

vision to guide economic, social, and environmental progress in the region."

Rather than stick with exclusively federal areas of jurisdiction, Harper's Conservatives would "Maintain the funding for the New Deal for Cities and Communities" and "Maintain the existing federal infrastructure agreements that have been entered into between the federal government, the provinces, and municipalities." There was a promise to "Support the development of the Pacific Gateway Initiative, designating at least $591 million to the Initiative, but giving greater freedom to British Columbia and the other partners to designate their priority projects without federal interference." In effect, the regions could get federal money without the political interference they had come to expect from Liberals.

And in a move that would leave Reform party founders shaking their heads, Harper pledged to "Ensure that the CBC and Radio-Canada continue to perform their vital role as national public service broadcasters," and to preserve "the role of the National Film Board, the Canada Council, and other federal arts and culture agencies."

The 2004 platform had been virtually silent on issues specific to Quebec or the French language. In 2006, Harper made these commitments:

- Establish a Francophone Secretariat within the Department of Canadian Heritage. Language is an integral part of culture and heritage and should form the basis of decision-making for the Francophone cultural and artistic community.
- Invite the Government of Quebec to play a role at UNESCO along the lines of its participation in la Francophonie.
- Facilitate provincial participation in the development of the Canadian position in the negotiation of bilateral, continental, hemispheric, or global trade agreements where provincial jurisdiction is affected.
- Support the Official Languages Act, ensuring that English and French have equality of status and equal rights and privileges as

to their use in all institutions of the Parliament and
Government of Canada.

• Work with the provinces to enhance opportunities for
Canadians to learn both official languages and to ensure the via-
bility of minority language communities within the provinces.

Even more significant to Quebec was a commitment that a
Conservative government would "work with the provinces in order
to achieve a long-term agreement which would address the issue of
fiscal imbalance in a permanent fashion." There was a commitment
(affecting federal investments) to "ensure that any new shared-cost
programs in areas of provincial/territorial responsibility have the
consent of the majority of provinces to proceed, and that provinces
should be given the right to opt out of the federal program with compensation, so long as the province offers a similar program with
similar accountability structures."

What Harper said on his campaign tour carried as much weight
as a platform document. No campaign event was more important
than the December 19 stop in Quebec City. Harper's speech was
important enough to warrant a title—"Open Federalism." As L. Ian
MacDonald noted, "Harper caught the interest of frustrated federalists and soft nationalists—the voters of the former Mulroney
coalition."[28] Indeed, Mulroney and his gang of Quebec Conservative
federalists, like Josée Verner, Lawrence Cannon, Paul Terrien, and
Hugh Segal, all contributed content and language for the speech.
Leading Quebec journalists like André Pratte admired not only the
speech but also the timing, which gave Quebecers the festive season
to reflect about what Harper was saying.

Many Conservatives and members of the media thought Harper
was wasting his time in Quebec. Even some inside the campaign
thought there were, best-case scenario, only 2 seats to be had in the
province. But Harper believed otherwise. So did Mulroney. More

---

[28] L. Ian MacDonald, "How Harper forced a Conservative Spring," *Policy Options*,
March 2006, 29.

important, so did Quebec premier Jean Charest, who told reporters he had taken note of what Harper was saying. Those on the ground knew something significant was happening. Campaigning in Montreal, Fred Loiselle told Bill Pristanski the party "had a shot at winning 10 ridings if the momentum continued." The endorsement of Harper by influential Quebec newspapers *La Presse*, *Le Droit*, and *Le Soleil* was more than Harper could have imagined.

As well as significant policy shifts to bring the regions and Quebec into his coalition, there were the five priorities: cleaning up government by passing the Federal Accountability Act; providing tax relief by cutting the GST; making streets and communities safer by cracking down on crime; helping parents with the cost of raising their children; and working with the provinces to establish a Patient Wait Times Guarantee. The five priorities were useful not just for giving perspective to the four-hundred-plus promises in the platform, but also as a contrast to the image of Paul Martin as a dithering and indecisive politician. That label was given to Martin by the reputable and widely read international magazine *The Economist*. Under the title "Mr. Dithers and his Distracting Fiscal Cafeteria," its February 17, 2005, editorial contrasted Martin the decisive deficit fighter with Martin the man not big enough to be an effective prime minister: "As prime minister, his faltering leadership has earned him the sobriquet of 'Mr. Dithers' . . . . [whose] main concern seems to have been to court popularity by parading a generous social conscience." *The Economist* concluded, "If Mr. Martin is to win that election when it comes, perhaps next spring, he will have to show more of his decisive leadership of old."

There was a reason to highlight five priorities: "It was partly a response to Paul Martin being Mr. Dithers, but it was also a result of an exhaustive study of other successful campaigns elsewhere; in Ontario, Australia, you name it," said Yaroslav Baran. "Lists have a good track record. It was certainly premeditated and part of the plan going in."

The promise to offer parents $100 per month for each child younger than six became significant only when Martin's communications chief scoffed on national television that parents might well use the money to buy "beer and popcorn." No Conservative could have more effectively articulated the differing philosophies of the two leading parties. The Liberals wanted to control how child care money was spent through agreements with provinces and institutionalized child care. The Conservative approach was to directly support parents and the choices they made for the care of their children. This Liberal gaffe enabled Harper to showcase the policy as part of a national child care plan, even though it was really a targeted tax measure. Economic conservatives would be drawn to the plan because of reduced taxes, and social conservatives would embrace the plan's design for giving recognition to parents who stay at home with their children. Harper would declare at every partisan rally that his plan was based on his party's consultation with the real child care experts in the country—parents!

The promise to reduce the GST immediately from 7 per cent to 6 per cent, and to 5 per cent before the end of the first mandate, was perhaps the most telling indicator that Harper was prepared to do whatever it took to win. How could an economist propose reducing the GST—a tax that discourages consumption—rather than cutting income taxes—which discourages work and productivity? This promise would violate every economist inclination Harper had ever held. Preston Manning sympathetically described Harper's conversion from economist to politician:

> What Stephen would have is two lists. His economist friends would give him a list of tax cuts and they will be listed in order of which one would give the biggest bang for your buck in terms of economic growth. At the top of that list would be capital taxes, income taxes, stuff like that. But then the political guys would come in and say OK, in order to get support for a tax cut we will list the taxes in the order of which a reduction would get you the most support with the largest number of people. At the top of that list would be consumption taxes. You have these two lists and you have to decide what you want: the

one that gives you the biggest bang for the buck or the one that
will maybe give you a mandate to even start the tax cutting
process. And they chose, understandably I guess, the latter of
the two.

The 2004 platform had not even hinted at a GST cut. The centrepiece
of that platform had been to reduce the middle-income tax rate by
more than 25 per cent. Liberal Finance Minister Ralph Goodale
must have thought Harper's 2004 plan had merit, because the
income-tax-rate policy was central to Goodale's 2005 spring budget
and fall economic statement.

The GST cut rankled economists, and it also discomfited
Mulroney loyalists who had taken the heat for introducing the much-
hated tax in 1991. And that made Harper's policy shift a stroke of
pure political brilliance. He distinguished himself from Mulroney
and painted Martin into a corner. What could Martin do: defend the
hated GST, the tax Liberals pledged to kill in 1993? The move was
also good street politics for Harper. Unlike income tax, which is
taken from Canadians without much of a fight, the GST is visible,
mostly unavoidable, and paid by every Canadian. Even children and
the poorest of the poor pay the GST.

Mulroney recognized a good political strategy when he saw one,
and offered no objections. Harper and his advisers had thought the
strategy through meticulously, even to announcing it when former
Mulroney finance minister Michael Wilson was in Boston, and there-
fore unavailable for media commentary. Even Wilson, the man who
had introduced the tax, was brought on side; he enthusiastically
embraced Harper and his platform at a campaign event in Wilson's
former riding in Etobicoke, Ontario.

A brilliant execution had convinced the press that Harper had
both command of his party and a winning formula. Even before
Christmas, when the Liberals held a comfortable lead, there was a
feeling in Harper's team, and in the media, that it would be a good
election for Conservatives. "Laureen [Harper] used to often ask me
during the campaign, 'Do you think we are going to win?'" said

Senator Marjory LeBreton. "From the day the writ was dropped I thought we would. You could see it and feel it at events. Our people were energized and showing up, which was something that wasn't happening for the Liberals." After New Year's, Harper gained a lead in the polls that he never relinquished.

Each and every morning, the Conservative campaign rolled out a new election promise, setting the agenda for the day's political dialogue. "It was a masterful strategy," said Bill Pristanski. "Every night on our CPAC panel I was speaking about another positive Conservative policy. When the Liberals tried to play catch-up and introduce new policy of their own, they fired with blanks. Martin tried to one-up Harper and his fight against urban crime by declaring that he would ban handguns, only to find out that handguns had been banned in Canada since 1934."

A Tory lead in the polls was just what the Liberals hoped for. Liberal Treasury Board president Reg Alcock thought a big Tory lead was better than a small one. "There's a lot of people who argue that we had to come down in order to activate what we need, which is people needing to stop Harper. In fact, if we're going to do better than last time—that is, get a majority—we'd rather be a bit lower than we are."[29] The Liberals planned to hit the replay button from 2004: fall behind, frighten voters away from Harper, and establish momentum when it counted most.

Liberal strategists wanted to give Harper more airtime to vent his "scary" ideas. Two debates, the Liberals thought, would be better than one. But Conservatives also wanted two debates. Harper's strategists thought the more people saw of the calm, reasonable, and articulate Stephen Harper, the less fearful they would become. Back in 1993, the PC debate team thought giving Manning exposure would be good strategy, and that had backfired. This time the Liberals made the same mistake. Liberal strategists also called a long writ period, thinking that over the course of a lengthy campaign

---

[29] Paul Wells, "Inside an epic battle: Secret strategies, backroom blunders and private crises: the untold story of the 2006 election," *Maclean's*, January 26, 2006, 27.

Harper would falter and trip. They had underestimated Harper and wildly overestimated Martin.

The Liberal team also erred when it agreed to a format change for the debates. The revised format played into Harper's strengths, allowing him more time and space to articulate his vision and policies for Canada. "The new format was far more receptive to Harper's calm and substantive approach. Having two sets of English and French debates fit well with our strategy," said Conservative debate negotiator Michael Coates.

Coates was one of many from the PC side of the family who took a leading role in the 2006 campaign. Harper also received advice from Brian Mulroney and Michael Wilson; Senator Marjory LeBreton travelled with Harper throughout the campaign, providing sage advice at every key juncture. Long-time PC volunteers were brought into the organization structure of the campaign. They included Paul Brown and Kellie Leitch, who were given jobs as provincial campaign co-chairs. Other key PC stalwarts pitching in included Perry Mielle on advertising and David Crapper, who helped with polling.

Coates described Harper as a man evolving over time from Alliance leader into a coalition-building, no-nonsense Conservative leader who shed rigid ideology to become prime minister. "Harper became a pragmatic politician who had a good idea what the public wanted. He made the adjustments that were required at each stage of the party's development to build a broader base. He is a very strategic thinker. He was also more relaxed and more confident in 2006."

Harper also spent less time worrying that his candidates and officials might make extreme and radical statements during the election. He instituted a policy that no one could speak to the national media unless they were from the national campaign. If the *National Post*, *Globe and Mail*, or CBC wanted to do a story on abortion, they would have to go to Harper or his designated spokespersons from national headquarters to get a quote. Candidates like Cheryl Gallant from the Ottawa Valley had learned their lesson from 2004 and refused to attend editorial board meetings where controversy might erupt. To ensure the ability to provide swift and direct communication to negate an emerging story, Calgary Southeast MP Jason Kenney was planted in national headquarters and was available to appear before the national media on a moment's notice, whenever a spokesperson was required.

Not that Harper had any unruly and radical caucus members who needed to be kept under wraps; it was just a solid organizational move. "It was not unlike any caucus I had seen before," said Senator Marjory LeBreton. "And that goes back to Diefenbaker. We had people in Brian Mulroney's caucus that were far more radical than what we had after the 2004 election."

Using marketing techniques that Canadian Tire or Tim Hortons might employ, Harper's brain trust developed a campaign targeted at what they called a "conservative universe." Inspired by Tom Flanagan and Patrick Muttart, and informed by recent successful conservative campaigns worldwide, the 2006 strategy was based on knowing where votes could be won while ignoring those that could not. The campaign assigned fictitious names to describe the archetypal Canadian voter, some in the Conservative universe and some not. "Dougie" was a hypothetical tradesman, single, who liked to hunt. He was in the universe but would vote only if motivated. "Zoe," on the other hand, was an urbane, single, cat-loving condo owner with a stud in her nose who drank a seven-dollar latte every morning. She was never going to warm up to Harper. "Eunice," an elderly senior, active in her community, rich in assets but not in cash, was in the Conservative world. "Marcus and Fiona" were high-income earners with an elevated social status. They went to expensive black-tie parties to help the needy and assuage their social conscience. They were assumed to be Liberal. "Mike and Theresa" had a young family, a minivan, and a home in the suburbs. They felt the pinch of high taxes and didn't use institutionalized child care. They resented a government that did not respect the choice they made for their children's care. They were swing voters and heavily targeted by Conservative strategists. Each policy plank, television ad, or phrase in a Harper speech was designed to reach a voter whom Flanagan and Muttart had identified as part of the Conservative universe. It was a far more sophisticated approach than the one Conservatives had cobbled together in 2004. "Last time we went on assumptions about who would vote for us. This time it was based on science. We had the numbers to paint the picture, which had a huge impact on shaping policy," said Yaroslav Baran.

Because it reached out to specific voters, the platform became more focused. Rather than speak of ideology, such as free enterprise and reduced taxes, platform planks would drill down to concrete measures likely to be noticed by a target segment. Dougie might gloss over the economic arguments for higher productivity, but offer him a tax credit for his tools and you were speaking his language. Mike and Theresa cared little about a party that stood for the principle of protecting family values, but offer them a monthly cheque to help with the costs of raising a family, and tax credits for transit passes and minor hockey expenses, and the volume on their minivan radio might well be turned up. The communications strategy was as much about influencing voter turnout from the Conservative universe as it was persuading those who routinely go to the polls. It was similar to the strategy designed by Karl Rove, the architect of George Bush's 2004 re-election.

There was one broad category of voters Harper pursued in 2006. Harper, the intellectual economist, was going mainstream middle-class Canada. He would not be the leader of the cold-hearted government-hating party of the far right. His language was plain and his sentences crisp. In this campaign, Harper would look and talk more like Don Cherry than Adam Smith.[30] "He was appealing to the lunch bucket crowd that read *Sun* newspapers rather than the *Globe and Mail*," said Baran.

Even when the Conservative campaign blundered, it had nothing but good fortune on its side. When the Conservative advertising agency sent out DVDs of approved television commercials to national media outlets, it inadvertently included some test commercials that

---

[30] Don Cherry is the colourful and outspoken commentator featured on the CBC's *Hockey Night in Canada* "Coaches Corner" segment. Adam Smith, who lived in the eighteenth century, is regarded as the original thinker behind modern economic theory.

had not been edited or approved. Realizing the error, the courier company scrambled to retrieve the DVDs, but one copy was already in the hands of the editors at the Sun Media chain. The Conservative war room placed a sheepish call to request the return of the DVD, but the *Sun* editor pre-empted the request with a complaint about the DVD. Apparently, none of the files could be opened. "That's why we're calling," came the reply. "To let you know that a new DVD is on its way."

It is worth remembering that when Stephen Harper forced the election, his party was 8 percentage points behind in the polls. He took a big risk. In Quebec, Conservatives were in single digits, whereas the Liberals were at about 30 per cent support. Polls showed that 65 per cent of Canadians thought Martin would return as prime minister, and only 18 per cent gave Harper a chance of winning. Despite Liberal scandal and Martin's dithering, Harper still trailed Martin as the best leader for Canada by a significant margin. If he had thrown the country into an election that did not meaningfully change the composition of Parliament or put Harper in charge, it would be the end of his leadership. "Had Stephen lost the election he would have left without having to be pushed or asked to leave," said Weissenberger. Harper proved himself a risk taker by taking the government down on November 28, 2005.

When Conservatives fell behind by as many as 15 percentage points early in the campaign, Harper did not panic or change course. Capitalizing on a series of Liberal blunders, including allegations of leaks from the November Economic Statement that led to an RCMP investigation, Harper followed the strategy he had laid out at the start. In Quebec, the campaign began to exceed even Harper's wildest expectations. Harper was tied with the NDP's Jack Layton as Quebec's choice for best prime minister at the start; by election day Harper was Quebecers' first choice, outdistancing second-place Gilles Duceppe by a factor of almost two to one.

During the federal election campaign, the Public Policy Forum held a weekly breakfast panel discussion series at the National Press Club in Ottawa to analyze its progress. Participants and presenters came from a wide range of disciplines. At the end of the campaign, Graham Fox of the Public Policy Forum and Nick Nanos of SES Research spotlighted three main lessons from the election.[31]

First, *hope trumped fear*.

> Tories did not build their campaign around corruption but instead focused on a number of policies that spoke to the real concerns of average Canadians. When the Liberals unleashed their second volley of attack ads against Harper the week of the second leaders' debates, there was nothing on the record that could act as a hook for the claims made in the ads. Quite to the contrary, some of the allegations made in the TV spots seemed so far-fetched that the party was forced to explain many and even withdraw one before it made it to air. Put simply, Harper and the Conservatives inoculated themselves from allegations of hidden agendas by being so specific and explicit about their plan for government.

Second, *competence trumped ideology*.

> It was clear from the opening salvos in the campaign that the Tories had made an explicit choice to run the election on a set of specific policy announcements targeted at particular groups within the electorate. In contrast, the Liberals and NDP countered with campaigns based on values. More specifically, both the Liberals and the NDP issued dire warnings to the electorate about the dangers of electing a Conservative government with a right wing agenda... By being so specific, the Conservatives left little to the imagination as to the priorities of their government. Thus, charges of "un-Canadian" Conservative values could not be substantiated—people knew what they would do and were responding positively to it. In contrast, values-based

---

[31] Graham Fox and Nik Nanos, "Trading Places: The Story of the 39th General Election," *Public Policy Forum*, February 2006.

campaigns give voters few specifics on which to take hold in tight races.

Third, *ideas mattered*.

> Perhaps the most surprising feature of the election was the prominent role ideas played in this campaign. Contrary to predictions, all parties presented substantial policy platforms that had an impact on voter choice. In this election, citizens could decide their vote based on their preference with regards to tax policy, child care programs or federal-provincial relations. In this respect parties fulfilled their most basic obligation to citizens and the democratic process: they provided voters with a meaningful electoral choice. In this sense, the election cannot be deemed to be anything but a great success.

It is ironic that one of the key lessons from the 2006 campaign—that ideas mattered—was the same conclusion offered by David McLaughlin in the final chapter of his 1994 book, *Poisoned Chalice*:

> The overriding lesson from the [1993] election is simple. Standing for something does matter. The New Tory understands this. Does the Progressive Conservative Party? If it does not, there is no role for it in Canada's firmament and few should mourn its passing. The 1993 election will truly have been the last campaign of the Progressive Conservative Party.[32]

The contribution made by Harper to a successful Conservative campaign cannot be overestimated. Stockwell Day knows from firsthand experience how tough it can be to lead a party and run in a national election. His observations about the evolution of Stephen Harper and Harper's ability to lead a winning team reflect nothing but admiration:

---

[32] McLaughlin, *Poisoned Chalice*, 304.

People knew Stephen better in 2006 than 2004. Stephen knew himself better. He was more mature. He wasn't afraid to impose discipline and proper and strict guidelines. He wanted to win in 2004, but he *really* wanted to win in 2006 and he wasn't afraid to be tough with whomever he had to. This is the party of Stephen Harper. He has worked to make it what it is today. It's a coalition of people who are like-minded in some ways and not like-minded in other ways. While he put his own distinct stamp on this, he also learned from the three Ms: Macdonald, Mulroney, and Manning.

Harper watched the election-night returns with his family. John Weissenberger and his wife were also there, and Preston and Sandra Manning dropped in for a visit. "It was quite emotional when Preston and Sandra came in," said Weissenberger. "They didn't spend too long, but it was nice to see them." There had been a lot of water under the bridge over the years, said Weissenberger. "Had Preston become prime minister we would have been happy for him and happy to work with him again. There was never any personal animosity."

On election night Weissenberger thought back to 1987 and a chance meeting he and Harper had with Manning. At the time, Weissenberger and Harper were Blue Tories, two voices trying to shift the PC party further to the right of the political spectrum. It was just after Harper had returned to Calgary from Ottawa, after he had served as a parliamentary assistant to PC MP Jim Hawkes, the man Harper would defeat in the 1993 election. "It was quite a surreal experience on election night 2006 to sit in the audience," said Weissenberger. "We were in the front row. Three rows behind us were Jim Hawkes and his wife. In the other section were Preston Manning and his wife. Clearly it was quite symbolic how people had come together."

The 2006 vote was historic for a number of reasons, but the most significant was that after more than twelve years of Liberal rule, Canadians had elected a Conservative government. Stephen Harper, who just two years earlier had been leader of the Canadian

Alliance, was the Conservative prime minister of Canada. Peter MacKay, who had surrendered his newly won position as leader of the Progressive Conservative Party of Canada, would soon represent the country internationally as Canada's Minister for Foreign Affairs.

Harper's Conservatives won 124 of 308 seats, 31 seats short of a majority. The Liberals retained a strong position in the House of Commons with 103 seats, but that was not enough for Martin to retain his leadership. The BQ was disappointed to fall to 51 seats, while the NDP was pleased to increase its members by a third, to tally 29 seats. To govern with the confidence of the House, the Conservatives would need the periodic support of Liberal or BQ members.

From 2004 to 2006, the Conservatives increased their popular vote by 6.7 percentage points. They had won with only 36.3 per cent of the voting public, slightly less than the 36.7 per cent Martin received in 2004. In many respects, the results of the 2006 election were largely a reversal of Conservative and Liberal fortunes from 2004.

Perhaps most impressive about the Conservative win was that for the first time since 1988 a Canadian government had strong representation from every region of Canada. Liberal governments from the previous four elections had heavily depended on Ontario voters to win power. The Conservatives had reasonable representation in every province but one. Prince Edward Island was the only province that did not return a Conservative to Ottawa. (It was not for lack of trying, however; Harper had visited the island province late in the campaign.) Conservatives held 9 seats in Atlantic Canada, a gain of 2. They elected 16 new members from Ontario, to hold 40 of 106 seats. As expected, they steamrolled the prairies and won 48 of 56 seats. British Columbia was the only sore spot: they lost 5 seats to the NDP, but with 17 of 36 seats, they retained a significant B.C. caucus. Most impressive of all was what happened in the province of Quebec. A political wasteland in the early days of the campaign, Quebec gave the Conservatives 10 of 75 seats. Their share of the Quebec popular vote increased by 15.8 percentage points from 2004, and they cut heavily into the vote of the BQ. BQ leader Gilles Duceppe had predicted his party would eclipse the 50 per cent vote threshold, the theoretical level they sought to win a sovereignty referendum, but they ended up with 42.1 per cent, a 6.7 per cent drop from 2004. Belinda Stronach's worries had been misplaced: defeating the Liberals was not bad for federalist forces. Some would call Tory success in Quebec a miracle, just as they had when Brian Mulroney swept the province in 1984. Had those 10 Quebec seats gone Liberal, the national result would have been 114 for the Tories to 113 for the Grits.

The gains made in Ontario, mostly rural Ontario, provided another startling difference from 2004. Conservatives were once again shut out in Toronto, just as they had been in every election since 1988. Conservatives also had unimpressive results in Canada's next two largest cities, Montreal and Vancouver. Harper's attempt to appeal to mainstream Canadians resonated mostly in rural Canada.

The new Conservative party had not only won government, but every part of the country was behind it and wanted it to succeed. The NDP and BQ extended offers to work co-operatively with the Conservatives in a minority Parliament. It was a far cry from their demonization of Harper when he was a member of the Reform party, led the Alliance beginning in 2002, and first ran as Conservative leader in 2004. Even Liberals conceded it might be best that they be given time in Opposition to redefine their party, select a new leader, and generate new ideas.

The election did not give them a majority, at least not yet. But it was the first time since 1984 that Conservatives had defeated a Liberal government. In fact, comparing the 1984 and 2006 elections, Harper would most assuredly have won a majority in 2006 had the BQ not been on the ballot.

Stephen Harper took a risk and became prime minister. Peter MacKay also took a risk, and he would think back to that fall morning of 2003 when he felt the burden of history. He had made the right choice for his party.

CHAPTER 16

NEVER TO BE REPEATED

W ITH THE WIN IN 2006, Conservatives had support in every region of the country, including English and French Canada. The party held moderate mainstream Canadian values and had quieted its radical elements. Conservatives of all factions embraced the party and were united behind its leader. More important, the party had proven to Canadians that it was fit to govern. The new Conservative Party of Canada had come an extremely long way from December 7, 2003, when Canada's Chief Electoral Officer had accepted its registration as an official party, to February 6, 2006, when it was sworn into government.

From another point of view, however, Conservatives had not come very far at all. In fact, they ended up looking a lot like the Progressive Conservative party that had triumphed under Brian Mulroney in 1984. Even Preston Manning could cite only minor differences in tone and policy:

> [The new Conservative party] has more of an appreciation for some of the ideas that have their strongest support in the West. It has a strong western influence, particularly on the fiscal conservative front and constitutional front. Maybe less so on the democratic front than I would like. I think the memories of people are fresh enough of remembering maybe some of the mistakes of the Mulroney era that they won't be inclined to repeat them.

Manning admitted that the democratic populist measures fundamental to the creation of the Reform party—voter-initiated referenda, constituent assemblies, MP recall—were nowhere on Harper's radar screen and had been stripped out of the party constitution:

> Whether that democratic component is going to decline or just not manifest itself, it's probably too soon to tell. That is the element that is up in the air. That will be one of the factors people will be watching here. [Reform] won B.C. seats that we took away from the NDP; we didn't win them on our fiscal policy or on the constitution, we won them on democratic reform.

In April 2006, Norma Greenaway, national affairs writer with the *Ottawa Citizen*, canvassed a number of MPs from the old Reform party and asked what from their former party could be found in Harper's Conservative government.[1] Not much, was their conclusion. Harper's appointment of Michael Fortier, his national campaign co-chairman, to the Senate, and of newly elected Vancouver–Kingsway Liberal David Emerson to his cabinet was enough to make former Reformers cringe. These were actions, they argued, that Manning would never have countenanced. Vowed retired Reform MP Deborah Grey, "I will hang fire and see if [Fortier] runs [in the next election]." The former Reformers admitted that the populist measures that drew them to Preston Manning in the first place were nowhere to be found. "We may have lost the battle," said Saskatchewan MP Gary Breitkreuz, "but I am not giving up on the war." Former Reform MP Lee Morrison added, "There's a little bit of Reform that has rubbed off on the Conservative party. But it has become a pragmatic institution. The principal policy, as with any political party, is let's get in and stay as long as we can." From Morrison's statement, Greenaway inferred that "without its populist pillars...the new party is virtually indistinguishable from Mr. Mulroney's Progressive Conservative party."

[1] Greenaway, "The Conservative de-Reformation."

Tony Seskus of the *Calgary Herald* examined what was left of the original 52 Reform MPs who had stormed Ottawa in 1993. As well as numbers, he wanted to know which of their ideals and polices survived in the new party led by Stephen Harper. Writing in the midst of the 2006 election campaign, Seskus reported that less than a third of Reform's original MPs remained, and that their ideals had been eroded. Those quoted in the Seskus article expressed the apprehension among former Reform MPs that Preston Manning's ideals were relegated to second-tier status.[2] Jason Kenny, first elected in 1997, made a plea to "keep that Reform spirit alive." Original Reformer Chuck Strahl concluded that the anger that fuelled Reform was no longer present. Another original Reformer, Bob Mills, expressed his worry this way: "I don't think I want to be an inhabitant of Planet Ottawa. We've become more professional, we've learned the ropes, so to speak. But I would hate to be thought of as part of the culture of entitlement." Calgary Northeast MP Art Hanger was not ringing alarm bells but did caution that conservative principles were being lost. "I think the only way you're going to do that is by grassroots movements, political action on the ground, that will keep the party from going too far to the centre. We have to make that adjustment very soon because we've wandered too far in many respects." Veteran commentator and former *Alberta Report* publisher Link Byfield lamented that it was already too late. "What exists today is quite different from what Reform envisioned. It's a very disappointing experience. I think they did their best. They did as well as anyone could. But it shows the federal system does not lend itself to reform." Michael Behiels of the University of Ottawa drew a similar conclusion. "The true believers in the Reform movement, the purists, the hardliners, have pretty much all stepped aside."

Preston Manning could sense an abdication of Reform's democratic populist roots in Harper's decisions. Asked about the defection of David Emerson from the Liberal party to the

---

[2] Tony Seskus, "Original Reformers mixed on their party's legacy," *Calgary Herald*, December 28, 2005, A5.

Conservative cabinet two weeks after the election, Manning was incredulous. "From a democratic standpoint my preference was, if you want to do that, fine. But go and resign your seat and tell your people you made a mistake . . . and then stand in a by-election. That would be a more democratically consistent way to do it than they way they did it."

Roxanna Benoit, a westerner and former director of PC caucus research, agrees with Manning that the new Conservative party jettisoned the populist dogma. She also believes the right-wing ideology has been largely abandoned. "My view is that we are back where we were with Brian Mulroney. The big difference is that we have a leader who is not from Quebec. But Alberta will not put the pressure on this government as they did the Mulroney government. The people out West have more realistic expectations and a better understanding. No one wants to see the last fifteen years repeated."

Don Mazankowski thinks there are some small differences between the Conservative coalitions of 1984 and 2006, but nothing significant. "They will learn from some of the mistakes we made and from some of the things we did well. Overall, I think there are a lot of similarities." Peter MacKay thinks the differences relate more to the passage of time than to any change in thinking or approach. "The party had begun to lose focus in the 1990s and there has been a turnover of people. But as far as the philosophic base is concerned, the party's constitution, the political infrastructure, it's pretty hard to find any significant differences."

The face of Harper's 2006 cabinet took on a decidedly un-Reform–like complexion. Including Harper, only three in cabinet came from the original Reform class of 1993. Four are from the ranks of the Alliance party, and the Progressive Conservatives contributed twelve: nine from the former federal party and three provincial PCs. There was one former Liberal and seven who came to federal politics only after the merger. Of the former PCs, four had served in the Brian Mulroney caucus. Other than the prime minister, who had left Reform in 1997, none of the original Reformers had been given a heavyweight portfolio in cabinet.

Senator Marjory LeBreton credits Joe Clark for helping the PC party MPs understand that the differences between the two caucuses were not worth fighting over. "By inviting the DRC people into the PC party, Clark helped move the merger forward. He made us realize we could work with these MPs, that they really weren't much different from us." If there is a difference, Stockwell Day believes it comes from an understanding that the new Conservative party needs to be respectful of its various parts. "At the least, the big family of conservatives today is aware if you get one part of the family really upset, it will leave, which will devastate everything we are trying to do. The memory of that means that when Blue Tories stand up in caucus they are listened to: same with the Red Tories. We need each other. The colours won't run but they do mix."

Reform party founder John Weissenberger thinks the differences are more at the top than in the grassroots. "The membership of the parties is not much different. If there is a difference, it is that the party and its leadership are more cautious in their approaches to Quebec . . . and we are much more cognizant of staying away from the sovereignists."

Weissenberger is likely correct when he suggests that the main differences boil down to issues of leadership and style. But even there, the similarities between Harper and Mulroney are surprising. Geoff Norquay worked closely with both men. "Brian Mulroney and Stephen Harper are similar in how seriously they take the issue of caucus management. They both listen carefully and let debates run." Norquay believes both men are inclined to be even-handed when making decisions. Mulroney was a consensus-seeker, and "Harper is not autocratic and has no problem calling votes in caucus or shadow cabinet. For what we went through over the past fifteen years I don't think anyone would accept anything else."

Senator Marjory LeBreton might have had the best perch from which to observe Mulroney and Harper in action. "Both are big-picture thinkers, value caucus, have a total focus on winning and a work ethic like you cannot imagine." But LeBreton also sees differences. "Brian Mulroney and Stephen Harper are completely different personalities and have won over caucus quite differently. Mulroney is gregarious and entertaining. Harper is more serious." About Harper, LeBreton added, "There is no phoniness. He is decent, honest, and direct. He does not hold back information, and asks lots of questions. He is also very decisive. Once he makes his mind up he does not back off." Harper, LeBreton speculated, would not have changed his mind in the face of a public outcry, as Mulroney did in 1985 when he backed off a budget measure to partially de-index old-age pensions.

The relationship between Harper and Mulroney is another indication of the similarities between the parties of 1984 and 2006. Harper came out of the closet in 2006 and identified Mulroney as his trusted adviser and role model. Harper revealed his admiration for Mulroney on April 20, 2006, when he introduced him at an event to honour Mulroney as Canada's "greenest" prime minister:

> History will be kind to Brian Mulroney. He led an energetic and ambitious government . . . On international matters, Canada consistently punched above its weight . . . On economic matters he was ruthlessly pilloried for policies which his successors quickly adopted and which laid the groundwork for the prosperity we see today . . . Mr. Mulroney played a discrete but primordial role in the negotiations and reconciliation which led to the creation of the new Conservative Party of Canada.

Harper referred to Mulroney as a confidant and role model:

> In our relationship Brian Mulroney has proven generous with his time and frank with his advice, while making impositions on neither my schedule nor my decisions. Brian has always urged as a guiding principle for any action I must take [that I pursue] the greater long-run interests of Canada. Perhaps most of all I am particularly appreciative . . . of the fine model that Brian Mulroney had provided as a family man, for a prime minister who is also a husband and a father.

Preston Manning could never bring himself to say a kind word about Mulroney. Harper was proving he was different. To Mulroney's great relief, there was a prime minister who was prepared to defend the Mulroney legacy.

The new Conservative party had come so far so fast that after the 2006 election the pre-merger factions held surprisingly few grievances or hard feelings. Legally, operationally, and strategically, the party was functioning as a single, integrated and cohesive unit. Some members who slugged it out in the 1990s do carry battle scars. However, those with the deepest scars are gone from the federal Conservative scene: Preston Manning is out of politics, Jean Charest is in Quebec, and Joe Clark is hard to find. Scott Brison, Belinda Stronach, Keith Martin, and David Orchard have discovered that, really, they weren't all that conservative in the first place. And while there are a few Progressive Conservative senators wandering the halls of Parliament, no one seems to care very much what they do. It is of enormous benefit that Harper has not been a target of PC anger, not only because he excused himself from the fray between 1997 and 2002, but also because of his very public disagreements with Preston Manning, public enemy number one of PC loyalists.

Senator Noël Kinsella believes the Conservative party reached a stage of maturity in 2006 and shows a respect for divergent views that is more characteristic of the Liberal party:

> Political parties are essential to our Westminster system of parliamentary democracy. Parties are the forums to debate ideas and perspectives. It is natural for people to get frustrated while engaged in this process. Contradictions are normal. In spite of the frustration, the signs of maturity are that people hang in and keep the party together. The Liberals have been better at this over the years than have Conservatives, although they are going through a re-generation at the moment. Conservatives are today at a stage of synthesis.

These observations point to an interesting distinction between the actions of Preston Manning, Joe Clark, and David Orchard. Even though Manning is a conservative, he never felt comfortable expressing his views from inside the PC party. In Kinsella's terms, he did not "hang in," or even "hang out." David Orchard, on the other hand, was not a modern-day conservative, but he was prepared to fight his battles from within, even if that meant losing many more issues than he won. Joe Clark stayed with the PC party as long as it kept right-wing conservatives at bay. As soon as he saw the party embracing views and people with whom he disagreed, he quit. Among the three, Orchard is the one most likely to have considered staying with the party.

There is, perhaps, one member of the Conservative caucus who continues to struggle with broken relationships. "The day we elected a Tory government my journey was complete," said Senator Gerry St. Germain. He spoke of his decision to leave the Tory caucus and subsequently join the Alliance: "If there is such a thing as vindication for what I had done, the merger was it." Nonetheless, St. Germain remains estranged from many of his former colleagues, including the man who appointed him to the Senate: "Despite the fact that I was right, I don't think some of those in cabinet will ever forgive me." St. Germain seems resigned to his fate: "There will always be people who will not embrace what I did. I don't know what Mr. Mulroney will do, but I am at a point in my life where I can look at myself in the mirror. I knew what I was doing and I did it. Mission accomplished."

The evidence is overwhelming and the conclusion inescapable. There are far more similarities than differences between the Mulroney-led Progressive Conservative party of 1984 and the Harper-led Conservative party of 2006. The fundamental realignment of federal political parties that Preston Manning attempted to achieve never materialized. Under the vision and leadership of Peter MacKay and Stephen Harper, the party of Sir John A. Macdonald and Brian Mulroney had been reborn. The Conservative party had come full circle.

WHILE THE GOVERNMENT OF Prime Minister Harper is rightly focused on moving forward on its priorities and extending its coalition, a united Conservative party would be wise to take note of past damage. Conservatives need to understand why they lost four consecutive elections; they need to glean whatever lessons they can from this period of darkness. Those in the party who might become impatient over a lack of progress on certain conservative issues must understand just how much the Liberals would like to see another Reform party emerge. It is thus essential to reflect on the impact the Reform party had on the Canadian political landscape.

Most observers offer one of two opinions on Reform's effect. The more positive is that Reform helped shift the thinking in Canada towards more fiscally conservative policies. The other, more frequent opinion is that Reform did nothing but elect three successive Liberal majority governments.

In their 1992 book, *Storming Babylon*, journalists Sydney Sharpe and Don Braid predicted, "In the end, the Reform Party's main achievement may well be gauged by its effect on public policy, rather than by its electoral achievement."[3] There is likely not a former Reform member in Canada who would not lay claim to the party having been the bastion and defender of conservative economic values during the 1990s. However, there is strong evidence that Paul Martin knew early in his tenure as finance minister that his success would be judged on his ability to balance the budget, and that prodding from Manning had little if any influence.

As Brian Mulroney would often say it was because of Preston Manning that Jean Chrétien was able to win majority governments "without breaking a sweat." Peter MacKay elaborated on Mulroney's colourful reference: "When they build Jean Chrétien's statue on Parliament Hill, they have to have Preston Manning standing right beside him, practically inside his jacket." What steams Senator

---

[3] Sydney Sharpe and Don Braid, *Storming Babylon: Preston Manning and the Rise of the Reform Party* (Toronto: Key Porter Books, 1992), 193.

Marjory LeBreton most about Manning was that he undermined Mulroney before the latter had much of a chance to govern.

Canadian voters construed conservative division as evidence that neither the PC nor the Reform parties was fit to govern. Over the 1990s, Reformers and PCs turned themselves inside out trying to find a formula that would establish their party as the sole legitimate conservative voice. Both failed. Reform went so far as to change its name and leader, to no avail.

Manning looks at his legacy not in terms of electoral success and failure, but in broader terms, such as how he helped change the way Canadians think about democracy:

> The way I would like it to be looked at, and I think the most inspirational interpretation on it, was that Reform was an exercise in taking the tools of democracy, imperfect as it is. Reform was an example of a small group of people—starting with five people in a room in Calgary—who said we are going to change the national agenda. And we are going to do it by exercising these old rights of freedom of speech, freedom of association, freedom to try and persuade people to vote this way instead of that way.

Manning's observation makes Reform sound like an experiment, a way to test what might happen by mucking about with political institutions and established structures. Manning admits he fell short of reaching his goal, but does not acknowledge the consequences. Falling short in this context might be the equivalent of a tightrope walker claiming credit for reaching the three-quarter mark in a traverse across Niagara Falls. Nonetheless, Manning hopes he will inspire others to take the same leap:

> We didn't of course accomplish our whole objective and agenda, far from it. But by golly within ten years we went from the five people to 2.5 million votes and at least enough seats in the Parliament to be the Official Opposition. What I say to

public audiences that want to reflect on the democratic nature of the Reform experience is that it ought to be inspirational. Whether people agree with our particular agenda or not, it still is possible using those tools to actually make some impact. And so I say to people that have other agendas or want to do something else, maybe there is something in this story about what we did right and what we did wrong. That would be an encouragement to you to trust the democratic process and to use it.

Encouraging and enhancing democracy is usually the work of a think-tank or foundation. And, no great surprise, that is precisely what Preston Manning has turned to in his post-political life. The vision of the Manning Centre for Building Democracy is "to create a democratic society in Canada whose governments are guided by conservative ideas and principles—individual worth, freedom of choice, acceptance of responsibility, limited government, and respect for Canada's cultural, religious, and democratic values."[4]

The Reform party experimented with the tools of democracy. But Manning heralds one other bold achievement for the Reform party. To claims that the emergence of Reform accomplished little more than to elect three liberal majority governments, Manning counterclaims that Reform saved Canada from destruction:

> The other thing we did was keep western Canada from trying to secede at the same time as Quebec. If that was the only thing we did, that's something. There is not a flicker of recognition of that in most circles in Toronto. We say, if we had not done what we did, you would have had a full-blown separatist movement at both ends of the country and you would have blown [Canada] apart. Not only would you not have had a Conservative national government today, you would have had no national government at all. That's my thesis anyway.

---

[4] The Council of Advisors to the Manning Centre for Building Democracy includes many former Progressive Conservatives, for example John Laschinger. See Manning Centre for Building Democracy website: www.manningcentre.ca.

If Manning's thesis holds water, most Canadians owe him a debt of gratitude. But there is no empirical evidence to substantiate his claim. Certainly saving Canada from the throes of western-based separatism was not a reason Manning gave in 1986 for launching his new western-based political party.

The answer to the question of Reform's impact on Canadian politics is simple and clear: three successive Liberal majority governments. Progressive Conservatives and Reformers went into these elections with not a scintilla of a chance to win. Further, for the better part of a decade, the nation was governed without an effective opposition and lacked a government in waiting.

ERNEST AND PRESTON MANNING planted the seed of political realignment at the federal level in 1967. Two decades later, Manning set his sights on what that realignment would look like: the Reform party as government and himself as prime minister. Manning would try his best to imitate at the senior level of government what his father's Social Credit party had done in Alberta. He planned to generate a nationwide populist uprising by appealing to disaffected voters from across the political spectrum. However, after running candidates across the land in two elections, he admitted his populist dream would never be realized. And this is something that Manning, a student of history, should have been able to predict. Given the breadth and diversity of Canada, populism born in any one region can go only so far. Conservatives from the Atlantic provinces and Ontario were never going to support the social conservative agenda advanced by Reform or the hard-line economic message that was fundamental to Reform party policy. Manning's views on the pure equality of all provinces, with no recognition of Quebec's distinctiveness, made Reform a non-starter in French Quebec. Reform supporters were able to elect members in western Canada and appeal to a modest number of Canadians elsewhere. But it should have come as no surprise to Manning that a national consensus on a so-called populist program was never going to fly. Manning's project was doomed to fail before it began.

Elmer MacKay thought Manning's ambition was driven by retribution for what the PC party had done to destroy Social Credit in Alberta.

> After failing to defeat the Liberals, Manning had to face the realization that if there was even a chance to form government, he would have to recreate the moderate, pan-Canadian party that he worked so assiduously to destroy. He was bitter that Peter Lougheed had decimated the party his dad had led and his egotism and bitterness brought him to undermine the conservative party. He is a chameleon beyond compare.

For at least two elections, Manning held to the view that Reform was not a conservative party, or even a party of the right. Whether Manning understood it or not, his stance was tantamount to fraud. The evidence shows that Reform party members were anything but garden-variety conservatives. They were among the more right-wing Blue Tory factions in the country. John Weissenberger would shake his head at the incongruity of Manning's position. "At the beginning Manning bent over backwards to never ever say the word conservative. But we had a conservative platform and a conservative membership." Stephen Harper would not subscribe to the populist myth, and he left Manning before his first term as a member of parliament was up. After two national elections, the scam was exposed, and Manning was left to lead the western half of Canada's conservative political movement. Half a movement cannot win an entire nation.

For Manning to achieve his goal of forming a government, Reform needed to achieve two intermediate objectives. First, eliminate the Progressive Conservative party and become the national voice for Canadian conservatives. Second, make Reform a broad, inclusive, moderate political force that would appeal to all regions of Canada, including Quebec. But Manning seemed more intent on winning an argument than on winning an election. He did nothing to build bridges with like-minded conservatives, and he heaped disdain on his most natural political ally. As a *National Post* editorial noted soon after the merger, "Mr. Manning could never bring himself to do the one thing that might have propelled him into 24 Sussex Drive: put the federal Tories out of their misery. An idealistic man, he was preoccupied with 'doing politics differently.' And so whenever Kim Campbell or Jean Charest or Joe Clark would stumble, Mr. Manning would hesitate to recruit talented Tories away from the older party or steal their donors, until finally the Tories regained enough strength that they could not be crushed or ignored."[5]

John Weissenberger was with the Reform party from the very beginning. He concluded that Manning was never going to form a government and that his plan was doomed to fail:

> Had he more effectively positioned Reform to displace the PCs then I think he would have had a better chance. He left enough room for the PCs to come back in 1997, and with their history some sort of accommodation was inevitable. He made several attempts to eat away at PC support with the United Alternative, but he missed his window from '93 to '97. It was not easy for him. He did not come from the PC family and didn't understand their history.

Manning cannot be criticized for poor intentions. While ambition is a fatal flaw in every politician, Manning genuinely believed in what he was doing. He is anything but the intolerant and radical extremist often portrayed in the media. But he is a different sort of thinker. His strategy of waiting till Mulroney came to power before launching his movement was a clever way to hive off votes in the far West. It was also a blue-ribboned gift for Liberals.

Reform's only chance to achieve its goals was lost when it failed to make peace with the Tories after the 1993 election. Instead, it denigrated Brian Mulroney. "It was hard to reach out to the PCs because

---

[5] Editorial, "Mulroney, the West and the last laugh," *National Post*, December 23, 2003, A19.

their brand was damaged. Manning was riding the wave of indignation against Mulroney," said Weissenberger. Consequently, Preston Manning guaranteed that he would never get his hands on the conservative franchise.[6] After the 1997 election, Manning had to face the fact that Reform needed to be part of a broad coalition of Conservatives if the Liberals were ever to be defeated. In other words, the Progressive Conservative party, or something just like it, would have to be re-created. Manning held on, hoping he could reach his goal by changing the Reform party name and putting his leadership on the line. "I had been arguing for the bigger broader tent since right after the 1997 election," said Manning. "I tried to use positive arguments to [urge them] to just get on with it. I argued that if you had a coalition of fiscal conservatives, [plus] some of the social conservatives that could work with other Reform-oriented federalists . . . you had the potential of getting a governing party if you had that form of a coalition." What Manning did not want to admit was that he had become the problem. As the prime architect of conservative disunity, there could be no healing of past wounds, and no coalition, as long as he had a role.

After the Conservative victory in 2006, Reform party stalwarts began to admit that the Reform party could never have achieved its objectives. Original Reform MP Bob Mills reluctantly concluded, "All of us realized, no matter how much we would have liked to have stayed Reform, that [the party] wasn't going to form the government."[7]

And Manning himself might never have believed it possible to win government. Shortly after Stephen Harper was elected prime minister, Manning was asked if the federal political realignment that he and his father wrote about in 1967 had in fact taken place. In

---

[6] An example of his disdain for Brian Mulroney and his former government: When the former prime minister was made a Companion of the Order of Canada, Manning was quoted as saying, "Well, at least they didn't appoint him to the Senate. Whether you like Mulroney or not, very few people get to be Prime Minister of Canada for nine years. I presume that's the reason he was given this." Jennifer Ditchburn, "Manning jabs at Mulroney's Order of Canada," *Edmonton Journal*, July 9, 1998, A3.

[7] Greenaway, "The Conservative de-Reformation."

other words, did he think he had achieved the goals he had set for himself and his movement? He replied:

> It is sort of in that direction. Our idea on realignment was for a purpose. It was not just a reshuffling of the deck for the sake of reshuffling the deck. The real answer to your question depends on what the new Conservative party actually does. In a way what's happened is a manifestation of the thinking [we had] thirty-five years ago.

It depends? Given the enormity of the effort and the number of elections handed to the Liberals, Manning's acceptance of this outcome is strikingly tepid. We might have expected that for his experiment to be considered a success something more structural, institutional, and transformative would have to have occurred. But other than leadership, even Manning could not point to anything that was meaningfully different between the Conservatives of old and the Conservatives of 2006.

Asked what he might have done differently with the Reform party to achieve its goals, Manning paused at length, something he is not prone to do, and ultimately observed:

> That's hard to say. I don't really think much about that. Some people said we tried to do too much and we should have focused more. We had systemic change proposals on everything from criminal justice, to the democratic system, to constitutional reform, to health care, to the fiscal side. There may have been some merit in a tighter focus.

> I tend to be more of a policy-idea person and not as much relying on personality and personal relationships to get things done. Some of the Quebec media guys used to say to me I was always trying to appeal to Quebec decision-makers on the grounds of some policy or idea; [and that] I could have gotten far more entry as Leader of the Opposition saying 'I want to

meet with you.' However, I don't know how successful you can be politically if you start behaving out of character with yourself either.

This response certainly does not reflect the "big thinking" for which Manning is famous. Nowhere does he say that, instead of denigrating long-serving Tories, he should have tried to build a coalition with the remnants of the PC party in 1993. Nowhere does he recognize the strategy of running candidates only in the West, where Reform was strong, and leaving everything east of the Manitoba border for the PCs to contest. The objectives of the Reform party would more likely have been achieved had the party carried its original mantra, "The West Wants In," to its ultimate conclusion. Had Reform run candidates in western Canada only, it might have denied the Liberals majority governments throughout the 1990s. It was part of Reform's original thinking to become the Bloc Québécois of the West: a protest party with a mission. Reform might well have held the balance of power in a minority Parliament that would have given them a chance to voice western ideas and issues. Such an arrangement works in Germany with one conservative party in Bavaria and another for the rest of the country.[8] Staying out of the East might have enabled the more moderate Progressive Conservative party to win enough seats to cobble together, with Reform, a minority coalition government; not ideal, but closer to the goals Manning initially wanted to achieve.

PC–turned–Alliance senator Gerry St. Germain, a key figure in the Conservative reunification, faults Manning for ill-conceived political strategy:

---

[8] "The Christian Democratic Union of Germany is the largest conservative political party in Germany. In Bavaria, the CDU does not exist; its role is played by the Christian Social Union (CSU). The CDU cooperates with the CSU at the federal level; although each party maintains its own structure, the two form a common caucus in the German Parliament and do not run opposing campaigns. Their combination is generally referred to as The Union." From Wikipedia (www.wikipedia.org/wiki/CDU).

He should have done what he did from within the conservative family that existed. He opted for something else. He said
the West wanted in. Had he stuck to that, I would have had a
lot more respect for him. I am a westerner and 6 Senate
seats for B.C. is not right. But he deviated from his principles
so quickly, which discredited him in my eyes: the limo, the
suits, Stornoway. I would never have joined him in the
Reform Party.

Don Mazankowski, who negotiated against St. Germain from the PC
side of the merger, offers a similar view:

If he had wanted to reform the institutions of the right, he
would have been better off to do it from within our party.
That's what I fault him for. Unfortunately, he had another mission to accomplish and he ended up becoming the best friend
the Liberals ever had. I think his intentions were good, but he
learned a lot being in Ottawa and I think he got to like Ottawa
quite a bit. But he took us on a trip that caused us to go around
a vicious circle.

It was left to Brian Mulroney to remark on the ultimate irony: in the
attempt to strengthen the hand of westerners in Ottawa, Manning
virtually guaranteed the election of the party that had given the West
the hated National Energy Program.

Could Manning have integrated himself into the PC party to
achieve the political realignment he sought? Mulroney claims he
would have welcomed Manning into the fold, although it is hard to
say where Manning would have fit on a team he did not lead. Given
his history, it is unlikely he could have made the compromises that
are inevitable in a large national caucus, or even accepted a role that
was beneath the level of minister of finance or deputy prime minister. While Mulroney was not averse to plucking outsiders and giving
them senior portfolios and substantial clout—Lucien Bouchard, for

example[9]—Manning is unlikely to have qualified for such treatment. He came from a region of the country where Conservatives dominated and were already well represented in cabinet. Because Mulroney had underestimated the strength of western alienation, Manning would not have been seen at the time as someone who could bring much to the table. He would have been a foot soldier; the prospect of Manning ever working within the PC party would have been somewhere between zero and zilch. Perhaps his only real chance at becoming prime minister was to run for leadership of the PC party when the job came open in 1993. But that was never going to happen: Manning was raised to be distrustful of traditional political parties.

Every political party is challenged by disunity. Internal wrangling and compromise are inevitable. However, Conservatives are unique in that they take disunity to a structural level. First, the Progressives came out of the West in the 1920s to split the conservative vote. Next, the Social Credit party claimed Conservative votes in Quebec and the West and contributed significantly to the defeat of both the Diefenbaker and Clark governments. Then—the most serious split of all—the Reform party emerged.

Some might judge it remarkable that the Reform Party of Canada rose so quickly to become Her Majesty's Loyal Opposition. But if there is anything Conservatives are good at in Canada, it is being in opposition. The ultimate goal of any political party is to form a government. Having never formed a government, the Reform party has to be judged by history as a failure. Worse, perhaps, its existence was futile, because its goals were never achievable.

FOR CONSERVATIVES TO WIN, they must fight as a team. Any faction that goes out on its own will undermine the entire movement.

---

[9] Mulroney appointed Bouchard Canada's ambassador to France in 1985 and arranged for him to enter politics through a by-election in June 1988. Bouchard served as Mulroney's minister of the environment until he left cabinet to launch the Bloc Québécois in 1991.

It is when the party, in its broadest form, is united and embraces all strands of conservatism that it has a chance to win. The Conservative party has failed frequently over its history because, unlike the Liberals, it has not focused on winning. Focused on holding power, Liberals have built coalitions, cornered opposition parties, and dominated a wide swath of the political centre.

The Conservative legacy is incessant internal debates, personality conflicts, and regionalism. The most important lesson Conservatives can learn from losing four consecutive elections is that disunity and division are a guarantee of failure.

The only consistently successful Conservative prime ministers—Sir John A. Macdonald and Brian Mulroney, both with back-to-back majorities—were master coalition builders. It is ironic that Mulroney, arguably the most conservative of all Conservative prime ministers, would see his coalition undermined by elements of a far-right faction from the West. It had happened before under Diefenbaker, and there is no guarantee that it won't happen to Stephen Harper.

Conservatives would be well advised to heed Preston Manning's warning that there is something in the "juices" of western Canadians that gives them a predilection for launching and supporting populist-style, leader-centric political movements. Provinces east of the Manitoba border have almost never been susceptible to Social Credit democratic uprisings, but the West and occasionally Quebec have a history of getting swept up in rash political movements. In other words, dismissing westerners who complain about what goes on in central Canada is done at some peril. Too, it doesn't seem to take much more than a spark to ignite the brushfire of prairie discontent. Witness western outrage over Mulroney's decision to overrule the award of the CF-18 maintenance contract to the winning bidder from Manitoba in favour of a company in Quebec. Conservatives need to understand that western conservatism is different from that practiced in other parts of Canada. Westerners are consistently further to the right than are conservatives in the rest of Canada, and more likely to carry a strong dose of social conservatism on their sleeves. If westerners fail to see their views reflected in decision making, in substance or, in appearance, they are unlikely to stay passive for very long.

While Manning is correct that Quebec has its own history of populism, the province was largely unaffected by the emergence of the Reform party. Nonetheless, Quebec has been a perennial problem for Conservatives. Perhaps as punishment for hanging Louis Riel during Macdonald's tenure, or failing to stand up for minority language rights in Manitoba at the end of the nineteenth century, or endorsing conscription during two world wars—Conservatives have only rarely shown signs of life in Quebec. Other than during a brief period in 1891–92, Brian Mulroney is the only Quebecer ever to hold the party's leadership. Conservatives need to overcome their inferiority complex and embrace Quebec, as Stephen Harper did in 2006. Because of resentment over the sponsorship scandal, Harper had the opportunity to make Conservatives the dominant federalist political party in Quebec, perhaps for some time. The Conservative party can claim to be national in scope and united in purpose only if it embraces Quebec.

The concluding lesson for any political party that wants to be successful is this: in a country as geographically, culturally, linguistically, and socially diverse as Canada, building coalitions and maintaining unity are essential. The other side of this equation is equally important: pay attention to early indications of discontent before they take hold. Mulroney failed to heed the warning signs that were readily apparent from the 1989 Reform by-election win, and his party and the country paid dearly.

IN THE TELLING OF HISTORY, it is as important to understand what drew the PC and Alliance parties together as what drove them apart. Preston Manning credits hardball politics for the merger:

> The argument that was most persuasive to Stephen Harper and Peter MacKay was when the pollsters came in to them when Martin was flying higher than a kite and just held them over the

cliff. [The pollsters said] "Peter, you guys will be wiped out. There will not be a single Progressive Conservative in the Parliament. Stephen, if Martin's numbers hold up you guys will be driven back to your western base with maybe 35–40 seats." That argument was more convincing to them, and maybe rightly so, than all the positive arguments that could be made. It's not flattering. But all these guys had those polls and neither of them are stupid.

However, the conditions to which Manning refers were not new. They were present during the 1997 and 2000 elections when Jean Chrétien won majority governments. Manning's argument, made in 2006, did not carry the day before these two earlier elections, which begs the question, what was fundamentally different in 2003?

In their 2001 book, *Gritlock: Are the Liberals in Forever?*, Peter White and Adam Daifallah wrote about the forces keeping the Tories and Alliance apart. "There is an embarrassingly simple answer to the simple question: their leadership."[10] The authors argued that the party leaders were not only failing to do their jobs, but also standing in the way of others who were working to bring the two parties together. White and Daifallah presented a road map that, in the absence of leadership, might lead to a full-scale merger. They maintained that the process would have to be member-driven, not leader-driven. The reason is obvious: What political leader, having endured the grind and paid the price to get the top job, would willingly sacrifice that status? Joe Clark, remember, made it clear he would have merged his PCs with the Alliance, but only if he was guaranteed the leader's position.

Remember also that at the 2003 PC leadership convention the delegates did not support the candidate who was running openly on a pro-merger platform. Yet seven months later that same party voted more than ninety per cent to ratify the Agreement in Principle signed by the Alliance and PC party leaders. As White and

---

[10] White and Daifallah, *Gritlock*, 72.

Daifallah maintained, the simple difference was leadership. And both leaders stepped up. First, Stephen Harper took a calculated risk on his leadership, and agreed to the conditions proposed by PC party negotiators during merger talks. More significantly, Peter MacKay sacrificed his leadership to achieve another goal: to do what was right for the country and restore meaningful democracy to Canada.

Both Harper and MacKay provided bold leadership, and then party members dutifully fell in line. In the end, it took people who were willing to lead and people who were willing to follow to get the job done.

CAN STEPHEN HARPER KEEP HIS coalition together? Can he build upon his beachhead in Quebec? Will he be able to convince all Canadians, particularly those in urban centres, that his government need not be feared? Can he win majority government? More to the point, can Harper govern Canada and still be conservative enough to keep westerners on side?

To bridge the distance between a minority and majority government, given the 2006 configuration, the Conservatives need to attract only four or five more out of every one hundred Canadian voters. Ever the master strategist, Harper knows enough not to extend his reach beyond the hypothetical "conservative universe."

Manning certainly wishes his former protégé well, but he remembers well his own difficulties with Harper and does not hesitate to speak of what he considers Harper's weaknesses as a politician:

> Stephen is a private person. He is not comfortable in many respects with people, particularly large numbers of people. That is still a struggle with him. He is working at it. He is doing everything he can to compensate on that area, both himself and by having others around him that have that strength. But, that will be his challenge. He has certainly matured. He is stronger in his strong areas than he was way back and he has done what he can to try to compensate in those other areas.

What Manning sees as Harper's greatest strength is his ability to analyze and formulate policy, something better suited to government than opposition benches.

> His strengths today, although they are far more developed, are the same strengths, at least that I saw in him, as a younger person. His greatest strength was his capacity to analyze public problems and come up with public policy solutions. He is a public policy person and is very good at it. That type of person actually does better in government than in opposition because they actually get to do things, not just talk about them.

It is interesting that compliments about Stephen Harper seem to come more easily from the PC side of the conservative family than from Preston Manning. Brian Mulroney is effusive in his praise for what Harper has accomplished. Don Mazankowski thinks Harper's decisiveness and discipline are just what the party and the country need. Mazankowski and Mulroney are well placed to judge leadership qualities and could contrast the decisive Harper with the dithering Paul Martin. Harper has less need to be popular than did Martin, which is a good thing, because Paul Martin bent over backwards any time a province or special interest group complained. By making popularity his yardstick, Martin is likely to be judged a failure as prime minister. Harper will not suffer that fate.

One of the more interesting challenges Harper will face is sustaining western conservatives in his coalition. Is it inevitable that every generation or so, western Canadians, distrusting political elites and driven by the need for a stronger brand of conservatism, will rise up, as they have done before? Will Stephen Harper, a western Canadian, be better equipped than was Brian Mulroney to squelch any western-based populist uprisings?

Senator Marjory LeBreton thinks the party has learned its lesson. "It's not likely to happen again. There is today a greater appreciation for all facets of the party." However, Manning maintains that the West is stronger than it has ever been before, and he believes

that strength makes it difficult to predict how westerners might ultimately express themselves politically:

> The West is just becoming this big aggressive well-positioned
> region to have national influence. It has a third of the popula-
> tion; it produces over a third of the GDP; it produces 50 per cent
> of the exports; it's got almost a third of the seats in the parlia-
> ment. It's got a large amount of influence that's not been
> recognized as much as it should be in the political arena. But it
> is certainly recognized in the business area. There are a lot of
> investors and decision makers in London, Tokyo and Washington
> that know as much or more about Edmonton, Calgary, and Fort
> MacMurray as they know where Ottawa is. I think the west's
> influence is growing. Along with that goes responsibility.
>
> If you are a big player you have to think about more than just your-
> self. You have to think about the country as a whole. That is the
> more dominant influence on western Canadian politics than the
> old politics of grievance; and we are the little underdog that can't
> do anything and we need Ottawa to take care of us. That is the
> major change. And what impact is that going to have politically?

With his western fingerprints all over the conservative travails and
divisions of the past fifteen years, it is perhaps fitting that Preston
Manning's answer to that question takes the form of an ominous
warning that all Conservatives should heed:

> As long as the West can see the national Conservative party as
> one it's helped to shape as an adequate vehicle for some of its
> bigger ideas, it will be content with that. If it starts to see it not
> as that, then there are more resources and capability here to
> generate something else again.

Something else again? If Conservatives can learn anything from the
past two decades it is this: division and disunity should never be repeated.

Building and sustaining a successful Conservative franchise is an immense challenge. The factions of conservatism in Canada run wide and deep, and offer a full range of conflicts, contradictions, and inconsistencies. If those factions choose to battle each other for supremacy, the conservative movement will lose every time.

It does not matter if the Conservative leader comes from the East or the West, is French or English, a Blue Tory or a Red Tory. To think it does is to miss the point. No Conservative leader can hope to succeed by preferring one faction over another. A successful Conservative leader bridges the gaps, inspires unity, and draws the party together in common cause. Success comes when Conservatives, in the widest possible universe, respect one another and work together to achieve a greater goal.

In any broadly based political party, internal battles are inevitable. Each faction will naturally want to get its way. However, ignoring or disrespecting any element of the conservative coalition is risky. History has shown us that seemingly small matters, such as a single government contract for aircraft maintenance, can irrevocably upset the balance.

Stephen Harper did not become prime minister because of increased western economic and political clout. As Harper wrote in 1997, "The fragments of Canadian conservatism must recognize that each represents an authentic aspect of a larger conservative philosophy." In formulating his platform and strategy for the 2006 election, Harper followed a road map laid out by a select few of his predecessors. By shedding his economist instincts, he displayed the maturity required to build a winning national coalition. And experience and research show that mainstream Canadians will embrace balanced conservatism when given the chance.

United, moderate, inclusive, national, mainstream, visionary, and conservative—these words describe the party led by Macdonald, Borden, and Mulroney. Now Harper has his chance to emulate their success. Having been Canada's natural governing party in the nineteenth century, it is entirely possible Conservatives could reclaim that mantle in the twenty-first.

APPENDIX A

CONSERVATIVE PARTY LEADERS

Jul 1, 1867–Jun 6, 1891	Sir John A. Macdonald
Jun 16, 1891–Dec 5, 1892	J.J.C. Abbott
Dec 5, 1892–Dec 12, 1894	Sir John Thompson
Dec 21, 1894–Apr 27, 1896	Sir Mackenzie Bowell
May 1, 1896–Feb 5, 1901	Sir Charles Tupper
Feb 6, 1901–Jul 10, 1920	Sir Robert Borden
Jul 10, 1920–Oct 11, 1926	Arthur Meighen
Oct 11, 1926–Oct 12, 1927	Hugh Guthrie (interim)
Oct 12, 1927–Jul 7, 1938	R.B. Bennett
Jul 7, 1938–May 13, 1940	R.J. Manion
May 13, 1940–Jan 27, 1943	R.B. Hanson (interim)
Nov 12, 1941–Dec 11, 1942	Arthur Meighen
Dec 11, 1942–Oct 2, 1948	John Bracken
Oct 2, 1948–Dec 14, 1956	George A. Drew
Dec 14, 1956–Sep 9, 1967	John G. Diefenbaker
Sep 9, 1967–Feb 22, 1976	Robert L. Stanfield
Feb 22, 1976–Feb 8, 1983	Joe Clark
Feb 9, 1983–Jun 11, 1983	Erik Nielsen (interim)
Jun 11, 1983–Jun 13, 1993	Brian Mulroney
Jun 13, 1993–Dec 13, 1993	Kim Campbell
Dec 14, 1993–Apr 3, 1998	Jean J. Charest
Apr 3, 1998–Nov 14, 1998	Elsie Wayne (interim)
Nov 14, 1998–Jun 1, 2003	Joe Clark
Jun 1, 2003–Dec 6, 2003	Peter MacKay
Dec 8 2003–Mar 20, 2004	John Lynch-Staunton (interim)

Jan 9, 2004–Mar 20, 2004	Grant Hill (interim—House of Commons)
Mar 20, 2004–Present	Stephen Harper

Reform Party (1987–2000)

Oct 31,1987–Mar 26, 2000	Preston Manning

Canadian Reform Conservative Alliance (2000–2003)

Mar 27, 2000–Jul 7, 2000	Deborah C. Grey (interim)
Jul 8, 2000–Dec 11,2001	Stockwell Day
Dec 12, 2001–Mar 19, 2002	John Reynolds (interim)
Mar 20, 2002–Dec 7, 2003	Stephen Harper

APPENDIX B

CONSERVATIVE PRIME MINISTERS OF CANADA

Term Served	Name	Party Name
Jul 1, 1867– Nov 5, 1873	Sir John Alexander Macdonald	Liberal-Conservative
Oct 17, 1878– Jun 6, 1891	Sir John Alexander Macdonald	Liberal-Conservative
Jun 16, 1891– Nov 24, 1892	Sir John Joseph Caldwell Abbott	Liberal-Conservative
Dec 5, 1892– Dec 12, 1894	Sir John Sparrow David Thompson	Liberal-Conservative
Dec 21, 1894– Apr 27, 1896	Sir Mackenzie Bowell	Liberal-Conservative
May 1, 1896– Jul 8, 1896	Sir Charles Tupper	Conservative
Oct 10, 1911– Oct 12, 1917	Sir Robert Laird Borden	Conservative
Oct 12, 1917– Jul 10, 1920	Sir Robert Laird Borden	Conservative
Jul 10, 1920– Dec 29, 1921	Arthur Meighen	Conservative
Jun 29, 1926– Sep 25, 1926	Arthur Meighen	Conservative
Aug 7, 1930– Oct 23, 1935	Richard Bedford Bennett	Conservative

Jun 21, 1957– Apr 22, 1963	John George Diefenbaker	Progressive Conservative
Jun 4, 1979– Mar 3, 1980	Charles Joseph Clark	Progressive Conservative
Sep 17, 1984– Jun 13, 1993	Martin Brian Mulroney	Progressive Conservative
Jun 13, 1993– Oct 25 1993	Kim Campbell	Progressive Conservative
Feb 6, 2006– Present	Stephen Joseph Harper	Conservative

TIMELINE
OF KEY EVENTS

July 1,1867[1]	Under the leadership of Sir John A. Macdonald, the Liberal-Conservative Party forms Canada's first post-Confederation government. Macdonald sustains a coalition that wins 6 of the country's first 7 elections. Macdonald dies while in office on June 6,1891.
1873–1911	Candidates for the party run under the banner of the Liberal-Conservative and Conservative party. By 1911, only the Conservative party survives.
September 21, 1911	Robert Borden is elected Conservative prime minister.
December 17, 1917	Robert Borden is re-elected, as leader of the Unionist Party. His coalition comprises Conservatives, some Liberals, and Independents.
July 10, 1920	Following Borden's resignation, Arthur Meighen serves as prime minister for eighteen months as leader of the National Liberal and Conservative Party.
December 6, 1921	The Progressive party elects 58 members of parliament. In subsequent elections their numbers would be reduced successively to 22, 11, then 3 before the party dissolved.
August 7, 1930–October 22, 1935	Richard Bennett serves one term as Conservative prime minister, with a majority government.
December 11, 1942	With the election of former Manitoba premier John Bracken, a former Progressive, as party leader the Conservative party changes its name to the Progressive Conservative Party of Canada.

---

[1] Sir John A. Macdonald was designated prime minister on July 1, 1867 and elected in August–September 1867.

June 10, 1957–
April 21, 1963

John George Diefenbaker wins a minority government. He wins an overwhelming majority in 1958 and is reduced to a minority in 1962. His defeat is as prime minister is caused, in part, by rising support for the Social Credit party.

November 8, 1965

Preston Manning runs for federal Parliament for the Social Credit party in Edmonton East and finishes a distant second to the Progressive Conservative candidate.

1967

Ernest Manning publishes *Political Re-alignment: A Challenge to Thoughtful Canadians*. Preston Manning is given credit for the research and original drafting of the book, which advocates a social conservative perspective not being offered by the PC party at the time.

May 22, 1979

Joe Clark's Progressive Conservatives win minority government. Six seats short of a majority, they are defeated on December 13, 1979, on a budget bill. The Social Credit party is instrumental in the defeat. The PCs lose government in the election held February 18, 1980.

June 11, 1983

Brian Mulroney defeats Joe Clark on the fourth and final ballot to take the leadership of the PC party.

September 4, 1984

Brian Mulroney's Progressive Conservative party is elected with a massive majority government. Mulroney earns more than 50 per cent of the popular vote and wins 58 of 75 seats from Quebec.

Stephen Harper comes to Ottawa to work as the legislative assistant to Calgary MP Jim Hawkes.

June 27, 1985

Michael Wilson announces the government is backing away from its budget proposal to de-index old-age pensions.

June 1, 1986

Stephen Harper returns to Calgary to resume studies at the University of Calgary.

October 17, 1986

Preston Manning meets with business executives in Calgary to make the case for "a new federal political movement dedicated to reforms that would make the West an equal partner in Confederation."

October 31, 1986

The Mulroney government overrides the contract award for the maintenance of Canada's CF-18 jet fighters from Winnipeg Bristol Aerospace to Montreal-based Canadair.

April 1987

Prime Minister Mulroney and all provincial premiers sign a constitutional accord at Meech Lake. The accord requires ratification by the federal and all provincial parliaments.

May 29–31, 1987	Preston Manning helps organize and lead the Western Assembly on Canada's Economic and Political Future, held in Vancouver and attended by about 650 people. More than 85 per cent vote to approve a new federal political party.
October 30–November 1, 1987	The founding convention for the Reform Party of Canada is held in Winnipeg. Stan Roberts walks out after allegations of irregularities in delegate registration and the handling of funds. Preston Manning is acclaimed leader.
November 21, 1988	Brian Mulroney's Progressive Conservatives are re-elected with a majority government. The Reform party elects no members, but receives 2.5 per cent of the national vote and 15.3 per cent of the vote in Alberta. Preston Manning runs a feisty campaign and loses to Joe Clark in Yellowhead, Alberta. Stephen Harper runs in Calgary West for Reform and finishes a distant second to Jim Hawkes, his former boss.
March 13, 1989	Reform party candidate and schoolteacher Deborah Grey wins handily in a by-election in the Alberta riding of Beaver River.
October 16, 1989	Coincident with municipal elections in Alberta, a vote is held pursuant to the Alberta Senatorial Selection Act. Brian Mulroney ultimately summons the Reform party winner, Stan Waters, to the Senate on June 11, 1990.
October 17, 1989	A Reform party convention is held in Edmonton. Delegates support free trade but oppose the Meech Lake Accord.
June 23, 1990	After Premier Clyde Wells of Newfoundland declines to seek ratification of the Meech Lake Accord, the Mulroney government concedes the accord is dead. Preston Manning and Pierre Trudeau are leading opponents of the accord.
January 1, 1991	The Mulroney government implements the GST.
April 1, 1991	The Reform party holds a convention in Saskatoon, attended by 1,400 delegates representing virtually every riding in western Canada. Delegates support a resolution to conduct a referendum on moving from a regional to a national political party.
June 3, 1991	Only 42.4 per cent of Reform party members vote in a referendum; 92 per cent are in favour of expanding the party nationally.
September 10, 1992	The House of Common accepts the Charlottetown accord by a vote of 233 to 12. Voting in opposition is Reform MP Deborah Grey. The Reform party organizes on behalf of the NO campaign for the coming referendum.

October 26, 1992	The national referendum on the Charlottetown accord goes down to defeat. It is the third national referendum in the history of Canada.
March 29, 1993	The Reform party releases its election platform, called "Zero in Three." The plan calls for the elimination of the deficit over three years by making changes to Canada Pension Plan, Employment Insurance, Old Age Security, transfers to provinces and individuals, subsidies to business and special interests, and general government waste and inefficiency.
March 31, 1993	The country records its largest-ever deficit: $39 billion.
June 13, 1993	Kim Campbell, MP from British Columbia, is chosen leader of the Progressive Conservative Party and becomes prime minister of Canada.
September 8, 1993	The writ is dropped for an election to be held on October 25, 1993. Kim Campbell has among the highest approval ratings of any prime minister and is tied with the Liberals in popular support. Polls place Reform with about 10 per cent support.
October 25, 1993	The Liberal party under Jean Chrétien wins majority government. The Bloc Québécois forms the official opposition. The Reform party, with 18.7 per cent of the vote, wins 52 seats. The PC party, with 16.0 per cent support, wins 2 seats. Stephen Harper defeats his former boss to become the MP for Calgary West.
December 13, 1993	Kim Campbell resigns as leader of the PC party, making way for Jean Charest.
April 6, 1994	Stephen Harper and other caucus members go public with criticism of Preston Manning for use of party funds for clothing.
October 30, 1995	A referendum is held in Quebec on a convoluted question of political sovereignty. The result is 49.4 per cent voting YES and 50.6 per cent voting NO.
May 25–26, 1996	Ezra Levant and David Frum organize the Winds of Change conference to promote co-operation among the PC and Reform parties.
January 14, 1997	Stephen Harper resigns his seat in Parliament and becomes president of the National Citizens Coalition.
June 2, 1997	Jean Chrétien wins a second majority. Reform wins 60 seats and becomes the official opposition. With strong representation from Atlantic Canada, the PC party rebounds with 20 seats. The campaign is marred by Reform party ads that place

	red slashes across the faces of politicians from Quebec. Peter MacKay wins his home riding of Pictou–Antigonish, Nova Scotia.
June 1997	After suggesting it could be used more efficiently as a "bingo hall," Preston Manning and family move into Stornoway, official residence of the Leader of Her Majesty's Loyal Opposition. The house comes with a car and driver.
March 26, 1998	Jean Charest resigns as leader of the Progressive Conservative Party of Canada and becomes leader of the Liberal Party of Quebec on April 30, 1998.
May 27, 1998	The Reform party holds its convention in London, Ontario. Delegates endorse Preston Manning's idea to form a United Alternative with 91 per cent approval. Manning's leadership is approved by 81 per cent of delegates.
February 20, 1989	United Alternative holds a convention in Ottawa with 1,500 delegates. Four options are presented. Delegates approve a plan to create a new political party.
June 10, 1999	Reform party members participate in a mail-in vote. With a 49.7 per cent response rate, 60.5 per cent of those voting agree to continue with the United Alternative process.
November 14,1998	Joe Clark becomes leader of the Progressive Conservative party. His main opponents are party stalwart Hugh Segal and organic prairie farmer and anti-free-trade crusader David Orchard.
September 13, 1999	Progressive Conservative Peter MacKay and Reform Ian McLelland co-host a conference, "Citizens' Empowerment in Government," which is attended by Joe Clark and Preston Manning.
October 1, 1999	With approximately 95 per cent support, Progressive Conservative party delegates pass the "301 rule," affirming that candidates will be fielded in every constituency in Canada.
January 29, 2000	Canadian Reform Conservative Alliance party is formed. At a coincident Reform party convention, Preston Manning receives the endorsement of 75 per cent of delegates.
March 25, 2000	Reform party referendum results are released on a vote to join with the Canadian Alliance. About two-thirds of the membership participate in the vote, with 92 per cent voting in the affirmative.
March 27, 2000	Preston Manning resigns as leader of the Reform party and becomes a candidate for leader of the Canadian Alliance.

July 8, 2000	Stockwell Day wins the leadership of the Canadian Alliance.
September 11, 2000	Joe Clark and Stockwell Day win by-elections.
September 25, 2000	Stockwell Day challenges the prime minister in the House of Commons to call a general election.
October 8, 2000	Canadian Alliance releases its platform document "A Time for Change."
October 22, 2000	Jean Chrétien calls a general election for November 27, 2000.
November 27, 2000	Liberals take 172 seats, a gain of 17. The Canadian Alliance maintains opposition status with 66 seats, a gain of 6. Progressive Conservatives hang on to official party status with 12 seats. Alliance earns 25.0 per cent of the popular vote, to 12.2 per cent for the PC party.
January 24, 2001	Stephen Harper and others publish the "firewall" letter in the *National Post*, calling for Alberta to protect itself from federal incursions into areas of provincial jurisdiction.
February 2001	Alliance and PC members meet informally to begin discussions about co-operation among the parties. John Williams from the Alliance and Peter MacKay from the PC party are prominent.
April 2001	Deputy leader Deborah Grey and House leader Chuck Strahl resign their caucus jobs and launch a public attack on Stockwell Day's leadership.
July 19, 2001	Twelve Canadian Alliance MPs leave caucus and establish the Democratic Representation Caucus (DCR).
August 17–18, 2001	The DRC meets with PC representatives at Mount Tremblant to explore methods of co-operation and mutual support.
September 24, 2001	The Speaker of the House of Commons recognizes the DCR and PC caucus members as the Progressive Conservative–Democratic Reform (PC–DR).
January 31, 2002	Preston Manning resigns his seat in the House of Commons.
March 20, 2002	Stephen Harper is elected leader of the Canadian Alliance.
April 9, 2002	Stephen Harper and Tory leader Joe Clark meet to discuss co-operation. The talks fail.
April 16, 2002	Democratic Representative Caucus ends when all but one of the former dissident MPs, Inky Mark, return to the Canadian Alliance Party.
August 6, 2002	Joe Clark announces his intention to step down as leader of the Progressive Conservative party.

May 29–June 1, 2003	Peter MacKay is elected leader of the Progressive Conservative party after signing a controversial agreement with David Orchard.
June 26, 2003	Peter MacKay and Stephen Harper meet to launch a process that seeks to explore co-operation between the parties. Emissaries are subsequently appointed to pursue talks.
August 21, 2003	The emissaries meet in person to begin discussions.
September 22, 2003	There is a second meeting of the emissaries.
September 28–30, 2003	A meeting scheduled for September 29 between the emissaries is cancelled. Harper updates his caucus and national council via memo of September 29; Peter MacKay releases a report from his emissaries on September 30.
October 3, 2003	On reading the PC emissary report, Alliance MP Scot Reid writes to Don Mazinkowski indicating that only one issue remains outstanding—leadership selection.
October 15, 2003	Peter MacKay and Stephen Harper sign an agreement, on behalf of their parties, respecting a merger. The agreement requires the ratification of members by December 12.
November 20, 2003	David Orchard and others file an application in the Ontario Superior Court of Justice seeking declarations that the scheduled vote and its various provisions to merge with the Alliance violates the party's constitution and a written agreement between David Orchard and Peter MacKay.
December 5, 2003	Members of the Canadian Alliance ratify the merger with affirmative votes of 96 per cent. Mr. Justice J. Juriansz rules that the vote of PC party members may proceed.
December 6, 2003	In a delegated convention, members of the Progressive Conservative party ratify the merger by a vote of 90.4 per cent.
December 7, 2003	Canada's Chief Electoral Office accepts the registration of the Conservative Party of Canada.
March 20, 2004	Stephen Harper is chosen Conservative party leader on the first ballot. Other contenders for leadership are former Ontario health minister Tony Clement and Magna International CEO Belinda Stronach.
June 28, 2004	With 135 seats, Paul Martin's Liberals are reduced to a minority government. Conservatives win 99 seats, an increase of 21 from the combined PC and Canadian Alliance total. A net gain

of 22 Tory seats in Ontario is offset with a net decrease of 3 seats in the rest of the country. The Conservative party holds 31 out of a possible 213 seats east of the Manitoba border, and none in Quebec. The popular vote, at 29.6 per cent, is well below the combined PC and Alliance vote from the 2000 campaign, at 37.7 per cent.

March 17–19, 2005   The Conservative Party of Canada holds a policy convention in Montreal.

May 17, 2005   Belinda Stronach crosses the floor to become a minister in Paul Martin's government.

May 19, 2005   A vote of non-confidence in the Liberal government ends in a tie and is settled in favour of the government by a vote from the Speaker.

November 1, 2005   Mr. Justice John Gomery releases his report, "Who is Responsible," on the Liberal sponsorship scandal

November 28, 2006   The Martin government is defeated on a motion of non-confidence. An election is scheduled for January 23, 2006.

January 23, 2006   The Conservative party wins minority government with 124 seats to 103 for the Liberals.

February 6, 2006   Stephen Harper is sworn in as Canada's twenty-first prime minister. Peter MacKay, former Progressive Conservative party leader, becomes Minister for Foreign Affairs and Minister for the Atlantic Canada Opportunities Agency.

SELECTED BIBLIOGRAPHY

Bliss, Michael. *Right Honourable Men: The Descent of Canadian Politics from Macdonald to Mulroney*. Toronto: HarperCollins, 1994.

Brimelow, Peter. *The Patriot Game: National Dreams and Political Realities*. Toronto: Key Porter Books, 1986.

Campbell, Kim. *Time and Chance: The Political Memoirs of Canada's First Woman Prime Minister*. Toronto: Doubleday Canada, 1996.

Diefenbaker, John G. *One Canada: The Tumultuous Years, 1962–1967*. Toronto: Macmillan, 1977.

Flanagan, Tom. *Waiting for the Wave: The Reform Party and Preston Manning*. Toronto: Stoddart, 1995.

Fraser, Graham. *Playing for Keeps: The Making of the Prime Minister*. Toronto: McClelland & Stewart, 1989.

Granatstein, J.L., et al. *Nation: Canada Since Confederation*. Toronto: McGraw-Hill, 1990.

Harrison, Trevor. *Of Passionate Intensity: Right-Wing Populism and the Reform Party of Canada*. Toronto: University of Toronto Press, 1995.

Johnson, William. *Stephen Harper and the Future of Canada*. Toronto: McClelland & Stewart, 2005.

Kheiriddin, Tasha, and Adam Daifallah. *Rescuing Canada's Right: Blueprint for a Conservative Revolution*. Toronto: Wiley, 2005.

Mackey, Lloyd. *The Pilgrimage of Stephen Harper*. Toronto: ECW Press, 1995.

Manning, Ernest C. *Political Realignment: A Challenge to Thoughtful Canadians*. Toronto: McClelland & Stewart, 1967.

Manning, Preston. *The New Canada*. Toronto: Macmillan, 1992.

Manning, Preston. *Think Big: My Adventures in Life and Democracy*. Toronto: McClelland & Stewart, 2002.

McLaughlin, David. *Poisoned Chalice: The Last Campaign of the Progressive Conservative Party?* Toronto: Dundern Press, 1994.

McTeer, Maureen. *In My Own Name: A Memoir*. Toronnto: Random House, 2003.

Newman, Peter C. *The Secret Mulroney Tapes: Unguarded Confessions of a Prime Minister*. Toronto: Random House, 2005.

Orchard, David. *The Fight for Canada: Four Centuries of Resistance to American Expansionism*. Toronto: Stoddart, 1993.

Segal, Hugh. *No Surrender: Reflections of a Happy Warrior in the Tory Crusade*. Toronto: HarperCollins, 1996.

Sharpe, Sydney, and Don Braid. *Storming Babylon: Preston Manning and the Rise of the Reform Party*. Toronto: Key Porter Books, 1992.

Taylor, Charles. *Radical Tories: The Conservative Tradition in Canada*. Toronto: House of Anansi, 1982.

White, Peter G., and Adam Daifallah. *Gritlock: Are the Liberals in Forever?*. Toronto: Essence Publishing, 2001.

Wilson, Michael H. *A New Direction for Canada: An Agenda for Economic Renewal*. Ottawa: Finance Canada, 1984.

INDEX